CLASSIC

# NEW ZEALAND

SHORT STORIES

DAN DAVIN

OXFORD UNIVERSITY PRESS NEW
ZEALAND
Oxford  New York
Athens  Auckland  Bangkok  Bombay
Calcutta  Cape Town  Dar es Salaam  Delhi
Florence  Hong Kong  Istanbul  Karachi
Kuala Lumpur  Madras  Madrid  Melbourne
Mexico City  Nairobi  Paris  Port Moresby
Singapore  Taipei  Tokyo  Toronto
and associated companies in
Berlin  Ibadan

OXFORD is a trade mark of Oxford University
Press

Introduction and selection copyright © 1953, 1976,
1997 Oxford University Press
First published 1953
Reissued 1976, 1997

ISBN 019 5583841

Printed by McPherson's
Published by Oxford University Press
540 Great South Road, Greenlane, PO Box 11-149,
Auckland, New Zealand

# Acknowledgements

The editor is grateful for permission to use the following copyright material:

David Ballantyne, 'And The Glory' from *Landfall,* June 1948, by permission of The Caxton Press. William Baucke, 'A Quaint Friendship' from *Where the White Man Treads* (1905) by permission of Wilson and Horton, Auckland. B. E. Baughan, 'An Active Family' from *Brown Bread from a Colonial Oven* (1912) by permission of the author and Whitcombe and Tombs Ltd., Christchurch. James Courage, 'After the Earthquake' from *Landfall*, December 1948, by permission of The Caxton Press, Christchurch. Dan Davin, 'Saturday Night' and 'The General and the Nightingale' from *The Gorse Blooms Pale* (1947) by permission of the author. Maurice Duggan, 'Race Day' from the *New Zealand Listener,* February 1952, by permission of the editor and of the author. Roderick Finlayson, 'The Totara Tree' from *Brown Man's Burden* (1938) by permission of the author, the Hogarth Press, and the Unicorn Press, Auckland. Janet Frame, 'The Day of the Sheep' from *The Lagoon* (1952) by permission of the author and The Caxton Press. A. P. Gaskell, 'The Big Game' and 'School Picnic' from *The Big Game* (1947) by permission of The Caxton Press. G. R. Gilbert, 'A Girl with Ambition' from *Free to Laugh and Dance* (1942) by permission of The Caxton Press. Alfred A. Grace, 'The Ngarara' and 'Te Wiria's Potatoes' from *Tales of a Dying Race* (1901) by permission of Chatto and Windus. John A. Lee, 'Man's Inhumanity to Man' from *Shining with the Shiner* (1944) by permission of the author. Dennis McEldowney, 'By the Lake' from *Book,* July 1947, by permission of the author and The Caxton Press. Eruce Mason, 'The Glass Wig' from *Landfall,* December 1947, by permission of The Caxton Press. O. E. Middleton, 'Coopers' Christmas' from *Landfall,* June 1950, by permission of The Caxton Press. John Reece Cole, 'It Was So Late' from *It Was So Late* (1949) by permission of The Caxton Press. Frank Sargeson, 'Last Adventure' and 'The Making of a New Zealander' from *A Man and his Wife* (1940) by permission of the author and John Lehmann Ltd. Helen Shaw, 'The Blind' from *Arachne,* December 1951, by permission of the author. Douglas Stewart, 'The Whare' from *A Girl with Red Hair* (1944) by permission of Angus and Robertson Ltd., Sydney, and the Sydney *Bulletin.* Greville Texidor, 'An Annual

Affair' from *New Zealand New Writing,* June 1944, by permission of the author. Anton Vogt, 'The Accident' from the *New Zealand Listener,* January 1947, by permission of the editor and of the author. Alice F. Webb, 'The Patriot' from *Miss Peters' Special* (1926) by permission of the author. Phillip Wilson, 'The Wedding' from *Landfall.* September 1952, by permission of The Caxton Press.

## EDITOR'S NOTE

Apart from the obligations to authors and publishers recorded above, the editor would like to make special acknowledgement for the help given him by Mr E. H. McCormick and Mr Frank Sargeson, in preliminary discussion of the problems of selection and in reading the proofs for press.

*September 1952*

# Contents

# Contents

# Introduction

Collections of New Zealand short stories have not been numerous; as this is the first, so far as the editor knows, in which the stories have been arranged in chronological order of subject, some prefatory explanation seems called for. The plan, then, has been to include stories which are complete in themselves and which are all, if not anchored, at least tethered to a time and place that is recognizably New Zealand; to arrange the stories so selected approximately in the historical order of their settings; and to ensure, so far as is possible to fallible judgement, that the literary quality of the stories affords more than a mere documentary justification for their inclusion. A disadvantage of this method is that stories by the same author are sometimes separated from each other; an advantage is that the collection, while not compiled for the historian, should throw a sidelight on the history of New Zealand which historical documents more narrowly conceived could hardly give.

This said, the obvious gaps and flaws must be confessed. In the first place, no claim is made for complete representation of periods or settings. The short story appears in New Zealand writing only in the later nineteenth century; and, although inclusion of A. A. Grace's 'The Ngarara' makes a rueful concession to the semi-mythical past, the earlier phases of European colonization must go by default. The intellectuals among the first colonists were too deeply implicated in pioneering to spare energy for anything except the didactic, the hortatory, the political, and the briefly poetic; even in Europe itself, we may remind ourselves, the vogue of the short story was yet to come. Thus the only well-known prose-writer of the nineteenth century to have attempted the form was Lady Barker. Her energy was one of Victorian abundance and, even so, the story given here was written in the comparative leisure which must have been hers after she returned to England.

Again, diligent search has gleaned nothing good enough to represent the nineties. The reasons can only be guessed at: the social and political ferment of the time, the agitations of the Boer War which closed the decade, the rawness of a society no longer English and not yet New Zealand—all this may have distracted potential writers or distorted their talents. If such an explanation be acceptable we must assume that rather similar conditions in the present century did not produce similar results because a tradition had begun to establish itself, because there were more writers, and because fewer of them were diverted into the blind alley of sentimental journalism.

To deficiencies of period must be added those of place. New Zealand's length sprawls for some thousand miles from north to south. If there are places not represented at all, or represented at one time rather than another, it is probably safest to resort to the truism that the winds which carry talent are always arbitrary. Yet, in spite of gaps and although the New Zealand scene is broadly homogeneous, the collection does suggest the range of local differences. To the New Zealand eye at least it will be plain that Auckland—urban or rural—has been sharply observed by Sargeson, Finlayson, Texidor, and Ballantyne; Katherine Mansfield's is a Wellington not yet changed beyond recognition; Anthony's cows still have to be fed during the Taranaki winter; the social gradations implicit in Lady Barker's picture of an early Canterbury persist today, and it will be noted from James Courage's story that even natural cataclysms are less unruly there; A. P. Gaskell's big game identifies Dunedin; and Davin's 'Saturday Night', though not the cotter's that might have been expected in a largely Scottish community, could have been set only in Southland.

The principles of selection already suggested account for other omissions more serious, or at least less inevitable. Where space must be considered, two stories which reflect similar periods or similar local settings can seldom both be included and this has meant the rejection of good work. The criterion of local setting itself has excluded much: the journal or the public for which an author wrote, especially in the earlier periods, often called for the exotic, an escape from the background the author and his public really knew. The author went to the Russian steppes or the South Seas or wherever else the familiar might be evaded; and so his story became irrelevant to this collection—and, too often, bad as well.

Writers as good as William Satchell or Robin Hyde, moreover, preferred the novel with its looser and more spacious form. When they resorted to the short story they seem to have done so to please an editor and the public rather than themselves; so that what they wrote has been found too melodramatic, journalistic, or commercial to be represented here. And, indeed, the necessity to earn a sudden guinea may be a further reason for the shortage of material in the earlier periods. When writers knew, or fancied, that seriousness and veracity were unmarketable, pocket had to be preferred to pride.

The absence of writers as distinguished as Jane Mander and John Mulgan will be noted. Neither wrote short stories. Jane Mander evidently found the novel gave her the scope she needed. As for Mulgan, before the war cut him off he published *Man Alone* and wrote *Report on Experience*. It would be ungracious to lament the things that a busy life and its premature close left him no time to give.

The preponderance of stories written in this century has already been indicated and in part explained. The explanation would not be complete without a reference to the prestige conferred on the form by the work of Katherine Mansfield; the example of tenacious devotion and careful craftsmanship set by Frank Sargeson; and the courage and encouragement of a few journals—*Landfall* the most conspicuous current instance—and less than a handful of publishers. These, and a discriminating though small public, do much to account for the fact that New Zealand has never had more, and more promising young writers than it has today. Some of these writers are not represented here. Their absence is due sometimes to difficulties of relevance or duplication; and sometimes to the confidence of the editor that their best is still to come.

This collection has been entitled *New Zealand Short Stories*. How far is that title justified? Obviously, from what has been said, the collection is not universally representative. So the charitable will attribute the title's apparent inclusiveness to the need for brevity and not to editorial arrogance. But in it other questions are ambushed. In what sense are these New Zealand short stories? What is a New Zealand short story? Is there such a thing at all?

Difficult things first. Clearly it would be imprudent to generalize from a collection which can hardly avoid the criticism that it is arbitrary and subjective. Still, it may be legitimate to look for something that would suggest a specifically New Zealand contribution to the form. Nothing of the kind seems to offer itself. The more ingenuous of the stories here collected—and it may be a modern snobbery which makes us find these among the earlier in date—are 'colonial' rather than particularly New Zealand in form.

Consider, for instance, the device of the first-person narrator. In the hands of Lapham it is only a step in innocence from the yarns swapped by station hands in an hour of leisure; an innocence that Lady Barker transcribes from life—with a Mother Hubbard over the language—in her inset shepherd's tale. But the same circumstances have produced the same device in Australian and American writing of a corresponding period.

True, the device is used elsewhere and later for increasingly more sophisticated purposes. With Baucke—'I am a colonial, and sweet to me are the scents of the land of my birth'—it is in part the voice of a personal manifesto, and not a bad one despite the Victorian ballad's intruding echo. Later still it is the device of the conscious artist anxious to shed self-conscious literary mannerisms and get closer to the truth of life as he knows it. 'Here I am, gumboots and all, like me or lump me' is part of the underlying motive. But this too is a 'colonial' attitude and the literary method it entails will be found wherever the mode of living provokes it.

In this collection the device can be seen so used in the story of Alice Webb—unsophisticated only in its conclusion—and more effectively still in F. S. Anthony's 'Winter Feeding the Herd'. For its consummation, however, it has to wait till in the stories of Frank Sargeson its superficial simplicity is used to express a meaning poetic in its subtlety.

But honesty, direct or implicit, is not a colonial monopoly; the first person singular narrator belongs to our time rather than to our country. Indeed scrutiny of the short stories in this collection merely bears out what is prima facie probable: there is no specific New Zealand contribution to form—for it would be provincial of us, if not parochial, to claim that Katherine Mansfield learnt her art anywhere but in Europe, though we may also assert that in her finest stories she turned back to her memories of New Zealand to use that art. All that can be claimed is that our writers have shown honesty and skill in learning from the techniques they have found in the universal literature of the short story and applying what they have learnt to the material and the life they knew. Nor need this provoke surprise. The New Zealand literary tradition, in so far as one exists, is still being created and has reached its present development in only two or three generations. In the literature of the whole world there have been few who mastered and bettered the form with which they began; and those few were men of genius.

The discerning eye will see the influence of many European and American writers reflected here—Maupassant, Chekhov, James, Sherwood Anderson, Joyce, Saroyan, Farrell, have all left their mark. And one or two of the later stories suggest that Katherine Mansfield has herself been closely conned. But in the main the influences have been assimilated and the individual writer, whatever he may have learnt from the technique of others, can always be distinguished. For all the simplicity, the obvious authenticity, with which Sargeson uses the speech rhythms and the vernacular of the anonymous every-kiwi, no-one could confuse a story of his with that of another writer. Katherine Mansfield is herself from the beginning. Lady Barker's limpid grace is peculiarly her own. And it is so, in varying degrees, with the rest.

If we cannot seek a special New Zealand quality in the form we may still find it in things less obvious than the settings. Editorial bias is surely not the only reason why almost all the stories here are about people at work or never very far from work. There are none which depend on wit and only one—'By the Lake'—which approaches fantasy.

Perhaps this, and the rarity of humour, is to be regretted; but the pervading seriousness may be significant. In part, of course, it is only what is to be expected of writers who write with often slender hope of publication, let alone of fame or even recognition. But it cannot be merely the result of a professional predicament. It has grown as the art of the short story has grown. And—Katherine Mansfield, as always, apart—the growing point was the depression. In this collection Gilbert's 'A Girl with Ambition' is the first unequivocal sign that the earlier optimism has gone. The struggle has become grimmer. The pioneers, fighting external nature, could afford exhilaration. Their posterity came with the depression to realize that the pioneers had cleared the preliminary minefields only.

When the conditions of the cruder conflict—in the bush, in football, or in war—are renewed, something of the old exuberance returns. But in most of these stories the scar is there and often the note is of a turning away. We shall never know who won Gaskell's 'The Big Game' because its author was interested in what happened before it and scorned the easy tension of the game itself. A Victorian would have given us the whole. For perhaps similar reasons Sargeson 'never went up to Nick's place', Stewart left 'The Whare' furtively by night, Texidor—unlike Lady Barker—did not enjoy 'The Annual Picnic', and Reece Cole, grieving for the happiness his childhood missed, cannot wrench it from the situation where it might still be.

The same gravity seems to underlie the stories where Maoris enter. (That gifted people has not yet given us imaginative writers in English.) Here, too, the post-depression authors have lost the innocence that shows in Grace, and the hint of remorse that appears in Baucke's 'A Quaint Friendship' becomes more open. Finlayson's 'The Totara Tree', though good-humoured, does not leave his sympathy for the Maoris in doubt. In 'The Whare' Stewart gets much of his tension from the contrast between the Maori, however abased still able to enjoy, and the pakeha, acquisitive but impotent for anything more than pleasure. And in Gaskell's 'School Picnic' remorse has changed to a partisan anger all the more effective because it is the reader who becomes the partisan; behind the implicit indictment of the school teacher's unawakened heart is an honourable jealousy that it is the Maoris who have remained alive.

It may be rash to associate with the seriousness of which I have spoken the nostalgic note recurring in these stories. Men are predisposed to believe the past better than the present. And in our time writers, like psychologists, have tended to look to childhood for the sources of their troubles, believing that the rose sickens in the bud. Yet the fact that so many of these stories turn back to the authors' early life, hinting so often like Lady Barker's Bob that 'Things are very different now', may have its special significance. In our civilization, so quickly achieved and so soon found wanting, there is a special place for the myth of the good old days when neighbours were people you spoke to and on whom you depended.

Not that neighbourliness is wholly a legend, or extinct even now. Cobbers, men working, playing, drinking, fighting together, are in the foreground of most New Zealand stories. Family, friendship, the people who know you, are never far away. Our writers, even when they fret against the tolerance or the censure of those who knew them when they were 'so high', are deeply rooted in the social life; it is perhaps not solely editorial imagination which discerns in their work a warmth and humanity which is less characteristic of older and colder cultures.

D.M.D.

*March 1952*

ALFRED A. GRACE

# The Ngarara

The canoe, carried helpless on the top of a big roller, grounded on the beach with a bump which shook the thwarts out of her and threw Kahu-ki-te-rangi and his companions sprawling on the sand.

Kahu' 's companions were Popoia and Kareao: they three were the sole survivors of a large fishing-party which had left Mamaku, a hundred miles and more down the coast, and had been blown out to sea.

Kahu', Popoia, and Kareao were almost dead with cold and hunger, and for a while lay stiff and motionless, till Kahu' rose and began to stamp his feet and chafe himself.

'Then, you are not dead, Kahu'?' said Kareao. 'I, too, have some life left in me;' and he rose, and began to run to and fro to restore his circulation.

Popoia got up last.

'I, too, am here,' he said; 'but my limbs are stiff like the branches of a tree.'

The sun just then broke out brightly, and the three men soon got warm, though they were hungrier than ever.

First they hauled the canoe high and dry; then they took their wet *korowai* cloaks and hung them in the sun. 'Now,' said Kahu', 'we will see what sort of food we can find in this place.' And he led the others up the beach.

They closely examined the vegetation which grew thickly along the shore, but could find nothing to eat—not so much as a berry. They had almost given up in despair, when Kahu', who was ahead of Popoia and Kareao, cried out:

'Come here! These look like wild *kumara.*'

'This is an old plantation which has been overgrown,' said Kareao.

'Anyhow,' said Popoia, 'we have found food.'

Some of the sweet tubers they ate raw, others they took to the place where they had come ashore.

'Now,' said Kahu', 'we will make a fire.' With a heavy stone he broke one of the canoe thwarts, from which he split a piece about an inch thick. This last he handed to Kareao. 'There,' he said, 'you take the *kaureure;* I and Popoia will hold the *kauati,*' which was what he called the rest of the thwart.

Kareao put the point of the *kaureure* upon the middle of the *kauati,* and worked it backwards and forwards with sharp, strong strokes.

'Ah,' he said, 'you two have the easy part, holding the *kauati.* You know that part; you have done it before. But I am the strong man—I have the *kaureure.* I make the *kauati* hot, I make the fire come. I am the man.'

The other two laughed.

But, all the same, Kareao grew tired, and was glad when Popoia rose to help him with the *kaureure.* When Popoia had got a good hold of the implement, Kareao let go, and helped to hold the *kauati.*

'Hah!' said Popoia. 'You are not the man, Kareao. With you the *kaureure* had no strength, no heat; but the *kumara* I have eaten give me power; I give the power to the *kaureure,* and the *kaureure* gives it to the *kauati.* But I have done that before, many times. I am the man with the burning *kaureure!'*

And the others laughed.

But at last Popoia grew tired, and his rubbing flagged. Kahu' rose and relieved him.

'Now,' said Kahu', 'you will see what I can do. So far I have been silent, but that was because I waited to see how you two would succeed. One, two, three, four! Hoo! ha! hoo! ha! Now watch. In my hands the *kaureure* is the begetter of fire. One, two; one, two. I do with the *kauati* what I please. See, it smokes! Hoo! ha! hoo! ha! It burns! Quick, Popoia! the dry grass!'

The *kauati* was now smouldering, and the charred wood and tinder were soon fanned into a flame: the men had made a fire, blazing and hot.

'Now,' said Kahu', when they had eaten as many roasted *kumara* as they could, 'we will look for water and explore the island. We will see what people live here.'

They walked along the beach till they came to high, beetling cliffs, where there was a big cave, and half a mile beyond this they found ruined huts and the remains of a *pa,* which was overgrown with fern and bushes.

'How is this?' said Kareao. 'Where are the people?'

'They have gone away,' said Kahu'. 'They have found a better fishing-ground.'

'You two are clever,' said Popoia; 'you answer a question before it is asked. But what is that at the edge of the clearing?'

A figure was moving from bush to bush, as though watching them.

'We see you hiding there!' cried Kareao. 'Come into the open.'

'We won't hurt you,' cried Popoia. 'Come and tell us who you are.'

'Why are you so frightened of us?' asked Kahu', as a bent and skinny old woman approached them.

'Aaaaah! *tena koutou,*' wailed she, seizing them by the hands. '*Tena koe! tena koe! Katahi te koa!*' she cried, as she rubbed noses with them one by one. 'You are strong handsome men, and I thought you were the Ngarara.'

'The Ngarara?' said Popoia.

'Who's he?' said Kareao. 'We don't know him.'

'What tribe does he belong to?' said Kahu'.

'The Ngarara—you never heard of *him*?' said the old woman. 'He is *the* Ngarara—the real one. Big body, eight feet long; big webbed foot; big wings like a bat's, with which he flies and catches fish; long tail like a *tuatara* lizard's, but bigger; skin like the bark of the red pine.'

'This is very strange,' said Kareao.

'You astonish us,' said Popoia.

'Is it really possible?' said Kahu'.

'He came to the island nearly four years ago,' said the old woman, 'and made his home in a cave which winds far into the cliff. No one but the Ngarara knows all the windings of the cave. When the people were on the beach launching a canoe or looking for *pipi,* out of his cave would rush the Ngarara and catch two or three with his claws, and carry them into his cave, where he would eat them up. Sometimes he would lie in the "bush" and catch them when they went to snare birds; he would seize the women as they were digging *kumara* in the plantation, and the men as they were fishing from canoes. He was fond of the Maori; he made *kai* of my tribe, of all but me—I am too old, too skinny—and my daughter Hinana.'

'Your daughter—why did he spare her?' asked Kareao.

'She is his wife. He keeps her in his cave.'

The men's faces were filled with horror.

'Your daughter is the Ngarara's wife!' exclaimed Popoia.

'We must take her from him,' said Kahu'.

'She was the prettiest girl on the island,' said the old woman. 'The Ngarara saw that—he keeps her for himself. But if you stay here inactive he will catch you, too, and eat *you* up! Yet, if you are brave, very brave, I will show you a way to kill him. We shall see—we shall see. Come down with me to the beach.'

The old woman led them through the 'bush' to a distant part of the island, where the smooth sand stretched half a mile.

'Now,' she said, as they stood in a group round her, 'you see that pile of driftwood lying just below high-water mark? You shall run a race to that and back again, and the man who wins shall have my daughter when we have rescued her from the Ngarara. One, two, three—go!'

Away raced the men across the soft, smooth sand, their feet leaving long tracks behind them, till the old woman's weak sight could no longer distinguish one runner from another.

When they rounded the driftwood they came back, each straining every muscle to reach the old woman first. But one man was far ahead of the others. It was Kahu-ki-te-rangi; he won easily.

'Very good,' said the old woman; 'you are a quick runner; you are rightly called Kahu-ki-te-rangi—"the Hawk in the Heavens". I will now show you the Ngarara.'

So they all went through the 'bush' to the other side of the island, and lay concealed on the top of a high cliff.

'The tide has turned,' said the old woman. 'When it is nearly full the Ngarara comes out to catch fish. His cave is underneath the spot where we are lying.'

What she said was quite true, for before very long they heard a terrific noise in the earth beneath them, and the Ngarara appeared on the sands below.

He was black all over. His great head was like a bird's, but featherless and bare, and ended in a huge tapering muzzle, which was armed with numberless sharp teeth. His body was like a great bat's, and his wings, which at first he held close to his sides, ended at the top in bunches of sharp claws. He ran down to the water's edge after the manner of a great sea-fowl, snapping his horrible teeth this way and that in his eagerness to catch his prey.

When he had waded into the water up to his middle, he stretched out his wings, which extended twenty feet from tip to tip, and scooped the fish first with one wing and then with the other into his open mouth. But when the fish fled in fear into deep water, the Ngarara flew after them like a bird, dived, and caught them with his immense jaws, which he snapped together so loudly that the sound reached Kahu', Kareao, and Popoia, as they stood on the cliff.

'It is time we went,' said the old woman. 'If we stay here any longer he will see us, and then he will certainly eat you up. Let us go and make the *taiepawhare* in which to catch him.'

'Urrrgh!' exclaimed Kahu', shuddering, 'it would be better to be eaten than to be the wife of such a monster.'

So they went into the heart of the 'bush', and there the old woman gave them heavy stone axes with which they cut down thick branches of the trees. These they placed firmly side by side, in two rows each, a chain long and six feet apart, and the roof, which was ten feet from the ground, they made of lighter boughs and *toé-toé*. Then they drove a strong stake into the ground so as to block one entrance, and heaped dry fern and *toé-toé* on each side of the *taiepa-whare,* and all the preparations were made for the reception of the Ngarara.

'Now,' said the old woman, 'there remains but one thing. Here is a *pouwhenua,* stout and strong, for each of you. You, Kareao, stand with this big spear on one side of the *taiepa-whare,* and you, Popoia, take this and stand on the other. Kahu', take yours and place it in the *taiepa-whare,* about the middle, and then go and do as I have directed. You are a good runner; now is the time to prove that you are indeed Kahu-ki-te-rangi, that you can run as fast as a hawk flies in the heavens. See if you can race the Ngarara.'

So Kahu' departed, alone and unarmed. He passed through the forest till he came to the beetling cliff above the Ngarara's cave, and there he called out:

'Cooooeeeeee! Cooooooooooooeeee! Cooooooooooooeeee!'

Soon there was a noise like rumbling thunder in the bowels of the earth, and out of his cave came the Ngarara.

First he ran this way along the beach, then he ran that, but could see nothing.

'Cooooooooooooeeeee!' called Kahu' from the top of the cliff, and in a moment the Ngarara caught sight of him.

Kahu' saw the great jaws open and display their lines of teeth, and he retreated to the shelter of the 'bush'.

There was a great flapping and the sound of falling rocks, and right over the face of the cliff came the Ngarara, with open mouth and scrambling feet and flapping wings.

Kahu' turned and ran.

The Ngarara pursued. First he stretched out one wing to scoop the Maori into his mouth, then he stretched out the other; but each wing caught in a tree, and Kahu' ran uninjured through the forest. But now the Ngarara folded his wings and ran, too. Kahu' could hear his heavy breathing, and smelt the horrible odour of his body. Again and again the Ngarara had almost caught his prey in his teeth, but Kahu-ki-te-rangi had not received his name for nothing, and he ran fast to the mouth of the *taiepa-whare*—on either side of which his comrades lay concealed—and disappeared inside of the trap.

The Ngarara, in his eagerness to catch his prey never noticed that the leaves on the boughs of the *taiepa-whare* were beginning to wither. He did not see Popoia and Kareao hiding behind the heaps of *toé-toé* and fern. He plunged straight into the *taiepa-whare* after Kahu'.

Kareao and Popoia immediately arose, each grasping his *pouwhenua,* and stood ready. Kahu' ran to the middle of the trap, where he found his weapon, and seizing this he turned and faced the Ngarara.

And now the great reptile was caught at a disadvantage. The constricted space of the *taiepa-whare* pressed his formidable wings close to his sides, and rendered his claws almost useless. His teeth were the only weapons he had left; but they were many, and sharp, and long.

With these he snapped menacingly at Kahu', but Kahu' never flinched, and bravely awaited the onslaught of the Ngarara.

Plunge! He had driven his big spear into the reptile's eye, and pinned the monster's great head to the earth.

The Ngarara lashed with his tail, and in his agony tried to burst the walls of the trap with the weight of his huge body; but his endeavours only made matters worse for him, for Popoia and Kareao could now see in what part of the *taiepa-whare* Karu' held him pinned by his head to the ground. From either side they plunged their stout spears into his belly, and transfixed him to the earth.

Thus they held him, calling to and encouraging each other, till the Ngarara was exhausted and could struggle no more.

Then Kahu' came out of the *taiepa-whare* and set fire to the fern and *toé-toé*.

The Ngarara was burned to ashes.

Throughout this exciting scene the old woman had stood behind a tree, praising the men and cheering them on; but when the Ngarara was dead and burnt she led them down to the mouth of the cave, and called:

'Hinana, come to us. The Ngarara is dead; nothing remains of him. Come to your mother and the brave men who have saved you.'

Softly and full of fear the girl crept to the cave's entrance till she caught sight of Kahu', Popoia, Kareao, and her mother.

'But I dare not come,' she said, crying. 'If the Ngarara were to know that I came out of the cave, he would kill and eat me as he did all my relations.'

'But the Ngarara is dead,' said Kareao. 'I plunged my spear into his body.'

'There is nothing left of him but a few charred bones,' said Popoia.

'You need not fear,' said Kahu'. 'If the Ngarara were alive we should not dare to come openly to his cave. When he last left you he pursued me into the *taiepa-whare,* and there I transfixed him with my *pouwhenua.* He is dead, and you are now *my* wife.'

'That is all true,' said the old woman. 'Come, Hinana, and greet your mother and your husband, and then we will show you the place where the Ngarara died.'

Convinced, Hinana came out of the cave and *tangi'd* with her deliverers.

'*This* is your husband, Kahu-ki-te-rangi, the man who raced the Ngarara,' said her mother. 'He will soon make you happy.'

'I am quite light-hearted already,' said Hinana, 'for you can imagine what joy it is to become the wife of such a brave *toa* after having been married to the Ngarara for nearly three years.'

LADY BARKER

# Christmas Day in New Zealand

A great deal of the success of mustering depends on the clearness of the weather, as it is of no use going on the hills if a mist is hanging about. Very often, in the early summer, the hills are covered during the night by filmy clouds, which do not always disperse until the sun has risen and shrivelled them into light, upward-floating wreaths by one touch of his lance-like beams. But it is a great disadvantage in a day's mustering to make a late start; the sheep have dispersed from their high camping grounds, and are feeding all up the gullies and over the hill-sides in scattered mobs; and it is of course much harder work walking under the burning sun than if his fiercest hour of mid-day heat found the men at the top of the range of hills, and with the sheep so well in hand, driving slowly before them, as to allow of the tired musterers sitting down under the shadow of a great rock (for there are no trees), and having a ten minutes' 'spell' and half a pipe.

We were in the middle of mustering on this 25th of December, and the weather had not been quite so propitious as usual. A great deal of rain had fallen among the hills at the back of the run, and very few mornings dawned as cloudless and clear as the musterers desired. Of course Christmas Day would be a complete holiday, and we had invited shearers and musterers, and all the odd hands which flock to a station at shearing-time, to come up to our house, which stood in a valley a mile or so away from the sheep-yards, wool-shed, etc., and attend first a church service and then a good dinner, the day to wind up with athletic games.

The bad weather had been such an anxiety to F—— for some days past, that he could not shake off the habit of watching the clouds at sunset, and I had laughed at him on Christmas Eve for going out late at night to see if 'Flagpole had put on his night-cap'. Flagpole was the highest hill on our run; in any other country it would have been called a mountain, being over 3000 feet high; but as one of the last low spurs of the great Southern Alps, it did not take any rank after those mighty monarchs. When Flagpole put on his nightcap of clouds he was never in a hurry to take it off again, and the surrounding lower hills thought it only polite, I suppose, to follow his example, for it was sure to be a misty morning until 9 or 10 o'clock, if Flagpole had drawn his nightcap well over his rocky ears after sunset.

'Never mind Flagpole,' I said; 'there will be no mustering to-morrow, so it does not signify what he does.' But F—— still loitered in the verandah, watching Flagpole's misty summit, until long after I was asleep and dreaming of the pies and puddings I had been so busy preparing all day for my Christmas dinner.

Such was the force of habit, that the first faint streak of daylight stealing into our bedroom woke both F—— and me wide awake, and our first thought forgetting in our sleepiness that Christmas Day had dawned, was, 'Is it a fine clear morning?' F—— tumbled out of bed, and, murmuring something about going to see, stepped sleepily out of the French window which opened on the verandah and commanded an exquisite view up the valley whose narrow entrance was guarded by Flagpole. It soon stole like a delicious whisper on my sleep-steeped senses that there was actually no occasion to rouse myself up, for that it was Christmas Day, and there would be no mustering, no getting up at 5 o'clock, no anxiety about the weather. Flagpole and his nightcap became matters of profound indifference to me as I settled myself comfortably for another nap; yet, drowsy as I was, I can never forget the excitement in F——'s face as he darted back into the cosy little bedroom. If we had been in the North Island, I should have imagined that a regiment of Maoris were encamped on the lawn; but in our peaceful Middle Island home we are not even afraid of thieves, still less of murderers. I certainly thought F—— had gone suddenly stark staring mad, for he made one bound to a stand of fire-arms which hung against the bedroom wall, seized his rifle, and merely gasping out the words, 'More cartridges!' dashed out as swiftly as he had entered.

Here was a rude awakening on Christmas morning! 'It can't be a hawk,' I thought to myself; 'what *can* it be?' But I jumped out of bed, flung on my dressing-gown, thrust my feet into my slippers, and taking as many cartridges as my hands would hold, out of their tin box, I stepped out of the window into the verandah. No F—— was to be seen; nothing but the quiet home-like scene of lawn and garden and paddock glistening with dew, and Sandy, the house cat, daintily moving about in quest of his breakfast, which invariably consisted of the early bird. Acting entirely on instinct, I peeped round the corner of the house, which commanded a view of downs rolling into a narrow gully, the flax swamp of which formed a natural boundary to one bit of the kitchen garden. A slender path made of very rough shingle and gravel wound among the sloping potato and strawberry beds, and along this path F—— was creeping, almost on his hands and knees, so as to keep well under cover of the gorse hedge at the bottom of the garden. It must have been the most painful progress ever made by sporting pilgrim, and it was certainly the most ridiculous sight which can well be imagined. Bare-headed and bare-footed, crouching down on the rough path until he looked only about four feet high, F—— held his way, his one white garment fluttering in the wind, and his right hand grasping his rifle. The moment I perceived him creeping warily along, I dodged behind a great bush of Cape broom laden with fragrant yellow blossoms, and from this cover I too peered out, not daring to glance at F—— for fear I should laugh aloud. A careful survey of the broken ground beyond the garden fence showed me a huge black boar tranquilly feeding with his back towards the gorse hedge. Fortunately the wind blew down from him to us, so his keen snout was no protection to him. If a cock should crow, or a dog bark, or even a duck quack, he would be off almost like a deer, up those hills and far away before man or dog could reach him.

Still F—— must have his cartridges; if he missed his first shot, a second might bring the great fierce brute down on his knees and give time for the revolver to be used. So I crept swiftly back into the verandah, got the loaded revolver, stuck it and F——'s hunting-knife into the muslin sash of my dressing-gown, and was out again behind the bush in a moment. During my short absence, F—— had made great progress, and was rapidly nearing the hedge from whence he would be able to take aim. I could not get up to him in time to be of any use without jumping into a wide wet ditch, whose high banks afforded excellent shelter. . . . My kid slippers stuck fast in the tenacious yellow clay and were nearly dragged off my feet, and I made myself in a fine mess in about two minutes. However, I struggled along, feeling rather ashamed of myself, and somewhat inclined to cry. By this time F—— had reached the gorse hedge, and was kneeling down on a tussock (which must have seemed like a velvet cushion after the gravel path) to take a leisurely aim. He glanced round, and beckoned cautiously to me; so I floundered on as quickly as I could until I reached the friendly hedge and could scramble out of the ditch. He took his cartridges from me with only a nod of thanks, for the faintest whisper would have reached the boar's sharp ears. It seemed ages to me before the loud crack of his rifle rang through the clear mountain air, and the boar gave a bound into the air—only to fall flat on his great side, shot through the heart.

F—— and I were over the hedge and wading through the flax swamp before we saw that our game was bagged; indeed, we did not know he was dead and approached him with the greatest caution, for a wounded boar is about the most dangerous animal to attack. When we were able to perceive his huge black side upheaving through the flax bushes we fell into our usual line of march when on sporting expeditions. F—— first, with his finger on the trigger of his revolver, and I as far behind as was compatible with my own safety, carrying the hunting-knife in a very shaky hand.

Our precautions were useless on this occasion, for poor piggy (I am always sorry for them as soon as they are hit) was quite stone dead. He must have been a great age: his gigantic tusks were notched and broken, and his thick hide bore traces of old scars, received in former battles with his enemies; for boars are very pugnacious and will not brook 'a rival near the throne'.

The report of the rifle had aroused the whole establishment. The dogs barked and bayed furiously, the inmates of the poultry-yard seemed to become distracted, to judge by their clamour, and from every window in the house and its outbuildings a bearded head was popped, whilst cries of 'What's up?' 'Wait till I come,' etc. etc., were heard amid the noise of the animals. High and clear, piercing through the Babel of sounds, my maids' shrieks came at intervals like minute-guns at sea. Whenever anything was the matter, from a cut finger to the chimney on fire, the two girls screamed at the pitch of their exceedingly shrill voices. So this Christmas Day was ushered very noisily into existence; but you will be glad to hear that I got back into my own room very cleverly before anyone could array themselves sufficiently to sally forth, so I was spared the disgrace of being seen by my small household with bare feet and muddy skirts.

F—— could not tear himself away from his victim quite so soon, and when next I peeped round the corner of the verandah, I saw him, looking more ridiculous than ever in his short white garment, the centre figure of an admiring and excited group of shepherds and shearers. Pepper, our head shepherd, recognized an old enemy in the dead boar, and declared that he and his dogs had bailed him up unsuccessfully 'many a time and oft'.

*       *       *

I was not sorry, as it happened, that the episode of the boar had aroused the whole household at so early an hour, for it enabled me to get a great deal done before breakfast towards the reception of our Christmas guests. As soon as I had dressed myself, I sallied forth with F——, following the windings of the creek until it led us far back into the hills, to a little wooded gully which nestled between two steep ascents. If only we could have seen that strip of green anywhere from the house! but alas! it was too securely hidden to be visible, and I lighted upon the lonely spot quite by accident in one of my many rambles. At this part the creek was quite as noisy as a Scotch burn, and, like it, rippled and chattered noisily over a stony bed, as it wound for a few hundred yards under the shadow of the trees. Its banks were beautifully fringed with many varieties of ferns, which even in winter were kept green and fresh by the sheltering bushes above. It was upon these lovely feathery ferns my raid was directed; and if F—— and I could have only come across a magical carpet, or that delightful horse in the fairy tale who was set in motion by a peg, either of which would have borne us swiftly across land and sea, we might perhaps have realized a handsome fortune in a few minutes by selling our enormous green bundles in Covent Garden that Christmas morning.

But what a cruel change it would have been for the beautiful ferns from their enchanted mountain nook with the wood-pigeons cooing in the trees above them and the little green paroquets flashing past their waving plume-like tufts, to a cold, raw Christmas morning in smoky London! . . .

When the little homestead was once more reached we deposited our huge armfuls of ferns in a shady hole in the creek, and went in to breakfast with splendid appetites. I am afraid there were no presents exchanged that morning, for we were fifty miles away from the nearest shop, and had not been down to Christchurch for months. However, we received and returned many hearty good wishes; and in that foreign land it is something to be among friends on Christmas Day, even if there are no presents going about.

After breakfast I filled all the vases, and decorated the hall, and covered up the stand of Indian arms with my beautiful ferns, each spray of which was a marvel of grace and loveliness, and then it was time to arrange the verandah for service, which was soon done by the aid of boxes and red blankets. But it was fated that our gravity was to be sorely tried long before the short sermon which F—— read us was ended.

I think I have told you before, that the shepherds who formed the principal portion of our congregation always brought their dogs with them, and these dear sensible animals behaved in the most exemplary manner, lying down by their masters' saddles and never moving aught but their intelligent eyes until church was over, when they greeted their owners with rapture, as if to congratulate them on escaping from some dangerous ceremony. Amongst our most constant guests were the Scotch shepherds of a neighbouring 'squatter'. These men, M'Nab and M'Pherson by name, were excellent specimens of their class. Sober and industrious, they were also exceedingly intelligent, and thoroughly enjoyed the privilege of an invitation to attend our Sunday services. I observed that they invariably took it in turn to come to us; and when I asked M'Nab to come over on Christmas Day, I added, 'Don't you think you could manage to put the sheep in some place from which they would be safe not to stray, and *both* of you come to us at Christmas?'

'It is na the sheep, mem,' replied M'Nab bashfully; 'it's the claes.'

'But your clothes are very nice,' I said, looking at the neat little figure before me, clad in a suit of Lowland plaid, which was somewhat baggy, but clean and whole.

'Yes, mem, but we've naight but the one suit between us. So we can only come one at a time, like,' said M'Nab turning red through his sunbrown.

'Dear me, how can you both wear the same clothes?' I inquired. 'M'Pherson is such a giant, and you are not very tall, M'Nab.'

'Well, mem, we made them our ainsells, and we cut them on a *between* size, you see, so they fit baith, fine. The trews were hard to manage, but 'Phairson wears 'em with gaiters, and I rolls 'em up; so though they're a deal too short for him and too lang for me, we manage first class,' said M'Nab, relapsing into colonial phraseology.

On this Christmas Day it was Long 'Phairson's (as he was generally called) turn to wear the Lowland suit, and he had appeared in due season, accompanied not only by his colleys, but by a small white bull-terrier, with a knowing patch of yellowish-brown over one eye, a most vicious turned-up nose, and a short upper lip.

Fortunately, 'Phairson's arrival had been early, so I contrived to collect my hens and chickens, and decoy them into the fowl-house, out of the reach of this ferocious-looking animal. At church time, therefore, I took my place in the verandah with no domestic anxieties to distract my attention from the beautiful service which had never seemed more beautiful to me than when held in that distant hidden valley with nothing but hills and mountains around us, and a New Zealand summer sky overhead. The great tidings of 'To us a Child is born', rang as sweet and clear and welcome in my ears, amid that profound unbroken silence, as they have done when pealed from organs or proclaimed to hundreds of gathered worshippers with all the pomp and ceremony of the most gorgeous cathedral.

We had even managed to get through a hymn with tolerable correctness, and the last page of the sermon had been reached, when we were 'ware' of an extraordinary scuffling and rustling beneath our feet, accompanied by violent thumps against the wooden flooring of the verandah. It was evidently a battle; but who could the combatants be? Our own dogs were securely fastened up in their kennels, our cat had prudently retreated to a loft as soon as 'Phairson and his dog Nip appeared, and the other colleys, though bristling with excitement at the strange sounds, lay motionless as statues in obedience to their masters' warning glances. I am sorry to own that, as the noise increased, our repressed curiosity and wonder became too much for us, and it was fortunate for the decorum of the congregation that F——'s discourse (borrowed from one of Canon Kingsley's volumes of Cottage Sermons) came to an end, for hardly was the service over before we were perfectly deafened by the thumps. What could they mean? Nip was concerned, no doubt, for M'Pherson looked guilty and nervous; but what unhappy object was he dragging from end to end beneath the verandah? No dog but himself could get beneath the flooring,—the cat we knew was safe. 'Oh! it's Betty, poor Betty!' I shrieked in dismay, as I remembered that a favourite white Aylesbury duck was sitting on her first nest beneath the flooring of the verandah. In vain I had tried to coax her into arranging her nursery elsewhere; she insisted on taking up her abode in a hole scatched by a tame rabbit which had met with an untimely fate some months before.

And so it was Betty, who soon appeared before us, dragged to M'Pherson's feet by Nip, in answer to his summons of 'Nip, ye scamp, come here, sir!' Not a vestige of tail was left to her, but still Nip held firmly on to her poor stump feathers. She had flapped against the boards with her wings as he ruthlessly dragged her up and down beneath our feet; but she must have been too terrified to cry out, for no 'quack' or sound did she utter under this ignominious treatment. In addition to her bodily suffering during the process of parting from her tail, she must have gone through much mental anguish at beholding her cherished eggs scattered and broken. When Nip released her at last with great reluctance, she lay at M'Pherson's feet too utterly exhausted to stir; her snowy plumage, of which she was so daintily careful, all draggled and dusty, her wings extended, and only her bright terrified eyes giving evidence that Nip had not succeeded in killing her. Poor Betty! I took her up in my arms, though she was an immense and very heavy bird, and carried her tenderly into the house, soothing her as well as I could; but still she remained gasping and unable to move. At last I remembered my medicine-bottle full of brandy, and I administered such a tremendous dose of the stimulant, that Betty choked and struggled back into life and movement. In fact, I believe she spent the remainder of Christmas Day in a box full of hay in the stable—very tipsy, but safe, and, I hope, happy. For many weeks no one could look at Betty's ridiculous tail, or rather no-tail, without laughing, but in my eyes it was a very sad sight and I asked M'Pherson never to bring Nip to church again.

As soon as we had restored some sort of gravity, and after Nip had been well scolded and Betty soothed, the men (for alas! there were no women, except my servants, who were busy cooking) adjourned to the washhouse, where F—— presided over a substantial dinner of beef and poultry, for the great point is to have no mutton at a party in New Zealand. We happened to possess a big musical box, which was wound up and set playing, and the dinner proceeded to the sound of a succession of old-fashioned waltz tunes. It was much too hot to remain indoors; so directly the huge dishes of cherries and strawberries (presents from my neighbours' gardens on either side of the ranges) had been duly emptied, the company adjourned to the only spot of shade out-of-doors, the south-eastern side of the stables. We could contemplate little plantations of tiny trees about three feet high, dotted over the low downs, and carefully fenced in from investigating animals. We could contemplate them, I say, and speculate as to how many of us would be in that valley on a Christmas Day in the far future, when these trees would have struggled up against their enemy the Nor'-wester, and attained sufficient stature to afford shelter from the afternoon sun.

Probably not one of the party then assembled will ever sit under those imaginary branches; but at the date I am telling you of, Tom Thumb could not have found shade enough to shield himself from the bath of golden sunbeams anywhere on the run, unless he had joined our party, seated on hen-coops, in the lee of the stable.

The question then seriously presented itself to my mind, of how to amuse my twenty stalwart guests from 3 o'clock until 7. I intended them to have tea again about 5, and quantities of plum cake if they could possibly eat it; but there were two hours of broiling heat to be got through, socially speaking, before they could be invited to eat again. After tea I knew there would be athletic games, so soon as Flagpole's mighty shadow had laid a cool patch over the valley. My guests would be affronted if I went away, and yet my presence evidently made them miserable. They all sat in rigid and uncomfortable attitudes, and blushed furiously if I spoke to them, trying hard all the time to persuade themselves and me that they were enjoying themselves. Even the unfailing pipes, which I had insisted on being produced, failed to create an element of contentment, for the smokers suffered incessant anxiety lest the light shifting summer air should send a puff of tobacco-smoke towards me. We were all very polite, but wretched; and I shall never forgive F——'s unkind enjoyment of the horrible dullness of this stage of my party. 'Dear me, this is too exciting,' he would whisper; 'don't let them all talk at once;' or else he would ask me if it was not 'going off' very brilliantly, when all the time it was not going off at all.

I began to grow desperate; my company would not talk or do anything, but sit steadily staring at each other and me. In vain I asked questions about subjects which I thought might interest them. Conversation seemed impossible, and I had firmly resolved to go away in five minutes, and see if they would be more lively without me, when some bold individual started the subject of gold-digging. Everybody's tongue was unloosed as if by magic, and all had some really interesting story to tell about either their own or their 'mate's' experiences at the West Coast gold-diggings. One man described with much humour how he had been in the very first 'rush', and how amazed a lonely settler in the Bush had been at the sudden appearance of a thousand men in the silence and solitude of his hut, which was built up a gully. When the eager gold-seekers questioned him as to whether he had found the 'colour' in the creek which they were bent on tracing to its rich source, he lazily shook his head and said, coolly, pointing over his shoulder, 'Me and the boys' (his equally lazy sons) 'have never earned no wages, no, nor had any money of our own. Whenever we wanted to go to the store'—about twenty miles off, and a wretched track between—'we jest took and we washed a bit among that 'ere dirt, and we allers found as much dust as we wanted.' The bed of that creek contained nearly as many particles of fine flake-gold as of sand; and that lazy old man could have made a fabulous fortune years and years before, if he had taken the trouble to see it, as it rippled past his log hut. He never found a speck of gold in all his life afterwards, for no sooner had he finished his dawdling speech than the diggers had flung themselves into the wealth-bearing streamlet and fought and scrambled for its golden sands, which glided away during the night like a fairy vision. Great boulders were upheaved by the gold-seekers in their first eager rush, so the natural dams being thus removed, when the next morning dawned the water had rushed away into a new channel, bearing its precious freight with it.

The spokesman took from his neck a little wash-leather bag as he finished his story, with the words, 'All gone—clean gone;' and opening it shook a few pinches of the sparkling flaky dust into my lap, saying, 'That's some o' wot I got evenin' before. It's beautiful, ain't it, mum?' I duly admired the shining treasure, and he bade me keep it 'for my Christmas box', and I have it safely put away to this day. But I very nearly lost it, and this is how it happened. A discussion arose as to the most successful method of washing sand for gold, and some new inventions were freely discussed. 'Well, I reckon I got them there nuggets'—the largest no bigger than a small pin's head—'by washin' with a milk dish.' How?' I asked. 'I'll show you, mum, if I may get a dish from the gals;' and he strode off towards the house, returning with a large milk-tin in his hands. He then proceeded to the side of the duck-pond, and, in spite of the 'agony of dress' in which he was arrayed, filled the shallow dish with mud and stones and grit of all sorts. At this stage of the proceedings he appeared intent on making a huge dirt-pie. Imagine my dismay when he pounced on the paper packet into which I had just carefully collected my gold-dust, counted the tiny flakes rapidly up to fifteen, and then scattered them ruthlessly over the surface of this abominable mess. He next proceeded to stir it all up with a piece of wooden shingle, and regardless of my face of dismay, said calmly, 'Now we'll wash 'em out.' I should have had no objection to seeing the experiment tried with anybody else's gold dust, but I must say I was very sorry to find that my newly acquired treasure was thus lightly disposed of. 'Lightly won, lightly lost,' I thought to myself, 'for I shall never see it again.'

Pratchard (that was the name of the quondam digger) now marched off to the creek close by, and in spite of the blazing sunshine we all followed him. He stooped down, and, scooping up some water, began shaking his great heavy tin backwards and forwards. By degrees he got rid of the surface mud, then he added more water, until in half an hour or so he had washed and shaken all the materials for his dirt-pie out of the dish, and disclosed my fifteen wee nuggets shining like so many flecks of sunlight at the bottom of the tin vessel. 'Count 'em, mum, if *you* please,' said Pratchard, hot, but triumphant; and so I did, to find not one missing. To me it seemed like a conjuror's trick, but Pratchard and the rest of my company hastened to assure me that it was not possible to wash away gold. It sank and sank, being so much heavier than anything else, until it could be perceived at the bottom of whatever dish or even plate was used to scoop up the dirt among which it was to be found.

We were more sociable now, but hotter than ever, and we returned gladly to the shade of the stable. As things looked more promising at this stage of my party, I suggested that everybody should, in turn, tell a story. Of course they all declared 'they didn't know nothing', but finally I coaxed old Bob, a shepherd, to tell me about one of his early Christmas Days in the colony, and this is his narrative, but not in his own phraseology. I wish I could spell it as he pronounced it.

\*      \*      \*

'Things are very different now,' said Bob, 'all over the country, though it is not so many years ago, not more than six or seven perhaps. We did not think much of Sunday in the early days; we didn't exactly work, such as digging or such-like on that day, but we did other jobs which had been waiting for a spare moment all the week. We used not to think any harm of breaking a young colt on Sunday, or of riding over to the next run with a draughting notice; or if it was wet we lay in our bunks and smoked, or p'raps we got up and sat on a bucket turned wrong side up, and mended our clothes. As for Christmas Day, we never thought of it beyond wondering what sort of "duff" we were going to have. That's colonial for a pudding, ma'am, you know, don't you? If we had a couple of handfuls of currants and raisins, we shoved them into a lot of flour and sugar, and we put a bit of mutton fat into the middle, and tied it all up together in the sleeve of an old flannel shirt and boiled it, and it used to come out a first-rate plum duff and we thought we had no end of a Christmas if we could manage such a pudding as that.

'But we could not always get even a holiday on Christmas Day, because of the shearing. Shearers were too scarce in those days, and wages too high to miss a day's work, so it often happened that we had to work just as hard, or harder on Christmas than on any other day of the year. I was working then up at Mr Vansittart's ('Vans-start's', Bob called his master), and we had hopes of getting finished by Christmas Eve, and having at all events a good lie-in-bed on Christmas Day; but as ill-luck would have it, a mob of wethers bolted

from the flat where Tom Duckworth was watching them, and got
right away into the hills at the back of the run. *He* said it was because
his dogs were new and wouldn't work properly for him, but I knew
better—he done it a-purpose. Tom's sheep were always coming to
grief. He couldn't cross 'em over a river without losing half the mob,
and never a week passed without his getting boxed. That's mixed-up,
ma'am,' explained Bob politely, observing a puzzled expression in
my eyes. 'We calls it boxing when your sheep go and join another
mob feeding close by, and you can't tell one from another except by
the brand or the ear-mark. It's a nasty business is boxing, and *werry*
trying to the temper. Even the dogs get out of patience like, and nip
the stupid sheep harder than they do at any other time.

'Well, ma'am, as I was saying, Tom Duckworth let a fine mob of
young wethers get away the day before Christmas Day, and started
to look for them with his precious dogs. They were the very last mob
which had to come up to be shorn, so, as he couldn't find 'em—I
never expected he could,—there was the skillions standing empty,
and the shearers lounging about idling when Christmas Day came;
and a werry beautiful day it was, just like this one. The boss, that's
Master Vans-start, he was at his wits' ends what to do. He knew right
well that if the wethers wasn't in the yards that night, the shearers
would be off across the hills to Brown and Wetherby's next morning
first thing. You couldn't expect men who had their two pounds a day
waiting for them to lose many days, especially as Brown and
Wetherby's was an "open shed", where any shearers that came were
taken on until there were hands enough, so they knew they might
lose the job if they didn't look sharp. The boss managed to keep
them quiet on Christmas Day, by pretending he always meant to
take a spell on that day. He got the cook to make a stunning duff, and
he sent a boy on horseback across the river to Mulready's for some
beef; he knew Mulready always killed a bullock about Christmas
and he served out some grog, so in that way he kept the shearers well
fed and rested all Christmas Day. He never let them out of his sight,
not even down to the creek to wash their shirts, lest any of them
should slip away.

'I didn't come in for any of these good things: so far from it, quite
the contra-*ry*;' and here Bob paused and took a pull at his pipe,
resting his hands on his knees and gazing straight before him with
regretful eyes, as the memory of his wrongs rose freshly to his mind.
'Tom Duckworth did, though, the stupid fool! He laid in his bunk on
Christmas morning and had his snooze out, and then he got up and
eat the best part of a cold leg of mutton for his breakfast, and he
came in for the duff, and the grog, and all the rest of it afterwards.

But I'll tell you how I spent my Christmas Day, ma'am, and I hope I'll never have to spend another like it.

'As soon as ever it was light, the boss, leastways Master Vans-start, he came into the kitchen where I was sleeping, and he says, "Bob, I must have that mob of wethers by tonight, and that's all about it. They're quite likely to have gone up into the back ranges, but unless they're gone up into the sky I'm bound to have 'em in the skillions tonight." You see, ma'am, when Master Vans-start put it in that way, I knew that mob had got to be found before nightfall, and that he was going to tell me off to find 'em. So I lay there and listened, as was my dooty to. "Bob," says Master Vans-start, "I'll tell you what it is, I'll give you a fiver," — that's a five-pound note, ma'am, you'll understand, — "yes, Bob, a fiver, over and above your year's pay when I draws a cheque for your wages next week, and you can go down to town and spend it, Bob, if you bring me in the whole of that mob of wethers by sundown. Take anybody you like with you and the best of the dogs, only you bring them in; for if you don't, I shall be three hundred pounds short in my wool-money this year, and I've got too heavy a mortgage on this run, Bob, to be able to afford to lose that much, and all through Tom Duckworth's sleepy-headedness."

'Well, ma'am, when the boss spoke so feelingly, and put it to me in that way, I knew it had to be done, so I said, "Right you are, sir," and then he only said, "I looks to you, Bob, for them sheep," and he went away. It was barely light enough to see your hand, and I knew that the *mistesses* (that was the way Bob pronounced mists) would be hanging about the hills for a good time yet, so I reached out my hand and I got my pipe and a match and I smoked a bit, whilst I considered which way I should go and who I should take with me. Men, I mean; I didn't want to know what dogs I should take, for if Sharp and Sally couldn't find 'em, all I could say was, they wasn't to be found. I'd a good mind to name Tom Duckworth to come, but I meant to give whoever went with me a pound a-piece, and I didn't want to tip him for giving all this bother; besides, he was just as likely as not to sit down under the lea of a rock and smoke the moment he got out of my sight. No, I wouldn't take Tom, but I'd take little Joe Smelt, who was as active as a kid on the hills, and Munro, who, although he belonged to the next station, knew every yard of country round, and who had the best head on his shoulders of any man I knew. Besides, Munro had always been a chum of mine, and was such a decent well-spoken fellow, it was a pleasure to have any dealin's with him.

'By the time I had settled all this in my own mind, I thought it was about time to get up, so up I got and I lighted the stove and put the kettle on to boil, and a whole lot of chops on to fry, and I got the pannikins out and the tin plates. I remember well I was so anxious to have a good comfortable breakfast ready before I called Joe and Munro, that I even cleaned up the knives and forks for 'em. How did I do that, is it you want to know, ma'am? Oh, very easy: I just stuck 'em into the soft ground outside the back door, and worked 'em up and down a bit, and they came out fine and clean. Well, as soon as I had got everything ready, I went into the men's hut, and I got out Munro and little Joe Smelt without waking up any of the others; and when they got on their boots and moleskins, saving your presence, ma'am, they come into the kitchen, and I showed 'em the breakfast all ready and smelling uncommon good, and I told 'em what the boss had said, and I lays it before 'em whether they likes to come up the hills with me and earn their pound a-piece, or whether they'd *pre*-fer to loaf about the station all day, whiles I goes out by myself and sticks to the whole of the fiver.

'Munro, he goes on eating his breakfast quite quiet-like—for that matter we was all pegging away pretty tidily—and then, after a bit, he says in his pretty peaceable way—I've told you he was a very well spoken man, ma'am, haven't I?—he says, "Well, Bob, I don't mind if I do come;" and then Joe Smelt says, as well as he can speak for a mouthful of damper, "The same here;" so then I knew it was settled, and I enjoyed my breakfast with the rest. We didn't dawdle too long, though, for it was getting light enough to see, though them mistesses was still too low to please me, but I thought we might be making our way up the river-gorge and smoke our pipes as we went. The sheep had gone up that way, I knew, and there was no way out. Besides, sheep don't like crossing the water oftener than they can help. Nine times we had to cross that there river on that there blessed Christmas morning. Get wet! I should just think we did: leastways I took off my Cookhams and worsted socks at each ford, because I knew right well that if I went up the hills and walked all day in wet things my feet would get that blistered I'd feel like a cat in walnut-shells. Joe Smelt found that out to his cost before the day was over. He started werry cocky and turned up his trouser-legs and walked right through the water, saying he couldn't be bothered to stop and take his boots off and on at each crossing. Munro, he walked through all nine fords in his boots; and then, when we had done with them for that day, he sat down on a big stone and took off his socks and his boots and drew out a nice dry pair of worsted socks, and put 'em on; then he poured the water out of his boots and shook 'em up and down a bit and put 'em on again, and laced 'em up werry tight. But still, long before the day was done, his feet was smartin' and his boots was all out o' shape, and wringing him awful. Joe and I couldn't have managed that way if it had been ever so, for socks wasn't plenty with us in those days. We just used to get one pair at a time from the nighest store, and wear 'em until they got into one big hole all over, and then we chucked 'em away and got another pair. Now, Munro, he had a nice little Scotch wife up at his place, and she was always a-spinning and a-knitting for him, and kept him as comfortable as could be. But Joe and me, we hadn't neither wives, nor socks, nor anything nice about us, but we just pulled through as well as we could.

'Well, ma'am, to come back to that Christmas Day. It was as beautiful a morning as you would wish to see, and not too hot, neither; the sun just beginning to shine, and drinking up them mistesses as if they was grog, till there wasn't one to be seen, and Munro's glass showed him every sheep on every hill within sight as plain as you see your hand now. Lots of sheep there were too, and werry cheerful it sounded their calling to each other, and werry good feed there was for 'em on those hills. But they was all too white for what we wanted. They'd all been *shored,* 'twas easy to see that, and the mob we wanted was still in their wool, and would have looked dirty and much larger among the fresh-shored ones. We could track 'em easy enough by their footmarks up to the head of the gorge, but there we lost all trace, and though we spent a good hour hunting. We felt sure they'd all keep together, for they'd be frightened at the sight of all their fellows so white and so bare, and likely as not travel away from 'em. They wasn't anywhere on the low hills, that was certain; there was no use funking it, we had got to separate and go carefully over the back ranges, and a long hot climb we had before us that Christmas morning; and, not to be too long about it, ma'am, a long hot climb we had if ever there was one in this world. I sent the dogs many and many a time after what I thought might be a part of the mob; but though I hunted as close as ever I could, never a sheep did I see, no, nor a sign of one. Well, ma'am, it was very disheartening, you'll allow that, and I was so vexed I couldn't feel properly hungry even long after dinner-time came, and I kept thinking whatever I should do if they wasn't to be found. You see, I had chosen the most likely place to search in myself, as was but nat'ral, so I never thought that if *I* couldn't find 'em anybody else could. There's where I deceived myself; because when I had worked all round that blessed range and come upon Davis's hut—that was the out-station where we had settled to meet some time in the afternoon—what should I see but Munro and Joe Smelt a-lying on the shady side of the hut as cool and comfortable as you please smoking their pipes, and the whole mob of sheep lying quiet and peaceable on the little flat, with Munro's dog watching 'em. Not that they wanted any watching just then, for sheep always take a good spell in the afternoon of a hot day, and lie down and go to sleep, maybe, until it gets cool enough to make it pleasant to wander about and feed before dark.

'As soon as ever I see that sight I flung up my hat and danced for joy, and I felt desperate hungry all of a minute. I can tell you, my mates, I didn't lose much time getting down that hill, though I come pretty quiet for fear of scaring the sheep.

'When I comes up to the men, before I could speak, Joe Smelt says, first thing, "Munro found 'em; I haven't been long here." And Munro smiles quiet and pleased-like, and says, "I had a mob once served me the same trick, and I thought I knew where to look for 'em, and sure enough they was there, reg'larly hiding; I had to bring 'em down uncommon easy, for it was a nasty place, and I didn't want half of 'em to be smothered in the creek."

'Well, of course I meant to ask and to hear all about it, but I thought it would keep until we had had a bit of dinner, for it was about two o'clock, and you must please to remember, ma'am, that we had breakfasted somewhere about five, and likewise that walking up and down them back ranges is hungry work at the best of times, besides being wearing to the boots. "Where's Davis?" was my first words. "Davis must have gone away altogether for a bit" they said, "for the hut is locked and fastened up until it can't be fastened no more, and unless we reg'larly break into it, we shall never get in it."

' "Drat the fellow!" I cried, "there ain't no bush-rangers about. Why doesn't he just lock his door and hang the key on a nail outside where anybody can see it, as I used to do when I was a back-country shepherd, and wanted to go away for a bit." But it was no manner of use pitching into Davis, not then, because you see, ma'am, he wasn't there to hear himself abused, though we did that same and no mistake. It *was* aggravating—now, ma'am, wasn't it? There was we three, and the dogs, poor things! as hungry as hungry could be; and we knew there'd be flour and tea and sugar, and likely a bit of bacon (for Davis was a good hand at curing a ham of a wild pig), inside the door, if we could only open it. Not a bit of it would stir, though, for all our kicks, and Joe Smelt ran at it with his shoulders until I thought he must burst it open; but no, the lock didn't give one bit. "Tell you what," said Joe, rubbing his shoulder after his last attempt, "Davis has gone and barred this 'ere door up on the inside, and then got out of the window and fastened it up outside afterwards." When we came to look, it seemed quite likely, for the shutter was driven home and kept in its place by good-sized nails; but we got a big stone, and we used our knives, and Munro worked away that patiently that at last down came the shutter, and we had the little bit of a window open in no time after that. We made little Joe get through first, and we laughed and said we felt just like real house-breakers, but we thought we'd keep our jokes until we had had something to eat. Before Joe had well unbarred the door—for it was fastened up as if it was never meant to be opened again—Munro and me had settled that he should make some flap-jacks as soon as ever we could get the fire to burn; that is, supposing there wasn't any bacon or mutton lying about.

'The minute Joe opened the door with a cheery, "Here you are," we looked round us like so many hungry wolves, and the first thing we see is a fine big shoulder of mutton on the floor. Well, it was easy to see how it had got there, for there were marks of rats' teeth and feet too, all over it. Davis hadn't been long gone that was easy to see—not more than a few hours likely, though he plainly intended to be away for some time by the way he'd fastened up everything; but still it was very neglectful of him not to have flung that shoulder of mutton outside before he went because you see, ma'am, in a day or two it would surely be very unpleasant. A neat man was Davis—a very neat man—and when we'd prized open his cupboard made out of old gin-cases, we found his couple of tin-plates and pannikins, and his tea and sugar, and his flour and his matches, and his salt, all as tidy as tidy could be, and there was a big packet of "Vermin Destroyer" too, open and half used. We gave that a wide berth, however, as you may fancy; but we had some sticks in the fire-place and the kettle on to boil before you could say "Jack Robinson." We found half a loaf of bread also in the cupboard, which we concluded to eat, lest it should get stale by the time Davis came back, and we told Munro we'd have his flap-jacks for second course. "Here's a capital Christmas dinner after all," said Joe; and he picked up the meat carefully off the floor, and blew the dust off, and we sat down to the table with that shoulder of mutton before us; and all I can tell you, ma'am, is, that long before the kettle boiled—and it had a good fire under it too—there wasn't a scrap left on the bone. Cooked! in course it was cooked; you don't think we was going to eat raw wittles on Christmas Day. No, no, ma'am, we weren't such cannibals as that! Davis had baked it as nice as could be, but it seemed uncommon funny that he should have taken so much trouble for nothing. However, there it was, or, I *should* say, there it wasn't, for we had eaten it up, every bite; and we told Joe Smelt to get the tea out of the cupboard, and throw a couple of handfuls into the kettle, which was beginning to boil. Joe got up, saying, "I haven't half done yet; I'm just as hungry as ever I can be;" and he went to the cupboard and began to rummage among the things in it. "Don't give us any pison by mistake, Joe," said Munro, joking. Just as he said the words, Joe turned short round, his face looking as white as death underneath all the sunburn and freckles, his very lips white, and his eyes open wider than I thought mortal eyes could open; and he said in a dreadful voice—a sort of whisper, and yet you might have heard it all over the place—"That's where it is, we're pisoned!" With that Munro and I jumped up from the table, and we gasped out, "Pisoned, Joe!" but we needn't to ask—we couldn't speak if we wished. Joe pointed to the bare mutton bone, and held out the half-used paper of the poison in the other, and never a word did he say but, "Rats."

'We guessed it all then. Davis must have been fairly bullied by the impudent hungry critturs, and he had taken the trouble to cook for 'em, as if they had been Christians, and then he'd quite likely as not rubbed an ounce or two of strychnine into that shoulder of mutton, and left it where the rats could get at it, and we'd been and eaten it all up instead o' they. Yes, ma'am, it's all very well to laugh,' said Bob, taking his hat off, and wiping his head with the handkerchief stowed away in its crown, looking into the hat afterwards as if he saw the scene he was describing pictured there—'it was the werry roughest moment of all *my* life. To be pisoned like a rat, and in a lonely gully, where no one would ever pass. Most likely we shouldn't even be found before Davis came back. It was lucky Davis didn't come back, though—not at that moment, I mean—for I'm certain that if he stood in his own doorway just then we'd 'a set on him and killed him without so much as saying "with your leave or by your leave." We couldn't have been whiter than Joe, not if we'd tried; but we was white enough no doubt. Munro was a good man, so he was the bravest of the lot, and he said, or he tried to say, for he couldn't speak very clear, "The will of God be done, my poor Jeanie!" and with that he threw himself down on Davis's bed and hid his face.

'I don't rightly know what poor little Joe did, for I felt desperate mad. I caught sight of half a bar of soap stowed away at the back of the cupboard, and I seized it as if it had been a life-buouy, and I'd been a drowning man. I couldn't have gripped it harder or held it tighter if it *had* been a buouy,' said Bob, shaking his head meditatively. 'And I runs down to the creek with it. I don't know why I went there, unless it was to be handy to the water to gulp it down with. Well, ma'am, I had picked up my knife off the table as I passed, and I cut great junks of that bar of soap, and bolted 'em, whole. I seemed to remember having heard some one say that soap was good as a hemetick: and so I found it; for by the time I had swallowed half the bar I felt desperate sick, and joyful I was to feel it, I can tell you; but still I wasn't bad enough to please myself, so I drank some water and had three or four slices more, and that about finished me, and I lay down among the tussocks by the water side; and what with the fright, and the early rising, and the long walk, and the heat of the sun, joined to the murmur-like of the creek, I went off into the comfortablest sleep as I ever had, and it wasn't till the sun had got right behind the high hills to the westward that I woke up. I reckon it was the barking of Munro's dog that woke me, for the poor beast found he had more than he could do to manage the mob of sheep. They must have been feeding some time, and now wanted to be off up the hill to their camping ground; for you must know, ma'am, that sheep never settle for the night on low ground. They always travel up as high as they can conveniently get, and camp on the top of a hill.

'The poor beast seemed quite joyful to see it was me coming to help him, as he thought, but I couldn't give my mind to the sheep, not just yet. I was rather empty and a bit weak, but as well as ever I felt in my life. I remember I took off my hat, and looked up to the sky and I thanked God in my own rough fashion for saving my life all along of that bar of soap, and I give you my word, ma'am, I meant it, even when I found out my mistake. I thought I'd look up Munro and the other little chap, but I was more than half frightened to go and see about 'em, for at that time you see, I thought I was wot you may call the sole surwivor. However, the others were surwivors too, and a very good job for 'em *that* was. Munro had pegged away into a bag of salt until he must have reg'larly *cured* his inside in more senses than one, whilst Joe had hemeticked himself by shoving his fingers down his throat. Poor Joe! he must have been desperate bad too. Well, they'd been to sleep as well as me, and there we stood staring at each other, awful pale and haggard-looking, but still safe and well so far.

'Munro was the first to recover himself, and he said, "Them sheep'll be off before we can count ten," so with that we went to help the dog, who was barking hisself off his legs. Joe Smelt hung back a bit at first, for he said he'd heard as how exercise caused pison to work, but Munro called out, "Do your duty Joe, and never mind the pison."

'So we got the sheep together, and we brought 'em down to the homestead, and right glad the boss was to see 'em. When I told him the story of the shoulder of mutton, he went nearly as white as we did, and he said he'd send for the doctor and tell him to bring proper hemeticks along, but we felt we couldn't stand no more not just then, and Joe says, says he, "It wouldn't be no manner of use, sir, not till we'd had some supper." With that the boss laughs and tells the manager to give us each a glass of hot grog; and very comfortin' it was. That's all, ma'am,' concluded Bob, getting up from his hencoop and making me a bow.

'No, no, Bob,' I cried, 'that isn't all; I must know the end.'

'There wasn't no more end than that, ma'am; leastways when Davis turned up, which he did by chance next day, at the home station, we werry nearly made an end to him when he lets out that there never had been no pison on the shoulder of mutton at all. He said he'd cooked it, meaning to take it in his swag for his supper that night, and was fine and mad when he found he'd forgotten it. Mr Vans-start, he said we ought to be downright thankful to Davis when we found he hadn't let us in for his pison, but we couldn't see it in that light no how, and we give Davis, one and all of us, a bit of our minds, and Joe Smelt offered to fight him the very next Sunday for five pounds a side. Poor Davis! he made us mad by the way he laughed and he tried to comfort us by telling us that if the "Vermin Destroyer" did us as little harm as it did the rats, we needn't to have cried out. "Why, they thrive on it," he said. "I lets 'em have it pretty often, and they comes about more than ever arter a dose on it.' "

Bob's story took a long time in the telling, for he told it very deliberately, and enjoyed a long word, or any pet expression, such as his life-buouy, so intensely that he repeated it over and over again, rolling the words in his mouth as if they were good to taste. By the time he had finished, the valley was in deep shadow, and the delicious crisp feeling in the air, which always follows a summer's day in our New Zealand hills, made us feel inclined for a change of occupation. The quoits were got out, and the iron pegs stuck in the ground, and some of the shearers were soon hard at work pitching the heavy circlets through the air. Another group were putting the stone or the hammer, whilst a few made themselves very hot by running races or having hopping matches. The constant open-air exercise, keeps men of all grades in New Zealand in such good condition that, even in such rough primitive sports as these were, I have seen far more surprising feats of strength performed by athletes who had had no other training than their daily hill-walks and frugal, wholesome fare, than in the *champ-clos* of a fashionable arena in the old country.

But to-morrow's work must begin with the dawn so whilst there was yet light to see their way home across the rolling downs which stretched like a green sea before us, the good-nights were said. I stood in the porch and shook hands with each guest as he passed, though the performance of this ceremony entailed deep blushes on the part of my stalwart company. 'Here's wishin' you the best o' luck, mum,' was the general adieu; but when they all got to the bottom of the paddock, they consulted together and gave a ringing hearty cheer, which woke up the valley's quiet echoes, may be for the first time since it emerged from the water-world. 'One more for Old Father Christmas,' were the last words I heard, as I turned indoors, leaving the joyous sounds to die gradually away into the deep perfumy silence which hung over that lonely valley of the Malvern Hills.

ALFRED A. GRACE

# Te Wiria's Potatoes

Villiers was on good terms with the dispossessed lords of the soil. He had a sort of romantic regard for them. He considered they were an ill-treated, down-trodden race; he used to tell his *pakeha* friends so; and when men met him in Auckland they would ask him how his protégés the Ngati-Ata were getting on. Of course he spoke the Maori lingo. He doctored the members of his pet tribe when they fell ill; bought their *kumara* at exorbitant prices; helped them in their land transactions with the grasping *pakeha;* gave them the use of his out-houses for sleeping in, and of his paddocks for their horses.

So far the Ngati-Ata had done nothing for Villiers in return, beyond warning him of the approach of pack-horses from the interior; bony, pinch-bellied pack-horses were the bane of his life and a menace to his clover-paddocks.

Villiers lived in an old *pa* close to the sea. Its earthern walls stood twenty feet high, and were surrounded by a ditch fifteen feet deep. The whole earthwork was overgrown with maidenhair fern and lycopodium, in token of the return of peace. In the middle of the *pa*, commanding a view of the sea, Villiers had built his house, and his farm stretched its rich acres all round.

He had grown a phenomenal crop of potatoes, but the question was, who would dig them up? He himself was turning sixty; his sons had gone to the Thames to dig gold; all the able-bodied men of the district had caught the gold-fever, too; worn-out old soldier Saunders and one-armed constabulary-man Murphy were the only men left.

*     *     *

Villiers stood on the *pa* bank and pondered. The bay stretched glittering before him; a gentle breeze stirred the trees in the orchard below and rippled the surface of the sea. Of a sudden, two big canoes came in sight round the nearest point, and made for the shore in front of the house. Villiers anticipated a day spent in *korero* and eating.

Two score Maoris came straggling up from the beach through the gap in the *pa* bank, and stood in picturesque groups on Villiers' veranda.

'We come from Tohitapu, our chief,' said the spokesman of the party, a huge fellow of sixteen stone. 'Tohitapu loves the *pakeha* people, but most of all he loves Te Wiria, his great friend. Tohitapu has stored up in his heart all the good things Te Wiria has done for the Maoris, especially for the Ngati-Ata *hapu*. Nothing can ever make Tohitapu forget the kindness Te Wiria has shown him and his *kainga*. Therefore Tohi' has said to us: "What can we do to show Te Wiria our thanks? How can we return this great *rangatira's* services? How can we preserve the regard of our *pakeha* friend for a long time? I will tell you. Te Wiria has a fine crop of potatoes, just ready for digging—Hakiri has seen them, and so has Titoré. But how will Te Wiria dig up his crop at this time, when all the *pakeha* have gone to the goldfields and men are scarce? Now, you men of Ngati-Ata, I will tell you what you must do. You must take the largest canoes you have, the biggest of all, and go over to Te Wiria, and dig up his *riwai* crop for him. Then we shall show that the Maori people love Te Wiria, and there will be great friendship between him and us." '

Villiers replied almost with tears. He was overjoyed to know that the Ngati-Ata had his welfare so near their hearts. He had tried to show that he looked on them as friends: they had come to prove that they were such indeed. They were good men; they thought of the needs of others. They deserved to enjoy plenty all their lives. Might they never lack *kumara* and potatoes, pigs and tobacco. As for his *riwai* crop, it was a good crop and ready for digging, as they had guessed. He would be glad to accept their generous offer. He considered Hakiri and Titoré and Haneke and the rest of them had shown a very proper spirit in coming over to help him just in the nick of time. It was what he might have expected of such generous fellows.

Forks and spades were taken down to the potato-field. The Maoris, men and women, began to dig for all they were worth.

\*          \*          \*

Towards mid-day Villiers' women-folk took down to the workers large quantities of pork and a huge iron cauldron. The Maori women, with many smiles, fixed up a cooking-place, and soon the *kohua* was sizzling over a bright fire. The pork was boiled with potatoes and thistles in the same pot. The Maoris gathered round, squatted on the ground, dipped their fingers in the stew, and ate till they were full. Then they stretched themselves. They praised Te Wiria, his house, his horses, his pork, his potatoes. And Villiers' little son, who had watched them eat, coveted their feeding capacities.

In the evening the work was finished; fifty sacks of potatoes stood piled in Villiers' sheds. With many flattering speeches, and laughter, and chattering, the Maoris got into their canoes, and disappeared round the cape.

Villiers went to sleep with a light heart that night—his endeavours to maintain friendly relations with the Ngati-Ata were not in vain. But at one o'clock his big kangaroo-hound began to bark with all its might, and tugged furiously at the bullock-chain that held it. The dog often barked at night—usually at wildcats or the moon. Villiers put his head out of the window, but could see nothing; so he went to bed again. But the dog barked on for hours.

*       *       *

Next morning Villiers went to the sheds to feast his eyes on his wealth of potatoes. He opened the door of shed No. 1—it was empty. He went to No. 2—there, also, not a sack was to be seen. His potatoes were gone.

Villiers did not go for the police—there were no police to fetch. He saddled his horse, and rode over to Tohitapu's *pa*.

Tohi' met him with all the dignity of the true *rangatira*, and his mouth full of pork—Villiers had arrived there at dinner-time. The *pakeha* quickly told his story. Tohi' listened with the deepest respect. Villiers pointed to some sacks, marked with a great red V, hanging on a fence near by. Tohitapu acknowledged that it was strange that they should be there—marked with a V, too. Beyond a doubt, some of his fellows were arrant rogues; he would see to it. Villiers pointed to a newly-dug *rua,* almost under his horse's feet. Tohitapu acknowledged that it had been dug recently. Villiers remarked that it was full of potatoes. Tohi' relinquished his hold on Villiers' rein, and called his people to him.

'You Ngati-Ata are a bad people,' he said. 'You always were a greedy, thieving set of men! I have long felt ashamed of you. Te Wiria here is my *pakeha;* he has long been my friend, and the friend of the Ngati-Ata. So you men there, Hakiri, Titoré, and Haneke when you hear that Te Wiria has got a fine *riwai* crop, you go to him and say that I, Tohitapu, told you to dig it up. Te Wiria is a guileless man—he let you do the work. You store the *riwai* in Te Wiria's sheds. You are a low-bred set of men, *taurekareka,* all of you. You have no shame; you forget that the *pakeha* thinks stealing is a sin; you forget that the *pakeha* people put thieves into gaol and make them *heréheré*—prisoners. So you go and take Te Wiria's *riwai* crop; you steal it in the night—you dare not go in the day. You are great cowards, you Ngati-Ata! And you bring the potatoes to the *kainga,* and say to yourselves: "It is well: we shall have plenty of food for the winter." *He ware te iwi nei!* You are a wicked, lazy lot of people; you are a set of cowards and thieves; you are an ungrateful tribe; you have disgraced me in the eyes of my *pakeha,* Te Wiria. I am ashamed to be your chief. Get out of my sight, every one of you!'

And Tohitapu strode through the spell-bound Ngati-Ata, and resumed his interrupted meal, his meal of pork and baked potatoes—Te Wiria's potatoes.

Villiers sat on his horse, wondering whether Tohitapu was a great actor or a great liar. He rode home wondering. He wondered till the potatoes had long rested in the capacious stomachs of the Ngati-Ata. He is wondering to this day.

HENRY LAPHAM

# A Member of the Force

'Come now, Archie, it's your turn for a story?' said Jack Conliffe.

Archie only turned his big form in closer proximity to the fire and, laughingly, replied:

'Well, you see, boys, I know nothing of babies either from practice or precept, and as all your yarns to-night have been about youngsters, and I can't follow suit, and it is too late to play a new lead—so I'll shout.'

'That you won't,' said Harry Clare, 'I've told my story, and now I'm going to stand treat; you've shouted for us already, so now you tell a yarn.'

'Weren't you with that Sergeant who was drowned in the Waikaia over on Switzers side?' asked Jack. 'Tell us about that. What was his name to begin with?'

'His name was Michael Brennan, and he was as fine a fellow as ever walked, although he was "a bobby". He used to have to visit Nokomai, so may be some of you boys have seen him.' 'No!' 'Well, he was a bigger man than me, and taller, with black hair and whiskers, and big dark eyes, a real jolly fellow as ever I came across. There was never a dance or a spree but Brennan was sure to be in it. Of course he had to take his fun quietly because of his billet, but he did have lots of jollity for all that. But there was one good thing about him, he did not drink. I don't mean that he was teetotal, you know—he would have his nip like any other man—but he only got real tight twice in all the time I knew him. Once was the first night he came to Switzers, and of course no one took any notice of that. The other time you will hear about before I've finished my yarn. I don't think any of you boys were at Switzers when Frenchman's Hill was going a-head. What, you have never been in Switzers at all! Well, it's not much of a place to look at now for the gold has pretty well run out; but, my word, it was a rare rowdy quarter in '66 or thereabouts. The township is planted right on the top of a steep spur; you must climb a hill to get at it on any side. And then it is almost an island, the Winding Creek being on one side, and the Waikaia River a little further off on the other. When I first saw it there must have been close on 2000 men working about, and the whole top of the hill was covered with houses just as close as they could stick, most of them of canvas and roofed with zinc, and nearly every second house was a "shanty" or a store. There was drinking and dancing, shouting and billiard-playing every night from dark till daylight. Everybody was making money and everybody spent it. I often sold my gold for £50 on Saturday, and on Monday had not a five pound note. Ah! those were rare old times! I don't think though that any of the boys made much out of it, though the "shanties" cleared their hundreds a week. I don't know how old Brennan stood it, for he was always in the thick of the fun, and I suppose he only had his fixed wages to go upon. Well, at this time I was mates with a young fellow called Jim Smith, a good enough lad as a mate, and would do just as big a day's labour as any man, but an awful chap for a rowdy spree, and when he was drunk he was an out-and-out scoundrel. Poor lad, he was my mate, but what I've said is only the truth about him. The Crown Hotel in Switzers had a bar-maid at the time—a regular plum, the boys were all just mad about her. A little thing she was but with the prettiest of round faces and brown hair, and the most bewitching eyes, and she used to throw a glance of them at a fellow and it was all over with him. What do you say, Jack? "You suppose I was smitten too." Of course I was, I never could resist a pretty woman, and no man living could withstand one arch look from Lily's brown eyes. But she had completely captivated the Sergeant and my mate. I don't believe she cared a bit for Jim, only she liked to flirt with him when no one else was handy; but with the Sergeant it was different. She would be as demure as possible when he was near her and you couldn't get a word of fun or chaff from her. Old Brennan just worshipped her, but he was a fool, for he thought Lily only cared for him, while everyone else knew she never was happy without half-a-dozen followers, and would string men on with mischievous glances and pretty words, and squeezings of her warm little hands, just for the fun of laughing at them. Well, one Saturday evening, Jim and I went down to the township. At this time we were working at a place called "Gow's Creek", over the river up among the hills, but we generally went to Switzers every fortnight or so to sell our gold and get stores. Of course we could not dream of going home without calling on Lily. So, going to the Crown Hotel we made at once for the little back parlour, sacred to Lily and her special friends. There was the little girl looking as neat and as pretty as a flower. I think that was Lily's greatest charm; she was always neat—her dress seemed better made than those of the other women, and the colours always blended nicely and tastefully. But here too we found the Sergeant, seemingly quite at home. I was glad to see him, but Jim looked as black as thunder, and was for going away. However, Lily would not have that; she came to him with both hands out, and her big eyes looking so pleadingly into his face. "Ah, Jim, don't go away. I've been wondering so that you haven't been to see me. I was beginning to think you didn't *care* to come. There, now, I will give you my own arm chair, and that I wouldn't do for any one else"—"Except *you*," she whispered to the Sergeant, who was handing her a chair. I heard the aside, although it was spoken low. The Sergeant and I now were together, and trying to make conversation, but I could scarcely help smiling to see him glancing every minute at Lily, who sat with her little feet up on the hob talking away merrily to Jim.

' "Really, Jim, I was quite angry to think you never came to see me when last you were down. You didn't know how much I missed you."

' "I don't think you can miss any one much," said Jim, moodily, "you seem to have plenty of friends always about."

' "I don't know what you mean. I have not nearly enough friends. What do you mean? tell me, Jim?"

'Jim chose to whisper his reply, a most convenient way, I thought, as he drew her pretty face so close to his own. Then Jim must needs admire her bracelet, and of course, had to hold her hand in his while examining the trinket. Perhaps the Sergeant thought the examination was lasting too long, for he called for "drinks", which necessitated Lily's rising to give the message to the barman. Then the Sergeant quietly slipped into her place and engaged Jim in some discussion about the price of gold.

'When Lily came back she took the vacant seat. Jim tried to right affairs by reminding the Sergeant of the change, but Lily merely said, "Oh, never mind, Sergeant, I would just as soon sit here," and forthwith began to talk to me, but every now and then darting a smiling, loving glance at Jim. However, the evening passed away very fairly; the Sergeant told Irish stories with a brogue and a wittiness that even Jim had to laugh in spite of himself, and he sung jovial songs in which we all joined in chorus whether we knew the tune or not. But at last, as bad luck would have it, Brennan pitched on "Molly Asthore", and put his whole heart into the song, singing at and for Lily alone, as every one could see, while that young lady made eyes at him and blushed and simpered just as conscious and as pleased as could be. Now, I don't wonder poor Jim was angry; it is hard lines to have to sit and listen to a big handsome fellow singing soft songs to the girl you like best, and that too with a voice that would charm the heart of a nun. But for all that, Jim need not have been such a fool as to sneer and mutter something about "a blathering Irish idiot". Brennan's face grew as black as thunder, but Lily patted his shoulder and said, "O thank you, Sergeant, such a lovely song. Now there's no use in any one trying to sing again after that, so we'll have a game of whist, and you must be my partner, Jim." Then she drew a chair quite close, settled herself down cosily, and said, smiling up into Jim's face—"Do you know, Jim, you are the only good partner I ever get—I wish I had you always."

' "Upon my word!" laughed the Sergeant, "I wonder is this leap year?" Then Lily got quite confused and said she did not mean anything at all, and did not know how she could have been so stupid, and it was hard to tell whose face was the reddest, hers or Jim's. But in spite of his pretty partner Jim managed to lose every game. Perhaps it was her fault, for she wouldn't attend to what was going on, but must needs be giving sly glances at the Sergeant, and making little signs to him. At last, when she was pretending to show him all her cards, Jim flung down his "hand" and with a thump of his fist on the table, swore he wouldn't play any longer with a couple of —— cheats. Up jumped Brennan, seized Jim by the collar, and dragged him into the middle of the room. I tried to interfere, but one push of the Sergeant's strong arm sent me flying. Then he said, speaking quite coolly and deliberately, "Now, my friend Mr Smith, that last remark of yours could only be meant either for me or the lady I was talking to; if it was me, I'll punch your head; if it was for her, I'll break your — ugly neck: now, speak out." Jim could not do more than struggle in the Sergeant's grasp, but if ever a man's thoughts were told in a look, Jim's face spoke "murder" as plain as words. However, to our great surprise, my mate suddenly turned quite polite and said "I beg your pardon, Mr Brennan, and I am very sorry for the remark. I was angry, and did not mean it for anyone. Come, forget it, and let us have a drink."

' "It's a good thing for your hide you have apologized," said the Sergeant, "but as for the rest, I drink with honest men, and not with a liar and a coward."

'Jim's face turned white at the words, but he only said, "Oh, well, please yourself, I'm off to bed." Of course that put an end to our pleasant evening. Lily had run away at the first symptoms of a row, and after a good-night "nip", the Sergeant left for the camp.

'Of course I thought Jim would clear out early next morning, but he didn't show up until after breakfast, and then went straight off to the camp, of all places in the world. I suppose he and the Sergeant made the quarrel up in some way, for he told us Brennan had promised to come up in the evening. Well, I never did think much of my mate as a man, but before I'd go and eat humble pie to the Sergeant or any other man he might break my neck, if I wasn't able first to settle him. Well, the Sergeant did not come until late, after ten o'clock, and we all, that is he, Jim, Lily, and I, gathered in the little parlour. But it wasn't comfortable. Lily was as quiet as a mouse, keeping an anxious eye on Brennan and Jim, and of course, after what had happened the night before, one daren't even mention cards. So we talked a little, and had several drinks, till Lily said she was tired and must go to bed. Then the landlord closed the house and came to join us by the fire. After a little he asked us what we were going to have, and the Sergeant, I remember, took some cordial—cloves, I think.

' "Don't disturb yourself, boss," said Jim, as the landlord was about to get up, "I'll get the drinks."

'Jim knew the bar well, and as the boss was stout and not very active, he was ready enough to sit still in his easy chair. Jim was so long over his work that when he did come back the landlord said:

' "Well, I began to think as you must have been brewing fresh beer for us, Jim?"

' "Oh, dash it all?" said Jim, "you've altered the bar since I was down last, and I couldn't put my hand on a thing."

'When we had finished our drinks, Brennan exclaimed—

' "I say, boss, that's infernally bad stuff of yours, it is making me quite sick."

' "Right you are, Brennan," put in Jim, "it is bad stuff, I had a nip of it this morning and it nearly killed me. You'd better take a drop of something strong to keep off bad effects."

' "Faith, I think you're right, Jim, I'll have a nip of whisky."

' "Oh, by jove! Sergeant, the whisky is worse than the other—try some rum."

' "All right, Jim, please yourself."

'This last supply of drinks had a very queer effect on Brennan. When he first came in he had been very gloomy and cross, but suddenly became quite jolly, laughing at nothing at all, singing song after song and telling all sorts of funny yarns. Of course there were two or three more "shouts", and at last I thought old Brennan was fairly going mad. The landlord tried to get us to bed, but the Sergeant would not hear of it, and Jim kept backing him up. At last Jim found a Jew's harp lying on the mantelpiece and began to tinkle out an Irish jig tune. Up got the Sergeant, and though he could not stand straight, he must try to dance. Of course he fell, right across the little table and smashed it down. But he was on his feet in a minute, seized a leg of the table that was hanging loose, and commenced to flourish it round his head with a wild "Hurroo!"

' "Go it, your sowl," shouted Jim. The Sergeant let fly at the mantelpiece, and crash went the vases and the big looking-glass on the wall above it. Then he rushed out into the bar, and in a very few minutes the place was strewn with broken glass, and pools of liquor flooded the floor. Next he went off into the passage, where, fortunately, the front door was locked. Jim followed him close, there was a slight scuffle, then a heavy fall, and when we got out, Brennan lay insensible, bleeding from a severe scalp wound. Jim said he had struck against the door handle in his fall. We got him to bed, where he slept motionless till late next day. Then he awoke to find his head all bandaged up, and the unpleasant memory of the last night's row. But when he knew all the damage he had done, he was in an awful state of mind. He sent for the landlord, and, of course, had to pay all breakages, and one way or another that spree couldn't have cost less than £25. But it was not so much the money he minded as the fear that some report would get to the ears of the Inspector of Police. Fortunately, there were only few persons present; the boss was glad to be quiet for the credit of his house, and I thought I might safely promise both for Jim and myself. Jim cleared out for home early next morning, and Brennan did not see him again.

'Just before I left for home, Lily said she wanted to speak to me particularly, so we went into her private parlour and she locked the door.

' "Wasn't it a strange thing the way the poor Sergeant got on the other evening?" she asked.

'I said it was the strangest thing I had ever seen. He had taken only three or four glasses when he was mad drunk.

' "Oh! it couldn't have been the *quantity!*" said the girl, "I have known him to take a dozen 'nips' in an evening without being the least the worse of it. No, Archie, it wasn't the *quantity.*"

' "Well, but what was it then?" asked I.

' "Will you promise not to be offended if I tell you something strange about your mate?"

'I told her she might say what she pleased about Jim so far as I was concerned.

' "Well, Archie, after I left you that evening I went to my bedroom; but I had some sewing to do, and as there was a good fire in the kitchen I went in there. By-and-by I wanted my scissors, and remembered they were lying in the parlour just opposite to this. I had a pair of old slippers on and came very quietly along the passage, but on opening the door of the parlour, to my surprise there was Jim. He had a tray of glasses, and was bending over them, but I could not see that he was doing anything more, only he put his hand into his pocket all of a sudden."

' "Well, Lily, and what more? Do you think Jim was doing anything with the drink?"

' "Yes, I do, there, that's plain enough. I think he was putting some doctor's stuff in them to make Brennan tight."

' "Lily, my girl," said I, "that is a very serious thing to say against a man. I never did think Jim an extra good fellow, but I doubt if he is blackguard enough for that."

' "Oh! isn't he? Well, he is blackguard enough to go about the place whispering nasty stories about me and the Sergeant, and a man that is mean enough for that will do anything, *I* think."

' "Yes, you are right enough there, Lil, but I don't like this poisoning idea."

' "Why should not a man murder another with poison as well as any other way?"

' "But you surely do not think Jim would murder Brennan?"

' "Yes, I do, if only he could do it safely."

' "Lily, Lily, I wonder if you would say this if any other man than the Sergeant was hurt?"

' "Yes, of course I would. Oh, I know what you mean, Archie, and at any rate I will say I like the Sergeant fifty thousand times better than a sneaking, murdering villain like Jim Smith."

' "That's right, Lily, don't spare him."

' "Wait till you hear the rest that I have to tell before you know if he deserves to be spared. You know the Sergeant says now that when he fell in the passage, he did not hit his head against the door, but that some one struck him with a stick."

' "Ah, but, poor old fellow, he was too far gone to be certain of anything that happened that night."

' "Perhaps so, but wait a little. Yesterday morning one of the girls was sick, and I had to help to do up the rooms. I got the room that Jim had slept in—perhaps I took it on purpose, but never mind. At any rate, I took the chance to examine it well. I thought he might forget and leave some bottles of his poisons about. I didn't have the luck to find one of them, but I'll show you what I did get."

'She produced from behind her table, a walking stick with a white bone handle, on which there was an ugly dark stain. It was a weapon that could be made to give a very nasty blow.—"And," Lily continued, "he had it so cunningly thrust away underneath the chest of drawers. It is the boss's walking stick, and always used to hang in the passage, just a handy place for Jim to get it that night. And look at that stain; what did that, do you think? No, of course, it never was there before, nor would be now, only Jim thought he could knock the Sergeant's life out with it. What do you think of your mate now, Archie?"

' "I think he's a low, bad scoundrel, Lily; but what are you going to do with the stick?"

' "Why, I am going to show it to the boss, and see if I can't get that brute punished as he ought to be."

' "Well, you will be foolish if you do, Lil. You see there is no proof that Jim either 'hocussed' the Sergeant's drink, or used the stick to hurt him."

' "Why, what proof more is wanted?" said Lily, indignantly, "doesn't everyone know that Jim hates poor Brennan like poison. See the way he looks at him with murder in his eyes? I don't want any more proof; I'm sure that Jim tried to murder the poor man; I'm *sure* of it."

' "But how can you *prove* it, Lil? Jim might say that the stick was in the bedroom before he came there at all, and as for the poor old Sergeant's assertion, about not striking his head, I'm afraid his word would go for very little, considering the state he was in that night."

' "Oh," rejoined Lily, with a toss of her pretty head, "of course you stick up for your mate, but I'm sure he did it on purpose."

' "But why are you sure?"

' "Oh because—because, well, just because I am."

'It is hard to reason with a woman, you know, boys; once let them get a thing into their heads and they'll stick to it right or wrong. So I said:

' "Well, perhaps you are right, Lily; but look here, supposing you go and speak to the boss about your suspicions, there will sure to be an enquiry into the affair, and what will become of poor Brennan? It will be hard enough for him to clear himself as it is, and if all the facts of the case came out he would lose his billet to a certainty."

'This idea seemed to frighten the girl. She stood awhile, tapping her pretty foot impatiently on the ground, then went off saying—

' "Well, I don't care what anyone thinks, I'm *sure* Jim Smith tried to murder the Sergeant that night. I'm sure of it, so there now."

'Still, I thought she would keep quiet for fear of injuring the man she was so fond of, and I was right. I cleared out for home next day, and found Jim very sulky, but not one word passed between us as to the "set to" in the town. There was one thing good about Jim (and even this was not of his own nature) he had received an excellent schooling. He could write like copper-plate and spell like a dictionary. Every evening, for the first few days after our return, he was writing letters, or, rather, writing one letter over and over again, and then seeing something wrong about it and tearing it up. This went on till at last I said:

' "That must be a mighty particular letter of yours, Jim, for you've wrote it over a dozen times. Is it a gushing love-letter?'

'He looked, and laughing unpleasantly, said:

' "Yes, you're right, Archie, it is a love-letter."

'He seemed to be satisfied with the epistle he concocted that night, and took it to the post next day. Well, it might have been a fortnight after this when I happened to be alone in the hut one afternoon, and to my surprise who should ride up but the Inspector of Police. I had seen him before once or twice in the township. He soon began asking me questions about the Sergeant, whether I was well acquainted with him, and what sort of a character he bore in the town; whether he was a general favourite there or not. I said I thought not, as he was too severe to be much liked. Then a few more "hums-and-haws", for the fellow was a mighty "haw-haw" individual, but not one word about the particular row in the Hotel. By-and-bye, he asked for my mate. I said he was away from home—and so he was, a couple of hundred yards away, working in the claim, but that I did not think necessary to explain. So very soon, my gentleman rode off, and I blest my stars that he was gone before Jim put in an appearance. Jim had not seen him come or go. I did not tell him, for somehow I had a misgiving that if he knew, he would be off to town and then would tell enough to ruin the poor old Sergeant. As it was poor Brennan came in for it, for in some way the Inspector had got hold of a mild account of the affair, but what he did hear was enough to get the Sergeant a severe lecturing, as well as to be reduced to the rank of constable, and lose his stripes. It was hard lines on him, poor fellow, but bless you, those that were fond of him liked him just as well with stripes or without. Somehow the notion arose in the town that Jim Smith had sent in the report which caused old Brennan to be disgraced—none of us had any proof of it, but, Lily like, we were *sure* for all that.'

\*     \*     \*

'Well,' said Archie, resuming his story, 'things went on very quietly after this till Christmas time drew near. Jim and I were working steadily, intending to wash up just before the holidays, and then go into the township for a spree. The winter had been a severe one, and the spring unusually late and cold, so that even in the beginning of December the higher ranges were still covered with snow. But summer came at last with a rush. Days so hot that one could scarcely live after the bracing cold weather we had been having, and warm soft winds blowing that sent the rivers and creeks up and kept them high. Jim and I were rejoicing over such plenty of water, and thinking what a good washing up we would have, when our proceedings came to a sudden stop in a way we little looked for. We went to work as usual one morning; I was down in the tail-race, and Jim working just under the face. We had been there perhaps a couple of hours, when all of a sudden I was startled by a loud sharp yell from him. I knew that something bad had happened, but, good Lord, boys, it was a terrible sight I saw when I reached him. A big boulder had slipped from the face, and striking him right between the shoulders, had pinned him to the ground. No, he wasn't dead, better for the poor chap if he had been, for I'll never forget to my dying day the awful look of his white face, half turned round from under the big stone, and one hand tearing in agony at the grass by his side. It took all my strength with the help of a lever to shift away the stone, and his moaning and crying made me as weak as water, and then how to get him home I didn't know, for there wasn't a soul to get help from nearer than the town. At last some way or another I put him into the barrow, wheeled him home as gently as I could, and got him on to his bunk. I made him as comfortable as possible with pillows and blankets doubled up, and then there was nothing for it but to ride away to the township for the doctor. It did seem cruel to leave the poor fellow there, all smashed and hurt so badly, but what could I do? There wasn't even so much as a drop of brandy in the hut to give him, so I caught my moke, and, though I never rode so fast before, it was late when I reached "The Hill", and the rain that had been threatening all day was then falling steadily, and after all my hurry I was sold, for the doctor had been called away to a bad case at some of the stations, and no one knew when he would be back. Of course it wouldn't do to wait and let poor Jim die meantime, so I went to a chemist fellow that had a bit of a shop, and told him all that had happened. He said there was little he could do, but he gave me a lotion, and then says he, "If your mate has any of that drug left he got here a few weeks ago it might be as well to give him a grain or two to make him sleep, but be careful, for it is very powerful." Said I, "I won't go meddling with no drugs, just you make up the right amount yourself, and I'll give it to him;" but I began then to fear that Lily's suspicions were only too true. When the medicine was ready and I came out of the shop, first thing I saw in the street was the Sergeant's big chestnut horse, tied to the post in front of the Crown Hotel. So I thought I would go in and tell him about the accident. He had just come home from a long ride, having been to bring the escort down from Nokomai. He was sitting in Lily's room, comfortably ensconced in a big arm chair before a blazing fire, and that young lady on the hearth-rug at his feet. And she did look killing, I tell you, with her black silk dress with crimson bow at the neck, and crimson velvet in her shiny hair, and the firelight dancing on her upturned face, with its big brown eyes, and her slender fingers clasped upon her lap. Oh, Lord! oh, Lord! I'm growing quite poetical as I think of it, so boss, hurry up and bring us some more "nips".'

The 'nips' satisfactorily dispatched, Archie went on with his tale.

'Well, I found the Sergeant had heard of the accident, and he said to me,

' "When do you start back, Archie?"

' "Now, at once," says I.

' "Well just wait till I get a nip and a handful of biscuits, and I'll go with you. I'm afraid no one can do much for him, but it won't do to let him die there alone."

' "Ah! now, Sergeant," cried Lily, with a pout that made her look prettier than ever, "Here you've been away three days, and now you are off again, and for a man that would—well, never mind, he is no friend of yours, to say the least of it."

' "Lily, my girl," said he gravely, "friend or not has nothing to do with it. I must go, and will, so you'll get me a handful of biscuits and fill this flask with P.B., and be quick, my dear. I do wish I could get a feed for the old moke, but he must just make the best of it."

'Lily got the things, and just as we were starting she called me back, and shutting the door, says in a soft voice, "Archie, do you think Jim is very badly hurt?"

' "I do, indeed, as bad as can be almost."

' "Oh, poor fellow, poor fellow," she said, with her sweet voice all a tremble and her eyes quite dim; "you'll tell him, Archie, I am so very sorry, please," and she looked so tender and kind and pitiful, that I just felt like taking her in my arms and giving her a good kiss there and then.'

'And may be you didn't do it, too?' said one of the listeners in a suggestive voice.

'Never you mind,' retorted Archie, 'that's got nothing to do with the yarn.

'The Sergeant was already on his horse, a regular brute, that plunged and reared, and at last tried a bit of bucking before he would be turned away from home.

' "Now mind, Sergeant," cried Lily as we started, "you've promised that you will be here for the Christmas dinner the day after to-morrow, and *nothing* is to prevent you."

' "All right Lily, sweetheart, nothing shall prevent me; but if you don't give me plenty of goose and apple sauce I'll never kiss you again."

' "Well, I'm sure!" exclaimed the lady, blushing all over her pretty face, "the impudence of you men! I think, indeed, you are goose enough already."

' "So I am, my dear, and you are my apple sauce," called out the jolly Sergeant as we rode away.

'It was a terrible evening to be out. For all it was summer time, sharp breezes came sweeping off the lofty hills which we were nearing every half-hour, and a soft, steady rain was falling, that soaked us to the skin. Neither of our horses was very fresh, and this made the ride more tiresome. We did not reach the hut till after ten o'clock. Taking the saddles from our horses, we let them go. The Sergeant said he could trust the chestnut, while my horse of course was at home. A cold shiver came over me as we got close to the dark, silent hut, for I could not help wondering whether we should find Jim stiff and cold or still alive, and it was a queer thing, but it was the dead Jim that I was frightened of. But when we pushed open the door we heard a low moan, and knew that he was able to suffer still. We soon had a light, and there lay poor Jim, just as I had left him, but with his eyes shut and his senses gone with the pain. We had first to try and strip him, and, do you know, it was wonderful to see how tenderly Brennan handled him. When I tried, my awkward touch made him yell and cry, but the big Sergeant moved him as gently as a woman could, and he never made more than a moan. I soon had a good fire alight, and in less than no time Brennan had some of our beef cut up and stewing for beef tea, and had given Jim a nip and then the draught, and he was fast asleep.

'The Sergeant said, "I don't think he's dangerously hurt, Archie, but I'm afraid he will have to suffer a lot yet. I wish to Heaven the doctor was here."

'By and by Brennan turned in to my bunk, for he was fairly tired out, and I was to watch the patient.

'Jim slept quietly till nearly morning, when he began to moan and stir uneasily, and by and by woke with a terrible shriek that roused Brennan, who said, "Ah! this was what I feared; he's delirious."

'All that day he raved and cried like a madman, and didn't know who either of us was. All of a sudden he seemed to take me for the chemist, and said he wanted to buy some drug; then he lay still awhile, muttering to himself very low. But at last he whispers, "Ah! this is the d——d brute's glass—there—that will make him tight enough, the——Irish fool, and you will know him, Lily, my girl."

'Then for a little while he lay quiet, then called out, "Sergeant! Sergeant!" in a voice so natural that I was certain he knew Brennan, who was seated behind him and holding him up. But Jim was only raving, for he went on, "I say, Sergeant, I nearly finished you that night. The drink nearly cooked you, and if your head hadn't been as hard as granite that rap would have settled you. The stick—where is it? Ah! take it away, Archie—burn it! burn it! See! it has blood upon it—the Sergeant's blood! Burn it, Archie! Quick—here's Lily coming—quick, quick."

'And so he raved on half the day, confessing all his villainy, while poor Brennan had to listen, but his face was as red as if he were overhearing something he ought not to. But he never left Jim, bathing his forehead with vinegar and giving him nips of brandy, while Jim mistook him sometimes for me, sometimes for a stranger, and at last for his own father, and begged him to pray God to save him from being hanged, with cries and wild words pitiful to hear. We gave him his sleeping draught, but it seemed rather to make him worse than better, till at last, in despair, the Sergeant began to sing. I suppose it was thinking of the sad state the poor fellow was in, and the near approach of Christmas-time, but it was a hymn he chose, one that I have heard my mother sing a score of times, about the "shepherds that were watching their flocks by night, all seated on the ground." The Sergeant sang very low and sweetly, with a curious tremble in his voice I never noticed before. The song quieted and soothed Jim wonderfully, and as for me I just sat looking out through the open door, till the dreary grey flat, with the heavy sky raining over it, faded quite away, and I was back again in the old home place, and could see the cosy old red brick farm-house, with its shingled roof, the big gum trees beside the gate, the honeysuckle round the windows, and my old mother a-sitting at the door in the twilight singing to us youngsters before we went to bed. Well, well, anyhow before the hymn was done poor Jim was sleeping like a child, and holding the Sergeant's hand fast in his own. He slept for hours, and the Sergeant managed to slip away, while I took his place. When Jim awoke he was quite sensible, but in terrible agony. It was dreadful to listen to the poor fellow's low constant moaning. He recognized Brennan as soon as he saw him, but seemed to grow restless and nervous all the time he was in the hut, and when he went out Jim said, "Archie, for God's sake get the doctor!"

'I told him I was afraid the river was now so high as to be impassable. When Brennan came in again Jim begged him to go for medical aid. The Sergeant hesitated, and said he did not like the look of the river.

' "What!" asked Jim, "are you so much of a coward to be afraid to swim a river to get help for a dying man?"

'Brennan's face got quite red at the thought of being called a coward, and he said, "I'll go, Jim, at once. Come and give me a hand with the moke, Archie."

'When the horse was ready I told Jim I was going to see the Sergeant cross the river, and would be back soon, so Brennan and I went down the flat. The river was an ugly sight to see. Flooded far beyond its banks, muddy and thick, it came pouring down in a yellow swirling stream. About ten yards below the usual ford is a steep bank, and beneath it a deep pool; and in order to avoid this by landing above it Brennan selected a place about twenty yards higher to go in. The current would sweep the horse down, but he thought he could guide the animal so as to land on a spit upon the other side. The chestnut did not like the idea of going into the water; I suppose the poor brute's instinct told him there was danger. In he would not go. He plunged, reared, bucked, and shied till Brennan got fairly mad.

' "Archie," said he, "go and break a big branch off one of the manukas, and if this devil won't go in next time let him have it hot and heavy."

'I got the branch, and the chestnut was tried again, but without success. Brennan sang out, and I came down with the manuka on the horse's back. He went in then. He gave such a jump that I expected to see the Sergeant shot off into the river. But Brennan sat firm, keeping the horse well in hand, and now the chestnut finding himself fairly in for it, struck out gamely. The yellow bubbling water was above the saddle, round the Sergeant's waist, and he leant a little forward clapping the horse's neck and encouraging him. They had got perhaps a quarter of the way across when I caught sight of something that made me sick with fear. It was a big tree being swept down, and I saw that if the Sergeant did not keep a little farther down the river it would be borne right against him. I shouted, and Brennan tried to look round, but either he mistook my meaning or got confused, for he turned the horse's head straight across the river. On came the tree, rolling over and over with a fearful strength and speed. In one minute more it was bang! against the chestnut's ribs. The horse gave a shrill neigh, a wild struggle, and the next thing I knew Brennan was off; and then I remembered that he could not swim a stroke. The horse plunged, gasped, and turned over on his side. His ribs were broken by that terrible collision. Poor Brennan only struggled a minute, then the current swept him off, his arms waved wildly once or twice, and once I saw his face; and, boys, never till my dying day will I forget that awful last look. I went away back to the station as hard as I could, and all the men there, the boss and all, turned out to search for poor old Mick. I must have been cranky at the time, for I forgot all about Jim, and only when we were on the point of starting did I remember. Then a lad from the station offered to go and look after him till we came back. We did not find Brennan for two days, and then a long way down the river. He was washed upon a sand bank, not bruised or discoloured. His one hand was under his head and his eyes closed, lying quite peaceable as if asleep; there was even something like a shadowy smile on his brave old face. When the terrible news was told to Jim Smith, he said nothing, but only lay without speaking all day. Lily, they said, was heart-broken, and cried her pretty face very red. Jim didn't die. The doctor said he had better be brought down to the township, and there were plenty of volunteers for bearers. He was carried to "The Crown", for there was then no hospital in Switzers. Lily seemed afraid of him at first, but gradually came to nurse him and attend to him more than any one. When Jim got able to move he went to Dunedin. Lily also went to town a short time after. But they came back together, and Lily was Mrs Jim Smith. I wasn't much surprised. A woman can't weep always for a first love when the second is young, good-looking, and well-to-do. She is a good little woman, and makes Jim Smith just as loving a wife as if she had never heard of such a person as Sergeant Michael Brennan.'

WILLIAM BAUCKE

# A Quaint Friendship

I was standing on the train platform of a smoker, watching the guard, one hand at his whistle and the other rising to make the semaphore signal 'All clear', when I heard a clamour and lament in Maori of 'Au-ee ka mahue au' (Oh, I shall be left behind). Looking in the direction of the voice, I saw a native woman desperately boring her way through the sea of faces lining the station kerbing at Frankton Junction, Waikato.

Blind in her anxiety to reach the train, she rushed for a carriage, and that being my smoker, frantically clutched the handgrasp just as the whistle of the guard, and the answering scream of the engine, gave her two seconds to wave my out-stretched arms aside and clamber up.

Now, I have been intimately acquainted with the natives all my life. I know their customs and language, so that I naturally speak to them in it when I meet them.

'Friend,' I said, 'you have come to the wrong carriage; this is for men who smoke.' Casting a searching glance at me, she replied, doubtingly, 'Probably you lie,' but opening the door, and seeing two solid walls of faces, dim in a panoply of smoke, cautiously closed it again, remarking humbly, 'It is true; but I can sit here'—and, triumphantly producing a pipe, continued, 'I also smoke.'

We had drawn out meanwhile, and were humming along at the reckless speed of about five miles an hour. After about twenty minutes' trifling with eternity, I suddenly remembered my companion. But she was quite oblivious of danger, and from her gentle crooning, that kept time with the swaying of our motion, I guessed that her thoughts were far away—away in the past of her forefathers.

Presently, looking up, she pecked her head at me and smiled, as who should say: 'I see you; I don't recognize your features, but I greet you all the same.' I smiled back, and looking down on the poor old face, studied it with many a kindly thought. Her features were well formed, on which the tracery of her tattooed chin must have shown a conspicuous embellishment in the lusty heyday of her life. And as I looked down on the wistful eyes my heart went out to her. I began linking her with a past, when the dear old face, now lined and shrunken, and like a last year's apple forgotten in the fruit loft—creased with countless wrinkles—was young and plump and kissable. And while I looked a magic hand rolled back the screen of years, and passing, touched and smoothed each line and crease. I saw her in her youth and prime, full of the virility of barbaric health and vigour, swift in affection, and swifter still for vengeance, when the heart is full of hate, when the pulse is quick and keen to feel the ardour of a love grown cold—when the eye is sharp to note the secret signals of a rival's advent on the scene; for never pang so deadly as the jealous thought that fills the native maiden's soul—He ceases to regard me!

The train had by now forgotten that it set out with the mission to tear up the rails, and we sauntered along in a pleasant, hand-in hand, lover-like dawdle. We knew that we should not reach our destination before five o'clock, and also that before we came to a standstill the driver would waken out of his reverie, and pull over the lever a notch or so. This gait suited those hard of hearing, for in these lulls a theme could be comfortably discussed and exhausted, and when interest began to flag, the sudden uproar of the stampede along uneven rails would shake up the system and quicken the faculties for a fresh subject.

My native acquaintance also took advance of the spell, for after a shrewd, sidelong inspection, she inquired if I objected to the smell of 'torori' (native tobacco); if not, why, then, she was hungering for a smoke. I told her not to regard me, as we were both in an unlawful place while the train was in motion, and pointing overhead, translated to her the caution there notified. 'Ugh; meaha tera, kei te pai' (Oh, never mind that; it is all right), she carelessly retorted, and forthwith began to unwind herself, and spreading out her knees began to discharge thereon the varied contents of her pockets. After a lengthly manipulation she produced a photograph, with the remark, 'Taku mokopuna' (my grandchild), then a silk hand-kerchief, a pocket knife, and finally about four inches of hard, smoked sausage. Holding this up with great pride, she said, 'My torori; I cured it; take some, try it.' I shuddered. I remembered one day when the tobacco hunger pinched me sore, and the choice stood—torori or suffer; how to please the giver I pretended that it was good; how that presently I felt moved to go outside and take the evil-smelling pipe, and dig a hole, deep and secure, and bury it; how I went to the creek and held my head under water, and protruded my tongue, to soak it, and cool it; how I covered myself with vows, as with a gravecloth, that henceforward and forever I would have patience, and humbly ask in prayer that the smok'ard's pain might pass! But I took her specimen and acted the shameless hypocrite. I told her that I found it a particularly precious sample, that it ought to be preserved as a trophy of her skill; that she must allow me to take half to show my friends—at all of which her dear old face crinkled with pleasure, and with infinite tenderness, she laid a detaining hand on my knee, saying, 'Just let me cut off sufficient to last me home, then take the rest, aye, take it all.' I have it still. I keep it in remembrance of my friend, and to preserve its special aroma and prevent its defiling the neighbouring contents of my Gladstone bag, I have enshrined it in two folds of bright tinfoil.

After several blasts she turned on me a smile of ineffable satisfaction and content, inhaling the foetid vapour, and discharging it again in an ecstasy of enjoyment most envious to look upon.

I should guess her age to have been 65, probably 70. Hunched up as she sat, her hands clasped round her knees, her petticoat was too short to cover her feet, which were bare; her head was covered with a man's serge hat, decorated with a rusty huia feather; a shawl of dubious pattern and age (but clean) round her shoulders, completed a figure quaint and ridiculous, but deeply interesting as I knew her more.

Our way lay over a dreary maze of rolling down and swamp—cheerless and depressing—manuka and fern—with here and there a patch of stunted raupo standing listless in its sour and stagnant ooze. Once in a while we would strike a run on a down hill grade. Then the engine would hearten up, and show off its paces to an admiring cluster of ancient cabbage trees; but directly they disappeared, we fell back into apathy and the ultimate desire to get off and help to push it along. Therefore, it was with a sight of relief we panted into Ohaupo. 'Now,' I said, 'we'll get into a carriage and be comfortable; you follow me.'

We were now rising, and as our horizon widened I turned to my companion for information. 'Friend,' I said, 'I am a stranger here, enlighten me.' With a countenance beaming with pleasure she replied: 'So you are a stranger here? And I looked on you as one of us, far gone into the white man's blood. That, yes, that is Pirongia,' and as she went on I was amazed at her unending flow of description. Instead of answering my questions in a desultory staccato, she slid her shawl from her shoulders, and poured forth a wealth of tribal history, amplifying it with anecdote, collateral incident, and ancient legend—of family quarrels and their results; of famous heroes of war, their names, and imperishable deeds of might—merging one with the other in proper order and sequence; and, forgetful of place and circumstance, wound up with a slap on my thigh, and the violent peroration: 'Those were men—men with juice of life in their bodies. What are the Maoris now?' She answered herself, and with a passionate contempt spat on the floor. 'He tetua (they are slaves)—slaves to the white man's abominations—to idleness, gambling, and the lecherous coveting of their neighbours' wives, and whenever they can get it the white man's stinking water. Ah! then is heard the boast of the precious ancestor, the battles he fought, the trophies he brought home, and the slaves that he made. But enough, why speak of it?' and like the typhoon that has suddenly spent its fury she said: 'What are those people looking so hard for, and whispering? I am not mad,' and snuggling herself into her corner gazed as one inspired, with eyes that saw but inwardly, and in a subdued voice, but which I could hear distinctly, intoned this plaintive monody:—'The white man came, he saw our lands; the white man went, we knew not where, few came at first, then more and more; they clamoured at our chiefs to let them have land; the churchmen came, with voices soft, and promised blessings to our race; at last we let them land upon our shore. And thus the white man came. He stepped ashore with humble tread, and cried, "Make room, make room for these," and threw down guns and stinking water at our feet. "Behold," he cried, "the blessings that I bring." We touched and tried, we smelt and drank, till all we saw looked red like blood, till we were mad with lust for more. "Kapai," he said, "you give me land, I bring you more." We gave him land, he wanted more. He felt his feet, and found them firm; he crooked his toes yet deeper in the soil. He tried his strength—then our eyes saw our mistake. But what cared he? He strained his loins and pushed; we also pushed. But we were weak, for in our veins, instead of blood, our fathers' blood, there welled a poison—the stinking water of our ruin'! After a silence she looked at me, and said, 'You understand!' Yes, I understood how much of truth there was, and how to place it; but this was not the time to analyse and explain. So I simply said, 'It is true, with some exceptions, but what avail? Would that the strangers' promises had been redeemed other than they have.' She smiled one of her dreary smiles, which said little yet implied so much, and, laying her hand gently on my arm, looked at me with eyes that had in them a suspicion of tears, and said: 'Listen, our people came from the rising sun, we are now going into its setting; we are hurrying into the night. As it gets darker we grope. The white man, who is far in the lead, calls back, "This is the way; come along!" But he travels too fast. He knows the road and where the boggy places are. He thinks that when he cries out from the darkness, "Hasten, but mind, here is a pit," we shall, when we come to it, avoid it. We don't. We are weary with long years of travel. We clutch at what we take to be guide-rails; but find, when we grasp them, that they are rotten sticks. Then we despair; we lie down—some never to rise again. Thus we thin out by the way; the road is dotted with our graves. Still the white man strides along. He comes to a hill. Is there a way round it? No; therefore he inflates his chest like a tui on the topmost branch; he bends his back; he breathes hard. Ah, he is at the top, and laughs! Ah, why does he laugh? He rejoices at his strength—then he is great. See, he looks at his arm; he crooks it, and smiles at the pattern of his tendons. He comes to a river. Does he look for a shallow ford? Not he! He says to himself, "My fancy is to cross just here," and he crosses there. We see his footsteps on the other side, and marvel. We venture closer; ha, of a surety has he crossed there! And how? Ask of the first-born of the gods!'

We had now reached the hill country, winding about with many a cunning turn. Here on the straight crossing a headland; there skirting a deep bayou of raupo swamp. On our right the setting sun gilded the nearer uplands with the restful lustre of mat gold, while the further ridges and the fore-shortened spurs cast looming shadows, here distinct and crisp, yonder blended and mellowed into blues and purples, making a dreamland panorama, transient here, to burst into fuller glory round yonder graceful curve.

Suddenly, like a slap in the face from an unseen hand, where one had looked for fresh wonders of forest beauty, spread a settler's recent burn! Gaunt and charred, prone on their mother's bosom, lay the mighty monarchs of the woods. Giants whom the storms of ages had battered at in vain, the tireless pecking of a pigmy two-legged creature with an axe had conquered and laid low.

And I heard a deep, resentful murmur at my side: 'There are his footsteps. That is where the white man treads!'

*       *       *

I was lazily wandering about, exploring its by-ways, and admiring the beauty spots of the King Country, when I discovered a nook of surpassing cosiness. It was a miniature valley whose uphill ended abruptly in a craggy steep, covered from foot to crown with plants, some dwarf, as became their source of nutriment; yet wherever a ledge afforded more generous sustenance, great ferns spread their arms to breeze and sunshine.

Down its centre tinkled a lively stream, clinking and gurgling on its merry way, as if revelling in the joyous thought that man might come, and man might go, but it went on for ever—aye, winter's rains might force it over bank, and summer's drought abase its fleeting pride, it stayed not once to moralize, to question this, or reason that; but hugged its mission to its breast, flowed gaily on, and will do so forever!

Suddenly the raucous barking of a distant dog disturbed my pleasant reverie. Following the sound I forced my way through man-high manuka, whose flowerets filled the air with an incense of long ago; for it brought back to me the days of my youth. I am a colonial, and sweet to me are the scents of the land of my birth.

Having crossed this Nature's plantation and brushed a cobweb from my face, I saw before me a native whare, in the low doorway of which—with head aslant, as of one who listens intently—I recognized the ancient dame whose friendship I had so curiously made some months before.

When she saw who it was that had intruded on her solitude, she stood forth and waved a hand in welcome, calling, in the voice I remembered so well, 'Haere mai, haere mai, e te manuwhiri ki te whare mate o aku tipuna' (welcome, welcome, visitor, to the deserted home of my ancestors), and, as is the habit of this people, when those meet, whose griefs have seen face to face, she took my hand and held up her nose.

Now, knowing the natives as I do, I make no pretence of fastidious delicacy, but conform to their custom of greeting—when they invite it—as strict courtesy demands. I therefore murmured, 'I greet you,' and crossed noses with her. Then, beckoning me to follow, she entered; but, turning on the doorstep, said: 'Tomo mai, otira kei te noho noaiho maua ko taku mokopuna' (enter friend, but I and my grandchild sit here empty), symbolizing thereby the regret that they had nothing worthy to set before the visitor. Expecting to see the grandchild, thus included in her apology, I cast an inquiring glance around, which she divining, smartly intercepted with the remark: 'He is gone to the township.'

Before hanging the kettle over the fire, she spread an absolutely clean mat over others equally clean, in a part bordered off from the rest of the house by a straight fern bole, secured in place by four pegs—two at each end—driven into the ground. 'Now,' she said, briskly, 'rest. He will be back soon, then you will see my grandchild. He has shot 25 rabbits, for which he will get sixpence apiece, which, counting two for one shilling, will come to 12s 6d; is it not so? He will bring home a loaf, and some butter, also he will buy some more cartridges and some cigarettes. Now this causes me much grief, because Dr Pomare has warned us that cigarette-smoking is very baneful to growing lads. I ask him to smoke my torori, which a friend has prized so highly (here memory smote me in the face, and left a bright accusing red, for I bethought me of my lies of months before) but he refuses. He says there is shame on his face when the white man sniffs, and says: "Young man, smoke not thy old soiled stockings, for the smell thereof is evil." But he is a good boy. He has been to school for a while. He can say "God damn" like a pakeha, as also other words, which I don't understand; but his dog does, for he obeys him at once with great fear.'

While, woman-like, she made conversation, I searched her face for some change, if any. There was the same old smile, only more pathetic; the wistfulness of eye more touching; the quiet submission to the fate of her race more patient; and the glow of idolatry more exalted whenever she mentioned her grandson—always her grandson! The remnant fruit of her body: he at one end, she at the other; but what of the space between? Husband, children, friends; love, pride, affection! And only her grandson left, with sorrow, and heartache, and a memory growing old with the years!

And, lo! there he stood in the doorway, having heralded his coming by viciously kicking a dog that lay sunning himself in the entrance, the everlasting cigarette in his mouth, and leaning against the door-post, without salute, stared rudely in while he inhaled the smoke and expelled it again through his nose, looking, when lit up by a sunbeam, like the simultaneous discharge of a double-barrelled gun, hat a-rake, a sweetbriar flower and cluster of berries in his buttonhole, boots with toes gaping unlaced—yet she looked up with a love which I envied him!

He was evidently ignorant of the fact that the visitor understood their language, for this uncouth chunk of truculence inquired: 'And who may this upoko kohua (pot head) be?' Lifting a deprecating hand, as if to ward me from a blow, she answered: 'He is a friend—our friend—who sees as men see, heart to heart; he loves us, for he sees in us the konini, whose leaves fall in the fading year; he is the friend I told you of that praised my torori, which you despise; come, shake his hand—so—Where is the loaf and butter?' And this graduate of a low white education threw down a parcel at her feet, reached for his gun, whistled to his dog, and lurched away.

After he had gone she sat silent, hurt at heart, may be, that the idol of her life had not made the most of his opportunity in the matter of good behaviour, and I felt that the furtive glances cast at me should be read as a dumb appeal to be merciful. Moved more than I care to tell, I reached over and gently stroked her sleeve, saying: 'Be comforted; he will remember your devotion in the years that are coming; he is young, and it is the way of youth; he is thoughtless. Now listen. His mistake is pardonable when you recollect that the white man of base and ignoble nature, in manner and speech, is of animal flavour; that the native youth, by such is much sought for, to learn from him phrases and words, which the decent keep secret. What marvel then that contempt for the white man in terms of derision finds utterance? For such is the bent of our curious nature, that we laugh at the joke with the joker, yet despise him in heart thereat after. That to touch what is evil is easy; but to grasp and exalt what is comely, means patient and painful endeavour. If what I have said in affection to your seeming is just and of savour, speak gently, in sorrow, not anger; rebuke in your grandchild his error. Yea, tell him that wit is not wisdom, nor rudeness a sign of high kinship; that white and black are equal in colour, if we judge by their shadow in daylight; that a guest is a guest by the token of a host being a host in his manner, and a visitor's rest when invited should be sacred as friendship, because of the inviter.'

'Yes, yes; all true,' she replied; and continued with a weary air, 'but you white people expect too much. Why burden our last few steps home with more than we can carry?'

Then she relapsed into dreamy repose. Her feet close together, her pipe in one hand, the thumb over the open bowl, the other clasped over it, and both clasped round her knees, her head tilted to one side—a far-away look in her eyes, staring hard and absently at the fire, as if waiting for the flickering of flame to light up the chambers of her memory. Then, speaking more in soliloquy than conversation, she said: 'Aye, what you have told me sounds good; that is my judgment on it.' Then she asked, 'Did I tell you that I had had two husbands? No? Then I will tell you now. The first I will not speak of; he was an evil man, and it is not meet to speak hard of the dead. The second was the light of my life. By him I had two children. The second was, I think, one year old when my husband left me. He left me, ah, woe of the day! You must know that the war was very grievous in the Waikato, at Rangiriri, at Orakau, and all the other battlefields of long ago, where many brave men went into the night. Though we Maniapoto had no direct quarrel with the pakeha, and the war never crossed our boundary, we heard that the pakeha intended to take all our lands, from Onehunga to Mokau, and drive us into the poor cold lands of Taupo, and to kill our wives and children. This report frightened us, and we said, "Let us guard our frontiers. We will set the river Puniu as our boundary, and no white man shall cross it; if he does we will kill him." So it came about that our best and strongest went away to lie in wait there. When those who had wives and children returned, they were relieved by others. At that time we never asked, "Where is So-and-So? Why did he not come home?" They had gone to the fight. For great was the fame of the leaders and heroes—Manga, Ngapora, and others. And the blood of their ancestors grew hot in their veins. So when news came of how the white soldiers, with the warrior from England (Cameron) had failed to storm Rangiriri, our messengers spoke with great freedom, and vaunted large boasts. That same night our young men met in council, and agreed to halve their forces—one to stay and watch our plantations and provide food; the other to join the heroes, who had at last shown the white man how the Maori can fight, or die. When we women heard this resolve, some cried; others were glad. You ask why some were glad? I will tell you. Every woman knows her man. All those who cried knew that their men were brave, and would go; and the others were cowards, and their women knew that they would stay at home, finding some excuse to do so. Ah! it was the winnowing of the grain; the chaff was blown away and the corn fell where all men might see it. It is many years ago; much has happened since then; but I see it all again now; and our speaking of fighting to-day has brought it all back to me. My man got up and went into our house, dug up the powder keg out of the corner, and began to make cartridges. All that night he made cartridges. He cleaned his "tupara" (double-barrelled gun), but never a word to me! I sat by the fire and watched him; and my heart was heavy. Oh! why did the pakeha covet our lands? When the children stirred I reached out and kept them away. Yet never a word to me! He looked not my way, but he saw me all the time! When I could bear it no longer I cried without noise, and when he heard me he tried to be blusterful and angry. That relieved me. Yes, such are the ways of the hearts of those that love, eh? But what of the glory—the name to be handed down to the children? Were not his ancestors brave, who suffered and said never a word? He looked my way at last—just one look! And I saw his hands tremble. Twice he dropped the bullet past the cartridge-case.

Then he ordered me out in a voice I knew not; and which failed to sound like anger. But I knew it was love, and therefore I went not: And when all was finished I went to his side and threw my shawl over his head, so that it covered us both. Then he cried in the voice of a man in terrible pain. For now when all was complete for the morrow it was meet we should chant the words that are sung at a parting! Then we unclosed our arms and sat silent. He thought my thoughts and I thought his! And to cheer me, and harden his feelings, he chanted the chant which the warrior recites before battle, and the chant was taken up by the others, who were also preparing for sunrise and travel.'

Here she sat silent so long that I thought she had ended, and I was on the point of making a remark when she continued. 'After twenty days—I counted them—a messenger came panting in, crying: "Prepare food; a party is at the turn of the road bringing in wounded." My heart turned white. I wanted to ask but could not. And I said, "Why should I shame his children by unseemly questions, and so much work to do?" But I knew, for my aitua (evil omen) whispered hard in my ear, "He cometh back as those who come home to their people to die!" Presently the messengers strode up and down, and recited the deeds, and the death of the fighting—the heroes, the dead, and the wounded! One instant I stayed my hand; it was powerless; five blinks of the eye, while the heart ceased its throbbing! For his name being called had palsied my living! Among the bravest he was, and how in the forefront of battle he had stood up and hurled his defiance, had singled out the foremost—also a brave, though a foeman, and shot him! Dead at his feet fell that foeman, just as two bullets struck at himself—one through the bridge of his nose, from a pistol, the other through both jaws, smashing through teeth and bone till his jaw hung like a beard to his face, cut thus by a bullet! "But you will see," said the orator, "he cares not. Yea, though he will die, he will joke at his blemish!"

'And truly he spoke, for there, when they brought him, he had stuck a huia feather through the hole in the bridge of his nose! Oh, my poor man! He never spoke—for how could he?—his tongue torn away and the wound all black with mortification. For we had nothing like the doctors of white men; only dock leaves, which we bruised and pressed the juice of into the wound, and thus laved all his terrible gashes. On the fourth day of his home-coming he died—died in my arms, where he lay from the day that they brought him till he went to rest in the home of his people. And his children are there! And the one that is left to me is one only—my grandchild!'

JOHN A. LEE

# Man's Inhumanity to Man

The sun was fierce and the sweat ran down the Shiner's face. His singlet was glued to his back although it kept climbing. His celluloid collar was slippery with sweat. The moisture from his brow was moistening the bleached dusty band of his straw boater and another layer of dust was gathering. It was a dry, hot, fierce heat, clear but too hot for a man warmly clad to be on the road carrying a swag and a heavy swag.

Harvest was coming at a rush. As he walked the road it seemed that the blue green of the wheat and oats turned to silver green, the silver green to yellow ears and straw. Two or three days and the farmers would be in the fields with their reapers and binders, working the clock around to get the wheat and oats in sheaf before a dry wind shook half the crop to the floor of the paddock. Man and beast would drive until the flesh was sore in those days before tractors eased the tension for the lovely horses.

In a few days he would go into the field himself. He always did respond to the call for harvest labour for a day or two. When everyone crowded into the fields to race the wind and the rain the social adventure of it all compelled a few days' loyalty from the most incorrigible of vagabonds. He would stook and he would help to stack and he would discourse learnedly on the quality and quantity of the harvest. He had better memory of such things than most of the farmers who were too busy fighting debt, whose nose was too near the soil for academic comparison of harvest with harvest.

Work was not so bad when it had a measure of novelty, of society, when man's race to gather the harvest before it was spoiled by the elements had a touch of adventure. But work for wages day after day, dull, unremitting, backbreaking, who wanted to work for wages when the glory had departed! So at every harvest he heeded the call. He spent a few days in the fields and then collected his money and hurried on, and that was the only time when he felt a trifle ashamed as he ran from a group who already had more than they could to do, a group who on Monday were inclined to think him a good fellow and on Friday chased his back up the road with curses and sneers as though they were kicking a dog in the tail.

Later, when the mills were coming out to thresh, he would throw his swag in again with a team and for a day or two be a man amongst men in the yearly novelty of the job, the whirr of the machinery, the vagabondage of other men. For half the mills recruited their crews off the road, men and swags.

He could fork from a stack to a mill with any man on earth when he was in the mood. It was because of his prowess that he achieved the pinnacle of notoriety as a loafer. He could and he wouldn't. The mood to show the world would come to him as he stood on a stack and looked down upon the mill feeder who, knowing the Shiner held the fork would have for him a measure of contempt. The attitude and tones of the mill feeder would say: 'Huh, the Shiner. Easy to keep ahead of this bird!'

So the Shiner would shower the sheaves down on him, or pile them up around him. The feeder had to set a fast pace for the mill. The Shiner would start to set an impossible pace for the feeder. The feeder would smile contemptuously at the start of the day but be a beaten man before the day was out, never quite able to win a fraction of a second between the arrival of the sheaves. And then the Shiner would smile even as he sweated, and maybe even as his hands blistered. And the feeder at last might be the one to plead for mercy.

'Steady!'

'You can't keep ahead of the Shiner!'

'Easy, easy.'

'When I was a lad feeders were feeders!'

But by the time the Shiner had convinced the feeder that he was the greatest forker from the stack in New Zealand, a sorely libelled man, he was getting toward the mood to loaf as prodigiously as he had worked. From then on he had to be coaxed, he could not be driven for he was the most imperturbable loafer in the land. He would slow up his delivery and the mill would pour out a diminishing stream of grain, and when the feeder called for speed he had been known to lean on the fork and ask the feeder if he had heard this one, until at last the millowner paid the Shiner off and sent him packing.

There were millowners who had been known to keep him hard at work for a couple of days, or until some other had come carrying his swag along the road, by sheer flattery. The Shiner would stay on the stack, in the spotlight as it were. But no engine driver could stand for a whole season gazing in admiration at the Shiner's prowess. There were jobs to do. Flattery can become real hard work.

Nevertheless the Shiner was feeling the call of harvest again as he tramped the road on this hot sweaty day. But he had a prior call. The road was dusty, his palate was dusty, his tongue was dusty, his lips were cracking like the mud in the drying creeks. This was no place where he could find cool shade in pine trees and pitch a tent, and loaf, and feed upon the country until the silver green straw and heads of wheat and oats turned to hard yellow, even if that moment was only a couple of days ahead. This was bad country for him to forage in. This was country in which he had played too many tricks, country in which he possessed notoriety and not fame.

He wanted liquor as he hadn't wanted it in a decade. And he did not want the bite but the bitterness of alcohol. He wanted beer, long bitter beer, not whiskey. He wanted alcohol and a sense of having alcohol, the gradual lubrication and easement of malt and hops and not the warm mellow forgetfulness of spirits. Oh for a beer, for a long, long, long, bitter, bitter, bitter beer. 'Be-e-e-r.' He said the word with a long deep 'e' and his desire became a fanaticism. 'Be-e-e-e-er.'

The idea was getting hold of him so thoroughly that he was in grave danger of being driven to work to secure the price. But the job would have to yield the price in advance. He couldn't wait!

'Be-e-e-er!'

He wanted beer so much that he felt sinful at the lack of it. He was an inferior. Without a pint in his hand he was conscious of an awful blasphemous nakedness. Beer he wanted until he was prepared to work for beer. And in the Shiner could there be greater proof of the intensity of craving? And he couldn't get beer anywhere. Along the road, and the country was thick with pubs, he tried to scrounge the bitter foaming liquor.

'How about a beer, boss?'

'It's the Shiner himself! Well, I'll make a bargain. Go out the back and chop wood for a couple of hours and I'll give you two beers and dinner.'

'One now. Can't you see I'm perishing?'

'You'll last it out. No one will give you anything around here in advance.'

It was as if the Shiner had got a craving for a brewery in the Sahara. Except that this Sahara was due to his own past bad behaviour. Be sure your peccadilloes will find you dry.

'Look, one glass!'

'The axe is sharp.'

'You can go to hell, you miserable cow!' The Shiner picked up his swag.

'I'll be seeing you, Shiner!'

Publicans. They had no sense of the fitness of things. Such a thirst derived from publicans and yet they baulked at a little human charity. They had no milk of human kindness, or could not understand that sometimes the milk of human kindness was a long beer. 'I haven't any money but will you take stamps?'

Alas, the story of the great stamp trick travelled so fast that he could not work it again. There are no copyrights about vagabondage. Publicans told the story and thought it wonderful because it celebrated the downfall of people easy to deceive like Mick Scanlan and Paddy Griffen. To demonstrate superiority to those weaklings was a point of honour.

'Now if you wanted a feed, Shiner.'

Beer. That was what he wanted. Bitter. Something to stimulate the glands that moistened the palate and something that would take aridity out of the soul. A feed. Who wanted a pie. Who wanted roast mutton, and baked potatoes, and bread and gravy, and cabbage and tea. He wanted beer. And there was no substitute.

'Just one long beer and I'll call back and pay you after harvest.'

'You fooled me once, Shiner!'

'But this is a pledge between gentlemen.'

'Gentlemen, indeed!'

Vagabond's thirst countered by publican's memory. What an awful predicament for a thirsty soul on a dry scorching day, on a day when the temperament is as parched as the throat. Publican's memory is as much an occupational disease as alcoholic's thirst.

Two, three, four hotels he tried in four or five miles. And all the publicans were scornful, even hilarious. They all knew him and had given the dog his bad name. No one begrudged the beer as much as they feared they would live to regret the slightest weakening.

'Give him a pint and he'll drink the pub dry!'

Not as bad as that but all had pitched him, neck and crop, into the dusty road on other days when he had quartered himself on the neighbourhood. You could never tell with that one. Treat him kindly, and end by a declaration of war, and maybe a storm of abuse before he walked down the road. And good customers would sometimes go to other places rather than be plagued with his insistence on free drink.

'I haven't had a beer for weeks!'

'Thought you were looking well.'

'You could stand me a beer.'

'I could. But I won't. Stick it out for another week and it'll become a habit. Never let it be said I started you again on the downward path.'

'Oh hell, I want a be-e-e-er!'

'I believe in helping a man to go straight when he's been trying.'

'Man, I'll die of thirst!'

'The only time my conscience ever pricked me was when a man died of beer in my own pub.'

'Have you no feeling for one of your victims?'

'Victim. You!'

For publicans from end to end of the country had been the Shiner's victims. And there were no men loitering around the hotels from whom he could cadge. They were out in the fields doing the work of the world. They were getting their reapers and binders turned over and ready. Nowhere was there someone with cash and his resistance half lowered and his geniality exaggerated by the goods he had imbibed.

'It's hell!' the Shiner said as he walked.

He always knew what hell would be like, for he was a believer and paid a measure of attention to the observance of his faith. Hell would be a terrible place where everyone would be hot and sweaty and would work on hot plates. They would be furry of tongue, and cracked of lip, and dry of throat. And Satan would be a fat leering publican. A fellow in shirt-sleeves and bowler and pasty of face and fishy of eye, and with a waistcoat that had to reach around twice as much circumference to cover the abdomen as to cross the chest. And in hell Satan would have vats of foaming cold bitter, and clean wide deep glasses. And the swine would laugh at the thirsty. Already on this day he was in purgatory. No. Satan would be no saturnine fellow with horns. He would be a hog fat publican, dull and mean.

The craving grew as the Shiner walked. At the start of the day his flesh had been parched. By late afternoon he could feel his soul being dehydrated.

'Sure I'm shrinking up and I won't expand until I can drink a bucket!'

He stood on a bridge over the muddy waters of a dredge-dirtied river and recited to himself: 'Water water everywhere, and all the boards did shrink; water water everywhere, and not a drop to drink.'

His thirst became as sizzling as a hot plate as he walked on. He failed to take his usual draughts of spring water and that made his plight worse. Nostalgia for beer and repugnance for water developed simultaneously. If he could only get fourpence for a pint. If he had threepence a publican would oblige, but when he had nothing and was known he had no chance. But he had an idea. There were four hotels in the town ahead and he would get a penny subsidy in all. They would go a penny but not a pint. He entered the first.

'I'm dying of thirst. If you'd give me a penny I'd have enough for a pint.'

'Give me the threepence then, Shiner.'

'No. Give me the penny and let me pay in full.'

'What's the game?'

'It's my dignity. I want to pay in full. Humour an old man!'

The publican opened the till and threw him a penny.

'Thanks.'

'What'll you have?'

'I've still got to get the other threepence.'

'You scoundrel!'

'You lent me a penny, didn't you. What are you screaming about?' the Shiner walked out.

'You thief!'

Let him bawl. He managed to work the trick in the next two hotels. Yes, it worked each time. They were all prepared to advance a penny to catch threepence. He didn't mind the abuse. His standing was at that zero at which beer freezes. He entered the last hotel. The publican, wonder of wonders, was a new fellow. An old enemy of the Shiner had moved on. The bar was empty.

'Good-day to you.'

'Good-day. Come far?'

'I'm really very sorry. I want a pint of beer and I've only got threepence.' He laid the pennies along the bar. 'Three pennies. Faith. Hope. Charity. Could you trust me with a penny. Faith. Hope. Charity. Benevolence, would be your penny.'

'Going to work in the neighbourhood?'

'Harvest. I'm the best forker in Otago and Canterbury.'

The publican filled out the glass and the Shiner pushed the three pennies across.

'Ah.' The Shiner sipped. Never let it be said he swallowed his beer at a draught. He wanted to taste and loiter over the wetness and bitterness of each drop. He had walked miles to win a pint. 'Ah.' A teaspoonful at a time, 'Ah. You keep the best beer around here.'

'You think so?' the publican was pleased.

'I don't think. I know. I'm an authority. Don't I bust my harvest cheque every year in this town?'

'You do. Have another!'

'Yes. The reapers and binders'll be going in a few days. Yes. Very good beer. I'll come here when I'm through.' As the Shiner sipped and sighed and ummed and ahed he saw a rat run out of a hole in the corner of the bar where someone had dropped a fragment of water biscuit.

'Rats. Cheeky. Ah.'

'There's dozens of them around here. I wish I could get rid of them!'

'You should see me kill rats.'

'Go on.'

'There isn't another ratter my equal in the whole country.'

'And you've got nothing to do for a couple of days until the harvest starts?'

'Nothing. I'm broke. Me time's all me own.'

'I'll tell you what. Pull into the hut at the back. You can have your food and there's a bed there. You kill the rats.'

'There'll be never a rat left.' The Shiner drank his beer at a draught. 'Give me another beer and put it on the slate. I'll square after a few days at harvest.'

'You can kill rats, you say?' The publican filled the glass again. He had to make a good impression as a newcomer to the district and was prepared for a little generosity as a business investment. Set a beer and catch a boozer.

'I'll clear them all out for you.' The Shiner meant what he said. He was the greatest ratter on earth. He knew it.

'Anything you want to clean them out?'

'Look. I'll tell you what. I'll get it from you. Cheese. And a quart of beer. No rat can resist——'

'Cheese and beer! It sounds as if you wanted to catch a man!'

'Rats are human. Feed them on what they're used to. They live like humans around here. Cheese attracts them. But welsh rarebit!'

'I'll put some in a bottle.'

'No. Put a drop in my billy.'

'You're sure!'

'Of course. Rats get used to beer and cheese around a hotel. Now if you make what they're used to savoury——'

'It sounds alright to me.'

The Shiner didn't loaf around. Someone might come in who knew him and that would spoil the place for him. He retreated to the hut and unrolled his swag. He walked all round and through the hotel, into every room and every shed, made a great show of finding the holes in the walls. He baited a few rabbit traps with cheese and left them about. The publican left him alone.

He retired to his hut at sundown. He did not want to be around the hotel when the evening customers came around. Someone would be sure to know him. He lay down to rest with the billy by his side. He was serene after nearly a day's frustration. Calm and cool after heat and storm. He lifted the billy to his lips and had a mouthful and said, 'ah,' and smiled at the roof of the hut. Good beer. Welsh rarebits for rats. Why should he teach hotel rats bad habits. If the rats got drunk it would take a policeman and not the Shiner to arrest them. And

what were a few rats around a pub. They ate the crumbs and that
saved a lot of sweeping. And they got many a customer used to what
he was going to see anyhow. That was all to the good. In fact it might
be better for some of the fellows if there were a few snakes around
for the same reason. His mind retraced the events of the day as he
sipped. It had been started in the desert but had ended in an oasis.

'Be-e-e-er!'

Yes. Good beer. Homeopathy worked wonders with the Shiner. A
couple of quarts of bitter in the stomach dissolved a lot of bitterness
in the heart. He would have to deliver some dead rats on the morrow,
but who organized life that far in advance. And, wonder of wonders,
most of the rats seemed to come from the store where the publican
kept the bottled spirits; they seemed to come from there even when a
man was sober. That was an inducement to go ratting.

In the morning he fooled around and fooled around. He had a
couple of rats to show, caught in his cheese baited rabbit traps.

'There are rats in the bottle store, dozens of them!'

'I know.'

'Well, let me in.'

'Have a glass of beer.'

'No thanks. You can't mix work and drink. I always believe in
getting my job done first. Mind you, it's kind of you, and I'm not
saying I wouldn't like it, the good beer you keep. When I get the
harvesting done I'll bring a dozen fellows down here. It's the best
pub in town!'

'Just a glass?'

'No. Work first. You just lock me into that store. I'll shut the door
tight so that nothing can get out and I'll move all the boxes. I'll find
out where all the holes are.'

'Right-oh.' He let the Shiner in.

'Lock me in. I'll knock when I want to come out.' The Shiner had a
little parcel in his hand.

'Sure you won't have a glass?'

'When I come out.'

When the door was pulled shut and locked, the Shiner put a
couple of cases against it. It opened inward so he was safe. He
opened his little parcel. It contained the two rats he had already
caught. 'Two and two make four,' he said sweetly. He had to make
some sort of showing.

He was in that store a long time and there was a great banging and
rattling as he bumped the floor and made pretence of a great shifting. And long spells of silence as he sat quietly waiting for the rats. In
truth he was soon sitting on a case making an odd bump on the floor

and drinking whiskey from the neck of a flask he had opened, a flask of the real mackay. He sat and he drank, as fast as he could drink. And then he slipped a quart bottle in his hip pocket. He scattered a few baits around before he shifted the cases and knocked again on the door.

'Look. I caught two myself while I was in there. I'll catch a hundred tonight now I know where they all are. With the bait.'

'You'll have a beer now?'

'Never a drop till my task is done.' The Shiner didn't want to kill the spirits with the ferment.

'A cup of tea' said the publican's wife.

'Sure. It's a lady after me own heart that you are. And are these your own scones made hot from your own hand?'

'Yes, they're mine.'

'Me own mother never made better scones and she could make scones.'

'A nice man,' said the wife to the husband.

'Steady fellow,' said the publican. 'He refuses to touch a drop while he's working.'

So the Shiner had a cup of tea and hot buttered scones and went back to his hut 'to give the bait a chance to work.' He took some water in his billy and thought he would have a dram. And since he hadn't been drinking spirits for many weeks the liquor made way with his caution. He had many drams. Although there was one precaution he never forgot to take. He filled the whiskey into his pannikin, enough for a dram or two, and always rolled up the quart bottle in his swag. If he was forced to retreat and went with his swag retreat had compensations. He had learned that trick across the years. Soon whiskey got the better of all but that one discretion. The descent was easy and glorious.

A customer came from the bar around the house to a place marked 'gents'. He heard a raucous voice singing.

> 'I'm out in the cruel world
> Out in the street
> I'm asking a penny
> From each one I meet
> I'm fatherless, motherless
> Sadly I roam
> What will become of me
> I have no home.'

The customer looked into the hut.

'Well, if it isn't the Shiner!'

'Hullo. Hullo. Hullo.'

'What are you doing, Shiner?'

'Catching rats.'

'Catching rats! Ha, ha. Seems to me as if you will soon catch rats alright. Watch you don't catch a few snakes too. Ha, ha.'

'I'm out in the cruel world,' the Shiner was more interested in himself than in his visitor and started to sing again.

'Come and have a drink with me, Shiner.'

'Sorry. But I never drink during working hours.' He was expansive, engaging, apologetic.

'What work are you doing?'

'I told you. I'm catching rats.'

'Catching rats, ha, ha, ha.'

His interrogator went back to the bar while the Shiner changed his song.

> 'Only a leaf
> Oh but what grief
> It caused in the
> Dim long ago
> Once it was red
> Now faded and dead
> And the woman
> Who wore it lies low.

'See you've got the Shiner in the hut out there,' said the customer to the publican.

'The Shiner. Where? Where?'

'Out in the hut. Drunk. Singing like mad. Says he's catching rats. He's making a good start. Watch he doesn't put a trick across you.'

'Is that the Shiner? What's the Shiner like?'

'Tall. Straw boater tied to coat with a bootlace. Celluloid collar. I thought everyone around here knew the Shiner!'

'Drunk as a lord you say? On what?'

'Smells like whiskey.'

'Come on.'

They stood outside the hut listening.

> 'It is ten weary years
> Since I left England's shores
> In a far distant country to roam
> How I long to return to my own native land
> To my friends and the old folks at home.
> Last night as I slumbered
> I had a strange dream——'

'You'll have a nightmare tonight, Shiner,' the publican put his head around the door. 'You won't have a drink?'

'Not during working hours,' said the Shiner. 'One that seemed to bring distant friends near,' he went back to his singing.

'Good-day, Mister Shiner,' the publican moved in. A dark, tough looking little cuss when he was riled.

'It is that. It is that.'

'Drunk. Where did you get it? You wouldn't have any beer. You didn't sneak any whiskey by any chance did you?'

'It's me rheumatic fever,' the Shiner grinned.

'Seen any rats yet?'

'Easy now. Easy. Can't you take a joke?'

'You promised to kill the rats.'

'Sure.'

'Well, kill them, or I'll kill the ratter!'

'Come on,' said the Shiner, unsteady on his feet but determined to carry it off, 'come on.' He walked out of the hut to the wood pile. 'Did I say how I would kill them? Did I now?'

'Welsh rarebit,' the publican was mumbling.

'Can't you see they are not water rats.'

'Welsh rarebits,' the publican was glowering. 'Well, get busy.'

'Sure I can kill all the rats,' the Shiner bent and lifted up a billet of wood. 'I'm ready to perform me contract now. You bring the rats out and hold their heads on the block and I'll knock the brains out of everyone of them. Bring out your rats.'

There was an audience of three now and they were tittering. The publican might have considered his experience cheap at the price had it not been for the audience, but he had some dignity too. He hit the Shiner in the stomach and doubled him over. And as the Shiner doubled he let him have a boot in the exposed haunches. The Shiner sat amid the sawdust and the chips gasping for breath.

'You — wind — ed — me.'

'Let me wind you again.'

'Sure you can't take a joke.'

'Stand up.' The publican was small but he had been a champion wrestler at Caledonian sports gatherings for years. 'Stand up!'

'If I stand up you'll knock me down.'

'If you don't stand up I'll knock you down just the same.'

'Publicans,' said the Shiner mournfully, 'are losing their sense of humour.'

'Stand up!'

'Not again.'

'Well I'll knock you flat if you don't.'

'I won't have so far to fall.'

The audience was laughing. The Shiner looked at them accusingly and recited—

'Man's inhumanity to man makes countless thousands mourn.'

The publican dragged the Shiner to his feet, picked him up, carried him to the road, and threw him ungently in the dustiest spot he could find.

His wife called to him and the publican turned to talk to her. The Shiner jumped and scrambled through the fence into the field opposite, leaving his boater in the dust. The publican sent it after him with a couple of kicks, one of which sent a toe through the crown. He went to the hut and got the swag and the billy and brought them and threw them across the fence. And the swag didn't leak. The bottle didn't break. The Shiner sat looking out on to the road mournfully, his straw boater with its ruptured top on his head.

'Now go catching your rats,' the publican went back to his bar followed by his customers. 'And if ever you want the Shine taken out of the Shiner call in on me. I'll oblige you.'

'Publicans without humour,' said the Shiner to his back as he sat looking through the fence.

But the sun was shining and the birds were twittering and harvest was coming and there was half a quart of whiskey in the swag. And half a quart and a flask in the Shiner, so he mellowed after a mournful inspection of his hat. He unrolled his swag and took out the bottle. There would be no rain for weeks and the ground was dry. And in his progress he had brought his billet of wood with him, grasping at it when he had been picked up, as he would have grasped at anything in reach. He drank and he sat in the field and bawled.

'Bring out your rats! Bring out your rats!'

Later in the day when twilight came he sat singing—

> 'I'm out in the cruel world
> I'm out in the street
> I'm asking a penny
> From each one I meet.
> Fatherless, motherless,
> Sadly I roam
> What will become of me
> I have no home.'

'The poor man,' said the publican's wife and she took him some tea and scones.

'Your scones are better than the ones me mother used to make.'

She gave him half a crown as well, but never told her husband.

'Man's inhumanity to man,' he said to her as he handed back the jug and took the coin, 'makes countless thousands mourn.'

That publican never did any good anyhow. His wife took pity on too many customers.

KATHERINE MANSFIELD     **At the Bay**

Very early morning. The sun was not yet risen, and the whole of Crescent Bay was hidden under a white sea-mist. The big bush-covered hills at the back were smothered. You could not see where they ended and the paddocks and bungalows began. The sandy road was gone and the paddocks and bungalows the other side of it; there were no white dunes covered with reddish grass beyond them; there was nothing to mark which was beach and where was the sea. A heavy dew had fallen. The grass was blue. Big drops hung on the bushes and just did not fall; the silvery, fluffy toi-toi was limp on its long stalks, and all the marigolds and the pinks in the bungalow gardens were bowed to the earth with wetness. Drenched were the cold fuchsias, round pearls of dew lay on the flat nasturtium leaves. It looked as though the sea had beaten up softly in the darkness, as though one immense wave had come rippling, rippling—how far? Perhaps if you had waked up in the middle of the night you might have seen a big fish flicking in at the window and gone again. . . .

Ah-Aah! sounded the sleepy sea. And from the bush there came the sound of little streams flowing, quickly, lightly, slipping between the smooth stones, gushing into ferny basins and out again; and there was the splashing of big drops on large leaves, and something else—what was it?—a faint stirring and shaking, the snapping of a twig and then such silence that it seemed some one was listening.

Round the corner of Crescent Bay, between the piled-up masses of broken rock, a flock of sheep came pattering. They were huddled together, a small, tossing, woolly mass, and their thin, stick-like legs trotted along quickly as if the cold and the quiet had frightened them. Behind them an old sheep-dog, his soaking paws covered with sand, ran along with his nose to the ground, but carelessly, as if thinking of something else. And then in the rocky gateway the shepherd himself appeared. He was a lean, upright old man, in a frieze coat that was covered with a web of tiny drops, velvet trousers tied under the knee, and a wide-awake with a folded blue handkerchief round the brim. One hand was crammed into his belt, the other grasped a beautifully smooth yellow stick. And as he walked, taking his time, he kept up a very soft light whistling, an airy, far-away fluting that sounded mournful and tender. The old dog cut an ancient caper or two and then drew up sharp, ashamed of his levity, and walked a few dignified paces by his master's side. The sheep ran forward in little pattering rushes; they began to bleat, and ghostly flocks and herds answered them from under the sea. 'Baa! Baaa!' For a time they seemed to be always on the same piece of ground. There ahead was stretched the sandy road with shallow puddles; the same soaking bushes showed on either side and the same shadowy palings. Then something immense came into view; an enormous shock-haired giant with his arms stretched out. It was the big gum-tree outside Mrs Stubbs's shop, and as they passed by there was a strong whiff of eucalyptus. And now big spots of light gleamed in the mist. The shepherd stopped whistling; he rubbed his red nose and wet beard on his wet sleeve and, screwing up his eyes, glanced in the direction of the sea. The sun was rising. It was marvellous how quickly the mist thinned, sped away, dissolved from the shallow plain, rolled up from the bush and was gone as if in a hurry to escape; big twists and curls jostled and shouldered each other as the silvery beams broadened. The faraway sky—a bright, pure blue—was reflected in the puddles, and the drops, swimming along the telegraph poles, flashed into points of light. Now the leaping, glittering sea was so bright it made one's eyes ache to look at it. The shepherd drew a pipe, the bowl as small as an acorn, out of his breast pocket, fumbled for a chunk of speckled tobacco, pared off a few shavings and stuffed the bowl. He was a grave, fine-looking old man. As he lit up and the blue smoke wreathed his head, the dog, watching, looked proud of him.

'Baa! Baaa!' The sheep spread out into a fan. They were just clear of the summer colony before the first sleeper turned over and lifted a drowsy head; their cry sounded in the dreams of little children . . . who lifted their arms to drag down, to cuddle the darling little woolly lambs of sleep. Then the first inhabitant appeared; it was the Burnells' cat Florrie, sitting on the gatepost, far too early as usual, looking for their milk-girl. When she saw the old sheep-dog she sprang up quickly, arched her back, drew in her tabby head, and seemed to give a little fastidious shiver. 'Ugh! What a coarse, revolting creature!' said Florrie. But the old sheep-dog, not looking up, waggled past, flinging out his legs from side to side. Only one of his ears twitched to prove that he saw, and thought her a silly young female.

The breeze of morning lifted in the bush and the smell of leaves and wet black earth mingled with the sharp smell of the sea. Myriads of birds were singing. A goldfinch flew over the shepherd's head and, perching on the tiptop of a spray, it turned to the sun, ruffling its small breast feathers. And now they had passed the fisherman's hut, passed the charred-looking little *whare* where Leila the milk-girl lived with her old Gran. The sheep strayed over a yellow swamp and Wag, the sheep-dog, padded after, rounded them up and headed them for the steeper, narrower rocky pass that led out of Crescent Bay and towards Daylight Cove. 'Baa! Baaa!' Faint the cry came as they rocked along the fast-drying road. The shepherd put away his pipe, dropping it into his breast-pocket so that the little bowl hung over. And straightway the soft airy whistling began again. Wag ran out along a ledge of rock after something that smelled, and ran back again disgusted. Then pushing, nudging, hurrying, the sheep rounded the bend and the shepherd followed after out of sight.

## II

A few moments later the back door of one of the bungalows opened, and a figure in a broad-striped bathing suit flung down the paddock, cleared the stile, rushed through the tussock grass into the hollow, staggered up the sandy hillock, and raced for dear life over the big porous stones, over the cold, wet pebbles, on to the hard sand that gleamed like oil. Splish-Splosh! Splish-Splosh! The water bubbled round his legs as Stanley Burnell waded out exulting. First man in as usual! He'd beaten them all again. And he swooped down to souse his head and neck.

'Hail, brother! All hail, Thou Mighty One!' A velvety bass voice came booming over the water.

Great Scott! Damnation take it! Stanley lifted up to see a dark head bobbing far out and an arm lifted. It was Jonathan Trout—there before him! 'Glorious morning!' sang the voice.

'Yes, very fine!' said Stanley briefly. Why the dickens didn't the fellow stick to his part of the sea? Why should he come barging over to this exact spot? Stanley gave a kick, a lunge and struck out, swimming overarm. But Jonathan was a match for him. Up he came, his black hair sleek on his forehead, his short beard sleek.

'I had an extraordinary dream last night!' he shouted.

What was the matter with the man? This mania for conversation irritated Stanley beyond words. And it was always the same—always some piffle about a dream he'd had, or some cranky idea he'd got hold of, or some rot he'd been reading. Stanley turned over on his back and kicked with his legs till he was a living waterspout. But even then . . . 'I dreamed I was hanging over a terrifically high cliff, shouting to some one below.' You would be! thought Stanley. He could stick no more of it. He stopped splashing. 'Look here, Trout,' he said, 'I'm in rather a hurry this morning.'

'You're WHAT?' Jonathan was so surprised—or pretended to be—that he sank under the water, then reappeared again blowing.

'All I mean is,' said Stanley, 'I've no time to—to—to fool about. I want to get this over. I'm in a hurry. I've work to do this morning—see?'

Jonathan was gone before Stanley had finished. 'Pass, friend!' said the bass voice gently, and he slid away through the water with scarcely a ripple. . . . But curse the fellow! He'd ruined Stanley's bathe. What an unpractical idiot the man was! Stanley struck out to sea again, and then as quickly swam in again, and away he rushed up the beach. He felt cheated.

Jonathan stayed a little longer in the water. He floated, gently moving his hands like fins, and letting the sea rock his long, skinny body. It was curious, but in spite of everything he was fond of Stanley Burnell. True, he had a fiendish desire to tease him sometimes, to poke fun at him, but at bottom he was sorry for the fellow. There was something pathetic in his determination to make a job of everything. You couldn't help feeling he'd be caught out one day, and then what an almighty cropper he'd come! At that moment an immense wave lifted Jonathan, rode past him, and broke along the beach with a joyful sound. What a beauty! And now there came another. That was the way to live—carelessly, recklessly, spending oneself. He got on to his feet and began to wade towards the shore, pressing his toes into the firm, wrinkled sand. To take things easy, not to fight against the ebb and flow of life, but to give way to it—that was what was needed. It was this tension that was all wrong. To live—to live! And the perfect morning, so fresh and fair, basking in the light, as though laughing at its own beauty, seemed to whisper, 'Why not?'

But now he was out of the water Jonathan turned blue with cold. He ached all over; it was as though some one was wringing the blood out of him. And stalking up the beach, shivering, all his muscles tight, he too felt his bathe was spoilt. He'd stayed in too long.

## III

Beryl was alone in the living-room when Stanley appeared, wearing a blue serge suit, a stiff collar and a spotted tie. He looked almost uncannily clean and brushed; he was going to town for the day. Dropping into his chair, he pulled out his watch and put it beside his plate.

'I've just got twenty-five minutes,' he said. 'You might go and see if the porridge is ready, Beryl?'

'Mother's just gone for it,' said Beryl. She sat down at the table and poured out his tea.

'Thanks!' Stanley took a sip. 'Hallo!' he said in an astonished voice, 'you've forgotten the sugar.'

'Oh, sorry!' But even then Beryl didn't help him; she pushed the basin across. What did this mean? As Stanley helped himself his blue eyes widened; they seemed to quiver. He shot a quick glance at his sister-in-law and leaned back.

'Nothing wrong, is there?' he asked carelessly, fingering his collar.

Beryl's head was bent; she turned her plate in her fingers.

'Nothing,' said her light voice. Then she too looked up, and smiled at Stanley. 'Why should there be?'

'O-oh! No reason at all as far as I know. I thought you seemed rather——'

At that moment the door opened and the three little girls appeared, each carrying a porridge plate. They were dressed alike in blue jerseys and knickers; their brown legs were bare, and each had her hair plaited and pinned up in what was called a horse's tail. Behind them came Mrs Fairfield with the tray.

'Carefully, children,' she warned. But they were taking the very greatest care. They loved being allowed to carry things. 'Have you said good morning to your father?'

'Yes, grandma.' They settled themselves on the bench opposite Stanley and Beryl.

'Good morning, Stanley!' Old Mrs Fairfield gave him his plate.

'Morning, mother! How's the boy?'

'Splendid! He only woke up once last night. What a perfect morning!' The old woman paused, her hand on the loaf of bread, to gaze out of the open door into the garden. The sea sounded. Through the wide-open window streamed the sun on to the yellow varnished walls and bare floor. Everything on the table flashed and glittered. In the middle there was an old salad bowl filled with yellow and red nasturtiums. She smiled, and a look of deep content shone in her eyes.

'You might *cut* me a slice of that bread, mother,' said

Stanley. 'I've only twelve and a half minutes before the coach passes. Has anyone given my shoes to the servant girl?'

'Yes, they're ready for you.' Mrs Fairfield was quite unruffled.

'Oh, Kezia! Why are you such a messy child!' cried Beryl despairingly.

'Me, Aunt Beryl?' Kezia stared at her. What had she done now? She had only dug a river down the middle of her porridge, filled it, and was eating the banks away. But she did that every single morning and no one had said a word up till now.

'Why can't you eat your food properly like Isabel and Lottie?' How unfair grown-ups are!

'But Lottie always makes a floating island, don't you, Lottie?'

'I don't,' said Isabel smartly. 'I just sprinkle mine with sugar and put on the milk and finish it. Only babies play with their food.'

Stanley pushed back his chair and got up.

'Would you get me those shoes, mother? And, Beryl, if you've finished, I wish you'd cut down to the gate and stop the coach. Run in to your mother, Isabel, and ask her where my bowler hat's been put. Wait a minute—have you children been playing with my stick?'

'No, father!'

'But I put it here,' Stanley began to bluster. 'I remember distinctly putting it in this corner. Now, who's had it? There's no time to lose. Look sharp! The stick's got to be found.'

Even Alice, the servant-girl, was drawn into the chase. 'You haven't been using it to poke the kitchen fire with by any chance?'

Stanley dashed into the bedroom where Linda was lying. 'Most extraordinary thing. I can't keep a single possession to myself. They've made away with my stick, now!'

'Stick, dear? What stick?' Linda's vagueness on these occasions could not be real, Stanley decided. Would nobody sympathize with him?

'Coach! Coach, Stanley!' Beryl's voice cried from the gate.

Stanley waved his arm to Linda. 'No time to say good-bye!' he cried. And he meant that as a punishment to her.

He snatched his bowler hat, dashed out of the house, and swung down the garden path. Yes, the coach was there waiting, and Beryl, leaning over the open gate, was laughing up at somebody or other just as if nothing had happened. The heartlessness of women! The way they took it for granted it was your job to slave away for them while they didn't even take the trouble to see that your walking-stick wasn't lost. Kelly trailed his whip across the horses.

'Good-bye, Stanley,' called Beryl, sweetly and gaily. It was easy enough to say good-bye! And there she stood, idle, shading her eyes with her hand. The worst of it was Stanley had to shout good-bye too, for the sake of appearances. Then he saw her turn, give a little skip and run back to the house. She was glad to be rid of him!

Yes, she was thankful. Into the living-room she ran and called 'He's gone!' Linda cried from her room: 'Beryl! Has Stanley gone?' Old Mrs Fairfield appeared, carrying the boy in his little flannel coatee.

'Gone?'

'Gone!'

Oh, the relief the difference it made to have the man out of the house. Their very voices were changed as they called to one another; they sounded warm and loving and as if they shared a secret. Beryl went over to the table. 'Have another cup of tea, mother. It's still hot.' She wanted, somehow, to celebrate the fact that they could do what they liked now. There was no man to disturb them; the whole perfect day was theirs.

'No, thank you, child,' said old Mrs Fairfield, but the way at that moment she tossed the boy up and said 'a-goos-a-goos-a-ga!' to him meant that she felt the same. The little girls ran into the paddock like chickens let out of a coop.

Even Alice, the servant-girl, washing up the dishes in the kitchen, caught the infection and used the precious tank water in a perfectly reckless fashion.

'Oh, these men!' said she, and she plunged the teapot into the bowl and held it under the water even after it had stopped bubbling, as if it too was a man and drowning was too good for them.

## IV

'Wait for me, Isa-bel! Kezia, wait for me!'

There was poor little Lottie, left behind again, because she found it so fearfully hard to get over the stile by herself. When she stood on the first step her knees began to wobble; she grasped the post. Then you had to put one leg over. But which leg? She never could decide. And when she did finally put one leg over with a sort of stamp of despair—then the feeling was awful. She was half in the paddock still and half in the tussock grass. She clutched the post desperately and lifted her voice. 'Wait for me!'

'No, don't you wait for her, Kezia!' said Isabel. 'She's such a little silly. She's always making a fuss. Come on!' And she tugged Kezia's jersey. 'You can use my bucket if you come with me,' she said kindly. 'It's bigger than yours.' But Kezia couldn't leave Lottie all by herself.

She ran back to her. By this time Lottie was very red in the face and breathing heavily.

'Here, put your other foot over,' said Kezia.

'Where?'

Lottie looked down at Kezia as if from a mountain height.

'Here where my hand is.' Kezia patted the place.

'Oh, *there* do you mean?' Lottie gave a deep sigh and put the second foot over.

'Now—sort of turn round and sit down and slide,' said Kezia.

'But there's nothing to sit down *on,* Kezia,' said Lottie.

She managed it at last, and once it was over she shook herself and began to beam.

'I'm getting better at climbing over stiles, aren't I, Kezia?'

Lottie's was a very hopeful nature.

The pink and the blue sunbonnet followed Isabel's bright red sunbonnet up that sliding, slipping hill. At the top they paused to decide where to go and to have a good stare at who was there already. Seen from behind, standing against the skyline, gesticulating largely with their spades, they looked like minute puzzled explorers.

The whole family of Samuel Josephs was there already with their lady-help, who sat on a camp-stool and kept order with a whistle that she wore tied round her neck, and a small cane with which she directed operations. The Samuel Josephs never played by themselves or managed their own game. If they did, it ended in the boys pouring water down the girls' necks or the girls trying to put little black crabs into the boys' pockets. So Mrs S. J. and the poor lady-help drew up what she called a 'brogramme' every morning to keep them 'abused and out of bischief'. It was all competitions or races or round games. Everything began with a piercing blast of the lady-help's whistle and ended with another. There were even prizes—large, rather dirty paper parcels which the lady-help with a sour little smile drew out of a bulging string kit. The Samuel Josephs fought fearfully for the prizes and cheated and pinched one another's arms—they were all expert pinchers. The only time the Burnell children ever played with them Kezia had got a prize, and when she undid three bits of paper she found a very small rusty button-hook. She couldn't understand why they made such a fuss. . .

But they never played with the Samuel Josephs now or even went to their parties. The Samuel Josephs were always giving children's parties at the Bay and there was always the same food. A big washhand basin of very brown fruit-salad, buns cut into four and a washhand jug full of something the lady-help called 'Limmonadear'.

And you went away in the evening with half the frill torn off your frock or something spilled all down the front of your open-work pinafore, leaving the Samuel Josephs leaping like savages on their lawn. No! They were too awful.

On the other side of the beach, close down to the water, two little boys, their knickers rolled up, twinkled like spiders. One was digging, the other pattered in and out of the water, filling a small bucket. They were the Trout boys, Pip and Rags. But Pip was so busy digging and Rags was so busy helping that they didn't see their little cousins until they were quite close.

'Look!' said Pip. 'Look what I've discovered.' And he showed them an old wet, squashed-looking boot. The three little girls stared.

'Whatever are you going to do with it?' asked Kezia.

'Keep it, of course!' Pip was very scornful. 'It's a find—see?'

Yes, Kezia saw that. All the same . . .

'There's lots of things buried in the sand,' explained Pip. 'They get chucked up from wrecks. Treasure. Why—you might find——'

'But why does Rags have to keep on pouring water in?' asked Lottie.

'Oh, that's to moisten it,' said Pip, 'to make the work a bit easier. Keep it up, Rags.'

And good little Rags ran up and down, pouring in the water that turned brown like cocoa.

'Here, shall I show you what I found yesterday?' said Pip mysteriously, and he stuck his spade into the sand. 'Promise not to tell.'

They promised.

'Say, cross my heart straight dinkum.'

The little girls said it.

Pip took something out of his pocket, rubbed it a long time on the front of his jersey, then breathed on it and rubbed it again.

'Now turn round!' he ordered.

They turned round.

'All look the same way! Keep still! Now!'

And his hand opened; he held up to the light something that flashed, that winked, that was a most lovely green.

'It's a nemeral,' said Pip solemnly.

'Is it really, Pip?' Even Isabel was impressed.

The lovely green thing seemed to dance in Pip's fingers. Aunt Beryl had a nemeral in a ring, but it was a very small one. This one was as big as a star and far more beautiful.

## V

As the morning lengthened whole parties appeared over the sand-hills and came down on the beach to bathe. It was understood that at eleven o'clock the women and children of the summer colony had the sea to themselves. First the women undressed, pulled on their bathing dresses and covered their heads in hideous caps like sponge bags; then the children were unburdened. The beach was strewn with little heaps of clothes and shoes; the big summer hats, with stones on them to keep them from blowing away, looked like immense shells. It was strange that even the sea seemed to sound differently when all those leaping, laughing figures ran into the waves. Old Mrs Fairfield, in a lilac cotton dress and a black hat tied under the chin, gathered her little brood and got them ready. The little Trout boys whipped their shirts over their heads, and away the five sped, while their grandma sat with one hand in her knitting-bag ready to draw out the ball of wool when she was satisfied they were safely in.

The firm compact little girls were not half so brave as the tender, delicate-looking little boys. Pip and Rags, shivering, crouching down, slapping the water, never hesitated. But Isabel, who could swim twelve strokes, and Kezia, who could nearly swim eight, only followed on the strict understanding they were not to be splashed. As for Lottie, she didn't follow at all. She liked to be left to go in her own way, please. And that way was to sit down at the edge of the water, her legs straight, her knees pressed together, and to make vague motions with her arms as if she expected to be wafted out to sea. But when a bigger wave than usual, an old whiskery one, came lolloping along in her direction, she scrambled to her feet with a face of horror and flew up the beach again.

'Here, mother, keep those for me, will you?'

Two rings and a thin gold chain were dropped into Mrs Fairfield's lap.

'Yes, dear. But aren't you going to bathe here?'

'No-o,' Beryl drawled. She sounded vague. 'I'm undressing farther along. I'm going to bathe with Mrs Harry Kember.'

'Very well.' But Mrs Fairfield's lips set. She disapproved of Mrs Harry Kember. Beryl knew it.

Poor old mother, she smiled, as she skimmed over the stones. Poor old mother! Old! Oh, what joy, what bliss it was to be young. . . .

'You look very pleased,' said Mrs Harry Kember. She sat hunched up on the stones, her arms round her knees, smoking.

'It's such a lovely day,' said Beryl, smiling down at her.

'Oh, my *dear!*' Mrs Harry Kember's voice sounded as though she knew better than that. But then her voice always sounded as though she knew something more about you than you did yourself. She was a long, strange-looking woman with narrow hands and feet. Her face, too, was long and narrow and exhausted-looking; even her fair curled fringe looked burnt out and withered. She was the only woman at the Bay who smoked, and she smoked incessantly, keeping the cigarette between her lips while she talked, and only taking it out when the ash was so long you could not understand why it did not fall. When she was not playing bridge—she played bridge every day of her life—she spent her time lying in the full glare of the sun. She could stand any amount of it; she never had enough. All the same, it did not seem to warm her. Parched, withered, cold, she lay stretched on the stones like a piece of tossed-up driftwood. The women at the Bay thought she was very, very fast. Her lack of vanity, her slang, the way she treated men as though she was one of them, and the fact that she didn't care twopence about her house and called the servant Gladys 'Glad-eyes', was disgraceful. Standing on the veranda steps Mrs Kember would call in her indifferent, tired voice, 'I say, Glad-eyes, you might heave me a handkerchief if I've got one, will you?' And Glad-eyes, a red bow in her hair instead of a cap, and white shoes, came running with an impudent smile. It was an absolute scandal! True, she had no children, and her husband. . . Here the voices were always raised; they became fervent. How can he have married her? How can he, how can he? It must have been money, of course, but even then!

Mrs Kember's husband was at least ten years younger than she was, and so incredibly handsome that he looked like a mask or a most perfect illustration in an American novel rather than a man. Black hair, dark blue eyes, red lips, a slow sleepy smile, a fine tennis player, a perfect dancer, and with it all a mystery. Harry Kember was like a man walking in his sleep. Men couldn't stand him, they couldn't get a word out of the chap; he ignored his wife just as she ignored him. How did he live? Of course there were stories, but such stories! They simply couldn't be told. The women he'd been seen with, the places he'd been seen in . . . but nothing was ever certain, nothing definite. Some of the women at the Bay privately thought he'd commit a murder one day. Yes, even while they talked to Mrs Kember and took in the awful concoction she was wearing, they saw her, stretched as she lay on the beach; but cold, bloody, and still with a cigarette stuck in the corner of her mouth.

Mrs Kember rose, yawned, unsnapped her belt buckle, and tugged at the tape of her blouse. And Beryl stepped out of her skirt and shed her jersey, and stood up in her short white petticoat, and her camisole with ribbon bows on the shoulders.

'Mercy on us,' said Mrs Harry Kember, 'what a little beauty you are!'

'Don't!' said Beryl softly; but, drawing off one stocking and then the other, she felt a little beauty.

'My dear–why not?' said Mrs Harry Kember, stamping on her own petticoat. Really–her underclothes! A pair of blue cotton knickers and a linen bodice that reminded one somehow of a pillowcase. . . . 'And you don't wear stays, do you?' She touched Beryl's waist, and Beryl sprang away with a small affected cry. Then 'Never!' she said firmly.

'Lucky little creature,' sighed Mrs Kember, unfastening her own.

Beryl turned her back and began the complicated movements of some one who is trying to take off her clothes and to pull on her bathing-dress all at one and the same time.

'Oh, my dear–don't mind me,' said Mrs Harry Kember. 'Why be shy? I shan't eat you. I shan't be shocked like those other ninnies.' And she gave her strange neighing laugh and grimaced at the other women.

But Beryl was shy. She never undressed in front of anybody. Was that silly? Mrs Harry Kember made her feel it was silly, even something to be ashamed of. Why be shy indeed! She glanced quickly at her friend standing so boldly in her torn chemise and lighting a fresh cigarette; and a quick, bold, evil feeling started up in her breast. Laughing recklessly, she drew on the limp, sandy-feeling bathing-dress that was not quite dry and fastened the twisted buttons.

'That's better,' said Mrs Harry Kember. They began to go down the beach together. 'Really, it's a sin for you to wear clothes, my dear. Somebody's got to tell you some day.'

The water was quite warm. It was that marvellous transparent blue, flecked with silver, but the sand at the bottom looked gold; when you kicked with your toes there rose a little puff of gold-dust. Now the waves just reached her breast. Beryl stood, her arms outstretched, gazing out, and as each wave came she gave the slightest little jump, so that it seemed it was the wave which lifted her so gently.

'I believe in pretty girls having a good time,' said Mrs Harry Kember. 'Why not? Don't you make a mistake, my dear. Enjoy yourself.' And suddenly she turned turtle, disappeared, and swam away quickly, quickly, like a rat. Then she flicked round and began swimming back. She was going to say something else. Beryl felt that she was being poisoned by this cold woman, but she longed to hear. But oh, how strange, how horrible! As Mrs Harry Kember came up close she looked, in her black waterproof bathing-cap, with her sleepy face lifted above the water, just her chin touching, like a horrible caricature of her husband.

## VI

In a steamer chair, under a manuka tree that grew in the middle of the front grass patch, Linda Burnell dreamed the morning away. She did nothing. She looked up at the dark, close, dry leaves of the manuka, at the chinks of blue between, and now and again a tiny yellowish flower dropped on her. Pretty—yes, if you held one of those flowers on the palm of your hand and looked at it closely, it was an exquisite small thing. Each pale yellow petal shone as if each was the careful work of a loving hand. The tiny tongue in the centre gave it the shape of a bell. And when you turned it over the outside was a deep bronze colour. But as soon as they flowered, they fell and were scattered. You brushed them off your frock as you talked; the horrid little things got caught in one's hair. Why, then, flower at all? Who takes the trouble—or the joy—to make all these things that are wasted, wasted. . . It was uncanny.

On the grass beside her, lying between two pillows, was the boy. Sound asleep he lay, his head turned away from his mother. His fine dark hair looked more like a shadow than like real hair, but his ear was a bright, deep coral. Linda clasped her hands above her head and crossed her feet. It was very pleasant to know that all these bungalows were empty, that everybody was down on the beach, out of sight, out of hearing. She had the garden to herself; she was alone.

Dazzling white the picotees shone; the golden-eyed marigold glittered; the nasturtiums wreathed the veranda poles in green and gold flame. If only one had time to look at these flowers long enough, time to get over the sense of novelty and strangeness, time to know them! But as soon as one paused to part the petals, to discover the under-side of the leaf, along came Life and one was swept away. And, lying in her cane chair, Linda felt so light; she felt like a leaf. Along came Life like a wind and she was seized and shaken; she had to go. Oh dear, would it always be so? Was there no escape?

. . . Now she sat on the veranda of their Tasmanian home, leaning against her father's knee. And he promised, 'As soon as you and I are old enough, Linny, we'll cut off somewhere, we'll escape. Two boys together. I have a fancy I'd like to sail up a river in China.' Linda saw that river, very wide, covered with little rafts and boats. She saw the yellow hats of the boatmen and she heard their high, thin voices as they called . . .

'Yes, papa.'

But just then a very broad young man with bright ginger hair walked slowly past their house, and slowly, solemnly even, uncovered. Linda's father pulled her ear teasingly, in the way he had.

'Linny's beau,' he whispered.

'Oh, papa, fancy being married to Stanley Burnell!'

Well, she was married to him. And what was more she loved him. Not the Stanley whom every one saw, not the everyday one; but a timid, sensitive, innocent Stanley who knelt down every night to say his prayers, and who longed to be good. Stanley was simple. If he believed in people—as he believed in her, for instance—it was with his whole heart. He could not be disloyal; he could not tell a lie. And how terribly he suffered if he thought anyone—she—was not being dead straight, dead sincere with him! 'This is too subtle for me!' He flung out the words, but his open, quivering, distraught look was like the look of a trapped beast.

But the trouble was—here Linda felt almost inclined to laugh, though Heaven knows it was no laughing matter—she saw *her* Stanley so seldom. There were glimpses, moments, breathing spaces of calm, but all the rest of the time it was like living in a house that couldn't be cured of the habit of catching on fire, on a ship that got wrecked every day. And it was always Stanley who was in the thick of the danger. Her whole time was spent in rescuing him, and restoring him, and calming him down, and listening to his story. And what was left of her time was spent in the dread of having children.

Linda frowned; she sat up quickly in her steamer chair and clasped her ankles. Yes, that was her real grudge against life; that was what she could not understand. That was the question she asked and asked, and listened in vain for the answer. It was all very well to say it was the common lot of women to bear children. It wasn't true. She, for one, could prove that wrong. She was broken, made weak, her courage was gone, through child-bearing. And what made it doubly hard to bear was, she did not love her children. It was useless pretending. Even if she had had the strength she never would have nursed and played with the little girls. No, it was as though a cold breath had chilled her through and through on each of those awful journeys; she had no warmth left to give them. As to the boy—well, thank Heaven, mother had taken him; he was mother's, or Beryl's or anybody's who wanted him. She had hardly held him in her arms. She was so indifferent about him that as he lay there . . . Linda glanced down.

The boy had turned over. He lay facing her, and he was no longer asleep. His dark-blue, baby eyes were open; he looked as though he was peeping at his mother. And suddenly his face dimpled; it broke into a wide, toothless smile, a perfect beam, no less.

'I'm here!' that happy smile seemed to say. 'Why don't you like me?'

There was something so quaint, so unexpected about that smile that Linda smiled herself. But she checked herself and said to the boy coldly, 'I don't like babies.'

'Don't like babies?' The boy couldn't believe her. 'Don't like *me*?' He waved his arms foolishly at his mother.

Linda dropped off her chair on to the grass.

'Why do you keep on smiling?' she said severely. 'If you knew what I was thinking about, you wouldn't.'

But he only squeezed up his eyes, slyly, and rolled his head on the pillow. He didn't believe a word she said.

'We know all about that!' smiled the boy.

Linda was so astonished at the confidence of this little creature. . . Ah no, be sincere. That was not what she felt; it was something far different, it was something so new, so. . . . The tears danced in her eyes; she breathed in a small whisper to the boy, 'Hallo, my funny!'

But by now the boy had forgotten his mother. He was serious again. Something pink, something soft waved in front of him. He made a grab at it and it immediately disappeared. But when he lay back, another, like the first, appeared. This time he determined to catch it. He made a tremendous effort and rolled right over.

## VII

The tide was out; the beach was deserted; lazily flopped the warm sea. The sun beat down, beat down hot and fiery on the fine sand, baking the grey and blue and black and white-veined pebbles. It sucked up the little drop of water that lay in the hollow of the curved shells; it bleached the pink convolvulus that threaded through and through the sand-hills. Nothing seemed to move but the small sand-hoppers. Pit-pit-pit! They were never still.

Over there on the weed-hung rocks that looked at low tide like shaggy beasts come down to the water to drink, the sunlight seemed to spin like a silver coin dropped into each of the small rock pools. They danced, they quivered, and minute ripples laved the porous shores. Looking down, bending over, each pool was like a lake with pink and blue houses clustered on the shores; and oh! the vast mountainous country behind those houses—the ravines, the passes, the dangerous creeks and fearful tracks that led to the water's edge. Underneath waves the sea-forest–pink thread-like trees, velvet anemones, and orange berry-spotted weeds. Now a stone on the bottom moved, rocked, and there was a glimpse of a black feeler; now a thread-like creature wavered by and was lost. Something was happening to the pink, waving trees; they were changing to a cold moon-light blue. And now there sounded the faintest 'plop'. Who made that sound? What was going on down there? And how strong, how damp the seaweed smelt in the hot sun. . . .

The green blinds were drawn in the bungalows of the summer colony. Over the verandas, prone on the paddock, flung over the fences, there were exhausted-looking bathing-dresses and rough striped towels. Each back window seemed to have a pair of sand-shoes on the sill and some lumps of rock or a bucket or a collection of pawa shells. The bush quivered in a haze of heat; the sandy road was empty except for the Trouts' dog Snooker, who lay stretched in the very middle of it. His blue eye was turned up, his legs stuck out stiffly, and he gave an occasional desperate-sounding puff, as much as to say he had decided to make an end of it and was only waiting for some kind cart to come along.

'What are you looking at, my grandma? Why do you keep stopping and sort of staring at the wall?'

Kezia and her grandmother were taking their siesta together. The little girl, wearing only her short drawers and her under-bodice, her arms and legs bare, lay on one of the puffed-up pillows of her grandma's bed, and the old woman, in a white ruffled dressing-gown, sat in a rocker at the window, with a long piece of pink knitting in her lap. This room that they shared, like the other rooms of the bungalow, was of light varnished wood and the floor was bare. The furniture was of the shabbiest, the simplest. The dressing-table, for instance, was a packing-case in a sprigged muslin petticoat, and the mirror above was very strange; it was as though a little piece of forked lightning was imprisoned in it. On the table there stood a jar of seapinks, pressed so tightly together they looked more like a velvet pincushion, and a special shell which Kezia had given her grandma for a pin-tray, and another even more special which she had thought would make a very nice place for a watch to curl up in.

'Tell me, grandma,' said Kezia.

The old woman sighed, whipped the wool twice round her thumb, and drew the bone needle through. She was casting on.

'I was thinking of your Uncle William, darling.' she said quietly.

'My Australian Uncle William?' said Kezia. She had another.

'Yes, of course.'

'The one I never saw?'

'That was the one.'

'Well, what happened to him?' Kezia knew perfectly well, but she wanted to be told again.

'He went to the mines, and he got a sunstroke there and died,' said old Mrs Fairfield.

Kezia blinked and considered the picture again. . . A little man fallen over like a tin soldier by the side of a big black hole.

'Does it make you sad to think about him, grandma?' She hated her grandma to be sad.

It was the old woman's turn to consider. Did it make her sad? To look back, back. To stare down the years, as Kezia had seen her doing. To look after *them* as a woman does, long after *they* were out of sight. Did it make her sad? No, life was like that.

'No, Kezia.'

'But why?' asked Kezia. She lifted one bare arm and began to draw things in the air. 'Why did Uncle William have to die? He wasn't old.'

Mrs Fairfield began counting the stitches in threes. 'It just happened,' she said in an absorbed voice.

'Does everybody have to die?' asked Kezia.

'Everybody!'

'*Me*?' Kezia sounded fearfully incredulous.

'Some day, my darling.'

'But, grandma.' Kezia waved her left leg and waggled the toes. They felt sandy. 'What if I just won't?'

The old woman sighed again and drew a long thread from the ball.

'We're not asked, Kezia,' she said sadly. 'It happens to all of us sooner or later.'

Kezia lay still thinking this over. She didn't want to die. It meant she would have to leave here, leave everywhere, for ever, leave—leave her grandma. She rolled over quickly.

'Grandma,' she said in a startled voice.

'What, my pet!'

'*You're* not to die.' Kezia was very decided.

'Ah, Kezia'—her grandma looked up and smiled and shook her head—'don't let's talk about it.'

'But you're not to. You couldn't leave me. You couldn't not be there.' This was awful. 'Promise me you won't ever do it, grandma,' pleaded Kezia.

The old woman went on knitting.

'Promise me! Say never!'

But still her grandma was silent.

Kezia rolled off the bed; she couldn't bear it any longer, and lightly she leapt on to her grandma's knees, clasped her hand round the old woman's throat and began kissing her, under the chin, behind the ear, and blowing down her neck.

'Say never . . . say never . . . say never——' She gasped between the kisses. And then she began, very softly and lightly, to tickle her grandma.

'Kezia!' The old woman dropped her knitting. She swung back in the rocker. She began to tickle Kezia. 'Say never, say never, say never,' gurgled Kezia, while they lay there laughing in each other's arms. 'Come, that's enough, my squirrel! That's enough, my wild pony!' said old Mrs Fairfield, setting her cap straight. 'Pick up my knitting.'

Both of them had forgotten what the 'never' was about.

## VIII

The sun was still full on the garden when the back door of the Burnells' shut with a bang, and a very gay figure walked down the path to the gate. It was Alice, the servant-girl, dressed for her afternoon out. She wore a white cotton dress with such large red spots on it, and so many that they made you shudder, white shoes and a leghorn turned up under the brim with poppies. Of course she wore gloves, white ones, stained at the fastenings with iron-mould, and in one hand she carried a very dashed-looking sunshade which she referred to as her *perishall.*

Beryl, sitting in the window, fanning her freshly washed hair, thought she had never seen such a guy. If Alice had only blacked her face with a piece of cork before she started out, the picture would have been complete. And where did a girl like that go to in a place like this? The heart-shaped Fijian fan beat scornfully at that lovely bright mane. She supposed Alice had picked up some horrible common larrikin and they'd go off into the bush together. Pity to make herself so conspicuous; they'd have hard work to hide with Alice in that rig-out.

But no, Beryl was unfair. Alice was going to tea with Mrs Stubbs, who'd sent her an 'invite' by the little boy who called for orders. She had taken ever such a liking to Mrs Stubbs ever since the first time she went to the shop to get something for her mosquitoes.

'Dear heart!' Mrs Stubbs had clapped her hand to her side. 'I never seen anyone so eaten. You might have been attacked by canningbals.'

Alice did wish there'd been a bit of life on the road though. Made her feel so queer, having nobody behind her. Made her feel all weak in the spine. She couldn't believe that some one wasn't watching her. And yet it was silly to turn round; it gave you away. She pulled up her gloves, hummed to herself and said to the distant gum tree, 'Shan't be long now.' But that was hardly company.

Mrs Stubbs's shop was perched on a little hillock just off the road. It had two big windows for eyes, a broad veranda for a hat, and the sign on the roof, scrawled MRS STUBBS'S, was like a little card stuck rakishly in the hat crown.

On the veranda there hung a long string of bathing-dresses, clinging together as though they'd just been rescued from the sea rather than waiting to go in, and beside them there hung a cluster of sand-shoes so extraordinarily mixed that to get at one pair you had to tear apart and forcibly separate at least fifty. Even then it was the rarest thing to find the left that belonged to the right. So many people had lost patience and gone off with one shoe that fitted and one that was a little too big. . . . Mrs Stubbs prided herself on keeping something of everything. The two windows, arranged in the form of precarious pyramids, were crammed so tight, piled so high, that it seemed only a conjuror could prevent them from toppling over. In the left-hand corner of one window, glued to the pane by four gelatine lozenges, there was—and there had been from time immemorial—a notice.

> LOST! HANSOME GOLE BROOCH
> SOLID GOLD
> ON OR NEAR BEACH
> REWARD OFFERED

Alice pressed open the door. The bell jangled, the red serge curtains parted, and Mrs Stubbs appeared. With her broad smile and the long bacon knife in her hand, she looked like a friendly brigand. Alice was welcomed so warmly that she found it quite difficult to keep up her 'manners'. They consisted of persistent little coughs and hems, pulls at her gloves, tweaks at her skirt, and a curious difficulty in seeing what was set before her or understanding what was said.

Tea was laid on the parlour table—ham, sardines, a whole pound of butter, and such a large johnny cake that it looked like an advertisement for somebody's baking-powder. But the Primus stove roared so loudly that it was useless to try to talk above it. Alice sat down on the edge of a basket-chair while Mrs Stubbs pumped the stove still higher. Suddenly Mrs Stubbs whipped the cushion off a chair and disclosed a large brown paper parcel.

'I've just had some new photers taken, my dear,' she shouted cheerfully to Alice. 'Tell me what you think of them.'

In a very dainty, refined way Alice wet her finger and put the tissue back from the first one. Life! How many there were! There were three dozzing at least. And she held hers up to the light.

Mrs Stubbs sat in an arm-chair, leaning very much to one side. There was a look of mild astonishment on her large face, and well there might be. For though the arm-chair stood on a carpet, to the left of it, miraculously skirting the carpet border, there was a dashing waterfall. On her right stood a Grecian pillar with a giant fern tree on either side of it, and in the background towered a gaunt mountain, pale with snow.

'It is a nice style, isn't it?' shouted Mrs Stubbs, and Alice had just screamed 'Sweetly' when the roaring of the Primus stove died down, fizzled out, ceased, and she said 'Pretty' in a silence that was frightening.

'Draw up your chair, my dear,' said Mrs Stubbs, beginning to pour out. 'Yes,' she said thoughtfully, as she handed the tea, 'but I don't care about the size. I'm having an enlargemint. All very well for Christmas cards, but I never was the one for small photers myself. You get no comfort out of them. To say the truth, I find them dis'eartening.'

Alice quite saw what she meant.

'Size,' said Mrs Stubbs. 'Give me size. That was what my poor dear husband was always saying. He couldn't stand anything small. Gave him the creeps. And, strange as it may seem, my dear'—here Mrs Stubbs creaked and seemed to expand herself at the memory—'it was dropsy that carried him off at the larst. Many's the time they drawn one and a half pints from 'im at the 'ospital. . . .It seemed like a judgmint.'

Alice burned to know exactly what it was that was drawn from him. She ventured, 'I suppose it was water.'

But Mrs Stubbs fixed Alice with her eyes and replied meaningly, 'It was *liquid*, my dear.'

Liquid! Alice jumped away from the word like a cat and came back to it, nosing and wary.

'That's 'im!' said Mrs Stubbs, and she pointed dramatically to the life-size head and shoulders of a burly man with a dead white rose in the button-hole of his coat that made you think of a curl of cold mutting fat. Just below, in silver letters on a red cardboard ground, were the words, 'Be not afraid, it is I.'

'It's ever such a fine face,' said Alice faintly.

The pale-blue bow on the top of Mrs Stubbs's fair frizzy hair quivered. She arched her plump neck. What a neck she had! It was bright pink where it began and then it changed to warm apricot, and that faded to the colour of a brown egg and then to a deep creamy.

'All the same, my dear,' she said surprisingly, 'freedom's best!' Her soft, fat chuckle sounded like a purr. 'Freedom's best,' said Mrs Stubbs again.

Freedom! Alice gave a loud, silly little titter. She felt awkward. Her mind flew back to her own kitching. Ever so queer! She wanted to be back in it again.

## IX

A strange company assembled in the Burnells' washhouse after tea. Round the table there sat a bull, a rooster, a donkey that kept forgetting it was a donkey, a sheep and a bee. The washhouse was the perfect place for such a meeting because they could make as much noise as they liked, and nobody ever interrupted. It was a small tin shed standing apart from the bungalow. Against the wall there was a deep trough and in the corner a copper with a basket of clothes-pegs on top of it. The little window, spun over with cobwebs, had a piece of candle and a mouse-trap on the dusty sill. There were clothes-lines criss-crossed overhead and, hanging from a peg on the wall, a very big, a huge, rusty horseshoe. The table was in the middle with a form at either side.

'You can't be a bee, Kezia, A bee's not an animal. It's a ninseck.'

'Oh, but I do want to be a bee frightfully,' wailed Kezia. . . . A tiny bee, all yellow-furry, with striped legs. She drew her legs up under her and leaned over the table. She felt she was a bee.

'A ninseck must be an animal,' she said stoutly. 'It makes a noise. It's not like a fish.'

'I'm a bull, I'm a bull!' cried Pip. And he gave such a tremendous bellow—how did he make that noise?—that Lottie looked quite alarmed.

'I'll be a sheep,' said little Rags. 'A whole lot of sheep went past this morning.'

'How do you know?'

'Dad heard them. Baa!' He sounded like the little lamb that trots behind and seems to wait to be carried.

'Cock-a-doodle-do!' shrilled Isabel. With her red cheeks and bright eyes she looked like a rooster.

'What'll I be?' Lottie asked everybody, and she sat there smiling, waiting for them to decide for her. It had to be an easy one.

'Be a donkey, Lottie.' It was Kezia's suggestion. 'Hee-haw! You can't forget that.'

'Hee-haw!' said Lottie solemnly. 'When do I have to say it?'

'I'll explain, I'll explain,' said the bull. It was he who had the cards. He waved them round his head. 'All be quiet! All listen!' And he waited for them. 'Look here, Lottie.' He turned up a card. 'It's got two spots on it—see? Now, if you put that card in the middle and somebody else has one with two spots as well, you say "Hee-haw", and the card's yours.'

'Mine?' Lottie was round-eyed. 'To keep?'

'No, silly. Just for the game, see? Just while we're playing.' The bull was very cross with her.

'Oh, Lottie, you *are* a little silly,' said the proud rooster.

Lottie looked at both of them. Then she hung her head; her lip quivered. 'I don't not want to play,' she whispered. The others glanced at one another like conspirators. All of them knew what that meant. She would go away and be discovered somewhere standing with a pinny thrown over her head, in a corner, or against a wall, or even behind a chair.

'Yes, you *do,* Lottie. It's quite easy,' said Kezia.

And Isabel, repentant, said exactly like a grown-up, 'Watch *me,* Lottie, and you'll soon learn.'

'Cheer up, Lot,' said Pip. 'There, I know what I'll do. I'll give you the first one. It's mine, really, but I'll give it to you. Here you are.' And he slammed the card down in front of Lottie.

Lottie revived at that. But now she was in another difficulty. 'I haven't got a hanky,' she said; 'I want one badly, too.'

'Here, Lottie, you can use mine.' Rags dipped into his sailor blouse and brought up a very wet-looking one, knotted together. 'Be very careful,' he warned her. 'Only use that corner. Don't undo it. I've got a little star-fish inside I'm going to try and tame.'

'Oh, come on, you girls,' said the bull. 'And mind—you're not to look at your cards. You've got to keep your hands under the table till I say "Go." '

Smack went the cards round the table. They tried with all their might to see, but Pip was too quick for them. It was very exciting, sitting there in the washhouse; it was all they could do not to burst into a little chorus of animals before Pip had finished dealing.

'Now, Lottie, you begin.'

Timidly Lottie stretched out a hand, took the top card off her pack, had a good look at it—it was plain she was counting the spots—and put it down.

'No, Lottie, you can't do that. You mustn't look first. You must turn it the other way over.'

'But then everybody will see it the same time as me,' said Lottie.

The game proceeded. Mooe-ooo-er! The bull was terrible. He charged over the table and seemed to eat the cards up.

Bss-ss! said the bee.

Cock-a-doodle-do! Isabel stood up in her excitement and moved her elbows like wings.

Baa! Little Rags put down the King of Diamonds and Lottie put down the one they called the King of Spain. She hard hardly any cards left.

'Why don't you call out, Lottie?'

'I've forgotten what I am,' said the donkey woefully.

'Well, change! Be a dog instead! Bow-wow!'

'Oh yes. That's *much* easier.' Lottie smiled again. But when she and Kezia both had a one Kezia waited on purpose. The others made signs to Lottie and pointed. Lottie turned very red; she looked bewildered, and at last she said, 'Hee-haw! Ke-zia.'

'Ss! Wait a minute!' They were in the very thick of it when the bull stopped them, holding up his hand. 'What's that? What's that noise?'

'What noise? What do you mean?' asked the rooster.

'Ss! Shut up! Listen!' They were mouse-still. 'I thought I heard a—a sort of knocking,' said the bull.

'What was it like?' asked the sheep faintly.

No answer.

The bee gave a shudder. 'Whatever did we shut the door for?' she said softly. Oh, why, why had they shut the door?

While they were playing, the day had faded; the gorgeous sunset had blazed and died. And now the quick dark came racing over the sea, over the sandhills, up the paddock. You were frightened to look in the corners of the washhouse, and yet you had to look with all your might. And somewhere, far away grandma was lighting a lamp. The blinds were being pulled down; the kitchen fire leapt in the tins on the mantelpiece.

'It would be awful now,' said the bull, 'if a spider was to fall from the ceiling on to the table, wouldn't it?'

'Spiders don't fall from ceilings.'

'Yes, they do. Our Min told us she'bhseen a spider as big as a saucer, with long hairs on it like a gooseberry.'

Quickly all the little heads were jerked up; all the little bodies drew together, pressed together.

'Why doesn't somebody come and call us?' cried the rooster.

Oh, those grown-ups, laughing and snug, sitting in the lamp-light, drinking out of cups! They'd forgotten about them. No, not really forgotten. That was what their smile meant. They had decided to leave them there all by themselves.

Suddenly Lottie gave such a piercing scream that all of them jumped off the forms, all of them screamed too. 'A face—a face looking!' shrieked Lottie.

It was true, it was real. Pressed against the window was a pale face, black eyes, a black beard.

'Grandma! Mother! Somebody!'

But they had not got to the door, tumbling over one another, before it opened for Uncle Jonathan. He had come to take the little boys home.

X

He had meant to be there before, but in the front garden he had come upon Linda walking up and down the grass, stopping to pick off a dead pink or give a top-heavy carnation something to lean against, or to take a deep breath of something, and then walking on again, with her little air of remoteness. Over her white frock she wore a yellow, pink-fringed shawl from the Chinaman's shop.

'Hallo, Jonathan!' called Linda. And Jonathan whipped off his shabby panama, pressed it against his breast, dropped on one knee, and kissed Linda's hand.

'Greeting, my Fair One! Greeting, my Celestial Peach Blossom!' boomed the bass voice gently. 'Where are the other noble dames?'

'Beryl's out playing bridge and mother's giving the boy his bath. . . Have you come to borrow something?'

The Trouts were for ever running out of things and sending across to the Burnells' at the last moment.

But Jonathan only answered, 'A little love, a little kindness;' and he walked by his sister-in-law's side.

Linda dropped into Beryl's hammock under the manuka-tree, and Jonathan stretched himself on the grass beside her, pulled a long stalk and began chewing it. They knew each other well. The voices of children cried from the other gardens. A fisherman's light cart shook along the sandy road, and from far away they heard a dog barking; it was muffled as though the dog had its head in a sack. If you listened you could just hear the soft swish of the sea at full tide sweeping the pebbles. The sun was sinking.

'And so you go back to the office on Monday, do you, Jonathan?' asked Linda.

'On Monday the cage door opens and clangs to upon the victim for another eleven months and a week,' answered Jonathan.

Linda swung a little. 'It must be awful,' she said slowly.

'Would ye have me laugh, my fair sister? Would ye have me weep?'

Linda was so accustomed to Jonathan's way of talking that she paid no attention to it.

'I suppose,' she said vaguely, 'one gets used to it. One gets used to anything.'

'Does one? Hum!' The 'Hum' was so deep it seemed to boom from underneath the ground. 'I wonder how it's done,' brooded Jonathan; 'I've never managed it.'

Looking at him as he lay there, Linda thought again how attractive he was. It was strange to think that he was only an ordinary clerk, that Stanley earned twice as much money as he. What was the matter with Jonathan? He had no ambition; she supposed that was it. And yet one felt he was gifted, exceptional. He was passionately fond of music; every spare penny he had went on books. He was always full of new ideas, schemes, plans. But nothing came of it all. The new fire blazed in Jonathan; you almost heard it roaring softly as he explained, described and dilated on the new thing; but a moment later it had fallen in and there was nothing but ashes, and Jonathan went about with a look like hunger in his black eyes. At these times he exaggerated his absurd manner of speaking, and he sang in church—he was the leader of the choir—with such fearful dramatic intensity that the meanest hymn put on an unholy splendour.

'It seems to me just as imbecile, just as infernal, to have to go to the office on Monday,' said Jonathan, 'as it always has done and always will do. To spend all the best years of one's life sitting on a stool from nine to five, scratching in somebody's ledger! It's a queer use to make of one's . . . one and only life, isn't it? Or do I fondly dream?' He rolled over on the grass and looked up at Linda. 'Tell me, what is the difference between my life and that of an ordinary prisoner? The only difference I can see is that I put myself in jail and nobody's ever going to let me out. That's a more intolerable situation than the other. For if I'd been—pushed in, against my will—kicking, even—once the door was locked, or at any rate in five years or so, I might have accepted the fact and begun to take an interest in the flight of flies or counting the warder's steps along the passage with particular attention to variations of tread and so on. But as it is, I'm like an insect that's flown into a room of its own accord. I dash against the walls, dash against the windows, flop against the ceiling, do everything on God's earth, in fact, except fly out again. And all the while I'm thinking, like that moth, or that butterfly, or whatever it is, "The shortness of life! The shortness of life!" I've only one night or one day, and there's this vast dangerous garden, waiting out there, undiscovered, unexplored.'

'But, if you feel like that, why——' began Linda quickly.

'*Ah*!' cried Jonathan. And that '*Ah*!' was somehow almost exultant. 'There you have me. Why? Why indeed? There's the maddening, mysterious question. Why don't I fly out again? There's the window or the door or whatever it was I came in by. It's not hopelessly shut—is it? Why don't I find it and be off? Answer me, that, little sister.' But he gave her no time to answer.

'I'm exactly like that insect again. For some reason'—Jonathan paused between the words—'it's not allowed, it's forbidden, it's against the insect law, to stop banging and flopping and crawling up the pane even for an instant. Why don't I leave the office? Why don't I seriously consider, this moment, for instance, what it is that prevents me leaving? It's not as though I'm tremendously tied. I've two boys to provide for, but, after all, they're boys. I could cut off to sea, or get a job up-country, or——' Suddenly he smiled at Linda and said in a changed voice, as if he were confiding a secret, 'Weak . . . weak. No stamina. No anchor. No guiding principle, let us call it.' But then the dark velvety voice rolled out:

> *Would ye hear the story*
> *How it unfolds itself . . .*

and they were silent.

The sun had set. In the western sky there were great masses of crushed-up rose-coloured clouds. Broad beams of light shone through the clouds and beyond them as if they would cover the whole sky. Overhead the blue faded; it turned a pale gold, and the bush outlined against it gleamed dark and brilliant like metal. Sometimes when those beams of light show in the sky they are very awful. They remind you that up there sits Jehovah, the jealous God, the Almighty, Whose eye is upon you, ever watchful, never weary. You remember that at His coming the whole earth will shake into one ruined graveyard; the cold, bright angels will drive you this way and that, and there will be no time to explain what could be explained so simply. . . . But to-night it seemed to Linda there was something infinitely joyful and loving in those silver beams. And now no sound came from the sea. It breathed softly as if it would draw that tender, joyful beauty into its own bosom.

'It's all wrong, it's all wrong,' came the shadowy voice of Jonathan. 'It's not the scene, it's not the setting for . . . three stools, three desks, three ink-pots and a wire blind.'

Linda knew that he would never change, but she said, 'Is it too late, even now?'

'I'm old—I'm old,' intoned Jonathan. He bent towards her, he passed his hand over his head. 'Look!' His black hair was speckled all over with silver, like the breast plumage of a black fowl.

Linda was surprised. She had no idea that he was grey. And yet, as he stood up beside her and sighed and stretched, she saw him, for the first time, not resolute, not gallant, not careless, but touched already with age. He looked very tall on the darkening grass, and the thought crossed her mind, 'He is like a weed.'

Jonathan stooped again and kissed her fingers.

'Heaven reward thy sweet patience, lady mine,' he murmured. 'I must go seek those heirs to my fame and fortune. . .' He was gone.

## XI

Light shone in the windows of the bungalow. Two square patches of gold fell upon the pinks and the peaked marigolds. Florrie, the cat, came out on to the veranda, and sat on the top step, her white paws close together, her tail curled round. She looked content, as though she had been waiting for this moment all day.

'Thank goodness, it's getting late,' said Florrie. 'Thank goodness, the long day is over.' Her greengage eyes opened.

Presently there sounded the rumble of the coach, the crack of Kelly's whip. It came near enough for one to hear the voices of the men from town, talking loudly together. It stopped at the Burnells' gate.

Stanley was half-way up the path before he saw Linda. 'Is that you, darling?'

'Yes, Stanley.'

He leapt across the flower-bed and seized her in his arms. She was enfolded in that familiar, eager, strong embrace.

'Forgive me, darling, forgive me,' stammered Stanley, and he put his hand under her chin and lifted her face to him.

'Forgive you?' smiled Linda. 'But whatever for?'

'Good God! You can't have forgotten,' cried Stanley Burnell. 'I've thought of nothing else all day. I've had the hell of a day. I made up my mind to dash out and telegraph, and then I thought the wire mightn't reach you before I did. I've been in tortures, Linda.'

'But, Stanley,' said Linda, 'what must I forgive you for?'

'Linda!'—Stanley was very hurt—'didn't you realize—you must have realized—I went away without saying good-bye to you this morning? I can't imagine how I can have done such a thing. My

confounded temper, of course. But—well'—and he sighed and took
her in his arms again—'I've suffered for it enough to-day.'

'What's that you've got in your hand?' asked Linda. 'New gloves?
Let me see.'

'Oh, just a cheap pair of wash-leather ones,' said Stanley humbly.
'I noticed Bell was wearing some in the coach this morning, so, as I
was passing the shop, I dashed in and got myself a pair. What are
you smiling at? You don't think it was wrong of me, do you?'

'On the *con*-trary, darling,' said Linda, 'I think it was most
sensible.'

She pulled one of the large, pale gloves on her own fingers and
looked at her hand, turning it this way and that. She was still smiling.

Stanley wanted to say, 'I was thinking of you the whole time I
bought them.' It was true, but for some reason he couldn't say it.
'Let's go in,' said he.

## XII

Why does one feel so different at night? Why is it so exciting to be
awake when everybody else is asleep? Late—it is very late! And yet
every moment you feel more and more wakeful, as though you were
slowly almost with every breath, waking up into a new, wonderful,
far more thrilling and exciting world than the daylight one. And
what is this queer sensation that you're a conspirator? Lightly,
stealthily you move about your room. You take something off the
dressing-table and put it down again without a sound. And everything, even the bed-post, knows you, responds, shares your secret. . .

You're not very fond of your room by day. You never think about
it. You're in and out, the door opens and slams, the cupboard creaks.
You sit down on the side of your bed, change your shoes and dash
out again. A dive down to the glass, two pins in your hair, powder
your nose and off again. But now—it's suddenly dear to you. It's a
darling little funny room. It's yours. Oh, what a joy it is to own
things! Mine—my own!

'My very own for ever?'

'Yes.' Their lips meet.

No, of course, that had nothing to do with it. That was all nonsense
and rubbish. But, in spite of herself, Beryl saw so plainly two people
standing in the middle of her room. Her arms were round his neck;
he held her. And now he whispered, 'My beauty, my little beauty!'
She jumped off her bed, ran over to the window and kneeled on the
window-seat, with her elbows on the sill. But the beautiful night, the
garden, every bush, every leaf, even the white palings, even the stars,

were conspirators too. So bright was the moon that the flowers were bright as by day; the shadow of the nasturtiums, exquisite lily-like leaves and wide-open flowers, lay across the silvery veranda. The manuka-tree, bent by the southerly winds, was like a bird on one leg stretching out a wing.

But when Beryl looked at the bush, it seemed to her the bush was sad.

'We are dumb trees, reaching up in the night, imploring we know not what,' said the sorrowful bush.

It is true when you are by yourself and you think about life, it is always sad. All that excitement and so on has a way of suddenly leaving you, and it's as though, in the silence, somebody called your name, and you heard your name for the first time. 'Beryl!'

'Yes, I'm here. I'm Beryl. Who wants me?'

'Beryl!'

'Let me come.'

It is lonely living by oneself. Of course, there are relations, friends, heaps of them; but that's not what she means. She wants some one who will find the Beryl they none of them know, who will expect her to be that Beryl always. She wants a lover.

'Take me away from all these other people, my love. Let us go far away. Let us live our life, all new, all ours, from the very beginning. Let us make our fire. Let us sit down to eat together. Let us have long talks at night.'

And the thought was almost, 'Save me, my love, Save me!'

. . . 'Oh, go on! Don't be a prude, my dear. You enjoy yourself while you're young. That's my advice.' And a high rush of silly laughter joined Mrs Harry Kember's loud, indifferent neigh.

You see, it's so frightfully difficult when you've nobody. You're so at the mercy of things. You can't just be rude. And you've always this horror of seeming inexperienced and stuffy like the other ninnies at the Bay. And—and it's fascinating to know you've power over people. Yes, that is fascinating. . . .

Oh why, oh why doesn't 'he' come soon?

If I go on living here, thought Beryl, anything may happen to me.

'But how do you know he is coming at all?' mocked a small voice within her.

But Beryl dismissed it. She couldn't be left. Other people, perhaps, but not she. It wasn't possible to think that Beryl Fairfield never married, that lovely fascinating girl.

'Do you remember Beryl Fairfield?'

'Remember her! As if I could forget her! It was one summer at the Bay that I saw her. She was standing on the beach in a blue'—no, pink—'muslin frock, holding on a big cream'—no, black—'straw hat. But it's years ago now.'

'She's as lovely as ever, more so if anything.'

Beryl smiled, bit her lip, and gazed over the garden. As she gazed, she saw somebody, a man, leave the road, step along the paddock beside their palings as if he was coming straight towards her. Her heart beat. Who was it? Who could it be? It couldn't be a burglar, certainly not a burglar, for he was smoking and he strolled lightly. Beryl's heart leapt; it seemed to turn right over, and then to stop. She recognized him.

'Good evening, Miss Beryl,' said the voice softly.

'Good evening.'

'Won't you come for a little walk?' it drawled.

Come for a walk—at that time of night! 'I couldn't. Everybody's in bed. Everybody's asleep.'

'Oh,' said the voice lightly, and a whiff of sweet smoke reached her. 'What does everybody matter? Do come! It's such a fine night. There's not a soul about.'

Beryl shook her head. But already something stirred in her, something reared its head.

The voice said, 'Frightened?' It mocked, 'Poor little girl!'

'Not in the least,' said she. As she spoke that weak thing within her seemed to uncoil, to grow suddenly tremendously strong; she longed to go!

And just as if this was quite understood by the other, the voice said, gently and softly, but finally, 'Come along!'

Beryl stepped over her low window, crossed the veranda, ran down the grass to the gate. He was there before her.

'That's right,' breathed the voice, and it teased, 'You're not frightened, are you? You're not frightened?'

She was; now she was here she was terrified, and it seemed to her everything was different. The moonlight stared and glittered: the shadows were like bars of iron. Her hand was taken.

'Not in the least,' she said lightly. 'Why should I be?'

Her hand was pulled gently, tugged. She held back.

'No, I'm not coming any farther,' said Beryl.

'Oh, rot!' Harry Kember didn't believe her. 'Come along! We'll just go as far as that fuchsia bush. Come along!'

The fuchsia bush was tall. It fell over the fence in a shower. There was a little pit of darkness beneath.

'No, really, I don't want to,' said Beryl.

For a moment Harry Kember didn't answer. Then he came close

to her, turned to her smiled and said quickly. 'Don't be silly! Don't be silly!'

His smile was something she'd never seen before. Was he drunk? That bright, blind, terrifying smile froze her with horror. What was she doing? How had she got here? The stern garden asked her as the gate pushed open, and quick as a cat Harry Kember came through and snatched her to him.

'Cold little devil! Cold little devil!' said the hateful voice.

But Beryl was strong. She slipped, ducked, wrenched free.

'You are vile, vile,' said she.

'Then why in God's name did you come?' stammered Harry Kember.

Nobody, answered him.

A cloud, small, serene, floated across the moon. In that moment of darkness the sea sounded deep, troubled. Then the cloud sailed away, and the sound of the sea was a vague murmur, as though it walked out of a dark dream. All was still.

KATHERINE MANSFIELD **The Voyage**

The Picton boat was due to leave at half-past eleven. It was a beautiful night, mild, starry, only when they got out of the cab and started to walk down the Old Wharf that jutted out into the harbour, a faint wind blowing off the water ruffled under Fenella's hat, and she put up her hand to keep it on. It was dark on the Old Wharf, very dark; the wool sheds, the cattle trucks, the cranes stand up so high, the little squat railway engine, all seemed carved out of solid darkness. Here and there on a rounded wood-pile, that was like the stalk of a huge black mushroom, there hung a lantern, but it seemed afraid to unfurl its timid, quivering light in all that blackness; it burned softly, as if for itself.

Fenella's father pushed on with quick, nervous strides. Beside him her grandma bustled along in her crackling black ulster; they went so fast that she had now and again to give an undignified little skip to keep up with them. As well as her luggage strapped into a neat sausage, Fenella carried clasped to her her grandma's umbrella, and the handle, which was a swan's head, kept giving her shoulder a sharp little peck as if it too wanted her to hurry. . . . Men, their caps pulled down, their collars turned up, swung by; a few women all muffled scurried along; and one tiny boy, only his little black arms and legs showing out of a white woolly shawl, was jerked along angrily between his father and mother; he looked like a baby fly that had fallen into the cream.

Then suddenly, so suddenly that Fenella and her grandma both leapt, there sounded from behind the largest wool shed, that had a trail of smoke hanging over it, *Mia-oo-oo-O-O!*

'First whistle,' said her father briefly, and at that moment they came in sight of the Picton boat. Lying beside the dark wharf, all strung, all beaded with round golden lights, the Picton boat looked as if she was more ready to sail among stars than out into the cold sea. People pressed along the gangway. First went her grandma, then her father, then Fenella.There was a high step down on to the deck, and an old sailor in a jersey standing by gave her his dry, hard hand. They were there; they stepped out of the way of the hurrying people, and standing under a little iron stairway that led to the upper deck they began to say good-bye.

'There, mother, there's your luggage!; said Fenella's father, giving grandma another strapped-up sausage.

'Thank you, Frank.'

'And you've got your cabin tickets safe?'

'Yes, dear.'

'And your other tickets?'

Grandma felt for them inside her glove and showed him the tips.

'That's right.'

He sounded stern, but Fenella, eagerly watching him, saw that he looked tired and sad. *Mia-oo-oo-O-O!* The second whistle blared just above their heads, and a voice like a cry shouted, 'Any more for the gangway?'

'You'll give my love to father,' Fenella saw her father's lips say. And her grandma, very agitated, answered, 'Of course I will, dear. Go now. You'll be left. Go now, Frank. Go now.'

'It's all right, mother. I've got another three minutes.' To her surprise Fenella saw her father take off his hat. He clasped grandma in his arms and pressed her to him. 'God bless you, mother!' she heard him say.

And grandma put her hand, with the black thread glove that was worn through on her ring finger, against his cheek, and she sobbed, 'God bless you, my own brave son!'

This was so awful that Fenella quickly turned her back on them, swallowed once, twice, and frowned terribly at a little green star on a mast head. But she had to turn round again; her father was going.

'Good-bye, Fenella. Be a good girl.' His cold, wet moustache brushed her cheek. But Fenella caught hold of the lapels of his coat.

'How long am I going to stay?' she whispered anxiously. He wouldn't look at her. He shook her off gently, and gently said, 'We'll see about that. Here! Where's your hand?' He pressed something into her palm. 'Here's a shilling in case your should need it.'

A shilling! She must be going away for ever! 'Father!' cried Fenella. But he was gone. He was the last off the ship. The sailors put their shoulders to the gangway. A huge coil of dark rope went flying through the air and fell 'thump' on the wharf. A bell rang; a whistle shrilled. Silently the dark wharf began to slip, to slide, to edge away from them. Now there was a rush of water between. Fenella strained to see with all her might. 'Was that father turning round?'—or waving?—or standing alone?—or walking off by himself? The strip of water grew broader, darker. Now the Picton boat began to swing round steady, pointing out to sea. It was no good looking any longer. There was nothing to be seen but a few lights, the face of the town clock hanging in the air, and more lights, little patches of them, on the dark hills.

The freshening wind tugged at Fenella's skirts; she went back to her grandma. To her relief grandma seemed no longer sad. She had put the two sausages of luggage one on top of the other, and she was sitting on them, her hands folded, her head a little on one side. There was an intent, bright look on her face. Then Fenella saw that her lips were moving and guessed that she was praying. But the old woman gave her a bright nod as if to say the prayer was nearly over. She unclasped her hands, sighed, clasped them again, bent forward, and at last gave herself a soft shake.

'And now, child,' she said, fingering the bow of her bonnet-strings, 'I think we ought to see about our cabins. Keep close to me, and mind you don't slip.'

'Yes, grandma!'

'And be careful the umbrellas aren't caught in the stair rail. I saw a beautiful umbrella broken in half like that on my way over.'

'Yes, grandma!'

Dark figures of men lounged against the rails. In the glow of their pipes a nose shone out, or the peak of a cap, or a pair of surpised-looking eyebrows. Fenella glanced up. High in the air, a little figure, his hands thrust in his short jacket pockets, stood staring out to sea. The ship rocked ever so little, and she thought the stars rocked too. And now a pale steward in a linen coat, holding a tray high in the palm of his hand, stepped out of a lighted doorway and skimmed past them. They went through that doorway. Carefully over the high brass-bound step on to the rubber mat and then down such a terrible steep flight of stairs that grandma had to put both feet on each step, and Fenella clutched the clammy brass rail and forgot all about the swan-necked umbrella.

At the bottom grandma stopped; Fenella was rather afraid she was going to pray again. But no, it was only to get out the cabin tickets. They were in the saloon. It was glaring bright and stifling; the air smelled of paint and burnt chop-bones and india-rubber. Fenella wished her grandma would go on, but the old woman was not to be hurried. An immense basket of ham sandwiches caught her eye. She went up to them and touched the top one delicately with her finger.

'How much are the sandwiches?' she asked.

'Tuppence!' bawled a rude steward, slamming down a knife and fork.

Grandma could hardly believe it.

'Twopence *each*?' she asked.

'That's right,' said the steward, and he winked at his companion.

Grandma made a small, astonished face. Then she whispered primly to Fenella. 'What wickedness!' And they sailed out at the further door and along a passage that had cabins on either side. Such a very nice stewardess came to meet them. She was dressed all in blue, and her collar and cuffs were fastened with large brass buttons. She seemed to know grandma well.

'Well, Mrs Crane,' said she, unlocking their washstand. 'We've got you back again. It's not often you give yourself a cabin.'

'No,' said grandma. 'But this time my dear son's thoughtfulness——'

'I hope——' began the stewardess. Then she turned round and took a long mournful look at grandma's blackness and at Fenella's black coat and skirt, black blouse, and hat with a crape rose.

Grandma nodded. 'It was God's will,' said she.

The stewardess shut her lips and, taking a deep breath, she seemed to expand.

'What I always say is,' she said, as though it was her own discovery, 'sooner or later each of us has to go, and that's a certingty.' She paused. 'Now, can I bring you anything, Mrs Crane? A cup of tea? I know it's no good offering you a little something to keep the cold out.'

Grandma shook her head. 'Nothing, thank you. We've got a few wine biscuits, and Fenella has a very nice banana.'

'Then I'll give you a look later on,' said the stewardess, and she went out, shutting the door.

What a very small cabin it was! It was like being shut up in a box with grandma. The dark round eye above the washstand gleamed at them dully. Fenella felt shy. She stood against the door, still clasping her luggage and the umbrella. Were they going to get undressed in here? Already her grandma had taken off her bonnet, and, rolling up the strings, she fixed each with a pin to the lining before she hung the bonnet up. Her white hair shone like silk; the little bun at the back was covered with a black net. Fenella hardly ever saw her grandma with her head uncovered; she looked strange.

'I shall put on the woollen fascinator your dear mother crocheted for me,' said grandma, and, unstrapping the sausage, she took it out and wound it round her head; the fringe of grey bobbles danced at her eyebrows as she smiled tenderly and mournfully at Fenella. Then she undid her bodice, and something under that, and something else underneath that. Then there seemed a short, sharp tussle, and grandma flushed faintly. Snip! Snap! She had undone her stays. She breathed a sigh of relief, and sitting on the plush couch, she slowly and carefully pulled off her elastic-sided boots and stood them side by side.

By the time Fenella had taken off her coat and skirt and put on her flannel dressing-gown grandma was quite ready.

'Must I take off my boots, grandma? They're lace.'

Grandma gave them a moment's deep consideration. 'You'd feel a great deal more comfortable if you did, child,' said she. She kissed Fenella. 'Don't forget to say your prayers. Our dear Lord is with us when we are at sea even more than when we are on dry land. And because I am an experienced traveller,' said grandma briskly, 'I shall take the upper berth.'

'But, grandma, however will you get up there?'

Three little spider-like steps were all Fenella saw. The old woman gave a small silent laugh before she mounted them nimbly, and she peered over the high bunk at the astonished Fenella.

'You didn't think your grandma could do that, did you?' said she. And as she sank back Fenella heard her light laugh again.

The hard square of brown soap would not lather, and the water in the bottle was like a kind of blue jelly. How hard it was, too, to turn down those stiff sheets; you simply had to tear your way in. If everything had been different, Fenella might have got the giggles. . . At last she was inside, and while she lay there panting, there sounded from above a long, soft whispering, as though some one was gently, gently rustling among tissue paper to find something. It was grandma saying her prayers. . . .

A long time passed. Then the stewardess came in; she trod softly and leaned her hand on grandma's bunk.

'We're just entering the Straits,' she said.

'Oh!'

'It's a fine night, but we're rather empty. We may pitch a little.'

And indeed at that moment the Picton boat rose and rose and hung in the air just long enough to give a shiver before she swung down again, and there was the sound of heavy water slapping against her sides. Fenella remembered she had left that swan-necked umbrella standing up on the little couch. If it fell over, would it break? But grandma remembered too, at the same time.

'I wonder if you'd mind, stewardess, laying down my umbrella,' she whispered.

'Not at all, Mrs Crane.' And the stewardess, coming back to grandma breathed, 'Your little grand-daughter's in such a beautiful sleep.'

'God be praised for that!' said grandma.

'Poor little motherless mite!' said the stewardess. And grandma was still telling the stewardess all about what happened when Fenella fell asleep.

But she hadn't been asleep long enough to dream before she woke up again to see something waving in the air above her head. What was it? What could it be? It was a small grey foot. Now another joined it. They seemed to be feeling about for something; there came a sigh.

'I'm awake, grandma,' said Fenella.

'Oh, dear, am I near the ladder?' asked grandma. 'I thought it was this end.'

'No, grandma, it's the other. I'll put your foot on it. Are we there?' asked Fenella.

'In the harbour,' said grandma. 'We must get up, child. You'd better have a biscuit to steady yourself before you move.'

But Fenella had hopped out of her bunk. The lamp was still burning, but night was over, and it was cold. Peering through that round eye, she could see far off some rocks. Now they were scattered over with foam; now a gull flipped by; and now there came a long piece of real land.

'It's land, grandma,' said Fenella, wonderingly, as though they had been at sea for weeks together. She hugged herself; she stood on one leg and rubbed it with the toes of the other foot; she was trembling. Oh, it had all been so sad lately. Was it going to change? But all her grandma said was, 'Make haste, child. I should leave your nice banana for the stewardess as you haven't eaten it.' And Fenella put on her black clothes again, and a button sprang off one of her gloves and rolled to where she couldn't reach it. They went up on deck.

But if it had been cold in the cabin, on deck it was like ice. The sun was not up yet, but the stars were dim, and the cold pale sky was the same colour as the cold pale sea. On the land a white mist rose and fell. Now they could see quite plainly dark bush. Even the shapes of the umbrella ferns showed, and those strange silvery withered trees that are like skeletons. . . . Now they could see the landing-stage and some little houses, pale too, clustered together, like shells on the lid of a box. The other passengers tramped up and down, but more slowly than they had the night before, and they looked gloomy.

And now the landing-stage came out to meet them. Slowly it swam towards the Picton boat, and a man holding a coil of rope, and a cart with a small drooping horse and another man sitting on the step, came too.

'It's Mr Penreddy, Fenella, come for us,' said grandma. She sounded pleased. Her white waxen cheeks were blue with cold, her chin trembled, and she had to keep wiping her eyes and her little pink nose.

'You've got my——'

'Yes, grandma.' Fenella showed it to her.

The rope came flying through the air, and 'smack' it fell on to the deck. The gangway was lowered. Again Fenella followed her grandma on to the wharf over to the little cart, and a moment later they were bowling away. The hooves of the little horse drummed over the wooden piles, then sank softly into the sandy road. Not a soul was to be seen; there was not even a feather of smoke. The mist rose and fell, and the sea still sounded asleep as slowly it turned on the beach.

'I seen Mr Crane yestiddy,' said Mr Penreddy. 'He looked himself then. Missus knocked him up a batch of scones last week.'

And now the little horse pulled up before one of the shell-like houses. They got down. Fenella put her hand on the gate, and the big, trembling dew-drops soaked through her glove-tips. Up a little path of round white pebbles they went, with drenched sleeping flowers on either side. Grandma's delicate white picotees were so heavy with dew that they were fallen, but their sweet smell was part of the cold morning. The blinds were down in the little house; they mounted the steps on to the verandah. A pair of old bluchers was on one side of the door, and a large red watering-can on the other.

'Tut! tut! Your grandpa,' said grandma. She turned the handle.

Not a sound. She called, 'Walter!' And immediately a deep voice that sounded half stifled called back, 'Is that you, Mary?'

'Wait, dear,' said grandma. 'Go in there.' She pushed Fenella gently into a small dusky sitting-room.

On the table a white cat, that had been folded up like a camel, rose, stretched itself, yawned, and then sprang on to the tips of its toes. Fenella buried one cold little hand in the white, warm fur, and smiled timidly while she stroked and listened to grandma's gentle voice and the rolling tones of grandpa.

A door creaked. 'Come in, dear.' The old woman beckoned, Fenella followed. There, lying to one side of an immense bed, lay grandpa. Just his head with a white tuft, and his rosy face and long silver beard showed over the quilt. He was like a very old wide-awake bird.

'Well, my girl!' said grandpa. 'Give us a kiss!' Fenella kissed him. 'Ugh!' said grandpa. 'Her little nose is as cold as a button. What's that she's holding? Her grandma's umbrella?'

Fenella smiled again, and crooked the swan neck over the bed-rail. Above the bed there was a big text in a deep-black frame:

> *Lost! One Golden Hour*
> *Set with Sixty Diamond Minutes*
> *No Reward Is Offered*
> *For It Is* GONE FOR EVER!

'Yer grandma painted that,' said grandpa. And he ruffled his white tuft and looked at Fenella so merrily she almost thought he winked at her.

# KATHERINE MANSFIELD **Her First Ball**

Exactly when the ball began Leila would have found it hard to say. Perhaps her first real partner was the cab. It did not matter that she shared the cab with the Sheridan girls and their brother. She sat back in her own little corner of it, and the bolster on which her hand rested felt like the sleeve of an unknown young man's dress suit; and away they bowled, past waltzing lamp-posts and houses and fences and trees.

'Have you really never been to a ball before, Leila? But, my child, how too weird——' cried the Sheridan girls.

'Our nearest neighbour was fifteen miles,' said Leila softly, gently opening and shutting her fan.

Oh, dear, how hard it was to be indifferent like the others! She tried not to smile too much; she tried not to care. But every single thing was so new and exciting . . . . Meg's tuberoses, Jose's long loop of amber, Laura's little dark head, pushing above her white fur like a flower through snow. She would remember for ever. It even gave her a pang to see her cousin Laurie throw away the wisps of tissue paper he pulled from the fastenings of his new gloves. She would like to have kept those wisps as a keepsake, as a remembrance. Laurie leaned forward and put his hand on Laura's knee.

'Look here, darling,' he said. 'The third and the ninth as usual. Twig?'

Oh, how marvellous to have a brother! In her excitement Leila felt that if there had been time, if it hadn't been impossible, she couldn't have helped crying because she was an only child, and no brother had ever said 'Twig?' to her; no sister would ever say, as Meg said to Jose that moment, 'I've never known your hair go up more successfully than it has tonight!'

But, of course, there was no time. They were at the drill hall already; there were cabs in front of them and cabs behind. The road was bright on either side with moving fan-like lights, and on the pavement gay couples seemed to float through the air; little satin shoes chased each other like birds.

'Hold on to me, Leila; you'll get lost,' said Laura.

'Come on, girls, let's make a dash for it,' said Laurie.

Leila put two fingers on Laura's pink velvet cloak, and they were somehow lifted past the big golden lantern, carried along the passage, and pushed into the little room marked 'Ladies'. Here the crowd was so great there was hardly space to take off their things; the noise was deafening. Two benches on either side were stacked high with wraps. Two old women in white aprons ran up and down tossing fresh armfuls. And everybody was pressing forward trying to get at the little dressing-table and mirror at the far end.

A great quivering jet of gas lighted the ladies' room. It couldn't wait; it was dancing already. When the door opened again and there came a burst of tuning from the drill hall, it leaped almost to the ceiling.

Dark girls, fair girls were patting their hair, tying ribbons again, tucking handkerchiefs down the fronts of their bodices, smoothing marble-white gloves. And because they were all laughing it seemed to Leila that they were all lovely.

'Aren't there any invisible hair-pins?' cried a voice. 'How most extraordinary! I can't see a single invisible hair-pin.'

'Powder my back, there's a darling,' cried some one else.

'But I must have a needle and cotton. I've torn simply miles and miles of the frill,' wailed a third.

Then, 'Pass them along, pass them along!' The straw basket of programmes was tossed from arm to arm. Darling little pink-and-silver programmes, with pink pencils and fluffy tassels. Leila's fingers shook as she took one out of the basket. She wanted to ask some one, 'Am I meant to have one too?' but she had just time to read: 'Waltz 3. *Two, Two in a Canoe*. Polka 4. *Making the Feathers Fly'*, when Meg cried, 'Ready, Leila?' and they pressed their way through the crush in the passage towards the big double doors of the drill hall.

Dancing had not begun yet, but the band had stopped tuning, and the noise was so great it seemed that when it did begin to play it would never be heard. Leila, pressing close to Meg, looking over Meg's shoulder, felt that even the little quivering coloured flags strung across the ceiling were talking. She quite forgot to be shy; she forgot how in the middle of dressing she had sat down on the bed with one shoe off and one shoe on and begged her mother to ring up her cousins and say she couldn't go after all. And the rush of longing she had had to be sitting on the verandah of their forsaken up-country home, listening to the baby owls crying 'More pork' in the moonlight, was changed to a rush of joy so sweet that it was hard to bear alone. She clutched her fan, and, gazing at the gleaming, golden floor, the azaleas, the lanterns, the stage at one end with its red carpet and gilt chairs and the band in a corner, she thought breathlessly, 'How heavenly; how simply heavenly!'

All the girls stood grouped together at one side of the doors, the men at the other, and the chaperones in dark dresses, smiling rather foolishly, walked with little careful steps over the polished floor towards the stage.

'This is my little country cousin Leila. Be nice to her. Find her partners; she's under my wing,' said Meg, going up to one girl after another.

Strange faces smiled at Leila—sweetly, vaguely. Strange voices answered, 'Of course, my dear.' But Leila felt the girls didn't really see her. They were looking towards the men. Why didn't the men begin? What were they waiting for? There they stood, smoothing their gloves, patting their glossy hair and smiling among themselves. Then, quite suddenly, as if they had only just made up their minds that that was what they had to do, the men came gliding over the parquet. There was a joyful flutter among the girls. A tall, fair man flew up to Meg, seized her programme, scribbled something; Meg passed him on to Leila. 'May I have the pleasure?' He ducked and smiled. There came a dark man wearing an eyeglass, then cousin Laurie with a friend, and Laura with a little freckled fellow whose tie was crooked. Then quite an old man—fat, with a big bald patch on his head—took her programme and murmured, 'Let me see, let me see!' And he was a long time comparing his programme, which looked black with names, with hers. It seemed to give him so much trouble that Leila was ashamed. 'Oh, please don't bother,' she said eagerly. But instead of replying the fat man wrote something, glanced at her again. 'Do I remember this bright little face?' he said softly. 'Is it known to me of yore?' At that moment the band began playing; the fat man disappeared. He was tossed away on a great wave of music that came flying over the gleaming floor, breaking the groups up into couples, scattering them, sending them spinning. . . .

Leila had learned to dance at boarding school. Every Saturday afternoon the boarders were hurried off to a little corrugated iron mission hall where Miss Eccles (of London) held her 'select' classes. But the difference between that dusty-smelling hall—with calico texts on the walls, the poor terrified little woman in a brown velvet toque with rabbit's ears thumping the cold piano, Miss Eccles poking the girls' feet with her long white wand—and this, was so tremendous that Leila was sure if her partner didn't come and she had to listen to that marvellous music and to watch the others sliding, gliding over the golden floor, she would die at least, or faint, or lift her arms and fly out of one of those dark windows that showed the stars.

'Ours, I think——' Some one bowed, smiled, and offered her his arm; she hadn't to die after all. Some one's hand pressed her waist, and she floated away like a flower that is tossed into a pool.

'Quite a good floor, isn't it?' drawled a faint voice close to her ear.

'I think it's most beautifully slippery,' said Leila.

'Pardon!' The faint voice sounded surprised. Leila said it again. And there was a tiny pause before the voice echoed, 'Oh, quite!' and she was swung round again.

He steered so beautifully. That was the great difference between dancing with girls and men, Leila decided. Girls banged into each other, and stamped on each other's feet; the girl who was gentleman always clutched you so.

The azaleas were separate flowers no longer; they were pink and white flags streaming by.

'Were you at the Bells' last week?' the voice came again. It sounded tired. Leila wondered whether she ought to ask him if he would like to stop.

'No, this is my first dance,' said she.

Her partner gave a little gasping laugh. 'Oh, I say,' he protested.

'Yes, it is really the first dance I've ever been to.' Leila was most fervent. It was such a relief to be able to tell somebody. 'You see, I've lived in the country all my life up till now . . .'

At that moment the music stopped, and they went to sit on two chairs against the wall. Leila tucked her pink satin feet under and fanned herself, while she blissfully watched the other couples passing and disappearing through the swing doors.

'Enjoying yourself, Leila?' asked Jose, nodding her golden head.

Laura passed and gave her the faintest little wink; it made Leila wonder for a moment whether she was quite grown up after all. Certainly her partner did not say very much. He coughed, tucked his handkerchief away, pulled down his waistcoat, took a minute thread off his sleeve. But it didn't matter. Almost immediately the band started, and her second partner seemed to spring from the ceiling.

'Floor's not bad,' said the new voice. Did one always begin with the floor? And then, 'Were you at the Neaves' on Tuesday?' And again Leila explained. Perhaps it was a little strange that her partners were not more interested. For it was thrilling. Her first ball! She was only at the beginning of everything. It seemed to her that she had never known what the night was like before. Up till now it had been dark, silent, beautiful very often—oh, yes—but mournful somehow. Solemn. And now it would never be like that again—it had opened dazzling bright.

'Care for an ice?' said her partner. And they went through the swing doors, down the passage, to the supper room. Her cheeks burned, she was fearfully thirsty. How sweet the ices looked on little glass plates, and how cold the frosted spoon was, iced too! And when they came back to the hall there was the fat man waiting for her by the door. It gave her quite a shock again to see how old he was; he ought to have been on the stage with the fathers and mothers. And when Leila compared him with her other partners he looked shabby. His waistcoat was creased, there was a button off his glove, his coat looked as if it was dusty with French chalk.

'Come along, little lady,' said the fat man. He scarcely troubled to clasp her, and they moved away so gently, it was more like walking than dancing. But he said not a word about the floor. 'Your first dance, isn't it?' he murmured.

'How *did* you know?'

'Ah,' said the fat man, 'that's what it is to be old!' He wheezed faintly as he steered her past an awkward couple. 'You see, I've been doing this kind of thing for the last thirty years.'

'Thirty years?' cried Leila. Twelve years before she was born!

'It hardly bears thinking about, does it?' said the fat man gloomily. Leila looked at his bald head, and she felt quite sorry for him.

'I think it's marvellous to be still going on,' she said kindly.

'Kind little lady,' said the fat man, and he pressed her a little closer, and hummed a bar of the waltz. 'Of course,' he said, 'you can't hope to last anything like as long as that. No-o,' said the fat man, 'long before that you'll be sitting up there on the stage, looking on, in your nice black velvet. And these pretty arms will have turned into little short fat ones, and you'll beat time with such a different kind of fan—a black bony one.' The fat man seemed to shudder. 'And you'll smile away like the poor old dears up there, and point to your daughter, and tell the elderly lady next to you how some dreadful man tried to kiss her at the club ball. And your heart will ache, ache'—the fat man squeezed her closer still, as if he really was sorry for that poor heart—'because no one wants to kiss you now. And you'll say how unpleasant these polished floors are to walk on, how dangerous they are. Eh, Mademoiselle Twinkletoes?' said the fat man softly.

Leila gave a light little laugh, but she did not feel like laughing. Was it—could it all be true? It sounded terribly true. Was this first ball only the beginning of her last ball after all? At that the music seemed to change; it sounded sad, sad; it rose upon a great sigh. Oh, how quickly things changed! Why didn't happiness last for ever? For ever wasn't a bit too long.

'I want to stop,' she said in a breathless voice. The fat man led her to the door.

'No,' she said, 'I won't go outside. I won't sit down. I'll just stand here, thank you.' She leaned against the wall, tapping with her foot, pulling up her gloves and trying to smile. But deep inside her a little girl threw her pinafore over her head and sobbed. Why had he spoiled it all?

'I say, you know,' said the fat man, 'you mustn't take me seriously, little lady.'

'As if I should!' said Leila, tossing her small dark head and sucking her underlip. . . .

Again the couples paraded. The swing doors opened and shut. Now new music was being given out by the bandmaster. But Leila didn't want to dance any more. She wanted to be home, or sitting on the verandah listening to those baby owls. When she looked through the dark windows at the stars, they had long beams like wings. . . .

But presently a soft, melting, ravishing tune began, and a young man with curly hair bowed before her. She would have to dance, out of politeness, until she could find Meg. Very stiffly she walked into the middle; very haughtily she put her hand on his sleeve. But in one minute, in one turn, her feet glided, glided. The lights, the azaleas, the dresses, the pink faces, the velvet chairs, all became one beautiful flying wheel. And when her next partner bumped her into the fat man and he said, 'Par *don,*' she smiled at him more radiantly than ever. She didn't even recognize him again.

## B. E. BAUGHAN

# An Active Family

The Post Office clock was just striking seven, that fine midsummer morning when 'Mother' and 'Dad' and I drove out of town and took the sea-coast road. 'Dad' was a spare, spry little man, somewhere between fifty and sixty, with a shock of grey hair and an eye of burning fire; 'Mother' was a buxom presence, comfortable and comforting, I just a stray guest; and we were all off, this rare mid-week holiday, to see how the up-country farm was getting on, and 'the children', who were in charge of it.

In less than five minutes the country spread all about us—the good, green, grassy country, rolling in gentle swells and undulations like a summer sea. Here and there one lonely cabbage tree stood up, curiously distinct; at long intervals we passed a squad of plantation-pines, or some homestead nestling in among the gentle hills; but otherwise all was wide sky and billowy grass, interspersed with browsing cattle. The skylark sang overhead; there was a fine fresh breeze; and away to the west, along the bright blue of the sky, there lay, straight and low, a dark blue band of sea.

Dad flicked the whip at Brownie with a nervous energy; he was 'in a bit of a rush to get home'. Always full of nervous energy was Dad, and more often than not 'in a bit of a rush'. He was a delicate man, who had survived, Mother alone knows how many 'bad turns', and he was often ailing and irritable, but never without a certain dash and vigour. 'More pluck than bulk', a neighbour once summed him up, and, 'You'd think he'd a fire inside of him,' agreed one of the listeners. Suppose it was so, then this fire had two flames—a love of music, and a passion for the soil.

The latter was paramount and urging. Dad, without capital, and with a numerous family, of which the eldest were but just emerging from school age, had nevertheless, some few years previously, managed, at last, to take up a bit of land; by dint of stern determination had ploughed and fenced and got it into some kind of going order; then, with the same sternness, had torn himself away from it. It needed money; that money he must make. The children were now growing up; they could manage things between them, and he would go back to town and earn. Accordingly, for the sake of his heart's delight, he banished himself from the sight of it all week long, and served in a grocery store, hurrying home, each Saturday night and every chance holiday, to take a general survey and issue orders. Mother would not leave him—of all her children he was the one who needed looking after most. 'So he's bachelorizin', an' I'm keepin' house for him,' she would explain, with a twinkle. And 'the children' managed the farm.

As we drove along, Mother related reminiscences—tales of the early days when she had just come out to New Zealand, and the Maori troubles in that part of the country were at their worst. 'Dad was ordered off, with all the rest of the men, the moment we landed, and all us women and children were herded together for safety,' narrated this Pilgrim mother. 'I remember how I sat down with my young one in my arms—he'd been born on board ship comin' out—an' cried an' *cried*. I was but only eighteen, and I'd made my mind up that we'd come out just to get killed. Things quieted down a bit after awhile, but for long enough they wasn't properly settled. Once, after we'd got us a house to ourselves, there was a band of Maoris come into it at the front door, just as I'd caught my babies together (two there was by then), an' run out into the flax-swamp by the back. Everything they could put their hands on they stole, them natives did; not a crumb of any one thing did they leave behind 'em; and, as I peered out from behind the flax and watched 'em go, I could see they was finishin' up with eatin', what do you think, now? *Soap!* Then, there was another time, and that was in the win-ter—bitter cold. I locked all the doors an' went without fire for a week, that they might think the house deserted, for there they was, bands of 'em again, goin' a-singin' an' a-screechin' up an' down the road. Hows'ever, none of 'em come in that time. . . . The babies? Nay, I lost 'em, dear. I never reared them two.'

So peaceful looked the smiling country all about us, so placid were Mother's soft tones, that it was hard to realize what danger and excitements, what sore straits at times, both land and woman had suffered in those bygone days—not bygone so very far yet, either.

The hills grew steeper as we proceeded, and the road rougher, but Brownie was a good horse, and she had a resolute driver. 'They'll have begun the stacking today, I shouldn't wonder,' Dad kept observing, whenever there was a pause in the talk; and we made good time. It was not yet quite nine o'clock, when we passed a hollow filled with glossy *karaka,* mounted the hill above it, up which ripe grasses ran before the wind—and there we were, at a white gate before a thick plantation, and—yes! they *had* 'begun the stacking'. Dad flung the reins to a girl who came flying out of the gate just as we stopped before it, kissed her somehow as he passed her, and bounded straight for the oat-paddock, pulling off his coat as he ran.

'Let him go!' says Mother with an indulgent smile, leisurely descending in her turn from the gig. 'Well, Flo, how's everybody?'

'Oh, fine!' says Flo, a big, broad-shouldered girl, of perhaps eighteen, with a happy face, a friendly smile, and two long plaits of rich dark hair hanging nearly to her waist. 'How do you do?' (to me) 'You must be pretty well starving, I'm sure! I'll take Brownie, Mum, you two go in. Nance is in the kitchen.'

So we leave Flo to unharness, and turn in at the gate. The path beyond it leads, first, through an avenue of breakwind pines, through which, turning for a moment to look back at Flo, I catch the smile of sunlit sea half a mile or so away; and then out upon an open space, bright with hardy flowers, and surrounding a ramshackle wooden house, with an overflow of outbuildings, all stained, rather than painted, with a various, weather-washed red.

'Nancy's flowers!' says Mother, stooping to smell a bit of lemon verbena, and to lift up a branch of fuchsia, all bowed down beneath its load of royal purple and crimson. 'That child would grow flowers in a dust-pan, I do believe—Ah, Nance, here you are!' as another girl comes flying out of the house—they all seem to take after their father as to movement, and carry the wind in their hair.

Nance is slighter than Flo, and fairer; perhaps she is a couple of years older. Her pale-green blouse is faded but spotless; and the untrimmed '*gégé*' hat tilted back upon her head frames in a face that is very nearly pretty, and so happy that it has the effect of being pretty quite; and that is a real triumph of mind over matter, since one cheek is red and swollen, and Nance's hand goes up to it, even as she smiles a charming welcome.

'Toothache?' asks Mother, sympathetically.

Nancy nods. 'But it'll go,' she says brightly. 'Come along in! The kettle's on the boil.'

'None of 'em really strong, someway,' Mother confides to me. 'But they all take after their dad—they won't give in till they must.'

The house door leads right into a large bare room, with a long table and some benches in it, all polished by much use, and a great open hearth, fit for burning huge logs of wood. The brown wood walls, guiltless of paint or paper, are decorated only with a couple of Christmas Supplement pictures, unframed; the floor is covered with a brown linoleum which lost its pattern long ago; the cupboard that occupies one corner, the dresser, hung with mugs and cups, that runs along one wall, the lounges underneath the two great windows, are all obviously home-made. But, frugal though its furnishing, there is a most comfortable *homeyness* about the place. A green jug upon the table, too, holds a handful of Canterbury bells, purple and white; plump cushions with bright covers mollify the lounges; there is plenty of light; above all, there is plenty of air, for both windows are open, and another door, opposite to that by which we entered, frames another glimpse of garden-green. Through this second door Nance disappears, while Mother smooths out an imaginary crease in the cloth laid at one end of the long table, and straightens the quite straight cups and plates.

'We've a cooking-shed outside,' she explains, as Nance returns with a tray and a steaming teapot. 'Where's Eva, Nance?'

'Eva? Oh, still at the butter, I expect,' says Nance. 'There's a splendid lot this week.'

It is hours since we breakfasted, and the delicious bread and butter and jam, all home-made, of course, are more than welcome, not to speak of the hot tea, and sweet rich cream.

'How about Dad, though?' says loyal Mother, as she takes her seat.

'Oh, Dad's all right,' Nance answers, putting brisk finishing touches to a great 'kit' covered in with a spotless tea-towel; 'I told Benny to be down for the lunch just about now'—and even as she says the words, in shoots a breathless, towheaded twelve-year-old. He smiles to his mother, nods to me, catches up the kit, together with a mighty billy by the door—and shoots out again.

'Who's up there?' asks Mother, 'and how are they gettin' along?'

'First-rate! They reckon to be done to-night,' says Nance. 'Benny's there, of course, and Bruv and Sandy; Flo and Bonny have been there most of the time, and . . . Hugh is helping.' Nance hesitated a little before that last name, and it seemed to me she blushed ever so slightly, too. If she did, however, Mother took no notice.

'That's good. And how's the ducks?' said she.

'There, now!' replies Nance ruefully. 'I do wish you hadn't asked; I was hoping to break it to you gently. All gone, mother! Poor Waddle, all her babies gone! Rats, we think; so we've moved Toddle and her little lot. But oh, Mother! what do you think? We've had somebody after the place!'

'That's good,' says Mother again, taking the translation of the little Waddles as equably as she takes everything else. 'Likely, d'you think?'

'Bruv says so,' Nance replies. 'Dad *would* be pleased, wouldn't he? He'd have us all up at that new Bush place in a twinkling. Only—you do get fond of a place you've done the settling of yourself, don't you, Mum? It'll seem a bit hard to move on.'

'Well, but after all that's what we settled it *for,* isn't it?' returns Mother comfortably. 'Bring out the sewin', will you? Machine still all right?' And, while Nance and I clear away, she establishes herself in a good light with a pile of dilapidated shirts, and a half-made white muslin blouse. 'Worst first,' says she, and begins upon the shirts.

The cups washed, Nance proposes that I should see the butter, and takes me over to the dairy-shed, where Eva, a second edition of Flo, though several years older, smiles merrily out at us from behind a great, pale-primrose-coloured hill. Long before breakfast, I learn, with the help of old Dobbin—harnessed to the cream-barrel, and steadily tramping round and round—the butter 'came' in about ten minutes; then it was copiously washed with clear, cold spring-water; and now, well worked and salted, here it lies upon the dark wood table, a mellow, shining mass, from which Eva is deftly wedging out, and weighing, and shaping, pile upon pile of 'regulation' pounds. Table and concrete floor are running with clean water; Eva has gumboots on her feet, her skirt, of dark-blue cambric, is pinned up, her snowy apron covers her from collar to hem. Bright are her great grey eyes, and her cheeks very pink and pretty. The very air seems clean and coloured in the dairy, and we stay there a good while, chatting.

Then, after a satisfactory inspection of affairs in the cooking-shed, Nance takes me up to the oat-paddock. 'For, though I am cook this week (Flo and Eva and I take it in turns),' she explains, 'the dinner's all on now, and, besides, Mother's here.' Watch, the old rough-coated dog, comes with us, and on the way there is yellow-haired Custard to be seen, with her six unparalleled pups. From the pigeon-cote above the cart-shed, a flock of snowy fantailed pigeons comes circling round our heads, not at all timidly; and Nance says, 'You can see they're pets, too, can't you? Everything we've got is a pet. You know, we don't believe in our animals working for us for nothing.'

Past the last of the many sheds, through the kitchen-garden, through the orchard, and then out, upon what a breezy hillock! High up it seems suddenly to have been lifted, and now to be held high up, all bare to the bright breezes. The view from it is all in breadths of blue and green—blue sky, blue sea, and another great green grassy knobs like itself; all the land on this side is hilly. Here and there a fire-blackened pole, or stubborn old grey stump, bears witness to the long-banished Bush, in one gully, tree-ferns spread their delicate pavilions. Up two more hillocks we climb, and chase each other down two gullies. Shouts and laughter greet our last ascent, and here we are, among the harvesters!

The crop is being carried. Benny, and Bonny, his twin-sister, whose flying fleece of yellow hair catches every sunbeam, are helping Flo to rake. Sandy is in charge of the sled, as Dobbin takes it back and forth between the rakers and the rick; while Bruv, the eldest of 'the children', is pitching, with the help of Hugh Miller, a neighbour's son. As for Dad, he is everywhere, of course. All the lads are well-grown, honest-looking and natural. Soft shirts with turned-down collars, blue dungarees, belts and great '*gégé*' hats make up their 'rig'—how they would laugh if one told them that it was picturesque! it is, though, all the same. Work is proceeding at top-speed; nevertheless, Hugh Miller, I perceive, finds time between his forkfuls for a word or two with Nancy, standing, with glowing face uplifted, close beneath the rick; and I do my best to engage that burning eye of Dad's elsewhere. But before very long there comes to my relief a prolonged 'BOO-OO!' rumbling through the racy air—the unmistakable sound of a horn. 'Dinner already? It can't be? cries poor Dad in dismay—nevertheless, dinner it is. In we all scamper, and lively presently about the kitchen door are the demands for 'more soap' and 'another towel'.

Mother has dished up; and now she and Nance take their stand at one end of the long table, and pass down, to any one who is seated, a generous plateful of roast pork, apple-sauce, and potatoes.

'We're rough, you know,' Dad says, apologetically, handing me the salt.

'And ready!' chuckles Sandy, falling to with a will upon his share.

'Roughest is best at times,' Mother placidly winds up.

But, in reality, there is very little that is rough about it. The cloth is clean, the set of sun-browned faces round it, shining with health and good humour, is a finer sight than any possible amount of silver on it could be, and the meal itself, though perhaps it might make a conscientious dyspeptic shudder, for the pork is followed by a hot plum-pudding, would likewise almost certainly make his mouth water, for it is excellently cooked. There is only one thing wrong, and that is, that every one of us drinks tea. Delicious, pernicious tea! When shall we of the back-blocks learn to do without you, anyway at dinner? No wonder that Nance has toothache, and patent medicines such a sale!

Dinner done, the harvest-hands take a brief 'spell' upon the lounges, while the rest of us clear away, and wash the dishes. Then, back they go to the paddock, Eva this time with them, Mother resumes her mending, and Nance and I proceed to bottle 'barm', Nance enlivening the task with a sketch of the family fortunes.

'At first, you know,' she says, 'we'd terrible luck up here. The cows *would* get milk fever, and the pigs took bad, and oh! we knew so little about it all! Then we'd a horrible scare about codlin moth (though I'm thankful to say that didn't come off ); and then, for two years running, we lost all the potatoes with blight. Next, the kitchen-shed caught fire—nobody knows how; and it burnt right down, and Dad had thought he could do without insuring. Luckily, it was like this one, right away from the house, but oh! the dairy nearly went as well! The water sizzled as we threw it on the walls, and once Bruv, who was drawing up the bucket from the well close by, gasped out, "I can't stand it any longer"—he was only sixteen. But Dad, who was really right inside the dairy, all smothered up in the smoke, shouted out to him, and said, "We MUST!" So, he did. I can see poor old Dad's face now. Oh, I was sorry for him that time; it fair broke him up—if the place had all gone, he'd have died, I do believe. Of course, to us kiddies it didn't really matter much—we didn't know enough, for one thing, and for another, as Sandy said, it was such a change! Anyway, you can pretty well always think how much worse things might have been, can't you?

'Oh, yes, thanks, they're ever so much easier now. We've fifty cows in milk, butter keeps up, and there's talk of building a factory four miles off. And then, if this man that's after the place now, you know, does take it, we'll be able to sell out well, and Dad can leave that hateful store.

'Neighbours? No, of course, we haven't many—nor much time, either, to go and see those that we have; but then, we're a host in ourselves, aren't we? and we can all sing, and most of us can play. That's one thing, though—I do want Eva to get away to town, and have some lessons; you ought to hear her; she *has* got a proper voice! And she's the only one of us all that doesn't like this life, and she tries to boss Bruv and Sandy sometimes, and naturally that doesn't do. Sundays? Oh, well, of course there isn't any church, and if there was, I doubt if we'd ever get, for we're mostly pretty tired, you see, by Sunday. So we just "doss" a bit, read a bit, eat a meal when one happens along, doss again, read again, and wind up with some music in the evening. You've got to milk on Sundays, of course, just the same as weekdays.'

I wondered what the reading was, and asked.

'Oh, just the papers—and a fool of a yarn sometimes. We've none of us got any brains to spare,' says Nance frankly. 'I can't stand reading dry stuff, anyway; can you? There! that's the last bottle; thanks! Now shall we go and pick up windfalls in the orchard? I want to make some apple-pies for tea.'

There was a certain foreigner who came to New Zealand not so very long ago—a Russian, if I remember rightly—and saw a good deal of our workaday doings; and at the end he broke out into this lamentable cry: 'Oh! you live so bad, you do live so bad!' It was not our material existence, nor, happily, our moral, that he intended thus to rebuke; it was the performance of our intellects and spirits. And, as I followed Nance into the orchard, his words came back to me, and I wondered whether, after all, he were not right; whether such as Nance and her family, toiling thus, year in, year out, were not actually, that the farm, forsooth, might prosper, being starved in brain and soul; whether, in fact, they could be said truly to *live* at all? Unlike the Old-World workers, we in this country have no burning wrongs to awake our energies and point us to ideals—or, at any rate, if we have, there are but few of us that have caught fire. Church and chapel, the immemorial 'way-out' from mere existence to so many of our labouring forefathers, mean (whatever the reason; I do but state the fact) very little to our younger generation. Art comes at all times scantly to the back-blocks; and with what hope can Literature appeal to brains exhausted already by the exhaustion of the body? While, on the other hand, what have we in the place of these, to exercise our higher faculties, and so give us, in addition to material existence, *life*? Oh dear! despite our soil and our sunshine, our independence and our labour laws, don't we some of us live really rather 'bad'? In our ardour for 'the land' are we not keeping our regard fixed rather too sedulously upon it? forgetting that the wide-winged air, the lofty sky, are also facts, and unconscious that man really cannot ever live by bread alone; no, not even with the agreeable addition of roast mutton and butter!

Well, it may be that no new country, after the first noble excitements of pioneering have died down, ever quite escapes this peril. It may be with healthy young nations as it is with healthy little boys, that the affairs of the soul interest them a very great deal less keenly than the affairs of the stomach—and, for the time being, rightly so. Nance's next words, moreover, showed that, for her at any rate, one gateway of escape into the larger life was always open—the universal woman's way, of the heart.

For, 'What makes it all so worth while, you see,' she observed confidentially, as down under the leafy fruit-trees we gathered our aprons full of fallen fruit, 'is, that it does make Dad so happy. When one feels dead-beat, you can't think what a stand-by that is. And then, I do love the country; don't you: the animals and flowers and things? We all do, Eva too. Besides . . . oh well!' finished up Nance rather abruptly, and as if she were taking a flying leap over a dangerous reason to a sound conclusion, 'I wouldn't change with any one, not if it was the Queen herself!' I could not help giving a guess at that reason she left in the gap, and unless I am greatly mistaken, the colour of its hair strongly favoured that of Master Miller's.

When we got back with our apples, there was afternoon tea to be prepared, both for paddock and house; then we made the pies, and then it was milking-time. I never knew the hours to fly so fast as they did on that farm. Nance put on a short old skirt and a cotton overall, and led me over to the yard. It was full of cows, creamy and mouse-coloured, brindled and red-and-white, deep chestnut, glossy black; the slanting sun-rays brightened and grew richer as they caressed those shining hides. Benny and Bonny, Flo and Eva had come down from the oats to milk; Mother, too, was quietly taking part with the bucket and stool as a matter of course.

Much to my surprise, there was no leg-roping, and hardly any bailing-up. Silky, Mima, Jewel, Fiddleface, and the rest, knew each her name, responded to the call of it, and stood to be milked, patient and contented, either in the open yard, or else in the paddock that led from it. It really was as though that spirit of willing good-nature which possessed the human members of the farm extended also to the animals—or rather, as Nance had said, they were obviously all pets. Fat old Pudding, the cat, waited for her evening meal in the most peaceful proximity to Watch, who, for his part, having brought in the cows from hillside and gully without any undue fuss or chasing, now lay by the yard-gate, more as a spectator than a sentinel. The very calves were tame already—far too tame, remarked Flo, as with a milk-pail in one hand and a stout stick in the other she dealt out mercy well-spiced with justice to their eager, jostling little host.

Barely were the calves fed, when down trooped all the harvesters, exultant—the oats were stacked! Tea was the next detail, and after tea Dad agreed that there was really time for an hour's music before we need start back for town. The boys had all fallen fast asleep upon the living-room lounges, and nobody had the heart to wake them; but when the dish-washing quickly despatched by our many hands, the rest of us had gathered together in the little sitting-room—furnished with a cottage piano, a few chairs, a big pile of music, and very little else—and Dad had begun to play (one of Schubert's *Moments Musicaux,* if you please!) one by one the missing members all crept in on tiptoe, rubbing their eyes, and mumuring under their breaths. 'That's it!' 'Go it, Dad!' or 'That's good!'

The Schubert ended, he began a glee; upon which the whole family, except Mother, who sat nodding her head while she knitted, but more, I fancied, in maternal than musical appreciation, burst spontaneously into voice, taking the parts and singing them together as though they had but one soul between them. Every note rang true, round, and rich, and Eva especially really had a beautiful contralto. After the glee, Bruv brought out a violin, Benny a 'cello, and Flo took her father's place at the piano, and played their accompaniment. Real music it was; the whole family had evidently a natural gift. Nobody spoke, every one was hanging on sweet sound. It was good to look round on all those absorbed faces; it was fine to feel that uplifted ending to a day that, arduous with toil, had nevertheless throughout been made lively with interest and sweet with love. Perhaps they did not actually 'live so bad' after all, these individual sons and daughters of the soil?

And then it was Good-bye, said lingeringly, and with regret. One felt for Dad, going back into exile. A load of butter and some apples were packed into the back of the gig, last congratulations were exchanged about the oats, and then we were off. An hour's downhill drive in the sweet starlight brought us back into town.

'Ay,' said Dad, as we parted. 'Good kids all, as you say; ne'er a scabby sheep among 'em. Won't be like some I know of, a-wantin' the State to keep their father an' mother in old age, I'll warrant. Only Hughie I s'pose 'll soon be wantin' Nance, an' that girl Eva has got to have lessons. Well, we shall manage. Glad you enjoyed yourself. Good night!'

JAMES COURAGE

# After the Earthquake

The earthquake happened late on a Saturday night in summer and shook all that coast by the sea and the coastal farms and townships for twenty miles inland, as far as the mountains. At the Blakiston homestead everyone had gone to bed and was asleep, but the shake woke Mr Blakiston immediately. When it was over he sat up in bed, lit his candle and looked about him at the bedroom walls and ceiling. Nothing seemed to be cracked or damaged, though the quake had been a sharp one and had heaved the house up for a moment or two and worried it as a dog worries a rabbit's pelt he cannot swallow.

'Are you all right?' Mr Blakiston asked his wife, who was now awake beside him in the double bed.

'Yes, dear, but you'd better find out if Walter's awake. The quake may have scared him.' She had been a good deal scared herself, waking from a dream of ships on the sea.

Her husband leaned up on one elbow, staring at the yellow candle-flame and listening so as to hear any sound from his son's room along the passage. Walter was six and had a room to himself near the head of the stairs.

'He'd call out if he'd been frightened,' said Mr Blakiston, hearing no sound in the house. He blew out the candle and lay back beside his wife. 'A nasty little quake, all the same,' he added. 'A hell of a nasty little quake.' Presently he was asleep again, lying on his back, snoring softly.

In the morning nothing was found damaged about the homestead, except for the old wash-house chimney, out at the back, which had collapsed on to the roof. Indoors, however, in Mr Blakiston's smoking-room, a thin china vase in which he kept hen-feathers for cleaning his pipe had fallen from the edge of the mantelpiece and shattered itself on the brick hearth. At breakfast time he brought the pieces of the vase to the table, in his hand, to show his wife and son.

'English china,' he explained to the boy, pointing to a delicate capital D on what had been the base of the vase. 'You don't get fine stuff like that made in this corner of the world. D stands for Doulton, the people who fired it.'

But Walter was less interested by the vase than by the news of the earthquake which had not wakened him in the night. 'Did the whole house rock?' he asked his father.

'Rocked a bit, yes, and rose a bit.'

'Will the quake have shaken down any houses we know?'

'Not many, I should think. A few ceilings and chimneys down, maybe.'

Walter ate his porridge. 'I'd like to see an earthquake shake down a lot of houses,' he said presently, 'then all the people in them'd get a good fright.'

'Walter,' said his mother, who sat with her back to the windows, at the end of the table, 'you oughtn't to say things like that, without thinking first. It's very selfish.'

'I did think first,' said Walter softly, to his plate.

'What did you say?' asked his mother. 'You know I've told you not to mumble.'

'I only said I wished I'd wakened up in the earthquake,' he said loudly.

That day was a Sunday. Mr Blakiston was a farmer and though there are jobs to be done on a farm all seven days of the week he usually spent Sundays near the homestead and in the home stables and paddocks, resting himself. On one Sunday out of every four the family went to church in the township below the hills of the farm. Today, however, Mr Blakiston, willingly helped by Walter, put on an old dungaree suit and set-to to clear the bricks from the roof of the wash-house, where the chimney had fallen in the night.

Walter always had questions to ask when he worked with his father. 'Do earthquakes happen in England?' he demanded now.

'Yes,' said Mr Blakiston shortly, 'but not often.' He was a practical man, enjoying the manual work, and slightly bored by the way his son always wanted to talk. The breaking of the vase that held his pipe-cleaners, the vase of English china, had taken his thoughts back to the Old Country and he would have preferred to think about it in silence. He had farmed in New Zealand for nearly twenty years but he still thought of England as home, his father's country, the original pattern. Colonial life was freer, less stiff, he liked it better, nevertheless something of the subtle flavour of the English way of living on which it had originally been founded was vanishing fast. The new climate was changing it, adapting its laws and forms to a younger society. And he himself had changed, and was changing, with it. Now, as he worked at heaving bricks from the wash-house roof to the ground, he realized that he would never go back to England, as he had once intended to. He was a colonial farmer for life. He was as pleased as though he himself, and not the years, had made the decision.

'Can I drive to the township with Mum in the morning?' asked Walter, beside him on the roof.

'Yes, if you want to. Ask her yourself. Now get down that ladder and pile those bricks by the wall, ship-shape.'

The following morning at eleven o'clock Mrs Blakiston had the horse and gig brought round to the front door by the odd-jobs man who was also the cowman and gardener at the homestead. Every fine week-day at eleven, wearing a flat grey hat with a veil tied under her chin, she drove to the township, four miles away, to collect the mail and the newspaper and to shop at the store. Summer or winter, she wore long elegant leather gloves to hold the reins.

On this Monday morning Walter went with her, happily hopping down from the gig to open the gates on the road as they came to them. On either side of the road lay wide flat paddocks of tussock-grass, divided by wire fences and burnt yellow by the sun. In the distance, in the summer haze, a mirage of heat flickered along the ridges of the hills. The blue reflection of the sea was on the sky.

When they reached the township, Mrs Blakiston drove the gig

along the straggling street of one- and two-storied buildings and pulled up before the verandah of Lakin's General Store.

'Can I go in?' asked Walter, preparing to jump down.

'Mr Lakin will be out in a moment,' said his mother. She opened her purse and found the list of groceries she wanted. 'We'll wait till he comes.'

Presently the store-keeper, wearing a white apron, came out from the shop-door under the verandah. He shaded his eyes against the morning glare and looked up at the gig. 'Glad to see you're all right after the quake, Mrs Blakiston,' he said in a high tinny voice.

'I'm very well, Mr Lakin, but it did frighten us a little, so late at night. Did you have any damage?'

'I slept through it, myself. A few broken bottles on the floor of the shop yesterday morning, though.'

Mrs Blakiston handed over her list.

'Have you heard about old Mrs Duncaster?' asked the store-keeper.

'Heard about her?' Mrs Blakiston was uncertain.

'The quake brought the plaster of the ceiling down on her. She died of shock, they say, early yesterday.'

'Oh, but what a dreadful thing, Mr Lakin—' said Mrs Blakiston. Walter saw her face tighten and her lips twitch in the sunlight. 'I'd no idea—'

'Well, it was a sudden end,' said the store-keeper, looking vaguely up the street. 'I thought I'd better tell you,' he added. 'I don't like my old customers dying.'

'Yes,' said Mrs Blakiston. 'Thank you, Mr Lakin. I hadn't heard about it, of course. I'll go and call on Miss Duncaster this morning.'

The store-keeper nodded and disappeared into the shop, Mrs Blakiston's list in his hand.

'The Mrs Duncaster who's dead,' said Walter, 'is she the one I know?'

'Yes,' said his mother. 'I'd no notion,' she added quietly. 'Yesterday being Sunday, of course, we didn't hear.

'Did the roof fall right on her face in bed?'

'I don't know, Walter. Don't ask silly questions. You heard what Mr Lakin said.'

'If she'd been properly under the blankets the plaster wouldn't have hit her.'

'She was very old. It's very sad that she's dead,' said Mrs Blakiston. She tilted his sun-hat down over his eyes and made him sit up straight on the hot leather seat of the gig.

'Are we going to visit Miss Duncaster?' he asked, after a moment.

'Yes, we must go and see her. She was very fond of her mother.'

After Mr Lakin had put a tin of biscuits, a bottle of methylated spirits and some smaller parcels into the back of the gig, under the seat, Mrs Blakiston drove up the street to the post office and collected the mail and the newspaper. She then drove straight to the northern end of the township, where the Duncasters lived in one of the oldest homes in the district. Made of cob and with a wooden roof, the small squat cottage was hidden by pine and eucalyptus trees from the road. Inside the fringe of trees a lawn of wild haylike grass, burnt almost red by the sun, bordered the short curving driveway that led up to the verandah.

'Somebody else is here too,' said Walter. He pointed to a saddle horse hitched by the bridle-reins to a hook in one of the verandah posts. The horse was a bay, roughly groomed and shaggy, a farmer's hack.

Mrs Blakiston looked at the horse for a moment as she drove up, then, carefully holding her long skirt, got down from the gig and knocked at the door of the cottage. She knocked twice, in the hot summer silence, before the door was opened by a tall woman wearing a dark grey dress with a white lace collar.

Walter watched his mother greet Miss Duncaster and kiss her on the cheek. He had hoped that Miss Duncaster might have tears in her eyes for a mother killed in an earthquake: he was disappointed that the light blue eyes and the long pink cheeks of Annie Duncaster looked as ordinary as ever.

'You must come in and have tea,' said Miss Duncaster's deep voice to his mother. 'And Walter with you. Please, please do. I'd like it.'

'But you have a visitor already,' hesitated Mrs Blakiston.

Miss Duncaster threw a quick glance at the saddled horse swishing its tail before the verandah. 'Nobody's here,' she said. 'Nobody at all. Do please come in.'

So Mrs Blakiston took the gig into the shade of the eucalyptus trees, tied up the horse, and took Walter with her into the cottage. 'You must be quiet,' she whispered to the boy in the doorway, 'and not ask questions.'

The inside of the cottage was dark and smelled cool after the hot morning. The tiny sitting-room behind the verandah was made even smaller by the glass cases of china and the shelves of books against the walls. A large, creamy-white ostrich egg hung by a string in a corner, by far the most interesting thing, to Walter, in the whole room. When Miss Duncaster had brought in the tea, he sat himself down so that he could gaze at this amazing egg while his mother talked.

'I've only just heard about your mother, Annie,' said Mrs Blakiston. 'I'm so very sorry.'

'Mother hated earthquakes,' Miss Duncaster said evenly. 'We had a bad one here, you know, just after Father and she had first come from England. She'd always been frightened of them since then.'

'They frighten me too. Did your mother die quite suddenly?'

'A little of the ceiling fell, you know, in her room, I got her out of bed and into a chair and ran downstairs to make her a cup of tea. When I got back she was dead.' Miss Duncaster put down her cup and gazed out of the window. 'It was all a great shock to me. The earthquake itself and then my mother dead.'

'I slept all through the earthquake,' put in Walter, 'didn't I, Mum?'

Mrs Blakiston ran her fingers over the gloves in her lap. 'Yes, dear, luckily,' she said.

Miss Duncaster, who had begun to sniffle, suddenly cheered up and said, 'Of course, my mother was no longer a young woman. Still, even at sixty, one likes to live. And she had had a wonderful life, you know. Young people like me can't hope for nearly so much.'

'Yes, Annie, I know,' said Mrs Blakiston, who knew also that old Mrs Duncaster had been seventy if she'd been a day and that her daughter was thirty-five. 'It is hard for you, being left alone,' she added.

Miss Duncaster got up, fumbling in her belt for her handkerchief. 'Oh, thank you, thank you. But I shan't let myself be lonely.' She glanced quickly out of the window, then moved to the door. 'I'd like you to come and see my mother now,' she said. 'She's lying upstairs in Father's old room. She looks beautiful.'

'Yes, of course I'll come up,' said Mrs Blakiston. 'Walter, you stay down here for a few minutes.'

'Oh, but I want Walter to see her too,' said Miss Duncaster. 'She always loved children, you know.'

The stairs were almost as narrow as a ladder and so dark that Miss Duncaster lit a candle to usher the boy and his mother round the stair-head and along the upper passage. The air, close under the roof, was as warm as the inside of a bird's nest.

'In here,' said Miss Duncaster, opening a door. She made Mrs Blakiston and Walter go in first, while she blew out the candle.

The small bedroom was crowded with dark furniture and lit only by a window in the slope of the roof. The bed was against the wall by the door, and on the bed, covered by a sheet up to her chin, lay the dead Mrs Duncaster. Walter was startled: the creamy-white, oval face was like the ostrich-egg downstairs, he thought, except that somebody had pinched into it a nose and mouth and drawn a grim line down each cheek. He hadn't remembered that old Mrs Duncaster looked so severe: she had always laughed at him and given him jujubes.

On a table at the head of the bed stood a vase full of green leaves and large open milky flowers that gave out a thick smell of lemons into the room.

'Magnolias,' said Mrs Blakiston gently, her head on one side. She loved flowers. 'Beautiful,' she added.

'I picked them from the garden,' said Miss Duncaster. 'Mother planted the tree the year I was born. It has grown up with me. I felt she'd like to have the flowers beside her now.'

'Yes,' said Mrs Blakiston, 'yes, Annie, of course.'

Walter turned aside from the bed to look at a box made of dark polished wood. It stood on the floor by the window, with brass handles and a lock of inlaid steel.

'That was Father's instrument case,' explained Miss Duncaster, beside him. 'He was a doctor, you know—the first doctor the district had. All his scalpels and things are in that box.'

'Did he come from England?' asked Walter.

'A long time ago, in a sailing ship, with my mother. Mother was home-sick all her life for England, but she didn't go back, even when Father died.'

At that moment Walter saw that one of old Mrs Duncaster's hands was showing under the edge of the sheet on the bed and that the hand held a book with an animal of some sort printed in gold on the black cover. 'What's that?' he asked, pointing.

'My mother's Bible,' said Miss Duncaster.

'No, I meant the—'

'Oh, the crest on the cover? That's a griffon, my mother's family crest. She was proud of that.' Miss Duncaster sighed, and added, to Walter's mother: 'I never knew any of the English family, of course. They meant nothing to me. I'm a colonial.' She pulled the sheet over the dead hand and straightened the magnolias in their vase by the bed. 'The funeral is the day after tomorrow,' she finished in a firm voice.

Presently they went downstairs, Mrs Blakiston said that she and Walter must be going home.

'You have been so kind,' said Miss Duncaster, smoothing her fair, fluffy hair. She seemed to be looking round the sitting-room for something to give them as a reward. 'Wait now and I'll cut you some magnolias from the garden, before you go. Yes, let me.'

The huge magnolia tree, with dark leaves shining in the sun and with white flowers high up like seabirds in the branches, grew at the back of the house. While Mrs Blakiston and Walter stood and watched, Miss Duncaster made big agile leaps to get at the flowering branches. She dragged them down and broke off the creamy heads, careful not to bruise the petals.

'They go brown so easily,' she explained. She laughed, with flushed and untidy face, handing over the bouquet to Walter. 'He's amazed I can jump so high,' she said to Mrs Blakiston, laughing again, this time at the boy's face.

'I only jump like that when I'm jumping for joy,' said Walter. 'Don't I, Mum? I can jump a hell of a height.'

'What did I hear you say, Walter?'

He had picked up the bad expression from his father. 'I can jump as high as my belt,' he amended softly, swinging the bunch of magnolias in his hand.

They walked round to the front of the house. While Mrs Blakiston went into the shade of the trees to fetch the gig, Walter was left with Miss Duncaster. He looked round and saw that the riding horse that had been tied to the verandah post was no longer there.

'Where's the horse gone?' he asked.

'What a funny boy you are,' said Miss Duncaster. 'What horse?'

He pointed with the magnolias. 'It was over by the verandah,' he said. 'We saw it.'

Miss Duncaster bent down and gave him a sudden sharp slap on the arm 'You're bruising the flowers,' she snapped. 'There was no horse.'

Mrs Blakiston drove up with the gig. 'Come along, Walter. Say good-bye nicely to Miss Duncaster.'

On the way home from the township with his mother Walter said: 'I didn't ask too many questions, did I?'

'No,' said his mother doubtfully, 'not as many as I expected.'

'Then why did she slap me?'

'I don't believe she did. You invent such things.'

That evening when Mr Blakiston came in from the farm to a late tea he glanced at the big bowl of magnolias in the middle of the dining-room table.

'Not ours, are they?' he asked.

'No.' His wife told him of their morning visit to the Duncasters and of Mrs Duncaster's death in the earthquake. While she talked she fiddled on the table with the broken pieces of the vase of English china that had held her husband's pipe-cleaners and that had fallen during the night. She was sticking them together with seccotine. Walter, his own tea finished, watched her and listened to her talking.

'Of course it's terrible for Annie, being left alone in that old cottage,' he heard her say presently to his father, 'though I must say she seemed very brave about it.'

'Brave?' Mr Blakiston paused. 'I should think she's damn well delighted! For ten years and more she's been cooped up at home looking after that old woman. She'll have a chance to marry now.'

'I don't think she's the marrying kind.'

'Don't you believe it. I hear more than you do.'

'Does Joe Sleaver ride a bay horse?' Walter put in suddenly.

Mr Blakiston looked surprised. He took his pipe from between his lips and studied the bowl of it before answering. 'Yes,' he said, 'now I come to think of it, he does ride a bay.'

'Walter,' interposed Mrs Blakiston warningly to the boy, 'you know what I said to you to-day, about not asking questions, don't you.'

'I only meant—' began Walter, and stopped.

'I wish,' said Mr Blakiston, 'I wish I knew what the devil you were both talking about. Why shouldn't Joe Sleaver ride a bay horse if he wants to?'

'Walter thinks he saw a bay horse tied up to the Duncasters' verandah this morning,' explained Mrs Blakiston.

'I did see it,' cried Walter. 'Mum saw it too!'

His father and mother exchanged a glance. Then, with his pipe in his mouth, Mr Blakiston leant forward and lightly took up from the table a piece of the vase his wife was mending with seccotine. 'Well,' he said offhandedly, grinning as he spoke, 'well, we don't have earthquakes every night.'

'I did see the horse,' insisted Walter, and felt that like all older people his parents were in some sort of conspiracy against his finding things out. 'I did see the horse.'

'Of course you saw the damned horse,' said his father suddenly. 'Shut up about it, that's all.' And he went on, to his wife, evenly: 'I was thinking yesterday, you know, I shall probably never go back to the Old Country. It's too far away now, too long ago.'

ALICE F. WEBB

# The Patriot

War had been declared some weeks before the news came as far as our place. It was mail day, and we were looking out of the door every few minutes to see who would get the first sight of M'Intosh's pack-horse on the far cutting. Nugget, the old white horse we used for odd jobs, had been saddled some time, and was standing with the reins on his neck, fast asleep. It was never any good to start to our mail box, a soap box nailed on the side of a high stump two miles from the whare, until the pack-horse was in sight coming down Gentle Annie, because he had to jog about three miles to the junction, driven by M'Intosh, who was never in a hurry, knowing as he did all the happenings in the outside world.

When mail day only comes round once a fortnight, the last hour or two before the mailman comes seems interminable.

We had, as was our custom, knocked off an hour early on mail day, and were busy preparing our dinner. I think on most back-block holdings mail day is kept as a kind of Sunday or holiday. I know it was with us. We kept Sunday, too, in a kind of half-hearted way; that is to say, we did not go on with the usual work, fencing or scrub-cutting or whatever we were doing at the time. Instead, we washed and mended our clothes and swept the house out, and sometimes hung our blankets out in the sun to air, if we thought of it. Jim used to mend our boots also: it was a day for quiet jobs and a change from our everyday occupations, and we had our dinner at twelve and made a plum duff because there was time to cook it while we were all about the whare. That was the best we could do for Sundays, but the real holiday of the week was Friday, the day when we got the papers and the letters from those dear to us from whom we were separated.

M'Intosh seemed to be later than ever that day. We had put the potatoes to boil, and the billy of fresh water for the tea hung over the fire also. It was my turn to ride across for the mail bag, so Jim was trimming the fat off the chips ready for frying, and throwing the trimmings to the dogs. At last he called to me, as I was behind the whare fetching an armful of dry wood up, 'He's coming.'

I did not take long about chucking that wood into the corner and getting on old Nugget, and Nugget, knowing the different manners of his riders, did not take long about waking up from his dreams and lumping himself along the track to the boundary gate either. M'Intosh, contrary to his morose habit of life, which usually induced him to thrust our mail into the box and slouch on down the main track with only a grunt for salutation, sat upon his horse waiting, and as I came within earshot he called, 'War is declared, Jack!'

'What war?' I said. 'Civil war in Ireland?' For the papers had been full of Home Rule and Irish unrest for weeks back, and as it was two weeks since we had seen a paper, and the newest we ever got were two days old when they reached us, there was time for quite a lot to take place in the world without our knowledge or consent.

'German war,' said M'Intosh briefly. 'Fools' war—madness, I call it. Picking a quarrel with all the world at once. Fools!' He gave a final grunt of farewell, and jogged heavily away after the pack-horse, now out of sight, on his way to the township, nine or ten miles away, where their journey ended.

I grabbed the mail bag and raced for home. At last there was a change in the monotony of things: life would begin to move, we should have real news to read and talk over. I arrived at the whare door in a hot state of excitement, shouting the news to Jim as I came, in much the same fashion that M'Intosh had used towards me. Like myself, Jim's first thought was of Ireland. He also gave a sigh of relief on being told that the trouble was elsewhere. Jim was older than I by some years, and had only missed taking a share in the Boer War by the, to him, unfortunate fact that peace was declared just as he succeeded in getting himself accepted for the last contingent. He had been across to South Africa, but was not able to remain there in the South African Constabulary, as he had hoped, for health reasons and family claims.

These claims and reasons would keep him at home still if there should be any volunteer forces used in the war now commencing. As we sat over our dinner, reading the papers and talking of the news contained in our home letters, we decided that there would be no need for colonial aid to England. 'Probably it is all over now,' said Jim. 'One week would be quite long enough to lay out Germany.'

But when his week had gone, and another week after it, and still Germany was not 'laid out', we began to consider the possibilities of a Dominion contingent, and discuss my chance of acceptance in it should I be able to offer myself. It seemed, somehow, impossible to keep quietly pegging away at our work. Anyway, I could not. Old Jim seemed to manage to give his attention to the usual dull round of work. The section we were working was nominally mine; that is, I was the lucky one who drew it in the land ballot. Old Jim was my partner, and it was his savings which had purchased the sheep we had on the place. We had got it ring-fenced, because, of course, the drawers of the adjoining sections had done their share towards that, and we had built the whare, or rather Jim had; I am not much of a carpenter.

Now we were busy with the second subdivision fence, which was to enclose about ten acres of extra good land near the whare, which we hoped to stump and plough ready for the sowing of turnips for the fattening sheep.

Somehow it seemed as if nothing of that kind mattered any more. It was all very well for Jim to say that it was a duty of every patriot to work harder than ever on his land, and to raise more fat stock and grow more wool, and all that sort of thing. To me it seemed more of a duty to get on my way to the front as soon as possible, and just finish up the war right at the beginning, because, of course, if a few of our Dominion boys got on to the Germans they'd have it all settled up quick and lively. Anyway, that was what I thought at the time, and I must say old Jim was jolly decent about it. He used to laugh at me a good deal, particularly when I kept making excuses to get off to the township, being unable to wait for mail day to come round and give us the news. And looking back on it all now, I see that he was awfully patient with me. There are very few chaps who would have just kept on pegging away at the fence alone, and done more than half of the odd jobs round too, and never a growl out of him all the time. And the work went on quickly too. By the time the Government had despatched the first lot of men, the crowd that went to Samoa, our fence was done, and the stumping was started.

I had quite made up my mind to offer to go with the next crowd that went to the front if I could get myself accepted. I remember as if it were yesterday my feelings on the night when I sent in my name to the Defence Force authorities. There had been what was called 'a patriotic social' in the township, which I attended—you know the kind of thing they have in these little places. There is a great display of red, white, and blue in the decorations, most of the people wear colours in their buttonholes, it is not thought rude to join in the chorus of any patriotic songs, and you have a jolly good supper, sometimes a dance too. For all this you pay 1*s*. or 2*s*. 6*d*. if it's a dance as well, and you have the time of your life, 'proceeds in aid of the starving Belgians' or 'to benefit the War Fund'.

All the same, I agree with Jim in thinking that the 'starving Belgians' would have got a shock if they had seen us stuffing our-

selves with cake and sandwiches in their interest, and that the War
Funds might have benefited to a larger extent if the money spent on
hire of halls, and lighting, etc., had been given straight out. I don't
count costs of advertising and so forth, because nearly all newspapers were doing that free for the good of the cause. Jim would not
go to any of the patriotic parties. He said he would give what he
could spare all the same, but he'd give it straight out. He had a map
with pins to mark the progress of events, on the wall by his bed, and
he used to be always poring over that when I got home, unless it were
very late, in which case he was fast asleep in bed.

Well, as I said, the night I sent in my name, I had been to such a
party. There were short speeches by various prominent men, and
much chorus singing and display of colours, and when the chairman
said that he had the needful forms of application to the Defence
Department in the little back room awaiting the signatures of any
who were offering, I went and put my name down, together with two
other fellows. For all their singing of 'Tipperary' and 'Rule Britania'
there did not appear to be an overwhelming rush from our district,
although people had given some horses, and more cash than you
would have thought could be raised in so short a time.

I rode home feeling very elated. If I were taken what a change I
was in for. All the pleasure of a real good holiday, all the excitement
of a fight, and the knowledge that my expenses would be guaran-
teed as well. I wasn't thinking then of the scanty rations, the damp beds,
sore feet, and wearing uncertainty which one who takes part in a war
has to bear as best he may. When I got home Jim was fast asleep, and
it struck me that he was growing awfully thin and haggard-looking.
And as I got into bed I began to think whether I had done quite a
fair thing in volunteering without consulting him (for though we
had spoken of my going it had been more as a joke than with any
serious intention); since, if I went he must be left to face the heavy
drag of the half-yearly payments still to be made on the section.

Still, it was done now, and one must be patriotic and serve one's
country in its hour of need. So I concluded that I was right after all,
and in the morning, when I told Jim about it, he said it was only what
he had been expecting to hear for a week or two back, and that he
thought he could manage all right by a little extra hard graft, if I left
him a power of attorney, and we put all our affairs in order. So that
day we both went into the township for once, and we made all our
arrangements, and I received a wire ordering me to report to the
nearest town for medical inspection, which I did, riding straight on,
while Jim went home alone.

In the town I got a bad disappointment for, having passed the doctor easily enough, I found the military authorities would not take my horse, as he was above the regulation height, and too heavy as well. This was a facer, because I had put my name down as bringing my own horse and saddle.

I went home feeling pretty sick about it, with orders to come into camp tomorrow, and go into training for the foot regiment if a horse was not procurable. Fancy me on foot; I don't suppose I had walked half a dozen miles at a stretch in my life.

I reached the whare about tea-time, full of gloom. With a decent horse I could be back the same evening and ready to go into Palmerston Camp with the other fellows from our part.

Of course if it had been Jim who had volunteered there would have been no difficulty. On his last birthday his uncle in Gisborne had given him a horse that—well it was a horse—just the right size and a good black. He had owned that animal nearly a year now, and the fuss he made over it amused all our neighbours. I knew he had refused lots of money for Dan, as he called it. He often said money would not buy that horse. Well, it was no good thinking of it; I should have to be a 'gravel scatcher' after all, but I did not feel half as patriotic as I had done the day before.

When I reached the whare I found Jim had got our meal ready, and had been putting my razor and a few handkerchiefs and socks and things together for me. 'Hurry up, Jack,' he said. 'Get your tea down and be ready. I've heard all about it from M'Intosh when he brought the mail in. I'll have mine later. You just hurry while I get your horse,' and he went out. I ate what tea I could, thinking that he was getting old Nugget for me to go up to the township and go on by coach. When I had finished I went out, and there was Dan ready with Jim's new saddle on, and my swag fastened on all ready. I could not say a thing. I just stared. 'You'll have to take my saddle, Jack,' said a sort of growling voice from the other side of the horse. 'Yours doesn't fit him. Good-bye, old man, good luck.' Jim emerged from behind Dan, shook me violently by the hand, and began fiddling with the bridle. I stammered something, I don't quite know what, but he would not listen to a word, so at last I mounted and rode away while he returned to the lonely whare and shut the door.

The time in camp was like a real picnic. I liked my camp mates, I liked the drill, the uniform, and all the military trappings amused me. Dan was beyond question the finest horse in our company and everything was just as lively and altogether good as my highest expectations. Old Jim wrote regularly and fairly cheerfully; he seeemd to be getting along with the work like a steam engine. As he stumped at one end of the paddock a neighbour had been engaged to begin ploughing at the other end, so that no time or weather should be lost. But the luck was not with him—it never was. Although he got the work finished and the seed in at the right time the weather wasn't right. The bright, hot days that made the camp such a cheery place kept the ground hard and dry, and the seed lay idly in the soil, making no sign of sprouting.

High winds raged day and night for a fortnight after the only shower those turnips had on them, and so that crop failed. The sheep that should have been sold fat were a drug in the market, as stores, and the money they should have brought was needed for that half-yearly payment due on the land.

Jim sold some of his private possessions to make up the shortage, although I did not know that at the time. He wrote me a hearty letter of good wishes just as we went on board ship to sail, in which he said the payment had been made all right on the due date, and not to worry, but to do my duty and serve the King as a man should.

There was a great public farewell to us all in the Basin Reserve in Wellington, and a procession through the streets afterwards. Women cried, and bands played, and men shook everybody near them by the hand whether they knew them or not, and what with all the cheering and excitement, we thought ourselves jolly fine fellows, I can tell you. 'Defenders of the Empire's honour' and 'Upholders of the cause of justice' and phrases of that sort are calculated to give a young fellow what is known as 'swelled head'. And then in the middle of it all I had a mental vision of Old Jim, doing two men's work and fighting an uneven battle in lonely dullness, and a heavy weight of unshared liabilities to face as best he could, giving up his cherished Dan, with the almost certain knowledge that he would never see him again, bearing it all so cheerfully and putting up such a plucky fight, and I said to myself, 'I wonder after all which of us is the Patriot?'

FRANK S. ANTHONY

# Winter Feeding the Herd

The year our swede crops were such a rotten failure, Gus Tomlins and I put our heads together and worked out a scheme for feeding our cows that winter. Gus slipped over to tea one night with a perfectly brainy proposition. While I was frying the steak over the fire he started to tell me about it.

Gus and I live about a mile from the Mount Egmont National Reserve, and Gus suggested why not bung about ten cows each up there and let them fossick for tucker in the bush. He said he saw four cows come out of there one winter, and they were simply rolling fat.

Everybody knew leaves were good for cows—hadn't I seen farmers feeding sick cows on leaves time and time again? I have seen that, but I was always under the impression they didn't happen to have any hay or turnips to give the cows. Gus said, No, it was medicine for them. That was the idea. While we were discussing the plan, Gus got his eye rivetted on a mouse that was balancing itself on the rim of my milk jug, trying to reach for a drink. He said he never came over to my place but what he saw something revolting.

I don't see any reason to be so superior over a little thing like that. As I showed him, the milk was too low down for the mouse to reach, and anyhow I often caught the little beggars like that. Gus said even if they couldn't reach down they left their feet marks on the rim, but what does that matter—a man can always pour the milk out of the side that hasn't any feet marks. That didn't suit Gus either. I had to wash out the jug, and get some fresh milk out of the milk can before he would have any.

I think myself, that when a man is out visiting he should take things as he finds them, and not go putting people to a lot of needless trouble. But that's Gus all over. Unless he has a man all on edge, he isn't satisfied. He went on about the plan again after I had satisfied his finicky mind over the milk, and said if we started in the morning and sorted ten of our youngest cows out, we could pop them straight up, and leave them there two months at least.

I wouldn't have been in on this proposition at all only a man had either to do that or buy feed, and I allowed Gus to persuade me.

Next morning we sorted our cows out and took them up to the reserve. It looked a pretty desolate sort of show to turn milkers into, miles and miles of swamp, boulders, and heavy timber, but not much of anything a cow could make a meal on. That was my opinion anyhow, but Gus said, 'What rot! That's just where cows would thrive. Look at the shelter.'

Cows can't live on shelter, in spite of what Gus tried to jam down my throat, but Gus said that would be all right; we would dog them well back on to the dry ridges, and they would have stacks of tucker there.

We dogged them back like that every day for nearly a week. Gus and I took turns, nipping up to the reserve every morning and shooting them back into the bush. Next morning they would all be back hanging over the fence again, and looking as hollow and haggard as if they were going through a great famine. I told Gus in the end that that sort of thing was no good to me. I wanted more than ten cows to milk next season, and if we left those up in the reserve much longer, they were going to pass out on us. Gus has a glimmering of commonsense now and again and he said, all right, we would both go up in the morning and bring them back home. When we got up there we got quite a surprise, because there wasn't a single solitary cow to be seen.

They had all left the fence and gone on a forage for something to eat in sheer desperation. Gus was as pleased as Punch about it. He kept rubbing his hands and stalking about, until he gave me the pip. 'There you are, Mark. What did I say? What did I tell you? Ain't I right, after all? By cripes, old man, if we'd done what you wanted instead of following my advice, look what a hole we'd have been in!'

I let him go on. I felt a bit pleased about it myself. It relieved my mind considerably not to have to feed those ten cows for two months. We decided to go up about once a week and keep a tally on them, although Gus reckoned it wasn't really necessary, because now they had settled down they would be as snug and safe as churches.

The first time we went up into the reserve to muster our stock we didn't hurry ourselves.

Gus came over and had some dinner with me first, and then we sat by the fire for an hour or so, while he explained exactly what steps we would take to get them together. I was to start off towards the mountain house, and then circle back and meet him. He arranged to take the other direction, and as we came across cows we were to leave them behind, but keep tally. If they were in good feed it was no use disturbing them. Gus complained all the way up about the taste of the curry I had given him for dinner. He kept making noises down in his throat, and belching and rolling his eyes about. If he didn't like the curry why did he eat it? That's what I asked him. I never invited him over to dinner, anyhow. I knew the curry was all right because I had used some three years before when I bought it first. I had it stuck on a shelf behind some other stuff, or it would have been used up long before. My own opinion about Gus is that he eats such a lot of bread and butter that if he gets a decent feed it makes him bilious.

When we got to the reserve he lay down under a tree, and I had to start mustering without him. I circled round to the right and then worked back, but no cows were about, so I decided they had all worked in the opposite direction. The Mountain Reserve is a pretty rough proposition. I found that out. If I wasn't getting bogged in some nightmare of a morass, I found myself getting into hopeless tangles of lawyers and supplejacks. It started to get dusk before I had found any cattle, and I knew if I left it till dark I could never find my way out, so I abandoned the search and made for Gus and the track.

On my way back I came across a beast tied up in vines. She was lying down in a wallow of mud, and I had to strike matches before I could identify her. It was a relief to discover that she didn't belong to either Gus or me, although I couldn't help wondering who had the cheek to run her in in a Government Reserve. They must have known it was not lawful, and I felt hurt about it. I cut her adrift with my pocket knife and she got on her feet and treed me in a tawa tree. I sat up there for an hour before I thought of cooeeing for Gus. I heard Gus cooee back and then he came blundering through the darkness towards me. He had been rambling about since dusk looking for me under the impression I was bushed. His last 'Cooee' brought him within a chain of me, and when he heard me answer he started to go crook.

He had just got to the place where I had a thick wooden head full of sawdust, when the cow took exception to his noise and charged. Only that she was a bit wobbly on her pins, I should have had to go home without Gus that night.

Then he settled himself on the branch of a small white pine, and I told him exactly what I thought of him and his Mountain Reserve.

While the cow did a war dance under Gus, I slipped out of my tree and gained a chain before she twigged me. Then while she superintended my climb up, Gus wriggled down and made a chain or two. We worked that stunt on her for over an hour, until we had almost gained the clearing, and then she suddenly gave a disdainful snort and toddled peacefully away.

It was a good job for Gus and me that we had a bright moonlight night to do our mustering in, or we should not have got out of that reserve that night. As it was we reached Gus's house after ten o'clock, and Gus asked me in to tea. He said he was as hungry as a hunter, and not having any dinner was no use to him any more. Next time he went up there, he said, he intended to have a good square meal before he started out, and take a snack up as well.

I pointed out that he had had dinner at my place that day, and he said, 'Oh, that!' and started to explain what a good job it was for him that his stomach had been strong enough to throw it up. He said he sat under that tree in the reserve and nearly broke a blood vessel; he was so sick. I hoped he would profit by such a lesson and not make such a gorging pig of himself another time, but nobody could have persuaded Gus it wasn't my fault.

While Gus was frying some bacon and eggs I took a look round. Gus has about twenty pairs of socks, and nineteen of them were hung on a string in front of the fire. As soon as the heat began to hit them they started to steam and smell, and once as Gus pulled the eggs off the fire to inspect them, a sock fell into the pan. I had to tell him about it. He said it was funny the silly little things I got upset about.

I don't profess to be very faddy about tucker myself, and if they'd been clean socks I wouldn't have minded, but Gus doesn't believe in washing socks. He says he has job enough laying his hands on a dry pair now, without going and deliberately wetting them. Another thing I don't like about Gus's house-keeping is the way he makes his tea. He boils the water in a big pot without a lid, and when he goes to ladle it out into the teapot, he has to navigate round with the ladle so as to dodge the dead matches, chips and things that are floating on top. I don't wonder he comes over to my bach so often—he does get a little decent cleanliness there.

After tea we discussed what we would do in the morning. Gus didn't attach much importance to the fact that I hadn't found any of our cows. He gave me the impression that it was just what he expected of me. Said it was a pity he hadn't been fit, it would have saved us another trip up there, but never mind, he would lead me right to them in the morning; they would all be together on a ridge he knew of. We made a fairly early start next morning and took our dinner up with us. Gus reckoned we had better stick together and the he wouldn't be worried out of his life looking for me, after he had found the cows. He kept finding ridges and saying, 'Ah! here we are,' until after one o'clock, but they all proved to be not the ridge he meant. After a snack, we set off again, only I took a different direction from Gus. Gus worked in a sawmill up Taihape way once, when he was about eighteen, and it gave him the notion that he was a qualified bushman.

How a man can fancy that a job of sawdust boy for a week or two can help him to locate cattle in Mount Egmont Reserve beats me, but when I told him so I got snubbed.

He asked me what bush experience I had ever had that I should sneer at a man who had made a living by it. When I pointed out that it must have been a pretty poor sort of living if he only lasted out a fortnight, he said, 'All right, you know so much, you take your own track and I'll take mine, only, by cripes, Mark, don't expect me to hunt round half the night finding you as I had to yesterday.'

He said that when he had counted up his ten cows, he intended to go home, and I could go to blazes; he was tired of keeping me out of trouble. I hooked off on my own and rambled aimlessly about until the sun was getting low, and then I made for the track.

Gus and I hit the clearing about the same time, and the first thing we saw was our twenty cows, camped alongside the fence, chewing their cuds. They must have come out to enjoy the sunshine, and probably been there for hours.

We felt just as pleased as if we had hunted them out ourselves, and Gus said now they were settled down, there was no need for us to bother them until we wanted to take them home. He said the reason he had missed them was because I had kept up such a discontented whine; it threw him off his scent, listening to me.

We didn't trouble ourselves for about six weeks after that. Gus was busy flying all over Taranaki on his motor bike, taking some red-headed tart to football matches and such like, and he said it would be dangerous for me to go up without him; I was bound to get bushed, and he was too busy to be bothered having to waste a day hunting for me.

When we did start up to get them the fun commenced.

Gus had been moping about with a face as long as crowbar for nearly a week, and the motor bike was getting a spell, so I knew what it was going to be. Whenever he gets like that, I have to keep quiet and listen to him going into ecstasies because he has had so much sense and kept single all his life. That sort of thing is all rot, anyhow. I know why I'm a bachelor; it's because I got disheartened and slung in the towel. Gus would have been tied up years ago, only for the girls.

Every time he gets the lemon he tries to put up a bluff, that his crash is according to programme, but he can't fool me about it.

I decided I was going a different way to Gus that morning. He could mumble and grunt to the trees and shrubs. I've had too much of that nonsense to volunteer for a whole day of it.

Gus and I hunted that reserve high and low and by nightfall had fifteen cows, seven of mine and eight of Gus's. We had to leave the rest till next day. We set out next day on another long stern hunt and found one. The next day I was crossing a gully and spotted one of mine down at the bottom with her neck broken.

Then we had two days' fruitless search, and on the third day we ran into a sad-faced settler from somewhere round Opunake side of the Mountain. He was looking for a brindle and a fawn. Had we seen them by any chance?

He told us he had run across three cows answering to ours about ten miles away, in terrible rough country, and gave us directions.

It was too late to go that day, so we made an early start in the morning and located them about three in the afternoon.

One of them had calved, and as soon as the calf spotted us, it disappeared into some low scrub, followed by its parent, and we had to leave them and bring out the other two. We got within a mile or so of the track when darkness set in, and we could get no further. Gus said if we left them they would hang about all right, and we could slip them out on to the road as soon as we came up next day, and then make back and get the cow and calf as well.

Next day it rained cats and dogs, and Gus sat by my fire all day critizing the way I had mismanaged the whole business.

If he hadn't been so busy that winter, Gus said those cows would all have been home long ago, but he trusted me to do my share and this was the result. I don't call taking red-haired girls about being busy, myself. I reckon it's just plain sloppy nonsense, but to listen to Gus one would imagine he'd been running Bill Massey's job all winter.

When we got into the reserve again, those two cows had disappeared, and we put in a soul-blistering week hunting them up again.

Every time Gus and I ran into each other while out searching we would commence to say a few things. Gus got the idea into his head I was following him round in case I got lost, and I had a suspicion Gus was stopping on one ridge loafing about, and every time I crossed the ridge I spotted him before he had time to hide. It was a good job for both of us when the cows turned up on the clearing one evening, although how they found that clearing again without running into Gus or I is a poser. Gus explained why, however. He said it was the habit I had of mooning about with my head down and my eyes shut—unless I actually ran into a beast I hadn't a possible chance of finding it.

Then we only had the cow and calf to bring home. I did three more days up there hunting for her, and then I slung my hand in. She belonged to Gus and he seemed to fancy a man ought to stick to it until we did get her, but I had a suspicion some settler from the other side of the mountain had found her running wild and annexed her. Anyhow, we never saw her again, and unless Gus hunts her up himself and brings her down off that reserve I never intend to see her.

The sickening part of the whole thing is the rotten attitude Gus took up about it. He seems to forget I lost a cow as well, and people get the idea, listening to him, that the reason he never got his cow out was because he trusted her to me while he hunted up two of mine.

FRANK SARGESON      # Last Adventure

The one and only time when I visited a certain seaside place in the far north of New Zealand was when I'd just left school. My mother had had an illness all through the spring, and towards Christmas the doctor ordered her away to the seaside. And as I was finishing with school that summer my father said I might as well have a decent holiday before I started on a job in his office early in the New Year.

In those days it was a quiet place up in the north there, a very old settled place with a row of Norfolk pines planted along the beach, and after living all my life in a country town I thought nothing could have been finer. Although to begin with my mother was rather difficult. She was far from being really well again, and she expected me to stay with her nearly all day while she sat in a deck chair in the shade of the pines. But later on we got to know some of the people in the settlement (they were nearly all retired lawyers and colonels, and people of that type), so most days I could get mother settled in her deck chair among the ladies along at the croquet lawn. They'd promise to keep an eye on her, and then I was free to go off and explore the coast. And it was on one of these occasions that I met the old man my story is about.

You had to walk a fair way along the coast before you came to where he lived. He'd built himself a shack among the sandhills, and he'd mainly used old pieces of corrugated iron. It was a hot sort of place to live in in summer, but then in summer he was hardly ever inside, and wintertime, he said, he could always keep a fire going with the driftwood that he picked up along the beach.

The first time I came on him he was in having a swim and he seemed to be enjoying himself. He was well sunburnt, and he had such an extraordinary growth of shaggy hair on his chest that when he stood up chest-high in the water, it floated on the surface like seaweed. He looked very old to me. He had on only a small pair of trunks and he was sunburnt all over, and I thought that at one time he must have been a lot heftier than he was then, as in places his skin hung in folds and reminded me of a rhinoceros that I'd seen in a zoo. Anyhow we said good-day to each other and he came out of the water and took me up to his shack and gave me a drink of his homebrew. It was the first time in my life I'd tasted any sort of brew, and I must say I found the taste to my liking.

But that first day he didn't open out much, although he told me that his name was Fred Holmes, and he seemed to like having me there to talk to, so it wasn't long before I got into the habit of always heading in his direction whenever I could leave my mother. He owned an old dinghy and he'd take me out fishing with him, although most of my time I'd have to spend in baling to keep us from sinking. And it was while we were fishing, or while we were lying in the sand after having a swim, that he told me about his life.

He'd been born in a Devonshire market town, and his father had been a solicitor (my own father was a public accountant, I told him) but when he was fifteen he'd cleared out and gone to sea in a wind-jammer. The trip had been across to New York and he'd got left there. It was over a girl. Her father kept a saloon on the water-front, and on the night the ship was sailing he thought he'd like to say good-bye to her just once more, even though he'd already said good-bye a good many times over. So he climbed up on some big pipes that were stacked endways underneath her window. But up on top he'd slipped down inside one of the pipes, and that had put the lid on things properly. The girl's father hadn't taken to him too kindly and he didn't feel like making a row, but there was no way of getting out. So he'd missed his ship, and for a time he'd had a tough spin living from hand to mouth on odd jobs he picked up on the waterfront. But later on he'd got another ship and finished up with her in Fremantle. This time he deserted on purpose. He thought he'd try his luck on the goldfields.

Well, he told me endless tales of his adventures and I suppose they were commonplace enough. I'd read any number of stories of such adventures and had many a wild longing to experience them myself, but they seemed so far removed from the everyday life of a small country town that I supposed I'd never have the courage to make the break. But it was somewhat different hearing them firsthand from Fred Holmes. He had a narrative gift that thrilled me as scarcely any book had ever done, and when I'd go back to the croquet lawn to help mother back to our boarding-house, and be offered a cup of tea when only an hour or so before I'd been drinking the old man's homebrew, I'd feel quite sick at the thought of how tame most people's lives were. Never in my life had I met anyone like Fred Holmes. But I was young, of course, and didn't know much.

The days passed and I could think of nothing but Fred Holmes and his adventures. And each fresh episode that he told me stirred me up more than the one before. His tales were of pearling and wild life in Broome, of life in the mounted police and on the goldfields. Later on he'd come further east and worked on boats running about the islands, for a time he'd run a banana farm in Queensland, and he'd first come to New Zealand in the hope of making a fortune out of picking up ambergris. He hadn't made a fortune, he said, but he'd done fairly well.

I remember particularly one bit he told me about gold prospecting. He told me about the way old-timers would cut a big potato in half and hollow out the centres, then they'd put their mixture of gold and quicksilver in the hollows, bind the pieces together with wire and put the potato in a heap of cinders. The heat would drive off the quicksilver and they'd open the potato and there'd be a lump of gold inside. It was wasteful of course, as you lost the quicksilver, but it was a way. And after a story like that I'd go back to the croquet lawn dreaming of enormous potatoes with enormous lumps of gold inside.

Other times he would tell me grim stories, and I could see that he had a great liking for telling them. There was one about when he was a constable in Boulder City and was sent out with a horse and cart to bring a corpse into town. He picked up the corpse and put it in the back of the cart, and after stopping at every hotel on the way he got back late at night. But when he looked in the cart the corpse wasn't there. So to save himself from getting into trouble he drove back over his route, but without finding the corpse anywhere. Then when he arrived back in the morning the corpse was found in the lock-up. It had fallen out of the cart outside the last hotel he had stopped at. Another constable had found it there, and thinking he was dealing with a drunken man had dragged him along to the lock-up.

But I'm afraid that such stories did not impress me very much. My life up till then hadn't brought me into contact with any corpses, and the sort of adventures that attracted me had no connection with them. And no matter how long I listened to the old man his grim stories would always seem much less real to me than his romantic ones. I much preferred to hear about potatoes with lumps of gold inside.

I had, in fact, almost made up my mind that I'd follow the old man's example and live a life of adventure. He told me that young people hadn't the spirit of adventure in them any longer, and it was a pity that in a new country like New Zealand it had died out so soon. He was quite proud of his life, particularly of the fact that he had been born in a humdrum market town in Devon, and into a very staid and respectable family, yet had struck out for himself and refused to live the tame easy life that he could have lived.

Nevertheless I had my doubts. I asked him whether he didn't wish that now he was old he could live in comfort, and that he's saved some of his money instead of always spending it on drinking and having a riotous time generally. But he said he had no regrets, and that if you had that attitude to money you'd never get the best out of life. When his time came he would die a free man just the same as he had always lived. Nor had he any intention of ending his days in his shack, he said. He'd been thinking of moving on for some while past, and there'd be lots of exciting times for him yet. It was just that in the meantime he was content to spend his time fishing and swimming and lying in the sun. And on such an occasion he'd always slap himself on the chest and declare that he was still as sound as ever he was. And certainly he seemed to be in the best of health, although there was one time when we were in swimming and after we'd raced over fifty yards or so he stood up rather pale and shaky. I said something about it, but he declared that it was only my imagination. Even so I noticed that he lay down, and was very quiet for a fair while after.

Then it happened that Christmas week began, and a few visitors turned up in the settlement, as well as some of the sons and daughters of mother's croquet-playing friends. So besides croquet there was tennis, and cricket on the beach, and mother insisted that instead of going off so much on my own I should make myself sociable by joining in. And as she was still far from well, and liable to be easily upset I had to fall in with her wishes as much as possible. Several days went by and I didn't get a chance to go along and see old Fred Holmes. But I was thinking of him all the time, and one day when a crowd of us took a launch trip round the Bay I got so sick of listening to back-chat that hardly went beyond tennis and dancing and cricket that I made up my mind. I decided that I would be like the old man and live a life of adventure. I didn't know how or when I would start on it, but sooner or later, start on it I would. And perhaps I was helped to make my decision by the launch's calling in at a place where overseas boats could come in to load timber. There was a big boat in loading at the time, and as we went past I watched the men working aboard. It made my heart beat. Lots of them, I thought, could tell of adventures as exciting as any of Fred Holmes's. And some of them looked very little older than I was. They might be cabin boys or apprentices, I didn't know what, but if they could get away on such boats so could I. And I imagined myself persuading Fred to let me have his dinghy so that some night I could pull out, climb aboard some such boat, and stow away. Perhaps I could persuade him to come too and it would be all right, I thought, to have him with me.

Anyhow, it must have been nearly a week before I got an opportunity to spend a day with my friend, and it was early one fine morning when I set out, wearing my bathing suit, and carrying only a towel and a parcel of lunch. But just before I was clear of the settlement I had to pass the little building that was known as the police station, although there was never any constable to be seen, and whatever duties were necessary were done by the local storekeeper. Outside was the storekeeper's old Ford truck, and as I passed the man himself came out of the building and asked me if I'd lend him a hand. I went inside and there was a coffin wrapped round with mourning crepe, and you could see it was just a long box made out of rough boards. Well, the storekeeper got me to help him to carry out the coffin and put it on the truck, and I felt rather uncomfortable having to do such a thing dressed only in my bathing suit.

The old bloke's not so heavy as I thought he'd be, the storekeeper said, and as he lit his pipe before driving off I said I supposed it was somebody local.

Yes, he said, the old bloke who was living just up the coast. Fred Holmes.

I was too upset to say anything. I just stood there and watched the storekeeper crank up and drive away, and there were so many ruts in the road I wouldn't have been surprised to see the coffin bounce off the back of the truck.

And thinking the matter over all these years I've never yet been able to decide why that sight of a coffin bouncing about on the back of an old Ford truck should have had such a profound effect on me. After all, an expensive funeral wouldn't have made things any better. I suppose it was just the shock of waking up to the fact that no matter what sort of life you have, there's always the catch at the end of it.

DAN DAVIN       # Saturday Night

'Yes,' said Mrs Connolly, ' "The Golden Calf" it was called. And so
naturally Mick and I thought it was a Bible picture. You know, like
"The Ten Commandments" or "Ben Hur".'

'You're right then,' said Mrs Fox. 'That's what anybody would be
thinking.'

'But you'd never guess what it really was.'

'Well, what was it then at all?'

Mrs Connolly lowered her voice and looked at the boy.

'It was about women's legs if you please. "The Golden Calf" was
women's legs.' Indignation ousted caution and she raised her voice.
'A pack of brazen hussies flaunting their bare legs.'

The boy did not look up. He was a practised eavesdropper.

'You don't say,' said Mrs Fox, and her spectacles glistened as she
leaned over the table. 'Well, and if it isn't a wicked world we're living
in!'

'A wicked world indeed. And so that's your pictures for you.
Disgusting, wasn't it, Ned?'

Ned started from his doze by the range.

'What's that?'

'That picture we saw, "The Golden Calf".'

'Disgusting,' said Ned. It was no matter for argument. He settled
into his chair again, the cat warm on his broad thigh and under his
hand. The cat knew who was the most stable member of the
household.

'Yes, them's your pictures for you, not fit for young people to see.'
Mrs Connolly raised her voice meaningly and looked across at Mick.
He did not lift his head from his book. The hand lifting the heavy
teacup to his mouth showed no sign.

But the battle was on. It was Saturday night. It was going to be a
job now to get the money. His mother had already committed herself
by this attack. Especially in front of Mrs Fox. His father would be no
use. He could always be silenced with 'The Golden Calf'. It was no
good Mick's pointing out that he didn't have the slightest desire to
see 'The Golden Calf', that there were other films on and in any case
he was fourteen and old enough to go out to the pictures at night at
least once a week anyway. Logic would be useless once his mother
was worked up like this, especially with that silly old gas-bag

urging her on.

Nellie came bustling out of the scullery and grabbed his cup. He grabbed it back.

'How much longer are you going to roost there, you and your old book? I've got to get ready for choir practice. Can't wait for you all night.'

He glared at her. On second thoughts better not give her a broadside. Not to-night.

He shut the book, got up and left the room.

In the bedroom he took down his navy-blue suit from the wardrobe, dug out a pair of clean socks, clean shirt and tie and gazed on them with satisfaction. His first suit of longs, all neatly pressed. He'd ironed them himself this morning. Not the sort of job you could trust women with. Socks nice dark blue, shirt light blue, a nice dark red tie. Not at all bad, really. Especially when you'd bought them all yourself out of rabbit-skin money; all except the tie, that is. The curse of it was, now he'd spent the money on the togs, he had to get the picture-money from his mother.

'Where are you going, Mick?'

Eileen had come in behind him.

'What do you want to know for?'

She ignored his crustiness. 'My word, you will look a sheikh. Going to the pictures?'

He was mollified. 'Yes.'

'Where are you going to get the money?'

'Oh, I'll get it.'

'Wish I was going. I get sick of Nellie always dragging me off to these silly old choir practices.'

'Eileen, Eileen!'

'There she goes again.' Eileen shot out the door.

Mick went over to the chest of drawers and opened his drawer. It contained a cross-section of his life history. Doughty marbles, cigarette cards, bits of shangeye as they called their catapults until they began to read *The Boys' Own Paper,* remnants of a fretwork phase and a photographic phase. But the latest stratum was at the bottom. From underneath the litter he drew a pack of 'Westward Ho' and transferred it deftly to the blue suit. From another cavern he produced a ferocious razor and some shaving-soap. He inspected the razor affectionately, heritage from Ned, already emancipated, picked up his towel and sauntered out in his shirt-sleeves.

His mother and Mrs Fox were deep in conclave.

'Gallstones,' Mrs Fox was saying. 'They took so many out of me I wonder I hadn't been rattling. I was like a quarry. It must have needed a wheelbarrow to carry them all away.'

Mrs Connolly did not look up as Mick passed. The gallstones story was an old favourite, and she was too comfortable. A person liked to sit quiet for a bit after tea and have a bit of peace.

Mick left the bathroom door ajar. The softening process first. He began to sing:

> 'Like a candle that's set in a window at night
> Your fond love has cheered me and guided me right.
> Every sorrow and care in the dear days gone by
> Was made bright by the light of the smile in your eye.
> I kiss the dear fingers
> So toilworn for me,
> Oh, God bless you and keep you,
> Mother Machree.'

The voice broke a bit on the high notes. But no harm in that. Showed how grown up he was. Better let it sink in a bit. The razor cut its swathe through the soft fur. Well, even if a man didn't have much of a beard he might as well get into the way of using a razor.

Better let fly again. No getting away from it, mothers were a blasted nuisance. Just wouldn't realize a man couldn't always go on being a boy just to please them. Ned had had just the same trouble. Frightful rows there used to be before she got used to him going out of a night. Mind you, he always took the bull-at-a-gate method. Mother Machree, he flattered himself, was more subtle.

'Mo-other Machree-ee.'

That should melt a stone.

'It's a beautiful voice the boy has, surely, Mrs Connolly.' Mrs Connolly bridled. 'Well, of course, he's at the awkward age now, Mrs Fox. Hobbledehoy, neither man nor boy.'

'Sure, and the boy is almost a man already.'

'Yes, they're all growing up on me. I only wish I had another one coming on. They're nicer when they're young. Not so bold.'

'Sure, Mrs Connolly, and it's a lucky woman you are to have such fine sons at all, and so clever they all are. It's a proud woman you must be.'

'Ah, well, and I suppose they might be worse. Though that Mick's a bit of a queer one. I had hopes of making a priest of him. But now I don't know at all, it's hard to know what he's thinking sometimes.'

'Ach, Mrs Connolly, the boy is a good boy and you know it. Many's the time when I've seen him up with the day bringing in the cows and feeding them at the fall of night I've been thinking to myself: It's a lucky woman you are, Mrs Connolly, to have such fine sons, so clever and so strong, a fine comfort for you when you're old and the nights are long and the winter hard. And it's wishing I am my own Andy had half the respect for his parents that your boys have.'

'Don't be fretting yourself with worry now, Mrs Fox, your own Andy's a good boy for all that. The young men will always be for drinking a drop or two when they're young and the blood's wild.'

'Still and all, Mrs Connolly, you'd be waiting a long time before you'd be hearing him sing the like of young Mick there—for all he has a good voice and all, the like mine was once. Just listen to the boy now.'

> 'Like a candle that's set in a window at night,
> Your fond love has cheered me and guided me right.
> Sure I love the dear silver that shines in your hair
> And the brow that's all furrowed and wrinkled with care.'

The bathroom door opened and Mick came out, his face shining, his walk elaborately casual. A quick whip of the eyes and he passed.

When he came back he was arrayed to perfection. He picked up the *Southland Times* and ostentatiously scanned the film advertisements.

'And where are you off to, all cocked up so fine?' his mother asked.

'I thought of going to the pictures.'

'Not to that "Golden Calf", I hope?'

'Good Heavens, no, not to that rubbish. There's a good film on at the Regent.'

'Well, fetch me my purse from the mantelpiece.'   He passed it over, worn, black leather.

'How much will it be?'

'Just a shilling.'

'Well, here's two shillings and you can buy yourself an orange drink.'

A packet of Capstan and still some money to spare!

His father was watching him. He had Mick's face with thirty years of hard work superimposed. You could not see his thoughts and he seldom spoke them.

Mick took the money. 'Thanks very much, Mum,' he said.

'Don't be late,' called Mrs Connolly. But he was already wheeling his bicycle round the corner of the house.

'After all, he's not a bad boy,' said Mrs Connolly.

'A fine strong lad and he is then,' said Mrs Fox.

Ned Connolly got to his feet.

'I'll just see that the cover is on Rosy. She's near calving.' He put on his gum boots.

'He's a sly one, is that fellow,' he said as he went out the door.

RODERICK FINLAYSON **The Totara Tree**

People came running from all directions wanting to know what all the fuss was about. 'Oho! it's crazy old Taranga perching like a crow in her tree because the Pakeha boss wants his men to cut it down,' Panapa explained, enjoying the joke hugely.

'What you say, cut it down? Cut the totara down?' echoed Uncle Tuna, anger and amazement wrinkling yet more his old wrinkled face. 'Cut Taranga down first!' he exclaimed. 'Every one knows that totara is Taranga's birth tree.'

Uncle Tuna was so old he claimed to remember the day Taranga's father had planted the young tree when the child was born. Nearly one hundred years ago, Uncle Tuna said. But many people doubted that he was quite as old as that. He always boasted so.

'Well it looks like they'll have to cut down both Taranga *and* her tree,' chuckled Panapa to the disgust of Uncle Tuna who disapproved of joking about matters of tapu.

'Can't the Pakeha bear the sight of one single tree without reaching for his axe?' Uncle Tuna demanded angrily. 'However this tree is tapu,' he added with an air of finality, 'so let the Pakeha go cut down his own weeds.' Uncle Tuna hated the Pakehas.

'Ae, why do they want to cut down Taranga's tree?' a puzzled woman asked.

'It's the wires,' Panapa explained loftily. 'The tree's right in the way of the new power wires they're taking up the valley. Ten thousand volts, ehoa! That's power, I tell you! A touch of that to her tail would soon make old Taranga spring out of her tree, ehoa,' Panapa added with impish delight and a sly dig in the ribs for old Uncle Tuna. The old man simply spat his contempt and stumped away.

'Oho!' gurgled Panapa, 'now just look at the big Pakeha boss down below dancing and cursing at mad old Taranga up the tree; and she doesn't know a single word and cares nothing at all!'

And indeed Taranga just sat up there smoking her pipe of evil-smelling torori. Now she turned her head away and spat slowly and deliberately on the ground. Then she fixed her old half-closed eyes on the horizon again. Aue! how those red-faced Pakehas down below there jabbered and shouted! Well, no matter.

Meanwhile a big crowd had collected near the shanty where Taranga lived with her grandson, in front of which grew Taranga's totara tree right on the narrow road that divided the straggling little hillside settlement from the river. Men lounged against old sheds and hung over sagging fences; women squatted in open doorways or strolled along the road with babies in shawls on their backs. The bolder children even came right up and made marks in the dust on the Inspector's big car with their grubby little fingers. The driver had to say to them: 'Hey, there, you! Keep away from the car.' And they hung their heads and pouted their lips and looked shyly at him with great sombre eyes.

But a minute later the kiddies were jigging with delight behind the Inspector's back. How splendid to see such a show—all the big Pakehas from town turned out to fight mad old Taranga perching in a tree! But she was a witch all right—like her father the tohunga. Maybe she'd just flap her black shawl like wings and give a cackle and turn into a bird and fly away. Or maybe she'd curse the Pakehas, and they'd all wither up like dry sticks before their eyes! Uncle Tuna said she could do even worse than that. However, the older children didn't believe that old witch stuff.

Now as long as the old woman sat unconcernedly smoking up the tree, and the Pakehas down below argued and appealed to her as unsuccessfully as appealing to Fate, the crowd thoroughly enjoyed the joke. But when the Inspector at last lost his temper and shouted to his men to pull the old woman down by force, the humour of the gathering changed. The women in the doorways shouted shrilly. One of them said, 'Go away, Pakeha, and bully city folk! We Maoris don't yet insult trees or old women!' The men on the fences began grumbling sullenly, and the younger fellows started to lounge over toward the Pakehas. Taranga's grandson, Taikehu, who had been chopping wood, had a big axe in his hand. Taranga may be mad but after all it was her birth tree. You couldn't just come along and cut down a tree like that. Ae, you could laugh your fill at the old woman perched among the branches like an old black crow, but it wasn't for a Pakeha to come talking about pulling her down and destroying her tree. That smart man had better look out.

The Inspector evidently thought so too. He made a sign to dismiss the linesmen who were waiting with ladders and axes and ropes and saws to cut the tree down. Then he got into his big car, tight-lipped with rage. 'Hey, look out there, you kids!' the driver shouted. And away went the Pakehas amid a stench of burnt benzine, leaving Taranga so far victorious.

'They'll be back tomorrow with the police all right and drag old Taranga down by a leg,' said Panapa gloatingly. 'She'll have no chance with the police. But by korry! I'll laugh to see the first policeman to sample her claws.'

'Oho, they'll be back with soljers,' chanted the kiddies in great excitement. 'They'll come with machine guns and go r-r-r-r-r- at old Taranga, but she'll just swallow the bullets!'

'Shut up, you kids,' Panapa commanded.

But somehow the excitement of the besieging of Taranga in her tree had spread like wildfire through the usually sleepy little settlement. The young bloods talked about preparing a hot welcome for the Pakehas tomorrow. Uncle Tuna encouraged them. A pretty state of affairs, he said, if a tapu tree could be desecrated by mere busybodies. The young men of his day knew better how to deal with such affairs. He remembered well how he himself had once tomahawked a Pakeha who broke the tapu of a burial ground. If people had listened to him long ago all the Pakehas would have been put in their place, under the deep sea—shark food! said Uncle Tuna ferociously. But the people were weary of Uncle Tuna's many exploits, and they didn't stop to listen. Even the youngsters nowadays merely remarked: 'oh, yeah,' when the old man harangued them.

Yet already the men were dancing half-humorous hakas around the totara tree. A fat woman with rolling eyes and a long tongue encouraged them. Everyone roared with laughter when she tripped in her long red skirts and fell bouncingly in the road. It was taken for granted now that they would make a night of it. Work was forgotten, and everyone gathered about Taranga's place. Taranga still waited quietly in the tree.

Panapa disappeared as night drew near but he soon returned with a barrel of home-brew on a sledge to enliven the occasion. That soon warmed things up, and the fun became fast and more furious. They gathered dry scrub and made bonfires to light the scene. They told Taranga not to leave her look-out, and they sent up baskets of food and drink to her; but she wouldn't touch bite nor sup. She alone of all the crowd was now calm and dignified. The men were dancing mad hakas armed with axes, knives and old taiahas. Someone kept firing a shot-gun till the cartridges gave out. Panapa's barrel of home-brew was getting low too, and Panapa just sat there propped against it and laughed and laughed; men and women alike boasted what they'd do with the Pakehas tomorrow. Old Uncle Tuna was disgusted with the whole business though. That was no way to fight the Pakeha, he said; that was the Pakeha's own ruination. He stood up by the meeting-house and harangued the mob, but no one listened to him.

The children were screeching with delight and racing around the bonfires like brown demons. They were throwing fire-sticks about here there and everywhere. So it's no wonder the scrub caught fire, and Taikehu's house beside the tree was ablaze before anybody noticed it. Heaven help us, but there was confusion then! Taikehu rushed in to try to save his best clothes. But he only got out with his old overcoat and a broken gramophone before the flames roared up through the roof. Some men started beating out the scrub with their axes and sticks. Others ran to the river for water. Uncle Tuna capered about urging the men to save the totara tree from the flames. Fancy wasting his breath preaching against the Pakeha, he cried. Trust this senseless generation of Maoris to work their own destruction, he sneered.

It seemed poor old Taranga was forgotten for the moment. Till a woman yelled at Taikehu, 'What you doing there with your old rags, you fool?' Look alive and get the old woman out of the tree.' Then she ran to the tree and called, 'Eh there, Taranga, don't be mad. Come down quick, old mother!'

But Taranga made no move.

Between the woman and Taikehu and some others, they got Taranga down. She looked to be still lost in meditation. But she was quite dead.

'Aue! she must have been dead a *long* time—she's quite cold and stiff,' Taikehu exclaimed. 'So it couldn't be the fright of the fire that killed her.'

'Fright!' jeered Uncle Tuna. 'I tell you, pothead, a woman who loaded rifles for me under the cannon shells of the Pakeha isn't likely to die of fright at a rubbish fire'. He cast a despising glance at the smoking ruins of Taikehu's shanty. 'No! but I tell you what she died of,' Uncle Tuna exclaimed 'Taranga was just sick to death of you and your Pakeha ways. Sick to death!' The old man spat on the ground and turned his back on Taikehu and Panapa and their companions.

Meanwhile the wind had changed, and the men had beaten out the scrub fire, and the totara tree was saved. The fire and the old woman's strange death and Uncle Tuna's harsh words had sobered everybody by now, and the mood of the gathering changed from its former frenzy to melancholy and a kind of superstitious awe. Already some women had started to wail at the meeting-house where Taranga had been carried. Arrangements would have to be made for the tangi.

'Come here, Taikehu,' Uncle Tuna commanded. 'I have to show you where you must bury Taranga.'

Well, the Inspector had the grace to keep away while the tangi was on. Or rather Sergeant O'Connor, the chief of the local police and a good friend of Taranga's people, advised the Inspector not to meddle till it was over. 'A tangi or a wake, sure it's just as sad and holy,' he said. 'Now I advise you, don't interfere till they've finished.'

But when the Inspector did go out to the settlement afterwards—well! Panapa gloatingly told the story in the pub in town later. 'O boy,' he said; 'you should have heard what plurry Mr Inspector called Sergeant O'Connor when he found out they'd buried the old woman right under the roots of the plurry tree! I think O'Connor like the joke though. When the Inspector finish cursing, O'Connor say to him, "Sure the situation's still unchanged then. Taranga's still in her tree." '

Well, the power lines were delayed more than ever, and in time this strange state of affairs was even mentioned in the Houses of Parliament, and the Maori members declared the Maoris' utter refusal to permit the desecration of burial places, and the Pakeha members all applauded these fine orations. So the Power Board was brought to the pass at last of having to build a special concrete foundation for the poles in the river bed so that the wires could be carried clear of Taranga's tree.

'Oho!' Panapa chuckles, telling the story to strangers who stop to look at the tomb beneath the totara on the roadside. 'Taranga dead protects her tree much better than Taranga alive. Py korry she cost the Pakeha thousands *and* thousands of pounds I guess!'

MAURICE DUGGAN     # Race Day

— Come on, Harry said.

— I've finished, Margaret said.

— Have you indeed, Mrs Lenihan said. And what's that on your plate?

— Get it down, there's a girl, Mr Lenihan said. It'll make your teeth curl and your hair white.

Margaret smiled, as at an old, old joke and bent over her plate where the cooling porridge rose like laval islands through the milk.

— Wait for your sister, Harry, Mr Lenihan said.

— I didn't hear anyone ask to leave the table, Mrs Lenihan said. But perhaps I'm going deaf.

— Say your piece son, Mr Lenihan said.

— Just this once, Grace, Mr Lenihan said. They're itching to get out.

— They're itching, Mrs Lenihan said. And who are they?

— Off you go, Mr Lenihan said.

And they edged around the table and ran through the house, but not until they were wedged, side by side in a space between the verandah posts, did they begin to believe that it was real, after all. But there it lay, a one day wonder, an oval of rich green in a summer-coloured oblong park, washed on one side by the tide which rose through the mangroves and held on the other by the shine of the harbour beach. Once each year they saw it as something wholly new. Their eyes looked out over the road and the sunken houses to where it lay, beyond and below, almost empty at this hour of the morning, but hung above with flags and rinsed in sun, a race-course for only one day in the year.

The sun warmed the wide rail on which they sat and the night's dew steamed still. Harry had his father's binoculars hung by their strap from his neck; as he leaned forward they knocked lightly on the wood. Below their dangling feet, a long way down, carnations tangled in the garden border.

\*  \*  \*

The line of traffic thickened until it was a solid stream, moving slowly, turning down the side road under the signalling whitesleeved arms of a policeman on points duty. The cars rolled richly over the spurting gravel.

Mr and Mrs Lenihan crossed the verandah and began to descend the steps; Mrs Lenihan in purple and white—huge flowers like stains of dry blood on the silk—and Mr Lenihan in a grey suit that would, later in the day, be much too hot. A *Members' Enclosure* card hung from Mr Lenihan's lapel.

— What are you sitting on top of one another for, Mrs Lenihan asked? There's plenty of room.

— Be good kids, Mr Lenihan said. Remember to back all the outsiders and you can't go wrong.

They laughed and arm in arm climbed down.

Mr Lenihan blithely hummed.

> Bet my money on a bobtail nag
> Somebody bet on the bay . . .

— Goodbye, he called.

And Harry put the binoculars wrong-end round to his eyes and watched his father and his step-mother descend, small, precise and a long way off, a flight of steps that went down and down until they seemed to plunge like a spear into the lawn. He changed ends and they were at the gate, so out of focus that his eyes watered as if in grief, and his father's hand was waving right up against the glass. The binoculars made no difference to voices. He turned them end for end again and swept them around in a wide arc so that the earth seemed to spin past, from left to right, and Mr Toms, swinging on crutches, three-legged through his garden, was appropriate denizen of a collapsing world.

— Please Harry, let me look, Margaret said. Please, before they are out of sight.

— And she too turned the binoculars on those retreating backs and watched her father cross to the outside of the pavement and extend his doubled arm and, although it was all too far away for her to have heard anything, she knew her father would be saying, mocking: And if I might have the honour Mrs Lenihan, in a brogue which, she did not know, he had preserved as carefully as the manner of his remarks in the years, a lifetime, since Dublin had seen him last. But had she known she would not have cared. What she saw was indistinguishable from what she felt and that brogue, telling tales, lay under her childhood like foundations of water. The tales seemed to be whispered to her now from the magic glass. And yet the grey back, turned solidly to her and moving away, mocked her as she looked.

\*      \*      \*

The race-course, outside the oval of track, had lost to bright fashion its summer colour and only inside the track, where a grey ambulance waited and a few men moved, was the grass still to be seen, brown and burned by the sun.

Margaret focused the glasses, won from Harry by promises which she could never keep, until the whole race-course lay, clear and close, almost under her hand. In the birdcage the horses for the first race circled and danced, perched on by jockeys as light and as perky and as gay as parakeets, and threaded out curving and sidestepping on to the unmarked track. Above the roofs of the buildings—the totalisator, the grandstand, the members' stand, the bar—the red balloon rode as no balloon ever rode, rigid from its mast, and away to the left the tide rose in patterns of light and shadow through the mangroves. The horses, rich as velvet, strained on tight reins past the grandstand, out to the barrier wires. Shredded by the breeze the tatters of music blew up, harsh and gay, to where the children sat, and with one arm hooked around the post Margaret stared through the binoculars.

— Can you see anything, Harry asked?

She did not answer.

Swinging and turning the horses came into line, broke, re-formed and burst away, running in silence, charging, while the wide line narrowed and beat against the rails and she saw them go into the bend and show again, smaller now, straining in the same amazing silence across the back-straight, and run towards her, colour after colour bright in the sunlight, to come to the hurdles where, still in silence, they stretched out and hung a moment as though carved from something solid and eternally still, and ran on. They raced in silence, or to a series of sounds—the banging of a gate, a radio playing, a car passing on the road—which served only to heighten the silence within that charmed lens. She felt that she had by some magic entered a world where, because of the silence, nothing human might ever enter again, and even Harry, shouting for his turn, could not disturb it.

Singly, in twos and threes, the horses rose and came on, fleeing across the confining circle until, when they were almost free, she shifted the binoculars and they were caught again. In the silence the billowing colours drummed and shone. She outpaced the running horses merely by moving her wrist and waited them at the double jump. The first horse rose to it and touched and rose again and was gone: the brush on the hurdle trembled. But before she too could swing away the following horses showered into the lens and, all grace gone, struck and fell, and a jockey in crimson and yellow silks and white breeches made an absurd clash of colour on the green grass.

Only when she took the binoculars from her eyes did the shouting beat up to her, blown, like the music, to shreds, whispering and roaring over the rooftops and the road.

— Could you see anything, Harry asked?

\*      \*      \*

The air was growing colder. A wind blew across the mangroves where now the tide had stolen from the muddy channels. They sat now out of their niche, on the top verandah step, and stared down: they had not spoken for a long time.

— How many have you got, Harry asked?

— I wasn't counting, Margaret said.

— I've got hundreds, Harry said. Not counting the people; they don't count.

— Not people, Margaret agreed.

— But horses and horse-floats do, Harry said. A horse-float is four and an ambulance is three—but I haven't seen one.

— There was one on the racecourse, following the horses round.

— A brewery lorry counts, Harry said.

— And jockeys, Margaret asked?

— Jockeys, but not proper people, Harry said.

— How much do they count for, Margaret asked? But she did not wait to hear.

Now the cars had begun to move again, nosing out into the main road and accelerating up the hill. The shadow of the house fell across the lawn and the road. A flag above the grandstand caught the last of the sun and stretched and flapped and the traffic policeman waved his white arms. Mr Toms swung through his garden of jockey-bright flowers, watering his plants with a hose; through the blowing spray a rainbow arched. Mr and Mrs Lenihan came through the gate.

— Hallo, cried Mr Lenihan, breezy and boozy, up from the gate. Have you made a pile?

— Hallo, they said in unison, descending.

— We nearly made a killing, Mr Lenihan said. But the judge was a blind man.

— A blind man on a left-hand course, Mrs Lenihan said, like someone repeating a lesson.

Remembering that Mr Toms had been almost blind since his fall Margaret looked to see if he had heard: she looked to where the spray was drifting back over the beds of flowers but Mr Toms had gone. She followed her father into the house, where his gaiety hammered in all the rooms. Under the gaiety she mused, nursing mournfully and yet with delight a vision of the silk and velvet colours falling spread out through the silent circle, falling to the silent grass. It might have been a vision—perhaps of death—multicoloured and fantastic and benign, from which—smothering her in wonder—the silence had taken all but the charm. But she did not know. On the short grass the gay colours had lain so still.

\*       \*       \*

Mr Lenihan was quiet. He pushed himself up from his chair and crossed the darkened room to where she sat. In a pale recollection of his former gaiety he smiled.

— Ah well, he said, the judge is a blind man and that's that. A blind man, he joked, to her wondering face.

G. R. GILBERT

# A Girl With Ambition

Round about 1933 things in New Zealand were not so good. You didn't notice them so much if your father owned a newspaper, it was having no money that made the difference. You noticed things more then, you felt that possibly capitalism was not operating as the *Dominion* and the *Evening Post* intended it to. In fact you felt hungry.

I didn't have a job either. But I was working on a relief scheme; three days a week I was filling in and digging up again a piece of ground in Hataitai. It was supposed to be a playing-field. The worst times New Zealand had struck, and all they could think of was to make playing-fields. They took great care to get the surface microscopically level and true—it took them and us months. Then they would decide to lower the whole thing six inches or so. It gave us work of course. If the slump had only lasted we'd have made all Wellington into playing-fields. We dug them out of the sides of hills, filled in valleys, diverted creeks and reclaimed swamps. All for playing-fields.

You got almost enough money to live on doing this. It wasn't bad digging until the murder, either. It was a great murder. I was extremely interested until it was decided that the girl's body was hidden under the spoil in our playing-field. I lost interest suddenly then. We were supposed to dig round for the remains, but I didn't feel like it—I didn't mind drowning kittens or cutting the head off a fowl if there was no one else, but digging round for a body was not my choice; why your spade might have gone into her and lifted her out in pieces. I hadn't been educated up to that sort of thing.

Leave her where she is, I said, forget about it. Why does one little body matter so much? It's quite unimportant and small; people die every day from more or less unnatural causes, particularly hunger. They die every day and it's all right. What does one little killing matter? Maybe she deserved to die, maybe he got mad at her for having the baby—wouldn't you? The silly kid having the baby and you no money and no likelihood. Two starve quicker than one you thought, and three a damsight quicker. She shouldn't have had him on. What would you do? and her buried so nicely beneath tons of spoil. Leave her there, damn it, I said, and forget about her.

But they ignored me and even got an excavator to work, so I quit and went up north. I got a job on a farm which lasted until the cocky decided to pay me less and less and practically no food, so I quit again and went further north. But that's by the way. What the story is about is this:

I was on the dole, on relief at about eighteen shillings a week in 1933, and things were worse than they had ever been. I had a small room in Cuba Street and some nights given the chance and the money I had dinner at Tony's. He was a Greek. They are all Greeks in Cuba Street, the restaurants have tins of spaghetti, parsley, bottles of soda-water and oysters-in-season in the window—they are very Greek. Inside you get boiled cabbage etc., and in some places the crockery was more cracked than others. The Greeks all wore black alpaca coats and shaven hair. They mostly spent their time standing behind the till collecting the shillings.

Eating at the same restaurant for long periods you get to know a bit about the waitresses. In this particular place, in Tony's, there were three, May, Sadie and Hettie. They were slightly different in detail as are all other people, but they all had the same intense way of calling out your order behind the screen.

At irregular intervals during the week and every Friday a fourth waitress appeared. And now the story is beginning because it is only about Lena, this waitress.

She was a lonely sort of dame. She had no great beauty, she was not the sort you longed to touch, she didn't walk very well and her hands were like the advertisement before taking Marvell Lotion for white hands. Yes, her hands were red.

But Lena and I got on pretty well after a while. I'd ask her about her boy-friend and was she going out tonight, and I bet she had a good time with the boys, and Lena would giggle and look pleased as though she had Prince Charming waiting in a V8 outside the kitchen door. It was Lena who kept me posted about the goings-on of Alexiouple the Greek, how he had married for the third time and his wife dead only two months, and how all the other children of his two previous marriages were indignant but they couldn't do anything about it, they all hanging round and smarming up to the old man, and his marrying again in spite of them. So they kept standing round in groups like stop-work meetings, all simmering with Greek hatred.

Lena was half Polish, at least half. Her father had come from somewhere near Tschenstochau; he had come out to New Zealand and died. It was peasant blood that Lena had from her father, you almost could see it running in her veins, snappy and sluggish; but it was good honest blood that made Lena like the earth and the growing things upon it. She had a window box to her room and used to grow daffodils. It made me feel good knowing that Lena grew flowers, it was something that she did—I felt proud of her. Once she brought me a daffodil from her garden. I put it in my button-hole and wore it proudly all that day although it looked rather peculiar. I'd have liked to be able to buy Lena a little farm with some pigs and a cow and a garden, she deserved it.

Lena looked after me well whenever she happened to be there. She saw I had the best, no scraggy endpieces for me, or messy left-overs for sweet.

What'll you have? she would say.

If I were you, she would say, I'd have mutton. The mutton's good but the beef—and she would screw her face up and shake her head—don't have the beef, have the mutton.

So I would have mutton.

Who's taking you out tonight? I would ask, and Lena would giggle; I bet you've got the boys on a string.

All this before we began digging for the body when I was still interested in the murder. Coming in from all that digging, and lifting the playing-field up and down so many inches, it was pretty good having a placid one like Lena, even though only once a week, to talk to. She was like a cow really, like a clean tame cow.

Lena, I said, would you like to live on a farm? A nice little farm with pigs?

Me on a farm, cried Lena, why me on a farm? I like my job where I am, I get great chances in my job, I get on. All the week I only wash dishes and sweep round in the back and the kitchen, I do work anyone could do. But on Fridays and when one of the girls is off I do work, skilled work. You got to be built that way to be a good waitress. Mr Alexiouple gives me my chance. All the week I only wash dishes but Fridays I am a waitress. Maybe sometimes I'll be a full time waitress. What would I do with a farm or pigs—I like it here, I got chances here—what would I do with a farm?

It was crazy that, and so wonderful. It was so damfool mad not to want pigs if you were a peasant. Having great ambition like that, you wanted to tell everyone about it, how great it was. If only a few had ambition like that how good things would be.

And all you with the assured positions and the cars, riding round in the cars, having homes on the hills with gardens and a view of the harbour, you laugh, you think of a poor polack being a waitress and having red hands. Only being a waitress once a week and thinking she's great. And you laugh. Well, you can laugh, but your laughter can't get us—we know how crazy beauty is, you only know soft things.

*     *     *

That was in 1933 and a few days after I went north because of the dead girl's body and digging for it.

**FRANK SARGESON**

# The Making of a New Zealander

When I called at that farm they promised me a job for two months so I took it on, but it turned out to be tough going. The boss was all right, I didn't mind him at all, and most days he'd just settle down by the fire and get busy with his crochet. It was real nice to see him looking happy and contented as he sat there with his ball of wool.

But this story is not about a cocky who used to sit in front of the fire and do crochet. I'm not saying I haven't got a story about him, but I'll have to be getting round to it another time.

Yes, the boss was all right, it was his missis that was the trouble. Some people say, never work for a woman, women'll never listen to reason. But that's not my experience. Use your block and in no time you'll be unlucky if you don't have them eating out of your hand.

But this time I was unlucky. This Mrs Crump was a real tough one. She and the boss ran a market garden besides the cows. She'd tie a flour-bag over her head, get into gum-boots, and not counting the time she put in in the house, she'd do about twelve hours a day, and she had me doing the same. Not that I minded all that much. The best of working on the land is that you're not always wishing it was time to knock off. Nor thinking of pay-day, either, particularly if there isn't a pub handy. I'm not going to explain. If you don't believe me, try it yourself and see.

But twelve hours a day, every day. I'll admit I used to get tired. Mrs Crump would see I was done in and tell me to stop working, and that was just what I was waiting for her to do. But there'd be a look in her eye. She'd say that I wasn't built for hard work, but she wasn't surprised because she'd never met a man she couldn't work to a standstill. Well, after she'd said that I'd just go on working, and if I was feeling cheeky I'd tell her I didn't mind giving her a run for her money. And before those two months were up I was feeling cheeky pretty often. Once she got going about my wages and everything else she had to pay out. She couldn't keep the wolf from the door, she said. Well then, I said, if you can't you'll just have to keep the door shut.

Now I'm running on ahead so I'd better break off again, because this isn't just a no-account story about how I began to get cheeky and put wisecracks across Mrs Crump. It's not about Mrs Crump, she only comes into it. I'm not saying I haven't got a story about her too, but it's another one I'll be getting round to another time.

What I want to tell is about how I sat on a hillside one evening and talked with a man. That's all, just a summer evening and a talk with a man on a hillside. Maybe there's nothing in it and maybe there is.

The man was one of two young Dallies who ran an orchard up at the back of Mrs Crump's place. These two had come out from Dalmatia and put some money down on the land, not much, just enough to give them the chance to start working the land. They were still paying off and would be for a good many years. There was a shed where they could live, and to begin with they took it in turns to go out and work for the money they needed to live and buy trees.

All that was some years before I turned up. The Dallies had worked hard, but it wasn't all plain sailing. They had about twenty-five acres, but it sloped away from the sun. They'd planted pines for shelter, but your shelter has to make a lot of growth before it's any use on land with a good slope to the south. And it was poor land, just an inch or two of dark soil on top of clay. You could tell it was poor from the tea-tree, which made no growth after it was a few feet high. Apples do best on land like that, so it was apple-trees the Dallies had mainly gone in for.

Of course Mrs Crump gossiped to me about all this. When I was there the Dallies weren't keeping a cow, so she was letting them have milk at half the town price. She didn't mind doing that much for them, she said, they worked so hard. And my last job each day was to take a billy up to the back fence. I'd collect an empty billy that'd be hanging on a hook, and I'd always consider going on and having a yarn with the Dallies. It wasn't far across to their shed but it would be getting dark, I'd be feeling like my tea so I'd tell myself I'd go over another time.

Then one evening the billy wasn't on the hook and I went on over, but the door was shut and there was no one about. The dog went for me but he never had a show. He'd had distemper, he couldn't move his hind legs and just had to pull himself along. I had a look round but there wasn't much to see, just two flannels and a towel hanging on the line, and a few empty barrels splashed with bluestone. Close to the shed there were grape vines growing on wires, then the trees began. They were carrying a lot of fruit and looked fine and healthy, but just a bit too healthy, I thought. You could tell from the growth that the Dallies had put on a lot of fertilizer. For a while I waited about, kidding to the dog until he wagged his tail, then I went back.

The next day one of the Dallies brought the billy over but I didn't see him. When we were milking Mrs Crump told me. He was the one called Nick, and the evening before he'd had to take his mate into hospital. He'd had a spill off his bike and broken some ribs and his collar-bone. Mrs Crump thought perhaps there'd been some drinking, she said they made wine. Anyhow Nick was upset. If his mate died, he said, he would die too. He'd have nothing left, nothing. And how could he work and live there by himself when his mate was lying all broken up in the hospital? Every afternoon he would leave off working and ride into town to see his mate.

There's a pal for you, Mrs Crump said.

Well, up at the fence the billy would always be on the hook, but if Nick was in town seeing his cobber I'd think it would be no use going over. Then one evening he was just coming across with the billy so I went over to meet him. We greeted each other, and I think we both felt a bit shy. He was small and dark, almost black, and his flannel and denims were pretty far gone the same as mine were. I gave him my tin and told him to roll a cigarette, and when he lit up he went cross-eyed. I noticed that, and I saw too that there was a sort of sadness on his face.

I asked him how his cobber was, and he said he was good.

In two days he will be here, he said. You could see he was excited about it and his face didn't look so sad. In two weeks, he said, it will be just as if it never happened.

That's great, I said, and we sat down and smoked.

How's the dog? I said.

He is getting better too, Nick said.

He whistled, and the dog pulled himself over to us by his front paws and put his chin on Nick's leg, and somehow with the dog there it was easier to talk.

I asked Nick about his trees and he said they were all right, but there were too many diseases.

Too much quick manure, I said.

He said yes, but what could they do? It would take a long time to make the soil deep and sweet like it was in the part of Dalmatia he came from. Out here everybody wanted money quick, so they put on the manure. It was money, money, all the time. But he and his mate never had any. Everything they got they had to pay out, and if the black-spot got among the apples they had to pay out more than they got. Then one of them had to go out and try for a job.

It's the manure that gives you the black-spot, I said.

Sometimes I think it is God, Nick said.

Well, maybe you're right, I said, but what about the grapes?'

Oh, Nick said, they grow, yes. But they are not sweet. To make wine we must put in sugar. In Dalmatia it is not done. Never.

Yes, I said, but you don't go back to Dalmatia.

Oh no, he said, now I am a New Zealander.

No, I said, but your children will be.

I have no children and I will never marry, Nick said.

No? I said, then your cobber will.

He will never marry either, Nick said.

Why? I said, there are plenty of Dalmatian girls out here. I bet you could get New Zealand girls too.

But Nick only said no, no, no, no, no.

If you were in Dalmatia I bet you'd be married, I said.

But I am not in Dalmatia, Nick said, now I am a New Zealander. In New Zealand everybody says they cannot afford to get married.

Yes, I said, that's what they say. But it's all wrong.

Yes, Nick said, it is all wrong. Because it is all wrong I am a Communist.

Good, I said. Well, I thought, spoil a good peasant and you might as well go the whole hog.

I bet you don't tell Mrs Crump you're a Communist, I said.

Oh no, Nick said, she would never be a Communist.

No fear, I said.

I will tell you about Mrs Crump, Nick said. She should go to Dalmatia. In Dalmatia our women wear bags on their heads just like her, and she would be happy there.

Yes, I said, I believe you're right. But Nick, I said, I thought you'd be a Catholic.

No, Nick said. It is all lies. In Dalmatia they say that Christ was born when there was snow on the ground in Palestine. But now I have read in a book there is no snow in Palestine. So now I know that they tell lies.

So you're a Communist instead, I said.

Yes, I am a Communist, Nick said. But what is the good of that? I am born too soon, eh? What do you think?

Maybe, I said.

You too, Nick said. You think that you and me are born too soon? What do you think?

He said it over and over, and I couldn't look him in the face. It had too much of that sadness . . . I mightn't have put it the way Nick had, I mightn't have said I was born too soon, but Nick knew what he was talking about. Nick and I were sitting on the hillside and Nick was saying he was a New Zealander, but he knew he wasn't a New Zealander. And he knew he wasn't a Dalmatian any more.

He knew he wasn't anything any more.

Listen, Nick said, do you drink wine?

Yes, I said.

Then to-morrow night you come up here and we will drink wine, Nick said.

Yes, I said, that's O.K. with me.

There is only to-morrow night, Nick said, then my mate will be here. We will drink a lot of wine, I have plenty and we will get very, very drunk. Oh, heaps drunk.

Yes, I said. Sure thing.

To-morrow night, he said.

He got up and I got up, he just waved his hand at me and walked off. He picked the dog up under his arm and walked off, and I just stood there and watched him go.

But it turned out I never went up to Nick's place. When I was having my tea that evening Mrs Crump told me about how a woman she knew had worked too hard and dropped dead with heart failure. But there's nothing wrong with my heart, she said.

No, I said, except that maybe it's not in the right place.

Of course it must have sounded like one of my wisecracks, but I was thinking of Dalmatia.

Anyhow Mrs Crump said she's stood enough from me, so when I'd finished my tea I could go.

I wasn't sorry. I stood on the road and wondered if I'd go up to Nick's place, but instead I walked into town, and for a good few days I never left off drinking.

I wanted to get Nick out of my mind. He knew what he was talking about, but maybe it's best for a man to hang on.

DOUGLAS STEWART     **The Whare**

It was six months since those fleas had tasted anything but Maori. They leaped at a white skin like a shoal of herrings at a loaf of bread. They came from the dust under the raupo mats and they were there in millions. Every ten minutes or so, when the irritation became unendurable, you could roll up your trousers and scrape them off like sand or bid-a-bid seeds. But attacking them was a waste of time, and unless a particularly savage pang forced you into action, you just sat and let yourself be devoured.

The old chief and his wife, with their hard, leathery skins, hardly seemed to notice them. Sometimes when the woman saw that I was in trouble she would say, 'Ah! You got te flea, eh?' and she would promise to boil a kerosene tin of water, shift the mats and scald the brutes to death. 'T'ose flea! We boil 'em, t'at te way to fix 'em!' If the chief on some rare occasion, sitting by the open fire in the whare at night, felt a pinprick through his hide, he said 'Flea! Bitem!' in a tone of pleased discovery. He took a pride in his fleas. Their presence cheered him, their habits interested him, and their prowess delighted him. They were his *lares et penates,* or the flocks and herds of a patriarch.

Maybe I exaggerate the importance of the fleas. In the long run, for there were processes of the mind more powerful than those ridiculous irritations of the flesh, I should probably have come to the same decision without their prompting. But I don't want memory, always a romantic, to sentimentalize them out of existence. They did force a decision.

*     *     *

I drifted into the Maori settlement with the greatest simplicity. It was trudging along the road in the sunny midday, heading north, when a tall native, riding bareback on an old grey mare, came cantering up the road behind me. He stopped short beside me, the mare grunting with relief and indignation, and said, 'You've got a heavy swag, Jack. Carry it for you?'

The morning seemed sunnier after that. It was good to be able to walk freely. The road wound along a ridge from which the ragged country, broken into gullies and patchworked with leaden tea-tree and an occasional acre of ploughed land or yellowish grass, fell with the slow sweep of a glacier into the shallow harbour of Kaipara. The water, so far away, had lost its quick sparkle and become some new element more like metal, a sheet of silvery tinfoil among the gigantic hills. It was hard desolate country, but it couldn't depress you when the sun was shining on the red clay cuttings and the mare's hooves were clip-clopping on the stones, and you had nothing to do but walk along the road and look at things.

The Maori, who seemed to be about thirty-five years old, was slim and sombre. He spoke little, and appeared to be turning something over in his mind. At last he said, 'My father will give you some lunch.'

I said 'Good!' and then wished I hadn't, for the monosyllable might have sounded like pidgin-English, and his own was perfect. He had probably been to one of the Maori colleges and then, as most of his people do, come back to the pa.

We plodded on until we caught sight of a tumble-down whare standing among the rushes of an upland swamp on a plateau above the harbour. 'That's my place,' said the horseman. 'You can sleep there if you like, have a rest for a day or two. I don't live there now. It's pretty rough,' he added.

He wasn't very enthusiastic. Afterwards I found out that various swaggies in the past had abused the hospitality of the little tribe, and I came to the conclusion that the young Maori resented it and that, although the tradition of welcome to the stranger was too strong for him to break, maybe his children would rebel against it.

The whare, like all deserted homes, was dirty and forlorn. The broken iron bedstead, the torn mats, the cook-pot lying on its side in the dust, the rain-sodden, long-dead ashes, the cobwebs and the rat-droppings—they were the apparatus of ghosts. Behind the building was the Maori's inevitable totem—a broken-down limousine, rusting into the grass. The Maori dropped my swag and we went back to the road and up to the settlement on the hill-side.

Half a dozen Maoris, squatting on the grass outside one of the whares, stared at us in good-humoured curiosity. They were all eating and drinking. One of the young fellows said something in Maori to a squat, dumpy girl, and she laughed. They went on eating.

The Maori took me to the whare door and introduced me to his father and mother, chief and chieftainess of the settlement. The woman, bent and skinny and weather-beaten like a twist of a withered grass, smiled a welcome. From her beaked nose her face fell away in a landslide of wrinkles to a toothless mouth, achieving some dignity again in a firm, tattooed chin. The old man had the stamp of aristocracy both in manners and features. His hair and moustache were grey, his brown eyes clear, his cheeks smooth. But for his colouring and his thick lower lip he could have passed for a European.

'Eh, Jack,' he said, 'you come a long way?'

'From Taranaki,' I told him.

'Eh, Tara-naki,' he drawled in soft amazement, as if I had come from the moon. His geography was vague. He had been to Auckland, though. He and the old woman had stayed with relations in the city—probably at that squalid settlement by the blue harbour—for several months, and then come back to the kumara patch and the whare. I imagined them labouring along Queen Street, staring in wonder and delight at the shops and the traffic. It would be like a visit to a foreign country.

The woman came out of the darkness of the whare with a mug of tea and a plate piled with pipis and something which looked like green string and which I was told was boiled watercress.

'You like te pipi?'

'Kapai!'

'Kapai!' She laughed. There was no fear of insulting her by using pidgin-English. Her pakeha vocabulary was small, and you had to speak simply and slowly to make her understand. She treated the barrier of tongues as a joke laughing with pleasure when she could comprehend and with amusement when she couldn't. Her conversation was full of expressive 'what-you-callums'.

Some sort of council-of-war, which I sensed concerned me, went on while I was negotiating the shell-fish and the boiled watercress (which tasted like barbed wire), and when it was over the young Maori went off on the mare and the old man said, 'You stay wit' me, eh, Jack? T'at other place no good. You stay here wit' me. The missus make you a bed in te whare-puni.'

That was better. The deserted whare would have given you the horrors. Only I had yet to meet the fleas.

That first night, sitting around the fire with the two old Maoris, I found everything, even the fleas, strange and exhilarating. It was an open fire built on the dust in a sort of alcove at one end of the whare, and the smoke, guided by the corrugated-iron walls of the alcove, found an uncertain track to a hole in the roof. Strips of shark meat and bunches of reddish corncobs hung on the walls, drying in the heat and collecting the savour of smoke and smuts. The firelight danced across the room, colouring the far wall and giving a touch of mystery to the Maoris' sleeping-place—a continuation of the main room, screened by a wall of mats. The narrow entrance and the black interior made it look like a cave. The room where we sat was full of moving shadows, with highlights glowing on the bare table and the wooden form beside it, and gleaming on a shelf of chipped crockery. Near the fire stood a kerosene tin of pipis. A big enamel teapot rested at the edge of the embers and an iron kettle swung over the flames.

We drank many cups of tea, ate pipis and smoked. The teapot, steaming by the fire day after day, was never emptied. When the black juice ran low, the old man would throw in a handful of tea-leaves and pour in boiling water.

The woman, washing dishes, mixing a damper or peeling kumaras, was always busy in a leisurely mechanical way. Sometimes, in a cracked voice, she sang a fragment of a Maori song. I asked her to sing the cradle song 'Hine e Hine' for me, and she was pleased, and sang the sweet air through. But she sang very badly. I talked to her about bird-voiced Ana Hato at Rotorua. She made a show of interest, but it was only her politeness. She wanted to peel the kumaras and sing to herself in her cracked voice and not to talk. I remembered the grey Tuwehirangi at Manutahi, reputed to be one hundred and fifteen years old, who would simply walk away when a white man talked to her. She wasn't interested. The old Maori women like to gossip with each other.

The old man, brightening at the mention of Rotorua, told me he had a cousin there. It was a peg to hang a conversation on, but the conversation wouldn't follow. There was no common ground on which we could meet, and, worse, no common background where the pakeha's way of thought could have commerce with the Maori's. Instead of asking him about the ancient legends of his race, I fell back on the fleas. We had them in common, anyhow.

When it came to supper-time, he said, 'You rest tomorrow, Jack. You done up. You don't do anyt'ing tomorrow and t'en we see. Maybe you stay wit' us for a while.'

He'd already begun to say that word 'Jack' in a different tone. At first, especially with the young Maori, it was the familiar, faintly contemptuous nick-name that would be fastened on a stray dog and a swaggie alike, and I had been inclined to resent it. Now it had become my name, not my nickname.

He led me over to the meeting-house, a long, low, gusty barn of a building where the old woman, by piling mats on an iron bedstead, had made me a sleeping-place. A cloud of sparrows stormed from the rafters, chirping in alarm. When the old man had gone, I lifted one of the mats and saw that here, too, the livestock abounded. There was nothing to be done about it; I lay down on the mats. Rats began to squeak and rustle and thump about the floor, and cautiously in twos and threes the sparrows came back.

Tired, and feeling security in the roof and the bed despite the rats and sparrows, I slept that night.

The next night was harder. I felt a bit foolish and out of place to be living with the Maoris, and lay awake thinking things over. My bloodthirsty bed-fellows made sleep impossible. In the early hours of the morning I put on an overcoat and sat out on the hill-side, looking at the harbour and waiting for day-light. The landscape had the dramatic, electric stillness of night, as if the hills as well as the sweet-scented moonlit tea-tree, stretching for miles, had awakened into some secret life quite different from their torpor in the daylight. The harbour, too, was brighter by moonlight than sunlight, a wash of pure silver around the dark bases of the ranges. A faint rushing sound might have been air dragging across the valleys, or the waves breaking on the coast, a long way off. I thought of Auckland asleep, and the two old Maoris asleep on the mats in the cubby-hole at the end of their whare, so remote from the city, lapped in this tranquility, as self-sufficient as the fallow deer on the ridges beyond Wanganui or the wild drake and his mate that nested on the cliff above the Waingongora at home.

I had loafed all day. The old man disappeared and came back in the evening and gave me a tin of tobacco he had bought for me at the store. I didn't want to take it, but couldn't refuse for fear of offending him. In the whare at night, breaking one of his long silences, he told me about the white woman—God knows who she was, and how poverty-stricken or how mad she was to be tramping the lonely road through the tea-tree—who had stayed at the pa all through the spring, and about a white man who had stayed for six months and then slipped away in the night, stealing their blankets and an axe.

'He need 'em, or else he wouldn't take 'em,' the Maori woman said.

'Aye, t'at orright,' the old man agreed. 'If he want 'em he can have 'em. He can come back again if he want to, t'at one.'

I began to understand something of Maori hospitality and of their outlook on life, simple but realistic, tolerant but not sentimental. It arose partly from the fact that understanding was easier than anger. They were happy and didn't want their happiness to be disturbed by the feeling that they had been let down.

It became obvious that they were expecting me to stay for a long time. They were hinting at that by telling me about the others. I had a notion they liked having a pet white man about the place. It satisfied their religious instincts in a way as well as their good nature.

You were at once a homeless dog to be comforted, a fabulous animal to wonder at, and a god to be propitiated. Owning you enhanced the chief's prestige in the pa, and gave the old couple something different to do, something different to talk about.

There was no effort of adjustment needed to settle into the life. You ate and slept and scratched and from time to time said something, not so much for its meaning but as a token of friendship. You said something to the old woman, or she said something to you, in the comradely way you'd talk to a dog you were fond of. The response was the same—a tail wagged in the mind.

On the second day I helped the tribe to store the kumaras for the winter. They gave me a black stallion to ride—not, unfortunately, a great proud snorting beast with a fiery eye and a flowing mane, but a typical product of Maori horse-breeding, a dusty, ragged, somnambulistic runt—and I made repeated trips from the whare to the field across the road where the women were digging the earthy red-purple sweet-potatoes. Taking their time about it, grubbing in the earth with their hands, they'd fill a sack and lift it up to me while I sat on the stallion. They cracked jokes to each other in Maori and laughed a lot.

The men had a pit dug at the back of the whare, lined with fern leaves. They tipped the kumaras into the pit and, when there was a fair-sized mound, laid more fern leaves around the sides and on top, then covered the pile with clay. It was easy work, very pleasant in the light May sunshine. The men smoked and lazed between trips. Nobody hurried. The little stallion was the only one tired enough to feel relieved when I brought the last load home in the dark and sent him off into the tea-tree with a smack on the rump.

Both the Maoris were sympathetic about the fleas that night. They would 'get te boiling water and kill 'em all for sure' one day—tomorrow. It wouldn't be long till the frosts came, and they weren't so bad then.

The futile promises were a bit irritating; the fleas were maddening. I'd get up and stamp about the room for relief, then sit down beside the old man and stare at the fire again. When the fleas had drunk their fill and were sleeping it off, there was something curiously attractive about the whare, especially one night when it rained and the big drops fell hissing into the fire. You thought of those miles of lonely wet hills, and it was good to be indoors. We sat for hours, it seemed, without talking, listening to the rain hammering on the iron roof. It drove us closer together, wove us into a primitive human companionship—three against the storm. I imagined the old couple sitting together by the fire year after year, and saw myself with them, staring at the flames interminably, not talking and not thinking, sunk in a dark tide of physical sympathy, with somewhere in the chasms of the mind a vague sadness. There was a touch of nightmare about the vision and afterwards it haunted me.

That wet night the woman, grinning, asked me, 'You got a girl, eh? You sad. You got a girl somewhere, a long way away? You leave te girl behind and forget her now?'

'Yes,' I told her. 'I've got a girl. She's a long way away.'

'Maybe you get te Maori girl, eh? How you like te Maori wife?'

Then she told me there was to be a dance at the meeting-house on the Saturday. 'You meet te nice girl at te dance. Plenty wahine!'

When I was alone with the rats and the sparrows, with the feeble light of the candle emphasizing the cavernous gloom of the whare-puni, I began to see that the woman had been testing me out. The old man that day had bought me another tin of tobacco and broached a great scheme whereby we were going to earn twelve pounds between us cutting rushes for a pakeha farmer down the road. Before the job started, we were to go down to the harbour and get in a store of pipis from the mud-flats. He was including me in all his plans as a matter of course. I had come to stay.

'You not want to go, eh? You stay here as long as you like. You stay wit' us. You not want to go away.'

I didn't work the next day. I felt restless and went for a walk along the road. A farmer—perhaps the one for whom we were to cut the rushes—saw me leaning over a bridge and had a yarn. He said if I registered on the unemployed he'd give me a job, with five bob a week added to the Government subsidy. I told him I'd think it over.

I was thinking everything over, and thinking with a queer urgency, almost panic, in the whare that night.

'Tomorrow we get te pipi.'

'We cut te rushes, contrac' for a fortnight; make twelve poun'.'

'Plenty nice Maori girl come on Saturday.'

'You not want to go away.'

Well, it would be interesting getting the pipis. I'd often watched the Maoris wading in shallow waters and reaching into the blue mud for the shell-fish, and it would be good to help them. I wouldn't mind rush-cutting, either. That would be something new and it ought to be as pleasant as scything the ragwort at Whangamomona. As for a Maori girl, the ukuleles and steel guitars and the rattle-trap piano all going like mad and the young bucks shouting the choruses—the way I'd often seen them—good!

Or would it be? Wouldn't you be isolated, mooching about on your own between dances, a stranger at the party? Maybe they'd be a bit antagonistic; certainly they'd be curious. Even if they gave you a good time and you joined in the singing, you'd be acting a part. You wouldn't belong.

'How you like te Maori wife, eh, Jack?'

I looked at the old couple nodding by the fire, the light on their dark faces. What did I really know about them? What went on in those secretive Maori minds? They weren't animals. They had their own thoughts, based on a conception of life beyond my understanding. What possible communion could there be between the white man and the native? The memory of that deep, mindless sympathy when we sat quietly by the fire on the wet night was uncannily disturbing, horrible. The friendly little whare was a prison.

'T'at flea! Tomorrow I kill te lot of 'em.'

When I went to bed they bit like devils. It was going to be a long, restless night. I thought of the Maoris' incredible kindliness. What lovable people they were! But I saw how their generosity was binding me to them. 'Tomorrow we get te pipis.' 'Next week we cut te rushes.' Next month, next year——

After a while I climbed out of bed and wrote a note.

Thank you to being so good to me. I hope I can repay you some day. I'm sorry to go away like this without saying good-bye. I hope you'll understand; it's just that I have to be moving on. Don't think I'm not grateful.

JACK.

Feeling as guilty as if I'd been the swaggie who stole the blankets, I packed my swag and crept out of the whare. There was a full moon, and the old mysterious enchantment in the vast hills and the tea-tree. Along the ridge above the glitter of the harbour, the road was white. I could have shouted for joy at the way it ran over the rise and disappeared into the country I'd never seen.

I walked hard all night, half expecting to see the young Maori come galloping after me on the indignant grey mare and force me to go back to the pa for fear of hurting his feelings.

A. P. GASKELL                    # The Big Game

The football match at Carisbrook was over. Dusk was already falling, and during the last part of the game the flight of the ball and even the movements of the players had been hard to follow in the failing light. Now, looking across the field, I could see the crowd dimly massing around the gates. Here and there a small yellow flame flickered where a smoker was lighting up, and the whole crowd moved under a thin blue haze of tobacco-smoke. After all the cheering the place seemed very quiet, and from the street outside came the noise of cars starting up and whining off in low gear, and a tram screeching round the corner under the railway bridge. Overhead the sky was clear with a promise of frost. A few small boys ran with shrill cries under the goalposts; the rest of the field lay empty in the grey light, and the smell of mud came through the damp air. I shivered and glanced down at my steaming jersey.

'Well, you'd better go and get changed,' said Betty. 'I don't want you to catch cold. You'll be playing Southern next Saturday now, won't you?'

'Yes,' I said. 'They were bound to win today. Beating Kaikorai puts us level with them.'

'Will you be too tired for the dance?'

'My old knee feels a bit sore but I'll ring you after tea. I must go and get changed now. So long.'

I trotted in under the stand. The lights were on, the unshaded bulbs threw a cheap yellow glare over the walls of the dressing-rooms, and up into the girders and struts above. My football boots clumped along the boards of the passageway. I stamped to get some of the mud off and pushed open the door chalked 'Varsity A.'

Inside the dressing-room there was a strong human smell of sweaty togs, muddy boots and warm bodies as the men came prancing back naked from the showers and stood on the seats drying themselves. The room was crowded. Togs and boots lay over the floor, clothes hung emptily from the pegs, and men were everywhere, shoving, jostling, reaching out their arms to dry themselves or climb into a shirt and taking up more room. Everyone was happy now that the strain was over, talking, yelling, singing, intent on their warmth and comfort and the clean feel of dry clothes. It was good to relax and know that we wouldn't have that feeling of before-the-game nervousness for another week. Next week it was going to be solid. The match against Southern was the Big Game.

'Shut that door,' roared Buck as I came in. 'Hello, it's Bennie. Did she think you played a nice game? Did she see my try? What did it look like from the stand?'

'They couldn't see it from the stand,' I said. 'They all thought you'd torn your pants when we gathered round you. Nobody knew it was a try.' I sat down and started picking at my muddy laces. My hands were too cold to grip them properly.

'Bloody liar,' said Buck amiably. 'It was a damn good try.' He had a very powerful voice. 'Boy oh boy oh boy,' he chanted, 'won't I knock back those handles tonight. You wait till I tell old Harry about my try. He'll shout after every round.'

'What try?' said Mac, our captain. 'Hell, you aren't going to claim anything for that bit of a scuffle? You were a mile offside.' His head disappeared into his shirt and came grinning out the top. He put on his glasses and the grin seemed more complete.

'Like hell,' shouted Buck, dancing about on the seat and sawing the towel across his back. 'I took the ball off him and fell over. When they all got off me there I was over the line. A clear try.'

'Offside a mile. Rabbiting. You handled it on the ground. I was walking back for the free-kick,' said the boys. They all liked Buck.

'Free-kick be damned,' he roared. 'It was a good forward's try. Right out of the book. Plenty of guts and initiative.'

'Yes, a typical forward's try,' said Bob, our half-back. He was small and very sturdy and freckled. 'Big bullocking bastards always mauling each other about. Why can't you do something nice and clean-cut like the backs?'

'The backs? The pansies? I sweat my guts out getting the ball for you and then you canter along very prettily about ten yards and then drop it.' He struck a chesty attitude standing naked on the seat. 'Do I look like a pansy?'

'Not with that thing.'

Someone shied a ball at Buck and left a muddy mark on his backside. I went out to the shower. I could hear Buck's voice as I trotted along the passage. One of the Kaikorai men was still in the shower-room.

'How are you now?' he said.

'Pretty tired. It was a tough game.'

'We didn't want you to have it too easy. You jokers will be playing off with Southern now.'

'Yes. The big championship. Next Saturday.'

'Think you'll lick them?'

'Hope so. We'll give them a good go, especially if it's a dry ground.'

'Their forwards are good. Pack very low. Well good luck.'

'Thanks.' I turned on the taps. There was still plenty of hot water left and it was great. Gosh I enjoyed it.

When I got back most of the boys were dressed and the coach was there talking to Mac. 'Shake it along Bennie,' said Bob, 'or we'll miss the beer. It's well after five now.'

'I'm practically there already,' I said. 'Don't rush me. Give me a smoke. Hell I feel good now.' I was in digs with Bob. 'What did the coach think of it?'

'He said you were lousy but the rest of us went well.'

I knew Bob was joking but I didn't like it much. I knew I wasn't particularly good and the coach was always on to me to put more vigour and initiative into my play. I was the heaviest man in the team and he would point out what the lighter forwards did and then what I did, and make me feel ashamed. If he thought I was lousy that meant I was in for a roasting at the next team-talk.

'He says you're to mark Jackie Hore on Saturday,' grinned Bob. 'You've got to dominate him.'

'I can easy fix Yackie,' I said. 'I bumped into him one game last season and he fell over. Fell right over from just a little bump. He's a softie.'

'Yes? Who was it broke your nose?'

'Aw that was just his knee. Everybody's got hard knees.' I struggled into my shirt.

'Listen! Listen!' Mac was yelling above the din. After the uproar the silence sounded immense.

'Well boys,' said the coach, 'You know you're for it now. It's either you or the Southern for this season's champions, and next Saturday you'll have the honour of playing off with them. It's up to every one of you to keep fit. It's going to be a long hard game and I know I can rely on you boys to go on the field fit. I know Buck will leave the beer alone tonight.'

'What,' roared Buck, 'why do you think I go tearing round there for ninety minutes if it's not to get a thirst?'

'I knew you wouldn't mind,' said the coach, 'especially after they presented you with that try.'

'Another one,' said Buck in mock resignation. 'Another one. The best forward on the ground and I get nothing but abuse. I'll chuck the game and take on ping-pong.'

'Well boys, I'll see you on Wednesday at practice. I want you all out early. Will they all be out, Mac?'

'Anyone who can't?' said Mac. No answer.

'O.K. then. Goodnight boys. Anyone coming my way?'

They all began drifting off. Mac waited on Bob and me. The Southern match was just a nice distance ahead. I could get a thrill out of thinking of it but no nervousness yet. I felt good.

'Well Mac,' I said, 'how does the skipper feel about our chances? Our great public would like to know. Would you care to make a statement?' We often did these cross-talk acts.

'I think I may say with all due modesty that we are quietly confident,' said Mac. 'Tell our public that the same spirit of healthy rivalry that has spurred on our predecessors will again be found animating the bosoms of this year's team. Tell them that the game of Rugby fosters the team spirit and is the basis of our democracy. Tell them to play up and play the game. Tell them to go to hell.'

'Very prettily put,' I said. 'And now who else can we help?'

'A message for the expectant mothers,' urged Bob.

Mac was going well. 'Tell them we favour the quick heel,' he said. 'Never leave an opening for your opponent. God save Sir Truby King. For Christ's sake hurry up Bennie.'

I was dumping my togs in the bag as the caretaker put his head round the door. 'You boys ready? I'm waiting to lock up.'

We went out with him. 'Think you can hold the Southern?' he asked. He called them 'Southeren.'

'We'll give them a good go for it,' said Mac. He was our spokesman on occasions like these.

'They've got a fine team. You'll need all your luck to beat those forwards of theirs—man!'

'We're going to play fifteen backs and run them off the paddock,' said Bob.

'Are you now? Ay? Well I'll be watching you, but I'll no say which side I'll be barracking for. Good-night.' He locked the gate after us.

It was quite dark now and all the street-lights were on. The air was keen and frosty. We went up under the railway bridge and stood in front of the lighted shops waiting for a tram. I was beginning to feel cold and stiff and tired now that the excitement was over.

'You know,' I said, 'football would be a good game if we could just play it on a Saturday.'

'Come up to date boy,' said Bob. 'This is Saturday. You remember yesterday? Well that was Friday. Today we've just beaten Kaikorai.'

'I bet he carries a calendar,' grinned Mac to me.

'No, fair go,' said Bob seriously. 'It's just general knowledge.'

'I mean it,' I said. 'It would be good if we could just play it on a

Saturday. I've just been thinking, here we are just after slogging through one hard game and before we're off the ground even, everyone wants to play next week's game with us. Why can't they give us a spell?'

'I suppose they're greedy,' said Mac. 'They just get over one sensation and they're greedy for the next. They don't like having nothing to look forward to.'

'Hero worship too,' said Bob. 'They like to air their views in front of the well-known Varsity skipper. It makes them feel big. Or perhaps they think we don't bother about much else, we just live for football.'

'We will be for the next week,' I said. 'We'll be playing Southern all the week and by the time Saturday comes we'll be so nervous we can't eat. It's one hell of a caper in a way. I'll be glad when the season's over and I can relax.'

'Did you get any knocks?'

'No worse than usual. The knee's pretty sore.'

The tram came along. It was good to sit down again. The conductor evidently recognized Mac. 'They'll make you run around next week,' he said. 'The Southern I mean. Be a good game.'

'How did they get on today?'

'Against Taieri? 46-3,' he said. 'How do you feel now?' He laughed and went to the back of the car. He came past us again later. '46-3,' he said again and winked.

The next Saturday morning I woke early in the digs and looked out the window. The sky was right down on the hills and there was a thick drizzle. Oh hell. I stretched down under the blankets again and tried to go to sleep but the thought of the match kept me awake. It had been a tough week as we were getting close to exams and I'd had a good deal of swot to do but I felt very fit. We'd been for a run every night after finishing our swot, usually about midnight, and on Wednesday there had been a really hard practice. The coach kept us packing lower and lower, scrum after scrum, and kept us down there with the strain on for so long that my muscles were all quivering and Buck who locked with me was groaning under the pressure, and when we stood up I felt dizzy and queer little lights slid down across my vision. It felt a good scrum though, very compact. The line-outs afterwards were plain hell. And then of course, the team-talk on Friday night. We used to hold it in a lecture room in the School of Mines. All around us on the wall were wooden models of pieces of machinery and charts of mines and geological strata. They made you realize the earth is very big and old, and goes down a long way. The coach would stand on the platform and start on his old game of building us up to fighting pitch. He was an artist at it, he could mould us just the way he wanted us. He spoke for a while about the traditions of the Club and then about the honour of playing off for the championship. 'To-morrow,' he said, 'We'll start off as usual by taking them on in the forwards. Here I am in the line-out. I look at my opposite number and I think, "You're a good man, but by Jesus I'm a better. To-day you've got no show." ' His voice takes on a stirring note. He moves about on the platform suiting actions to his words. 'Into them! Dominate them! And every man when he sees where that ball goes, he thinks "There's Buck in. I'm in too." Into them! And every man is thinking the same and we're all animated with the same spirit, we're going in to dominate them and we pack in tight and we're giving all our weight and strength and we're thinking together and working together and no one lets up. Dominate them.' And he goes on acting the part, words pouring out of him in that stirring tone and we watch him mesmerized, so that he takes us with him and we're there in the game too playing with him, working as a team. We leave the lecture room with a feeling of exaltation.

Then, on the other hand, there were the football notes in the paper. I know it was silly to take much notice of them, but I always read them. Referring to the Kaikorai game, the reporter said that I 'went a solid game but lacked the fire and dash that would make all the difference to his play.' The best thing I'd done, the movement where, to my mind, I had shown fire and dash was credited to Buck as 'one of his typical dashes'. Of course we are very much alike in build, but all the same I felt disappointed. The papers make people think that we are a sort of entertainment troupe, a public possession. Actually, I suppose, we'd go on playing if there were no public; we'd relax and enjoy our football much more.

It's one hell of a caper really, I thought, stretching out under the sheets. I was lucky to have a girl like Betty who was keen on football. Some of the girls used to go very snooty when the blokes couldn't take them to the Friday-night hops.

Well, this is the day. A few hours and it will be all over. This is it. It's funny how time comes round. For ages you talk of something and think of it and prepare for it, and it's still a long way off. You keep thinking how good it will be, and then suddenly, bang, it's there, you're doing it and it's not so enjoyable after all. I think football's like that, better before and after the game than in it.

Well the day had come. I wasn't keen to get up and face it but anything was better than lying in bed and thinking a lot of rubbish. I put on dressing-gown and slippers and padded round to Bob's room. He was still asleep. 'You won't look so peaceful in eight hours time,'

I said. 'They're queueing up at Carisbrook already.'

He raised his head from the pillow with a start. 'Eh?' He rubbed his eyes. 'What's wrong?'

'Jackie Hore just rang up to see how you are. He said their forwards are going to break very fast today, so he probably won't have an opportunity to ask you after the game because you'll be in hospital.'

He grinned. 'Then it's all bluff? I thought it was.'

'What?'

'About you forwards dominating them. I didn't think you could. I've never seen you do it yet. Just a bunch of big good-natured guys.'

'Not us,' I said. 'A pack of wolves just a-howling for prey. That's how we'll be to-day.'

Bob yawned and stretched his arms above his head. 'I must watch you. It would be interesting for a change. Have you eaten yet?'

So we went down for breakfast. Afterwards I cleaned my footy boots and packed my gear, and there was nothing to do but wait. I had no lectures on Saturday morning and I couldn't settle down to swot. The weather began to clear and a watery sun showed through the clouds so Bob and I went for a stroll. The town would be full of football talk and trams placarded, 'Big Game To-day, Carisbrook 3 p.m., Varsity A v Southern,' so to get away from it we went down to Logan Park and climbed up above the quarry. It wasn't so cold in the sun and the harbour looked glassy. There was no-one about. We threw stones down into the quarry. It was good watching them. They dropped away from us, slowly getting smaller and smaller, then suddenly they struck the bottom and exploded shooting fragments out sideways, starlike.

At twelve we went back to the digs for an early lunch. I didn't feel very hungry, and while we were waiting for the food, Bob kept tapping with his knife on the table. We caught the quarter past one tram out to the ground. It was better to watch the curtain-raiser than hang about the digs. The tram was packed and rows of cars were already making for the ground. Everybody looked very jolly and expectant. We saw Buck and Mac on the tram and that cheered us up a bit. It was good to realize that there were others who had to go through with it too. Buck didn't care a hoot about it all.

'Think you can win?' an old man said to him.

'Win?' Buck seized the old fellow's hand. 'Be the first to congratulate us on winning the championship. Get in early. Do it now. Be the very first.'

The old chap pulled his hand away looking a bit silly.

At Carisbrook we joined the crowd around the gates and pushed through to the players' entrance. I could see people nudging one another and nodding towards Mac. We showed our passes and went in along behind the stand and in underneath to the dressing-rooms. Most of the boys were early, there were other bags lying on the seats.

'Shall we go up for a while?' said Mac. We went out in front of the stand to see the final of the Junior Competition. The stand was packed and the bank opposite was dark with people. We stood about watching the boys playing with a sort of detached interest and then at half-time we went underneath to change. The strain was getting to me a little—I'd take things off and then forget where I'd put them. I had to undo my pants and look to see whether I'd put on my jock-strap. Most of the chaps were pretty quiet, but Buck kept going and we were pleased we had him to listen to. Mac was roaming round in his underpants looking for his glasses.

'Like to make a statement before the match?' I asked him.

He just looked at me. 'I can't find my bloody glasses. I suppose some bastard will tread on them.'

'Just a picture of quiet confidence,' said Bob. My face felt very tight when I tried to grin.

Soon the trainer came in and started to rub us down. The room was filled with the smell of eucalyptus and the rapid slap slap slap of his hands. It was a great feeling being done, he made us feel nice and loose and warm and free-moving. Then Jackie Hore, the Southern skipper came in to toss and we looked at him. There he was, the man we had been talking about all the week. He lost the toss and laughed. He looked a good deal smaller than I'd been imagining him. Of course we had played against him before, but the strain makes you think silly things. We felt better after he'd gone.

'He doesn't look so soft,' said Bob to me.

'Poor old Yackie. I'll try and bump into him again to-day and you just watch.'

'Never mind,' he said, 'unless you do it from the other side and straighten your nose up.'

I strapped up my weak knee and when the vaseline came round plastered it on my face to prevent scratches. The coach came in and we packed a scrum for him.

'That looks all right,' he said. 'Well now listen boys. Remember you're going out now as the Varsity boys have done for many years now to play off for the championship, and a lot of those old players are out there to-day watching to see how good you are. Don't let them down. Remember the first ten minutes in the forwards. Hard!' He punched his open hand. 'Go in there and dominate . . . .' But the referee was in the room to inspect the boots and the coach's exhortation was lost in the movement.

'Righto boys. One minute to go,' said the ref.

We took off our coats and handed round chewing gum. Buck and I put on our ear-guards. Mac found the ball and we lined up in the passage. The Southern players were there already, skipping about and rubbing their hands. They felt the cold too. The whistle blew, there was a glare of sunlight, and we were outside going out into the field, right out into the open. A roar from the crowd rolled all around enveloping us. A cold easterly breeze blew through our jerseys as we lined up for the photographers, squinting into the low sun. The Southern players looked broad and compact in their black and white jerseys. We gave three cheers and trotted out into the middle. The turf felt fine and springy. We spaced ourselves out. I took some deep breaths to get charged up with oxygen for this first ten minutes. A Southern player dug a hole with his heel and placed the ball.

'All right Southern? All right Varsity?' called the referee. Both captains nodded. He blew the whistle. The Southern man ran up to kick.

'Thank Christ,' I thought. 'The game at last.'

A. P. GASKELL                 # School Picnic

Miss Brown dismounted at the school gate. She hoped the bicycle saddle was not making the seat of her tweed skirt shiny. It was damn good tweed and black-market prices were terribly high. She pushed her bike into the wood-shed and took her case off the carrier. Oh hell . . . Joggling across those blasted sleepers had shaken open the powder-compact in her handbag. She shook it out and glanced at her watch. A quarter past and those damned Maoris had said they would be here at ten. Now after all her bustle she had to wait. As she lit a cigarette she noticed that she had chipped the varnish off one nail. Talk about roughing it.

She went round the front into the sunshine, unlocked the school door and entered. The sunlight was flooding the room through the windows and doorway, showing up the roughness of the match-lined walls and low ceiling. Little heaps of borer-dust lay on the desks, and as she entered a tiny stream of it filtered delicately down from the ceiling, through the slab of sunlight. The place some 30 years ago had been built as a cookhouse for the old sawmill, and no quantity of desks and blackboards, of 'Rules for Writing' or lists of 'Joining Words' could make it look like the city schools she was used to. It wasn't even painted inside.

She dusted her chair and sat down, pulling impatiently at the now pink-tipped cigarette. Me of all people, she thought, stuck away out here in this god-forsaken hole, and two weeks to go yet. I'm just halfway.

She had been sent to relieve for a month at this small King Country school, four miles 'by cycle track' from a station she had never even heard of. She had to board with the railway porter and bike it each day. The cycle track was simply a mark in the pumice that wound through the tea-tree and led to a crazy swing-bridge over the river. If she watched the boards as she bounced across, the water sliding beneath them made her feel dizzy as though she were falling sideways. The other half of the track was along the sleepers of an old bush tramway which wound through the scrub and blackberry above the river until it finally reached the clearing where the charred wreckage of the sawmill stood near the school. Beyond that, another swing-bridge led across the river to a flat wilderness of grey scaly tea-tree, fire-blackened in places. Somewhere in that mess of second growth the pupils lived. She often saw wisps of smoke rising against the bush on the hills at the back. Somewhere in there too the men were working. Sometimes she heard a lokey puffing, but where it was or what it was doing she neither knew nor cared. It was quite enough being expected to teach their snotty-nosed little Maori brats. She couldn't bear to touch them. One of them smelled smoky, just like an old roll of bacon. Jabbering at her in their excited pidgin English.

And to crown it all the damned School Committee had to pick on this Saturday for their school picnic. The first time she had seen old Araroa and big fat Terari was the day she arrived. She had thought they were rather cute then. The two of them met her at the gate. Old Araroa was still very erect, white-haired, his face wrinkled like a dried apple, blue markings on his chin, his eyes looking so very old and brown and tired. He spoke softly to her in Maori, leaning on his stick and gesturing with his free hand. The skin was very dry and shiny and stretched tight over the bones. After the old man finished, Fatty rolled his eyes at her and said, 'Hello, Miss Brown. The old man he say you be very happy here while the mahita away.' Fatty wore an old hat, disgraceful pants that folded back under his belly, showing a filthy lining, and a thick black woollen jersey with short sleeves. His arms were bigger than her legs. He had long yellow teeth like a horse. He was so much like the comic Maori of the illustrated papers that she felt safe and reassured at once. But she wasn't so pleased when they visited her again to tell her about the picnic. Fatty was rather excited himself at the idea. 'We give the kids the jolly good picnic eh?' he said. 'The old man here he say pretty near time we give the kids the picnic. Have the feed eh, and the races. You don't worry Miss Brown, we fix him all up. These jolly good worker these committee. We have him on Saturday.'

'On Saturday?' Of all days. Her voice was shrill.

'Saturday,' the old man whispered, and apparently satisfied, turned and walked off. Fatty stayed to reassure her. 'You don't worry Miss Brown. These committee fix him. You be here ten o'clock.'

And of course Saturday was the worst possible day. She had intended to have the day in Taumarunui, to go to the matinee and see Joan Crawford who always wore such stunning dresses and really did look wizard when she sat round sipping cocktails. She had really been looking forward to that. It was a pity Taumarunui was dry. She could do with a few spots herself to take away the taste of these last two weeks. Besides, she needed to have her hair set again, some of the rolls were coming out of place. At any rate she would feel a bit civilized again for a day at least.

She threw her butt in the empty fireplace. One of the schoolgirls usually cleaned the place. The sunlight outside was just pouring down and glinting off the pumice bank. She had to squint to see properly. Damn it, she should have brought her sunglasses. George didn't like wrinkles.

How the gang at home would laugh if they could see me now, she thought, awaiting the pleasure of a tribe of Maoris. I wonder if George has thought of me at all. Lucky devils, I suppose they'll all be going out on George's launch again. They'll probably have a few in by this time too, and boy, would I like to be the same. If it's fine George will be taking them up to his crib. George was a nice job, beautifully muscled. He had dark wavy hair, white teeth, and he oiled his body before he lay in the sun. Sometimes he would let her do it for him. His swimming shorts were always tight around his small hips and flat stomach. He knew what he wanted and had a lot of fun. She was trying to do a line with George but the competition was so keen. Still, just before she left she had thrown a spanner in Vonnie's works. She told George there was a rumour that Vonnie had a dose. George would keep well clear of her. Anything like that, even people with skin trouble, made him feel sick.

A shadow darkened the doorway. 'Hello, Miss Brown,' cried Terari, his big belly bulging out above his pants. 'You the first one here? Look nobody else here. You pretty keen on these picnic eh?'

'You said ten o'clock, and look at it, nearly eleven.' Her eyes focussed, hardened.

'Crikey, that late? By golly I ring the bell. Wake them up. Those lazy Maori must sleep in eh? You can't trust those Maori. Always late.' A dark smell of sweat preceded him into the room. 'You didn't light the fire?'

'I certainly didn't light the fire.'

'Nemind. We put him outside. If those fellow come you tell him off eh? They shouldn't be late.' He lumbered out and began striking the length of iron railing that hung from a tree near the door. The strong sound dinned and vibrated around her and rolled back off the hills. He was grinning in at her again. 'Just like school eh? You give them the strap for late.'

She heard the sound of his axe at the back.

A small head was thrust round the doorpost. 'Please Miss Brown.'

'Hello Lena. Are you the first one? Have you got a clean nose this morning?'

Lena sniffed and licked her upper lip. She came shyly into the room, barefoot but clean, with her hair drawn back and plaited tightly. Two even smaller children stayed at the door looking in at the teacher.

'Please Miss Brown, we gotta hundred pies.'

'My word that's a lot. You'll all have the bellyache. It's a pity they don't get you some decent food.' The poor kid had hardly a sound tooth in her head.

'Fizz,' said a small voice at the doorway.

'And please Miss Brown we gotta hundred fizz.'

'Fizz?'

'And straws,' cried the child at the door.

'Who are these, Lena?'

'Please Miss Brown, these my cousin. This Gwendoline and that one Harris. They Mrs Patutai baby. They coming to school maybe next year.'

'Mrs Patutai? I haven't heard of her.'

'Please Miss Brown, she live over at Tokaanu. Our last baby die so these one come and live with us. She got too many.'

I don't blame her, she thought, for giving them away. If this is populate or perish, I'll take perish. There were more voices outside. She went out to look. The children at the door stared at her as she passed. They both had running noses. 'Wah. Red hands too,' she heard one of them say. 'That's varnish,' came Lena's voice. 'I done mine with blackberry. Look. I done my mouth too but I lick him off. Sour.' Miss Brown decided to ignore it. After all you could hardly blame them, they were so out of touch with civilization away back here.

At the end of the building, where the sunlight made the white-washed wall hard to look at, three middle-aged women in dark cotton dresses were squatting. One was Terari's wife, a big fat wahine, barefooted, with a rug around her and a sleeping baby's head on her shoulder. The others she didn't know. They were talking softly, making guttural noises to one another in Maori, and smoking. They smiled up at her. 'Tenakoe.'

'A lovely day Miss Brown,' said Mrs Terari. 'We come early to do some work but they never brought the stuff yet. Get things ready for the picnic.'

'Picnic,' the others smiled and nodded.

'My husband here?'

'Yes. That's him chopping round at the back.' She was wondering what to say. These old dames were hard to talk to. She stood uncomfortably before them. One of them looked up and caught her eye. 'Picnic.' She smiled and nodded again.

Some children were running about in the paddock, the boys looking very clean in white shirts and with their hair plastered down. They were, as usual, being aeroplanes, dive-bombing and making zooming noises. One of the women called out sharply to them. Mrs Terari pointed to her. 'This lady's son was killed in Crete. He go to this school before.'

'Aie, Crete.' The mother covered her face with her hands, then broke into rapid Maori. Fatty came round the corner. 'Wah. You here? Where all those other fellow? Those damn lazy Maori, they no good for nothing.' He went and struck the rail again. Just then there were shouts at the gate, and men and women came in carrying parcels and boxes. 'Hey, you fellow,' he called. 'Miss Brown give you the strap for late.' Mrs Terari shrieked with laughter. The place was suddenly crowded with voices and movement. The children all gathered round, guessing what was in the boxes.

After that everything happened quickly. The women all went inside to arrange the food. The men grouped round the fire, talking and laughing. They were a cut-throat looking crew. Miss Brown wished she could understand what they were laughing so much about. Telling dirty yarns probably.

Fatty went out in the middle of the paddock and started the races. The boys ran fiercely, showing their teeth and straining hard especially when the men cheered. Fatty gave her an old notebook and asked her to take down the results. 'For prizes. This afternoon.' She stood there for ages, watching the children run and writing their names down. The men got excited, the children were hot, and when they grouped round her she could hardly breathe. She always deodorized herself so carefully too.

An elderly woman, tall, very thin, with blue markings on her nose and chin and a dark shawl over her hair came towards the group, shrilling angrily at them. They fell silent. She seemed to be picking on Fatty. He began to expostulate but she brushed past him and inclined her head very graciously to Miss Brown, 'Haeremai, haeremai,' and smiled showing empty gums. She took Miss Brown's arm and led her over to the school. I hope her hand's clean, thought Miss Brown. I'll have to wash this sweater now. 'My son-in-law got no manners,' said the old lady. 'He shouldn't left you out there with all those men. My name Mrs Te Ahuru. You come in and see all our baby. Nice for the girls to have the lady teacher.'

The schoolroom seemed crowded with women of all shades of brown and all ages. Sunken-cheeked old crones squatted against the wall in the sunlight under the windows, rolling cigarettes. Flash young things with lipstick, long-legged in high-heeled shoes, stood silkily, smoking tailormades. The desks were covered with food, buns and cakes on plates, and sandwiches in boxes and on newspapers. Boxes of pies stood near the fireplace and rows of red and yellow fizz bottles along the wall. Old Mrs Te Ahuru led her in and said something in Maori lingo, ending up with 'Miss Brown.' They all looked up and smiled and nodded. She didn't know what to say. 'How do you do?' she said. 'Isn't it a lovely day.' Everyone seemed pleased. Smiles in all directions.

She was taken round to admire the babies. It was agony. She wasn't interested in babies. All she could see of most of them was a small brown head lolling out of a blanket on the mother's back, or staring big-eyed over the mother's shoulder. She tried to say something nice. And there was Micky, her smallest primer, a little wizened creature with sad eyes like a monkey. 'Hello Micky. Why aren't you out running races?'

Micky grinned, crossing his legs with embarrassment but his eye was on the fizz. A youngish woman beside him answered; she was rather nice-looking but had very bad teeth. She spoke so pleasantly that Miss Brown decided she must have been somewhere to a Maori High School and then come back to the mat. Another baby hung on to her skirt and a third stared over her shoulder.

'I don't want Micky to run round,' said the young woman. 'He must keep quiet. He going to die soon.'

'To die!' Good Lord. And so matter-of-fact about it too. In school Micky was always full of beans.

'Yes.' The young woman fixed serious eyes on her. 'You know that Chinese doctor who come around with all the medicine?'

Miss Brown nodded. Some peddling herbalist had been around just before she came, she had heard the kids talking about him.

'I took Micky to see him. Micky not well, he so thin.'

'And what did he say?'

'When I go in the room he just look at me. He don't speak, he just look for long time. He got sharp eyes too. Then he say "You Mrs Pine?" I say "Yes." He say "Your husband name Joe?" I say "Yes." He say "I can tell all about you. Your husband fall off his horse and break his shoulder. He can't chop the trees now." He say "Your second baby die and this one Micky not Joe's baby. This Micky very sick." He keep looking at me all the time and I get frightened and think I go out but he say "Don't go out. I tell you about Micky." So he say Micky all twisted up inside and pretty soon he die. He give me some medicine in the little bottle.' She showed the size with her finger and thumb. 'Seven and six. But I don't get many bottle. Too dear. So I suppose Micky going to die.' She rubbed Micky's head gently with her hand. 'That doctor right about those other things. You think he right about Micky too?'

'Good Heavens no,' said Miss Brown. 'That's terrible. Why don't you tell the police?'

'He make me frightened. Those sharp eyes they go right in me.'

'But, but really you mustn't take any notice of all that nonsense. You get the nurse to look at Micky next time she's round. I don't think there's much the matter with him.' Poor thing, how terrible. She must have believed it all too, the way she was looking. They were all so damnably ignorant of civilized procedure. 'I'll tell the nurse about it.'

The clang of the iron railing was reverberating through the room. 'Come and get it,' yelled Mrs Terari. 'Heigh-oh Silver,' called one of the men, and they all came trooping in. The smell got stronger. They moved about, pushing, laughing, calling, helping themselves. Each child was sucking fizz through a straw, even the tiny ones. Miss Brown worked her way through them to the table, and from her case took her small lunch wrapped in a clean white serviette.

'Here Miss Brown, you sit down.' Fatty was offering her a chair. 'Wah, the poetry eh? By golly I say the poetry. Here Miss Brown, you sit down. Here Miss Brown, you sit down.' He roared with laughter. Fragments of half-chewed food lay on his tongue. She shuddered and looked away.

'Miss Brown, you have this nice pie.' Old Mrs Te Ahuru held out a clean plate with a pie on it. 'I keep him for you. And these sandwich.'

'But I have my own lunch here.'

'That leetle bit. You eat more, that's why you so thin eh? You have this nice pie.'

'Oh no really I. . . .'

'Oh but you must. You shouldn't brought your dinner. You come to our picnic you eat our dinner.' She turned to her son-in-law. 'You get Miss Brown the nice cup of tea. In the clean cup.'

Somehow she got them down. There were so many things she couldn't bear to watch—the old women mumbling soft sandwiches, Fatty eating pies enormously, the children with the wet under their noses mingling with the sticky wet round their mouths and chins from the fizz. Somehow the lunch ended and they went outside. Half-way, she thought. I've got the worst half over.

The sky was clouding, and a cool breeze came rustling across the tops of the tea-tree.

'By golly we better hurry before the rain,' shouted Fatty, and they ran the races in a frenzy of haste and shouting. The cheering was deafening for the grown-ups' races. Some of the men were going out into the bushes just outside the gate and coming back wiping their mouths. When the unmarried women ran with their skirts tucked up above their knees the men whistled and cat-called.

Miss Brown sneaked away to the girls' lavatory but when she tried to open the door there was a whiff of cigarette smoke and a guttural voice muttered something. She paused in indecision and an old crone came out and held the door for her, smiling gummily. She went in but could not bear to sit on that seat. After a decent interval she went back to the sports. Large isolated drops of rain were falling and rolling, still globular, in the dust. There was a sighing in the tea-tree as a grey curtain of rain moved towards them.

Soon they were all inside again. It's beer they've got out there, thought Miss Brown, sniffing. Fatty lit the fire inside and carried in kerosene tins of water for another cup of tea. The tins looked small when he held them. Old Araroa had arrived and was standing there leaning firmly on his stick, white-haired, full of gentleness and dignity, handing out the cheap toys for prizes. The children were rather in awe of him. He spoke softly, knowing most of the names. When all the prizes were gone and Micky was left standing beside his mother, the old man beckoned him over and gave him some money out of his pocket. The other kids crowded round. 'How much you got, Micky?' but he wouldn't show them. He couldn't count it.

No one knew what to do next. The rain was rattling on the roof and splashing against the windows. One young woman opened her blouse and began feeding her baby.

Fatty was approaching. 'The old man like to hear the kids sing.' Even he spoke quietly. 'You make them sing something?' Miss Brown finally had them in their desks, all self-conscious, pushing and showing off a little, looking to the sides to see who was watching.

The singing started, school songs for a while with Miss Brown beating time, then requests for popular songs and Maori tunes. Some of the men and women joined in. They began to warm up. The girls went in front and sang an action song. Even Lena went with them. The small girls moved stiffly, but the bigger ones were relaxed, their hands fluttered delicately, moving easily and clapping exactly in time. They finished and blushed at the applause. Some young women came out. More familiar cheering and whistling followed their number. Then the men lined up and started a vigorous song. The old ladies round the wall were nodding and smiling and moving their hands. Fatty was out in front leading the men with actions. Miss Brown was feeling out of things, when she noticed Fatty's eye upon her. Oh hell, here he was, coming over, showing the whites of his eyes, his tongue, jerking and posturing about, wobbling his big belly, quivering his hands. She shrank back against the wall while he performed in front of her. She could smell beer. The crowd was shrieking with laughter. She felt her throat and cheeks burning. The big fat bastard, making a laughing-stock of her. Suddenly and savagely she smacked his face. There was a sudden silence, then a scream of laughter. His face was hanging there before her, utterly astonished, his mouth hung open, his hands slowly sank. She was amazed at what she had done and very frightened, but he turned and saw the mirth, then clowning, clapped his hand over one eye and staggered back shouting with laughter. Old Mrs Te Ahuru was beside her. 'You serve him right,' she was shouting. 'You serve him damn well right.' She shooed some children out of a desk. 'We sit here.'

The show went on, there was no stopping them now. A new man was out in front leading a haka. The men shouted, smacked, jumped, stamped, the beat thundered round the room. The veins stood out on their throats and foreheads. The old women around the walls were mouthing, twitching, jerking their hands, grimacing. First one then another got up and moved jerkily across the floor, keeping in time with the beat, to join the line. Everybody was doing it, the kids too. The din was immense, the building shook, borer-dust showered down, dust rose from the floor. Crash! The climax. Sweaty faces smiling, all coughing in the dust.

'Tea, tea,' called old Mrs Te Ahuru beside her. 'Water boiling. We make tea.'

Miss Brown felt overpowered, helpless. These people were of another kind altogether. She was utterly alone among them. She felt suffocated. She couldn't stand it. She got her case and made for the door. A hand on her arm. Old Mrs Te Ahuru. And Fatty too.

'You can't go. Look. It's still raining.'

'I must. I've got to be back early.'

'But raining. You get wet through.'

'I can't help it. I can't stay any longer.'

'You got no coat?'

'No.'

'You take my rug.' Old Mrs Te Ahuru was unwrapping it. 'Look, I show you how to wear it.'

'No, no, please.'

'You want some coat?' Fatty turned and called to the crowd. A girl came forward with a raincoat. 'Here. You bring him back on Monday eh?'

They helped her into the coat. 'You come and see us some more,' said Mrs Te Ahuru. Old Araroa was approaching but she picked up her bag, got her bike. The rain was cold on her face and neck but oh, the air was clean and sweet, and she was away from them. Oh Christ, she thought, I must get out of it. I must get George somehow, get him drunk, have a baby even. Anything.

After all, she thought, they're nothing but a pack of savages. Not even civilized.

The rain was very steady, and by the time she reached the porter's house she was wet through. All the rolls were washed out of her hair and her make-up was streaky.

All this for a pack of bloody savages, she thought.

# An Annual Affair

It almost seemed to be blowing up for rain. Every minute or two the wind came across the paddocks, like a lorry changing gears, and round the lonely store corner. The store looked lonely because it was closed for Boxing Day. The orange drinks and weeties in the window and the country scene with stout letters, KEEP FIT, cutting across made you feel sad, as if you had eaten too much. The wallops from the wind made you feel tired. Joy sat on the step of the store.

Come on, get up now, her Mum said. You don't want to dirty your dress before we start.

Joy got up. The wind passed again blowing up dust and rain. It was late. It was nearly nine. Mum reckoned Auntie Laurel was holding them up.

Before the lorry came round the corner they could hear the kids screeching. It was like a cage of cockatoos on wheels. Uncle Nick was in front with Dad. Behind, besides the kids, there was Auntie Laurel and a flash lady from town. She had brought something for the children for Boxing Day. It was some crackers, but they couldn't pull them because Mum said it wasn't the proper time. Mum didn't think much of crackers.

The Domain in front of the hotel was packed out with cars and lorries. Dad growled because the place near the fence where they always parked, was taken. Mum only said, I thought we were going to be late. The cars looked funny all packed round the hotel because there was plenty of room along the beach. The hotel stood by itself away from the baches. It was tall and a dark red colour like the one in Joy's Granny's picture, *The Broad Way*. They didn't have pictures like that in Joy's home. They had one of a bunch of pansies and one of a cathedral. In Granny's picture the hotel had a Union Jack on top and through the windows you could see the people inside, playing cards and dancing. But the real hotel windows were always closed. It looked as if nobody lived there, but round at the side there was a small door and men going in and out.

The old jetty was standing over the mud with only its last two legs in the water. Brian and the boys made a dash for the trolley, that was used for loading timber in the old days, and started to push each other up and down, but Mum yelled to them that they'd fall in the water, and Auntie Laurel said the jetty was dangerous and ought to be seen to.

Mum and Dad and Miss Jenkins, the flash lady, sat down on the step of the lorry. Miss Jenkins had several rows of rolls on top of her head, and slacks which were tight behind, and dark red finger-nails. She said how pretty everything looked after the rain.

Dad kept looking hard at Miss Jenkins's finger-nails, then looking away.

Everyone seems to think it's nice down here in the summer, Mum said, of course we're used to it.

I suppose you always come here, Miss Jenkins said.

We always manage to get down for the picnic, Dad said. It's an annual affair.

Mum said, It looks as if we've been unlucky with the weather though.

Dad said, It's generally like this round about Christmas.

But anyway, Mum said, it does make a change and the kiddies do enjoy it.

Dad took out his cigarette case and offered Miss Jenkins one but she said, No thanks. She did occasionally, but not just now.

Dad said, Excuse me, he had to meet a chap, and went over towards the hotel.

It began to rain a bit and the wind was chilly. Mum said they might as well go for a walk as it wasn't lunch time yet, and Miss Jenkins could see the view from further up. Everyone always said it was rather nice, only of course the tide was wrong now.

Joy had to fetch Terry and Mavis. Mum was nervous about them falling into the mud. They were right at the end of the jetty pretending to fish. Jim was there too, he had rigged up the lines for them.

Jim didn't come round to Joy's place any more. Dad reckoned that scholarship he won hadn't done him much good. He had just picked up a lot of weird ideas and was always slinging off at everything. Dad would say, Where's the Red Flag? And Jim couldn't be bothered with Dad, so he didn't come round any more.

But the first Christmas Joy could remember he was there, and gave her a bell that was meant to be put on a tree and soon got broken. What she remembered about that Christmas was the colour of the bell. Auntie Laurel said that it was a nile green, but it wasn't at all like a nile green dress Joy had. She never could get it with her paints either, so after the bell was broken she never saw that particular colour again.

They had the socials at the station hall then, and Mum and Dad still went out together sometimes, and the imaginary man came at night to keep away danger. He wore historical clothes and was called Mr Charles but he looked very like Jim.

And after that nothing much except the picnics. Jim went away to the town and didn't come home very often. He was saving up for a trip to Europe, he said.

The kids didn't want to stop fishing, and Joy had to promise they could come back later on. I'll be seeing you later on, she said to Jim.

With Terry and Mavis dragging behind they walked along past the baches. The baches were mostly empty, and as they hadn't been painted for years, were grayish-white like the sky.

The Dacres were coming. They talked away to each other looking along the ground, not seeing Mum and her friend till they got quite close. Then they stopped and smiled and were introduced to Miss Jenkins. They said the glass had gone up quite a bit this morning.

When the Dacres were out of sight Miss Jenkins said she *would* like a smoke now, so Mum suggested they climb up the bank and sit under the pines where they would be sheltered from the drizzle and not be seen. Mavis slipped down the bank and dirtied herself but Mum was quite calm about it. She had brought another dress and panties for Mavis to change to for afternoon tea.

You keep them so nice, Miss Jenkins said with a smile.

When they got back to the lorry it was lunchtime. Auntie Laurel was there with the rest of the kids, waiting. She said she hadn't seen Uncle Nick all morning. He's always Hail fellow well met, she explained to Miss Jenkins.

They sat on the grass on coats and macs. Mum took off her hat with the felt feather. Whew, isn't it hot, she said. The sun had come out and it was stifling hot between the cars. Mum unpacked the peanut-butter sandwiches, and the date scones she had baked on the Happywork stove Dad gave her for Christmas. Well we might as well start, she said, as Dad hasn't come. She sent Brian of for the hot water from Mrs Withers. Then she passed the scones to Miss Jenkins. I baked them before we started this morning, she said.

Miss Jenkins took one. Oh aren't you clever, she said. I must confess I often pop round to the Cosy Cake Shop for scones and things, you know how it is in the city. She didn't look at all ashamed of it though.

They say our baker bakes a fair fruit cake, Mum said, but I prefer my own. You know what's in it.

I suppose you do, Miss Jenkins said.

Dad came and sat down and started fooling with Terry, turning

him over and pretending to smack him. Terry didn't know what to
make of it but he laughed till he turned red and hiccoughed. Dad
had red patches on his cheeks and his eyes were swimmy.

Brian came back with the teapot. In his other hand he carried the
broken off spout wrapped in a handkerchief. Mum couldn't let fly at
him with Mrs Jenkins there. Dad took it as a joke.

The tea was terribly strong and Miss Jenkins said, Couldn't we
borrow some hot water from the hotel? But Mum said, I don't care
about asking favours when we don't know them.

You needn't trouble for me, Dad said. He wouldn't have a scone
either. He ate one sandwich quickly, then started telling one of his
funny stories to Miss Jenkins. He said he knew some better ones than
that, but he didn't think he could tell them. This made Miss Jenkins
laugh but Mum was rather quiet. She was handing round some of
the Christmas cake. This year it had white water-icing and desic-
cated coconut, but as Mum said herself it had turned out rather
plain. No one took any. Terry was being a bad boy because Dad had
been taking notice of him, he was wanting his banana now, but Mum
said, No, you know they're for later on. But he howled so loud she
had to give him one and then the other kids grabbed bananas too out
of Mum's bag, which was bulging with bathing togs and things to
change and knitting and Miss Jenkins's *Gone with the Wind,* and
other things for later on, and ran off to the shore. Mum called after
them not to play in the mud and not to go on the jetty.

Miss Jenkins said she'd had such a lovely lunch and she thought
she'd retire to the lorry and have a smoke. Dad offered to go along
with her. Only in fun of course.

Pull your skirt down a bit Joy, Mum said. The Reverend Allum
was walking over their way. He sat down on the grass beside Joy and
smiled all round. He always smiled in a special way as if he were
much happier than everyone else. Joy looked away so as not to be
hooked with his smile and be asked something. She'd been in his bad
books since she let out that she was reading the Bible verses at night.
The verses to be read were marked on the card and if you were
regular you could get right through the Bible in five years. Only the
morning wasn't really a good time, Mum was tired after having done
so much before breakfast, and the kids had to be got off to school.
But the verses are your armour for the day, the Reverend Allum had
said. You wouldn't put on your armour when you lie down to sleep
would you now? Whoever heard of such a thing as that?

Do have some tea, Mum said, it's rather thick I'm afraid.

Thanks but I've had a cup with Mrs Withers, people are so
hospitable. I only wanted to enquire about your little laddie. The one

who wasn't at Sunday School last week.

It was only a cold, Mum said, but they hate to miss. It's nice for the kiddies having the Sunday School so near.

Yes and for Mum and Dad too, Joy was thinking, they can have a lie down on Sunday afternoons.

Miss Jenkins came out of the lorry and was introduced. Dad stretched out his legs on the grass till his foot was touching hers, then said, Oh, beg pardon.

Quite a good crowd down here today, Mum said. But the Reverend Allum's smile was for Miss Jenkins.

I expect you must find it pretty quiet, he said.

Oh no, she said, I love a day in the country.

You're right too, the Reverend Allum said. When she was younger Joy had used to think that when the Reverend Allum said You're right too, she'd hit upon something clever. It always turned out though, when he'd enlarged on it, that it wasn't what she had said after all.

The Reverend Allum took a deep breath in and a long look all round him. Yes, he said, on the out-going breath, when all's said and done nature takes a lot of beating. Jim was walking past, carrying a bottle with a straw stuck in it. They all looked away and pretended they hadn't noticed but Auntie Laurel said quietly to Mum, Fancy bringing it out here, where everyone's having their lunch.

But the Reverend Allum went on as though nothing had happened. We country-dwellers now, I sometimes think we're apt to forget perhaps. He looked all round him again. His all-embracing glance skipped the hotel and threaded its way through the cars to the strip of shore. The tide was nearly out. There was only a gray snake of water in the channel, and the steep mud-slopes were steaming off in the sun.

Yes, it's a pity Muriel and Winnie couldn't get down, Mum said. They've been in hospital with their appendixes, she explained to Miss Jenkins. Doctor thought they might as well have them done together and get it over.

Yes, We only see the sunny side of life over here, the Reverend Allum said. It's difficult to imagine what it must be like over there.

Dad had his eyes closed and a dribble of spit on his chin. Joy gave him a quiet agonized poke and he opened his eyes and smiled, looking like Terry. Mum was getting on with her fancy work. Yes. Quite a good crowd here today, she said, but a lot of them have to leave early for the milking.

I don't know what others' opinions may be, said the Reverend Allum, but personally Miss Jenkins, I like to think of this little affair as a sort of commemoration. The settlers in these parts landed here. Quite near where we are sitting now I believe.

There wasn't anything here then, Mum said, her eyes on the hotel.

The settlers had faith, said the Reverend.

Too right, said Miss Jenkins, putting her hand to a yawn.

Dad had found a pair of pink art silk panties that Mavis had had for Christmas. They had been in Mum's bag for Mavis to change to. Dad kept holding them up and squinting between the legs in a comical way. The Reverend Allum went right on about the settler who had stuck in the mud and they never found the body, but Joy felt hot all over. As if somethink awful might happen. She got up quietly and walked away to be out of sight of Dad and the lot of them.

She said hello to the Dodds, the Band of Hope Dodds, they always came early and got the best place nearest to the hotel, and went round to the yard. The hotel backed on to the shore and the yard was quiet and secluded, with empty cases to sit on and a nice view over the inlet. Jim was there smoking cigarette with the cider bottle and the straw beside him.

Hello, she said, what are you doing here?

Oh, nothing, he said.

I thought maybe you had a date.

Who with? he said.

Joy pulled little bits off the straw, wanting to cry. Mum had stuck to it that the navy was just as smart and safer for washing, and the perm she could have next year when she worked at the store. Next year it would be all too late. The other girls had florals, the kind with elastic round the waist that fits almost anyone, and their hair nicely set with steel clips and invisible hairnets. Merle had blossomed out with lip-stick too, but really it didn't look so hot with her pimples.

Cheer up, Jim said. How's old stick in the mud?

As usual, Joy said, he's on the settlers again.

And your Dad and the others?

As usual, she said. Dad's had a few of course. You know what he always says, It's a free country.

The curfew shall not ring, but Dad shall turn the wringer tomorrow. He'll have to take his headache to church as well.

Jim was always making fun of Dad and Mum. It wasn't true either, Dad didn't go to church any more. There was only the wringer. It was always like that with Jim. Just as you were settling for a nice yarn he would start slinging off at Dad, or his Dad, or the capitalist system, so that it never came to anything. Still, of course, there would never be anyone else.

It was sunny and quiet in the yard. The people walking up and down, up and down, between the hotel and jetty, stopped and turned back where the metalled path ended. Joy moved along closer to Jim on the box. The people seemed far away. It had to happen then that Murrey popped his head over the fence, grinning at them, showing his black stumps. A horrible boy Murrey, with filthy tricks.

It's only Murrey, Joy said. He'll be having his new teeth when he leaves school, his mother says.

The big thrill that only comes once in a lifetime. Well, my big thrill will be getting out of this. I might get my trip to Europe after all.

More likely land up in the desert though, Joy said. Why couldn't you help your Dad milking and get exempted? You don't want to go and get killed do you?

Get killed for these stick in the muds? But you have to think of the future. A lot of chaps are relieved to get into camp. It's a change from mowing the lawn and all that. It's going to be more of a change than they think though. A change is going on all over the world. Before the war governments had to make camps because the prisons couldn't hold the political prisoners. It's never happened like that before. The bosses are hoping it will blow over, the war will give people something else to do. It was only the old red spectre walking again, they think. But the change that is coming is rising like the tide. It will reach even this little place one day. But I'm going to be on the spot when the big things happen. You have to think of the future.

Joy was looking at the hills across the inlet, not thinking of the future, thinking the hills looked empty and strange today. She had always meant to go over there some time. It looked lonely, but pretty and peaceful, the grass a soft green, not the metal green of the properly fertilized paddocks, the hills split softly into creeks full of scrub and shadows. There were Maori lands over there. Better than on our side, Dad said, they are dirty and carry diseases. There wouldn't be much to see over there, he said, but Joy had always wanted to go some time.

The sun was bright and a cool wind blew from the coast. It was a lovely day now. Cheer up, Jim said. Joy sat still, for fear of disturbing his hand settled on hers, feeling his cool fingers and the heat inside her hand where the straw was crushed.

A man came out of the hotel back door. He was little and sandy, and walked slowly and sadly. He must have lost his way.

He crossed to a box and sat carefully down. Then he remembered something and got up again with a nervous look round the yard. He saw them but it was just too late by then. He took out his false teeth and was sick on the ground.

Joy got up. Jim said he'd have to be getting along too. Outside the yard they ran into the Young Men's Bible Class and the Reverend Allum in bathing togs. They were larking and making funny remarks like a boys' school story. Come along in and have a good swim, they shouted to Jim as they passed, it would do you good.

I'm afraid I haven't been introduced, Miss Jenkins said to Jim when she overtook them, but I've heard such a lot about you. Joy introduced them and she got confidential at once. Rather a queer idea for all the men to go in swimming together, Bible Class or no Bible Class, she said. And it was pretty hard to keep up a conversation with some people, and she asked him, had he read, *Gone with the Wind*?

Jim said, Well, yes, but he had to be going himself now. He started up his motor bike with a bang and rode off up the hill, the bike making scornful explosions.

After that there was nothing much to do. It began to rain again, and Mum sat on a box in the bathing shed with her fancy work, pegging away at the big rose in the middle she had promised herself she was going to finish today. Joy could see there was something wrong but Mum said it was only her legs.

They swelled up, generally in the evenings, about the time Dad came home, and she would say to him, Just look at my legs again, it's from being on them all day.

You must have got up too early, Miss Jenkins said.

Oh no, I always get up at five, Mum said. I like to get things done before breakfast.

It's a puzzle what you find to do all the rest of the day, Miss Jenkins said.

I find plenty to do thank you, Mum said, as if she'd been offered something she didn't like.

You must have a gift for it, Miss Jenkins said. And she laughed.

Like some people have a gift for fooling round with men, Mum said. Joy felt as if something horrid was going to happen. But Mum couldn't have meant Miss Jenkins.

The Bible Class was swimming still in the rain, and the other unmarried men must have been in the pub.

When it cleared up it was time to get Mavis changed and line up for the ice-cream. Mrs Dodds, Murrey's mother, and Mrs Chapman were doing the refreshments this year. Mrs Dodds always got first prize at the show with her sponge surprise, or else with her ginger kisses. But when Mum tasted the ice cream she said there was nothing in it but those powders, and Auntie Laurel said, Mrs Dodds and Mrs Chapman might have put in a bit more sugar and a drop of cream for the kiddies. And only those cheap soft drinks.

The soft drinks were mixed in two kerosene tins. One of the drinks was red and the other green. There was plenty of it and some of the boys got as many as ten drinks. To end off with there was an orange, but Mum said that was extravagant at the price they were now.

Then Brian was sent to fetch the hot water again, and Mum and Miss Jenkins and Auntie Laurel had afternoon tea again with the rest of the Christmas cake. The kids hung round, pestering to go in swimming and Mum kept saying, No you might get in the current. You know you can't go without Dad.

Mrs Chapman passed with her husband. We're off home, she said.

You've got him well trained, Mum said. That was one of her jokes.

Terry getting sleepy, worrying to be taken notice of, was saying over and over again, Where's Dad?

Now what did you promise me this morning? Mum said. What am I going to tell Dad when he asks if Terry has been a good boy all day?

Daddy's having his tea somewhere, Miss Jenkins said.

But Terry said, I know where he might be. Drinking beer in the hotel.

Mum suddenly gave him such a crack on the side of the head that he couldn't even yell for a minute or two.

The tide's about right in, Joy said. It made noises like smacking kisses under the banks where the kids were sitting looking down at the water. After a while Mum came over and said as the sun was going and Dad hadn't come yet, they could put on their togs. But they mustn't stay in for long, it was getting chilly. The boys rushed off to the shed to change. Joy and Mavis undressed in the lorry.

Terry stood on the bank and cried while the others were in. He hadn't been allowed to paddle because of his cold. The sun was off the water now but he cried so long that Mum undressed him and put on his bathing pants, but when he got down to the water he wouldn't go in.

Joy rubbed down Mavis and dressed herself quickly and walked away along the shore as if she were meeting someone. Passing the Withers she saw the dinghy tied to a post by the beach, and got in and let it drift into the mangroves. The wind had died down. It felt like a warm damp hand across her hair. The ugly old twisted mangrove trunks were all covered up and only the branches with dark green leaves were showing. The water made roads between the tops of the trees. Joy moved along the roads and little lanes till a branch scraped the bottom of the boat. Then it was not a road but only all that water underneath, enough to cover a tree.

She began to row out across the inlet. The sun had set and the valleys and creeks on the other side were smoothed out. The hills were black and flat, like the advertisement letters across the picture, painted across the sky for some reason.

When the boat swung in the current she turned. The kids had stopped shouting on the jetty and everything was quiet, and over towards the sea a crack in the sky opened into a still shiny lake, exactly the colour of the Christmas bell.

When Joy got back Brian and Mavis were sitting in the lorry because it was getting chilly, playing I Spy. Terry was asleep on the floor. He had a blue mark down the side of his face. Mum was walking up and down inside. She said Auntie Laurel and Miss Jenkins had gone home hours ago with somebody else.

It was quite dark when Dad came out at last. He said he had had to stay for Uncle Nick who was not feeling too good. Mum wanted to have it out with him but he only smiled. Might as well be the wind blowing, she said. But perhaps you'll be feeling differently tomorrow.

Mr Chapman, who hadn't gone home after all, sat in front with Dad. Uncle Nick was inside. He was carrying on about his kidneys, how bad they were, they didn't seem to get any better, he was sure he wouldn't pass the medical test, and everyone ought to do their bit, and the loved ones at home. He got so worked up about it he started to cry.

The kids feeling a bit awkward, piped up, *Roll out the Barrel, We'll have a Jolly Good Time*, just to change the subject. I wish it was next year, Brian said, for the picnic.

Joy said nothing. Brian was such a kid. He never stopped to think that everything might be different next year.

JANET FRAME

# The Day of
# the Sheep

It should not have rained. The clothes should have been slapped warm and dry with wind and sun and the day not have been a leafless cloudy secret hard to understand. It is always nice to understand the coming and going of a day. Tell her, blackbird that pirrup-pirrupped and rainwater that trickled down the kitchen window-pane and dirty backyard that oozed mud and housed puddles, tell her though the language be something she cannot construe having no grammar of journeys.

Why is the backyard so small and suffocating and untidy? On the rope clothes-line the washing hangs limp and wet, Tom's underpants and the sheets and my best tablecloth. We'll go away from here, Tom and me, we'll go some other place, the country perhaps, he likes the country but he's going on and on to a prize in Tatts and a new home, flat-roofed with blinds down in the front room and a piano with curved legs, though Tom's in the Dye Works just now, bringing home handkerchiefs at the end of each week, from the coats with no names on.

— Isn't it stealing Tom?

— Stealing my foot, I tell you I've worked two years without a holiday. You see? Tom striving for his rights and getting them even if they turn out to be only a small anonymous pile of men's hand-kerchiefs, but life is funny and people are funny, laugh and the world laughs with you.

She opens the wash-house door to let the blue water out of the tubs, she forgot all about the blue water, and then of all the surprises in the world there's a sheep in the wash-house, a poor sheep not knowing which way to turn, fat and blundering with the shy anxious look sheep have.

— Shoo Shoo.

Sheep are silly animals they're so scared and stupid, they either stand still and do nothing or else go round and round getting nowhere, when they're in they want out and when they're out they sneak in, they don't stay in places, they get lost in bogs and creeks and down cliffs, if only they stayed where they're put.

— Shoo Shoo.

Scared muddy and heavy the sheep lumbers from the wash-house and then bolts up the path, out the half-open gate on to the street and then round the corner out of sight, with the people stopping to stare and say well I declare for you never see sheep in the street, only people.

It should not have rained, the washing should have been dry and why did the sheep come and where did it come from to here in the middle of the city?

A long time ago there were sheep (she remembers, pulling out the plug so the dirty blue water can gurgle away, what slime I must wash more often why is everything always dirty) sheep, and I walked behind them with bare feet on a hot dusty road, with the warm steamy nobbles of sheep dirt getting crushed between my toes and my father close by me powerful and careless, and the dogs padding along, the spit dribbling from the loose corners of their mouths, Mac and Jock and Rover waiting for my father to cry Way Back Out, Way Back Out. Tom and me will go some other place I think. Tom and me will get out of here.

She dries her hands on the corner of her sack apron. That's that. A flat-roofed house and beds with shiny covers, and polished fire-tongs, and a picture of moonlight on a lake.

She crosses the backyard, brushing aside the wet clothes to pass. My best tablecloth. If visitors come tonight I am sunk.

But no visitors only Tom bringing cousin Nora, while the rain goes off, she has to catch the six o'clock bus at the end of the road. I must hurry I must be quick it is terrible to miss something. Cousin Nora widowed remarried separated and anxious to tell. Cousin Nora living everywhere and nowhere chained to number fifty Toon Street it is somewhere you must have somewhere even if you know you haven't got anywhere. And what about Tom tied up to a little pile of handkerchiefs and the prize that happens to-morrow, and Nance, look at her, the washing's still out and wet, she is tired and flurried, bound by the fearful chain of time and the burning sun and sheep and day that are nowhere.

— But of course Nance I won't have any dinner, you go on dishing up for Tom while I sit here on the sofa.

— Wait, I'll move these newspapers, excuse the muddle, we seem to be in a fearful muddle.

— Oh is that today's paper, no it's Tuesday's, just think on Tuesday Peter and I were up in the north island. He wanted me to sell my house you know, just fancy, he demanded that I sell it and I said not on your life did you marry me for myself or for my house and he said of course he married me for myself but would I sell the house, why I said, well you don't need it now he said, we can live up north, but I do need it I said, I've lived in it nearly all my life, it's my home, I live there.

Cousin Nora, dressed in navy, her fleecy dark hair and long soft wobbly face like a horse.

— Yes I've lived there all my life, so of course I said quite definitely no. Is that boiled bacon, there's nothing I like better, well if you insist, just the tiniest bit on a plate, over here will do, no fuss, thank you. Don't you think I was right about the house? I live there.

What does Tom think? His mouth busies itself with boiled bacon while his fingers search an envelope for the pink sheet that means Tatts results, ten thousand pounds first prize, a flat-roofed house and statues in the garden. No prize but first prize will do, Tom is clever and earnest, the other fellows have tickets in Tatts, why not I, the other fellows take handkerchiefs home and stray coats sometimes, why not I, and Bill Tent has a modern house one of those new ones you can never be too interested in where you live. Tom is go-ahead. In the front bedroom there's an orange coloured bed-lamp, it's scorched a bit now but it was lovely when it came, he won it with a question for a radio quiz, his name over the air and all——

Name the planets and their distance from the sun.

Name the planets.

Oh the sun is terribly far away but of course there's only been rain today, pirrup-pirrupping blackbirds, how it rains and the sheep why I must tell them about the sheep.

Nora leans forward, Nance you are dreaming, what *do* you think about the house?

— Oh, always let your conscience be your guide.

(Wear wise saws and modern instances like a false skin a Jiminy Cricket overcoat.)

— That's what I say too, your conscience, and that's why we separated, you heard of course?

Yes Nance knows, from Nora herself as soon as it happened Dear Nance and Tom you'll hardly believe it but Peter and I have decided to go our own ways, you and Tom are lucky you get on so well together no fuss about where to live you don't know how lucky you are.

No fuss but lost, look at the house look at the kitchen, and me going backwards and forwards carrying dishes and picking up newspapers and dirty clothes, muddling backwards and forwards in little irrelevant journeys, but going backwards always, to the time of the sun and the hot dusty road and a powerful father crying Way Back Out Way Back Out.

— Oh, Oh I must tell you, there was a sheep today in the wash-house.

— A what?

— A sheep. I don't know where he lived but I chased him away.

— Oh I say, really, ha ha, it's a good job we've got somewhere to live, I in my house (even though I had to break with Peter) and you and Tom in yours. — We *have* got somewhere to live haven't we, not like a lost sheep ha ha. What's the matter Tom?

— 74898, not a win.

The pink ticket thrust back quickly into the envelope and put on the stand beside the wireless, beside the half-open packet of matches and the sheaf of bills and the pile of race-books.

— Well I'm damned, let's turn on the news, it's almost six.

— Oh it's almost six and my bus!

— So it is Nora.

Quick it is terrible to lose something for the something you miss may be something you have looked for all your life, in the north island and the south island and number fifty Toon Street.

— Goodbye and thank you for the little eat and you must come and see me sometime and for goodness sake Nance get a perm or one of those cold waves, your hair's at the end of its tether.

Here is the news.

Quick goodbye then.

Why am I small and cramped and helpless why are there news-papers on the floor and why didn't I remember to gather up the dirt, where am I living that I'm not neat and tidy with a perm. Oh if only the whole of being were blued and washed and hung out in the far away sun. Nora has travelled she knows about things, it would be nice to travel if you knew where you were going and where you would live at the end or do we ever know, do we ever live where we live, we're always in other places, lost, like sheep, and I cannot understand the leafless cloudy secret and the sun of any day.

DAN DAVIN

# The General and The Nightingale

With two bivvies joined together and open along one side Plugger
Holmes, the General's batman, had made himself a snug little
shelter. After to-day's surprise shelling he'd thought he might have
to move to some place with a deeper soil under it. But when he dug
down he'd found there was enough depth for a shallow slittie before
you got to solid rock. So he was staying on. It wouldn't have been
easy to find another spot so well sheltered from the wind and
tactically it was nicely placed. Without getting out of his blankets he
had observation on the three vital points, the General's caravan, 'A'
Mess, and the Car Park.

Not that there was any need to keep an eye on them just now. The
G.O.C. was still away at Brigade. When he did come back he'd
probably make straight for the Mess where the Mess Corporal could
be relied on to look after him for a while. And Plugger had guests,
the A.Q.'s batman and the G.I.'s batman, especially invited to
sample the latest parcel from home. A panful of whitebait fritters
was already crackling over the Primus under Shorty's care and
Pongo Rose was just bringing the water to the boil. As host, senior
batman and provider of the rations, Plugger had nothing to do but
supervise.

'Billy's boiling, G.I.,' he announced. 'Make the tea, will you? And,
A.Q., I like my fritters well done on both sides. You'd better turn
them over, hadn't you?'

It was the General's voice and manner, exactly mimicked but with
asperity slightly exaggerated. And there was something of the
original's authority.

'There we are, sir,' said Shorty Evans, caricaturing his own master,
'We'll just give her a minute to draw and she'll be jake.' And he set
down three mugs beside the black boiling of tea, took out the twigs
which plugged the two holes in the Highlander Milk tin, and tapped
the sides of the billy with the handle of his knife. The leaves began to
settle down from the surface where they had floated like the debris of
an ants' nest.

'Come on, A.Q.,' said Plugger, sitting up on the blanket he had
disposed over the edge of his slittie and letting his legs dangle. 'Can't
wait all night, you know. They look well enough done now.'

'Yes, sir, yes, sir,' Pongo began to shuffle the fritters out on to three enamel plates. Fortunately, they divided evenly by three and there was no argument.

'Shall we have our plonk now, sir, or wait till afterwards?' Pongo added, looking at his mug.

'What sort of Mess were you brought up in Pongo?' said Shorty. 'You know the General never takes red vino with his fish.'

But like all great men Plugger didn't like to think he was an open book to his subordinates. Or to be anticipated. He eyed the half-full demijohn. 'I don't see why we shouldn't make an exception this once,' he said. 'Hardships of the field, you know. Eh, A.Q.?'

'Yes, sir,' assented Pongo with enthusiasm.

'I suppose you're right, Plugger,' said Shorty, and he pushed forward his mug, too. He wasn't very good at this game, not as good as if he'd been General, and he constantly forgot the rules.

'You know, G.I.,' said Plugger, who never forgot, eyeing the last of his fritters sadistically, 'I really think it's time you went back to your regiment for a spell. After all, it's selfish of me to keep you away from your men and regimental life so long.'

'That's right, sir,' said Pongo. 'He'll never get the V.C. here. And you've given him the Other Bastards' Effort already. I don't suppose he wants to be mentioned in dispatches again.' Pongo was apt to labour his points. 'Nothing like the regimental life,' he went on, after another look at Shorty, 'keeps you close to reality.'

'Nothing like it.' Shorty's lugubrious emphasis gave the phrase a more sinister meaning.

But Plugger believed in the balance of power.

'Yes, A.Q.,' he said, 'I suppose you do miss the excitements of the old life. The friendly shells screaming by, the comradeship in danger, the old nebels. Those were the days, eh?' He picked up his mug of tea, blew on it and gazed reflectively towards the Car Park.

'Jesus,' he suddenly said and put down his mug. 'There's the Old Man's jeep. He's back early.'

The others stared in the same direction. The sun was already down behind the Casole hills which the French had bitterly fought for that winter. But there was still enough light in the basin that held the camp for them to make out the Divisional Commander's flag on the bonnet of the jeep. And as the jeep passed the Provost on point duty saluted with unmistakable smartness.

'Well, his bed's made and everything's O.K.,' said Plugger. But care had returned to his face. Once the General was within the borders of the camp he was Plugger's responsibility. And Plugger had to watch him like a hawk to make sure he was kept in good trim and didn't want for anything. It wasn't a sinecure because the General combined absent-mindedness with considerateness so that you couldn't tell which was which. And he had a trick of asking you what you would do if you were Kesselring, which was a bit tough, especially before breakfast. So you had to keep on your toes. Anyhow, if he hadn't kept one jump ahead and been thinking while the General was taking off his trousers which ones he'd wear to-morrow, Plugger would have felt the way the General himself would feel if one of his brigades went short of ammo or lost more blokes in a scrap than they need have done.

The General had got out of his seat beside the driver. The G.I. and the A.D.C. vaulted from their perch in the back of the jeep and then bent over it again to get their map-boards. All three began to climb up the slope towards 'A' Mess. The driver, left alone in the jeep, swung her round and drove off towards the Car Park. Plugger and the other two watched him get out there and stand for a moment looking towards the men's cookhouse. There'd be something kept hot for him. But then he half turned and his gaze swivelled across the slope. It stopped on them. He began to walk firmly in their direction.

'Nose like a bloody bloodhound,' said Plugger. 'Well, here goes for the last of the whitebait.' With resignation, no longer General, he began to prepare more fritters.

'We've got the wood on him to-night, anyhow,' said Pongo. 'He can't come that Terelle Terror Ride stuff on us once he hears we've been getting pasted ourselves.'

But the other two shook their heads and Shorty said sourly: 'That'll be the bloody day when Alec lets himself be trumped. What's an 88 bursting in Rear Div. cookhouse to his imagination? Just a provocation that's all. If he'll even listen.'

'Well, you pack of bludgers,' was Alec's greeting. 'Can you spare a bite for a front-line troop? Nothing fancy. Anything will do for a man who's been in the saddle since dawn.' His eye had taken in the frying pan and his nostrils were twitching.

'Bludgers, what the hell do you mean, bludgers?' said Plugger. 'You're the bloody bludger round this outfit. Touring round the country all day and bludging their rations off the brigades and now you come and take their last bite from your old cobbers who used to know you when you were nothing better than the sanitary corporal's assistant. Don't think you're getting a clean plate, though, even if you have been hobnobbing with the big shots. You can pig it off mine. And he flapped a couple of fritters on to the plate.

'Good old Plugger,' said Alec. 'Too old to be anything but a base-wallower himself but never lets the fighting-man down.'

'Jesus, just listen to him, will you,' Shorty reached over for the loaf of bread Plugger had scrounged. 'He'll be telling us he's a soldier next.'

'He wouldn't be talking so big if he knew what a day we'd had here, would he, Shorty?' said Plugger.

'My bloody oath he wouldn't. D'you know what those bloody Teds have been up to? They've been bloody well shelling us. Airburst at that. On top of all the nervous strain of an important H.Q. job we've got to put up with air-burst. Takes a man back to Sidi Rizegh, doesn't it, Plugger? But, of course, you were only a bloody redarse in those days, weren't you, Alec?'

'So that's it,' said Alec. 'I thought I noticed a lot of new holes dug. Place looks like a Klondyke gold rush. Suppose no one thought of digging one for me?'

'Well, you know,' said Plugger, 'you being such a glutton for it and all that, we thought you wouldn't want us to bother.'

'Not after to-day. I'm a changed man.'

'Why, what happened to-day? You ought to be used to the Terelle Terror Ride by now. We are, hearing you talk about it every day since we got here. Hey, Shorty, go easy on that Cocky's Joy. It's not every day my old woman sends me a tin of that stuff.'

Shorty went on spreading the Golden Syrup. 'She wouldn't send you any at all if she knew what you did with the last tin,' he said when he had finished.

'Have a heart, Shorty, the poor girl was starving.'

'Lonely, too, I suppose. She seemed to need quite a lot of company, even after you left Naples.'

Alec had finished his fritters and skipping the tea, which by now had an oily film on its surface, armed himself with a mug of plonk. He put this beside him and began to roll a cigarette from Plugger's makings.

'So nobody's interested in my day of peril,' he remarked bitterly.

'Not if it's one more of those yarns about how with a savage twist of the wheel you wrenched the jeep away from the bursting shell and tears came into the General's eyes as he thanked you,' said Pongo. The others said nothing.

Alec looked at the three of them sorrowfully. Clearly he would have to shift the emphasis of his speech away from himself.

'You know he's a queer old cove, the General,' he said and took another dip into his mug. When he looked up the others were watching him. He had his audience.

'What's he been up to now?' Plugger asked.

Alec was away.

'Well, you know how it is,' he said. 'There we were as usual this morning at sparrowfart, me with the jeep pulled up in front of the General's caravan, the G.I. hurrying across from the Mess and wiping the bacon fat from his mouth, the A.D.C. scuttling about getting the map-boards together and covering them with a ground-sheet so the sun won't shine on them when we come under observation from the Jerry O.P.s on Cifalco. Then out bursts the G.O.C. from his caravan, looking at his watch. Time to get cracking, he says, come along G.I., come along, Harry. And all three of them bundle into the jeep. Then he spots one of the Intelligence blokes shaving outside his truck. "What's the news, 'I,' " he shouts, "any-thing fresh?"

' "No, sir," says the "I" bloke, "nothing much. There was a raid on the International Post early this morning, that's all. We took a couple of P.W. and lost no one. They were from II/132, as I thought."

' "Good," says the General and rubs his hands. "Tell me all about it when I get back to-night. But what about the Russians?"

' "Rokossovsky's rounded up another Corps, sir. Claims 10 000 killed, according to the B.B.C."

' "Good, good," says the Old Man. "Killed, eh? You did say killed?"

' "Killed, sir."

' "Good, good. Drive on, Alec. Thank you, 'I.' "

'And so away we go with him sitting beside me, that jaw of his as set as if he meant to go off and get 10 000 on his own.'

'And he would, too,' said Plugger, recognizing the will for the deed. The General had so often made the two identical.

'Well, we decided to go by the Inferno track because old Ted's been knocking hell out of the top road lately. Got all those loops absolutely taped. So the next thing we're belting through Acquafondata and then on to the Inferno. I thought the General might kick up a bit about the way I took that one in five down-grade part but there wasn't a murmur out of him. He never did like wasting time. But it was bad luck on old Harry and the G.I. in the back. They were bouncing about like fleas.

'At that rate, it wasn't long before we were at the Hove Dump. You should have seen the glare the Old Man gave at all the burnt-out trucks and stores. As if he'd like to have wrung the neck of the Jerry that got his guns on to the dump that night.'

'He would, too,' said Plugger, and the others nodded their heads.

'Well, from there it wasn't long before we were out in the Bowl. I must say, it looked as pretty as a picture. All the mud's dried up now, and the corpses in that knocked-out Sherman have stopped stinking

and there are poppies all over the place. You could see Cassino as
close as if you were looking through glasses and the old Monastery
up on top looked as if it was full of monks instead of Fritzes. But I
must admit I wasn't thinking much about the scenery just then.
That's the worst part of the trip, just round there. There's no cover,
just the flat and the road going through it and you know you're in
plain view of every O.P. he's got from the Monastery to Mount
Cifalco. Not to mention that bloody great Mount Cairo. Makes you
feel very queer in the guts, believe me, to think that if the O.P. officer
has had a bad night on the booze and wants to work it off on
someone he can bring Christ knows how many guns down on you in
a God-awful stonk.'

'Not for just one jeep,' said Shorty. 'He can't spare the ammo. At
least, that's what Geordie, the I.O.'s batman, says.'

'All bloody well for the I.O.'s batman. You wouldn't catch him out
in the bloody Bowl by himself though, let alone with a General in his
jeep. Anyhow, that's what I was saying to myself, too: It's not worth
their while to crack down on a single jeep. But when I saw that
stretch of flat all round us, as bare as a baby's bottom, and thought of
those bloody Jerries up there watching us through their glasses and
perhaps getting a fire order ready just for fun, I put my foot down on
the old accelerator and gave her the gun just the same. And just as I
was thinking to myself: only another mile and then the Terelle
staircase road and we're jake till the return trip, what do you think
happens?'

He paused.

'You hear the whine of a shell. With a savage twist of the wrist——'

'Don't be a bloody fool all your life, Shorty,' said Plugger.

'I hear the G.O.C.'s voice,' said Alec, ignoring Shorty. 'And he
says: "Stop, Alec, stop."'

'Well, you know, when the Old Man gives an order there's only
one thing to do about it—do what you're told. So I stopped. And
there we were, in a miserable bloody jeep under all those guns, a
sitting shot. No one says a word. I couldn't see how Harry and the
G.I. were in the back but I could sort of feel they were thinking along
the same lines as I was. As for me, my ears were pricked waiting to
hear that shell coming and my eyes were swivelling all over the place
looking for some hole in the ground to make for when the time came
to bolt.

' "Listen," says the General, as if we weren't listening already. I
reckon we could pretty near have heard the Jerries sliding the shells
into the breeches of those guns of theirs. We could hear them eating
their breakfast sausage up in Belmonte. I could hear Kesselring say

to his own A.D.C.: "Isn't that Alec Kane down there?" Yes, we were listening all right. We must have been sitting there a full minute, as stiff as statues except inside, listening.

'Then the General pipes up again: "Was that a nightingale I heard?" he says.

'Well, I thought to myself, it comes to us all sooner or later, I suppose. Only most of us don't have to start hearing little birds to know it's a mug's game. But he deserves a rest if anyone does. He's had a tough war, two tough wars, in fact. And then the Sangro and Cassino on top of everything else and a stinking bad winter. Making this Terelle Terror Ride twice a day every day this month has just about sent me crackers myself.

'But I wasn't so crackers I wasn't still listening for that bloody stonk to come screaming down on us.

' "I think it was a blackbird, sir," said Harry at the back of me. Good for you, Harry, I thought to myself. You're not an A.D.C. for nothing. Humour him, that's right. That's the presence of mind that makes an officer. If I had my way I'd make you G.I. Now we can get cracking to hell out of here.

'But I ought to have known the Old Man better. And the G.I. too, for that matter. He was too shrewd to make Harry's mistake. Because, of course, it only made the old Man determined to prove he was right.

' "Nonsense, Harry, nonsense," he says. "I know a nightingale when I hear one. Of course it was a nightingale. Listen!"

"So we start listening again. As if we'd ever stopped. Suddenly I gave a jump and so did the two in the back. It was only a mortar away over in Mortar Alley but all strung up like that we didn't have time to stop ourselves.

' "Keep still, will you," says the Old Man to me. "You'll frighten the bird."

'I ask you, frighten the bird. When I was in such a state that I'd have taken off myself if only I'd had the wings.

'And then out of a bit of a bush about fifty yards away we hear it. And it's a bloody nightingale all right, singing away as if he'd burst. I haven't heard a nightingale sing like that since that morning we skeltered through Athens trying to get to the beaches before the sun and the Stukas were up.

' "There you are, Harry," says the General. "I told you so. Didn't I, G.I.?"

' "That's right, sir," answered the G.I. in that poker voice of his. "Drive on, Alec," says the General. And, believe me, no one ever got into top gear quicker than I did and, by Jesus, we were half-way up the Terelle staircase road before I remembered to change down.'

'The old scamp,' said Plugger with delight. 'Isn't he an old scamp?'

'Well, I suppose I might as well have another jorum of your plonk before my hair turns white,' said Alec, reaching out.

A low-flying plane grumbled slowly overhead, looking for a target. It was now quite dark. The General must have come to the door of 'A' Mess. They could hear that peremptory, carrying voice.

'Put out those lights.'

They covered their cigarettes. All over the camp chinks in the blackout suddenly disappeared, the way a life goes out.

'The old scamp,' said Plugger.

BRUCE MASON                  # The Glass Wig

My early memories of Lachlan Fyffe are somewhat scattered. I first saw him from behind, at a naval medical board in 1942, and stared amazed at the thickest neck I have ever seen—it seemed to begin from the shoulders. Then he turned round, and I saw for the first time that big face, the small dull eyes with their slightly baffled look, and the little red mouth, compressed in a way which sharpened the chin, and lent to the face, not firmness, but a dour pixie quality, and I remember wondering how it was that someone not after all huge, could give so clear an impression of thickness and bulk.

Then I remember Lachlan on passage to England, sitting in his cabin sewing and darning while we played Crown and Anchor; Lachlan inflating suddenly and bursting into vehement song: can I forget the Sunday morning when Church parade was being held on deck, and Lachlan sang 'I'll Walk Beside You' to my accompaniment? The ship was rolling in a long swell and oh the agony of having to be straight-faced and calm while he sang, clutching a wire above his head, clambering slowly uphill to me, then racing down to the gunwale which he hit with a thud that left him breathless and made his song into a pneumatic, explosive, chanson triste. Lachlan at Colon, where we went to see the thing they called 'exhibish'—it was squalid and boring and left most of us cold, but Lachlan was suddenly sick on the floor and we had to get out quickly when the proprietress made at us with a knife.

But I never really knew him well until we went to a cruiser in the Home Fleet to do our seatime as matelots. There were eighteen of us, all New Zealanders, a little sheepish on our first day at sea. We were sent first to the Fleet Air Arm mess, which was used to holding only six, so we made a great mound of our kits and hammocks and sat on it, until the broadcast began to shout at us to report to sick bay, to the Commander's cabin, to the torpedo workshop, and what time we had left was spent on fruitless errands for the Pommie matelots, for whom any officer candidates were meat, even if we were Kiwis, and a long way from home. On the second day we were given messes, and I found myself with Lachlan on the Focsle mess deck. We arrived at Smoko time, and there were eight matelots sitting drinking their tea. One of them said 'Take your caps off', and we obeyed quickly. Another hoped we knew how to work because by Christ we were going to, and a leading seaman asked our names and put us on the duty lists. 'They don't make a man too welcome,' said Lachlan later. I felt they were just sizing us up. At this stage we were just C.W. candidates, and the Kiwi hardly showed through. But after a few days when Lachlan had fallen down a hatch, and I had been nearly drowned getting out the starboard boom, they seemed ready to receive us, and by the time a cake had arrived for Lachlan and the boys had all eaten of 'his moother's boon', we were proper matelots.

And now Lachlan seemed suddenly to bloom. Among us Kiwis he was large certainly, but beside the boys from Bolton and Leeds, he looked like a bear with his cubs. And began to feel like it too, I think. When the messdecks held their regatta, Lachlan's 'Come on, Focsle!' was heard at the start, half a mile down Scapa Flow. Action Stations, which was being exercised daily, took on the quality of a rite. As soon as he heard the pipe, Lachlan would drop everything, shout 'Come on, men!' and dash like a corsair up ladders and through hatches, bearing us along with him on a rising tide. And then, one night, Lachlan last up switched out the light and swung into his hammock with a series of satisfied grunts. I could hear around me the long regular breathing of men on the threshold of sleep. Then came Lachlan's voice, 'Well, goodnight, men,' it said. There was a sudden hush and the regular rhythms broke up. I gritted my teeth. Why oh why did Lachlan have to do these things that made one writhe with shame? I hoped nothing would happen, but after a moment of uneasy silence, rather gruffly, altogether, they chorused: 'Good-night.'

Lachlan was acknowledged. He was established.

Then we went on a northern convoy, and it was about three weeks before we returned to Scapa. Here one of the boys was drafted to barracks, and he left the day we got back. His relief was to arrive after supper the next day. We were still sitting over it, when we heard a roar at the hatch.

'If this is Scapa Flow, you can keep your Scapa bastard Flow!' A kit bounced down the ladder, then a hammock. They were followed by a pale, spare little man who pattered down into the mess and advanced on us. 'Twenty Mess? Hughes, vice Nicholls. Any tea in the dixie?' Someone poured out a cup and pushed it over to him. He sat down and began to drink. I saw that he kept his hat on, pushed right down to his eyebrows, and I wondered who would speak first.

'Take your cap off ', said Lachlan. He gave Lachlan a quick look, then removed it in the two precise movements which follow the order Off Caps at Divisions. We all stared at him. I had noticed a queer, set look about him, and now I saw why. He was quite bald; not a lash, not an eye-brow, not a hair on his skull. His head was all of one neutral, yellowish colour with a dull glow beneath the skin. He had a deadpan look in repose, but when he talked, his teeth and eyes made his face leap into a sudden grimacing life. His name was Gefyd Hughes, from Cardiff no less, this was his first ship for a year, and he didn't go much on it so far, whatever. I listened for the first time to the Welsh lilt, and its slight minor feeling at the end of a phrase. At pipe down, there was a furtive interest in him as he undressed, but as far as I could see, he was as smooth all over as a brass Buddha.

Next morning, as the broadcast was shouting wakey wakey and I could feel myself being dragged from some warm, vague shore, I saw that Lachlan was already up and dressed, moving from hammock to hammock, saying his cheery: 'Now then, men, once you start it won't be so bad,' and the men groaning and tumbling out, though I never knew why they didn't tell him to go to hell. Some sort of inertia perhaps—it was easier to obey his appeals to decency than risk the challenge of his honest, manly reproach. Now he was at Hughes' hammock. I watched with a slight tenseness. Lachlan seemed to diminish, he had a tentative look: that irresistible conviction was evaporating. Trial by ordeal, I thought. He put his hand on one of the ropes and shook it.

'Well now, Hughes, what about getting up, eh?' God, I thought, no. This won't do at all. Hughes opened one pale eye. 'What is it?' he said. 'You see,' said Lachlan gamely, 'We like to be first up in this mess. No waiting for the Crusher here. So what about it, eh?' Hughes sat up and looked at us. 'The leading seaman of the mess, is it?' Someone said no. 'Then what's biting you, chum?'

There it was, the question we had all baulked at, what's biting you? One might well ask, but somehow one never did. He was too difficult to gainsay, even more difficult to snub. I wondered what would happen now. Hughes went on: 'I'm not scared of the Crusher, look you,' and he rolled over out of sight. Lachlan shrugged and moved on to the next hammock. But he was too late. We had seen the standard of freedom hoisted, and silently had all ranged ourselves behind it. No one moved in answer to that obdurately cheerful call, though we might have spared him our loud callow snores. He had to retire, defeated, and began to lash his hammock with tight lips and a chin that was sharper than ever.

The sneak in me rejoiced at his rebuff. Often, when he'd done something that made me squirm, I had tried to wound him by some cheap irony, sarcasm or just plain rudeness, but I had never got anything through that tough, armadillo hide. Now he had been unseated by a little runt of a hairless Welshman and he wouldn't be cutting the same figure again. At least, not here. It was only remarkable he'd been able to hold some of these painful stances so long. I had tried several times to form a picture of Lachlan's home—what ground had husbanded this tough plant? What devious permutations had ended in him? I learnt little. Only child, both parents from north of the Tweed, and implacably Presbyterian; father a bank manager, and mother an indefatigable cook; a member of the Wellington Choral Union where he had once sung the baritone part in Hiawatha, and a leader of the Junior National Party. That was all.

As for Hughes, the mess embraced him as a deliverer. When at breakfast on that first morning, Hughes in one short sentence used the same expletive as adjective, noun, verb and adverb, and even sandwiched it inside a word, another little spell was broken. Instantly and magically, the convention of obscenity was re-established in the orotund vigour which had greeted us on our first day aboard. For three days I had not been able to listen to that blast of cussing without a thrill of guilt; after that it began to numb and ceased to shock. Lachlan had never expressed open disgust but he had somehow contrived to discredit it, and by an agreement never openly acknowledged, swearing had been in partial abeyance. It was a spontaneous tribute to a forceful will, backed by two hundred pounds avoirdupois, by the diffused image of the Presbyterian Church, and by the persuasive, if slightly alien authority which clings just now to the colonial in his parent country. But to a local saviour, no foreign tribute was necessary, and now, with joy and exuberance the men burst through their flimsy, self-imposed barrier, and let themselves go. For a few moments, the air seemed to have edges. Then Lachlan said 'Pass the butter please,' and it sounded so stark and pedantic that we jeered at him for his niceness. He rose and left us without a word.

It was Sunday, and we began to make ourselves 'tiddly' for Divisions. Hughes unpacked his kit to find his number ones badly crushed, and cursing, he went in search of an iron. We were already lined up on deck when he arrived and passed quickly down between the ranks. The Divisional Officer gaped. We stood aghast. On his head was a monstrous blond wig, which looked like silk, but we learnt later was of spun glass, and on top of it, sitting there like a little black wart, was his tiddly hat, strapped round under the chin. There was a buzz of excitement, but no time to talk as the Captain was already on inspection, and a moment later had reached us. He passed up the first rank without comment, and began the second from my end. Our eyes followed him down the line and we hardly dared breathe. I treasure the memory of the sudden tightening of the Captain's neck muscles and the little jerk of his eyelids flicking wide apart as he came level with Hughes. He murmured something to the Divisional Officer, who fumbled, clearly at a loss, then turned back to Hughes. We couldn't hear what was going on, but didn't need to. Hughes was a master of mime. He took off his hat, swept off the wig, and bent forward to show the barren polished top of his skull, then put them on again with perfect self-possession. The Captain did not lose his composure—that was inviolate—but he did appear to be under a slight strain. He said something which sounded like 'Carry on', returned the Divisional Officer's salute, and left us.

The story was soon all over the ship, and there was no chance to get our heads down that afternoon, as the mess was full of visitors eager to try on the wig. Lachlan, who was discovered full length on one of the benches, made way for the intruders with a bad grace. 'Like a ruddy exhibish,' he muttered, as Hughes was persuaded to drop his pants and justify the label of 'Taff, the hairless wonder'. Watching the way he dealt with all this, I decided that I liked him. He had something I couldn't put a name to: honesty? Not quite. Modesty, then. Hardly. It was more a kind of innocence, a refusal to see guile or deceit where others found it patent. He did not seem to feel for example that Lachlan had taken a dislike to him, instant and intense. Listening to Hughes in the mess bewildered and enraged him. For there was no doubt that Taff had quite a talent, and a genuinely literary one. His images, however obscene, were always precise, and in a way disinterested—they seemed to have a life of their own. It was this knowledge of having to deal with things rather than the man which puzzled Lachlan. 'I don't see what he gets out of it,' he said one day. 'I mean, what's the point? A man gets a bit cheesed off with the same thing all the time.'

It was strange in the next day or two to watch Lachlan trying on Hughes the same strategy I had bungled so often: goading him with the most inept sarcasms, anything which would penetrate and hurt. But Taff seemed to feel nothing. He would look at Lachlan with his bland, light eyes, and give him a straightforward, literal answer to his laboured ironies, which left Lachlan fretful.

He seemed to lose heart. No bounding out in the mornings now; the Crusher had to dig for us. No songs, no manly enthusiasms, no wild charges when the bugle called; only this shadow across his soul. He was as painstakingly down as he had been up. A tin of shortbread had arrived for him, which he put in his locker, and we never saw it until just after supper each night, when he would place it on the mess table, select three pieces, eat them dourly, and lock it away again.

After Hughes had been on board a fortnight, we upped anchor and went to Glasgow for repairs, asdic trouble I think. Our watch got shore leave the night we arrived, and Lachlan and I decided to have a meal somewhere, and then go to a film. It was wet, and Glasgow seemed cheerless and ugly. We got back about eleven, I suppose, and found some of the boys just slinging their hammocks. I was not listening to them directly but realized after a moment that they were talking about Hughes.

'There we are, standin' in the blackart an' the wet, like a lotta lorst souls, when sudden 'e orfs caps, and stands there shinin' like a bloody beacon, an' strite you could see it a nundred yards orf. Then we 'ears a voice. "Ullo Jack" it says, "goin' far?" We springs t'attention. "Take yer pick," I says. And 'oo d'ya think she goes for? Joe 'ere, or that big bastard in eight mess? Nah. It's Taff, little sawn-orf, knee 'igh to a grass 'opper Taff. "I'll take blondie, 'ere," she says, a norf they goes, the long an' the short of it, 'appy as Jacksy, an' 'im with 'is wig blazin' like Eddystone Lightarse. So we stands there, gettin' wet, too late for the flicks, an' the Judies takin' a night orf, so we make for the Y.M. an' the fuggin' tea's cold, a norl 'cos a little runt of a Taffy's got no 'air.'

I saw Lachlan listening with the moist, avid look of a dog held from its meat. I couldn't look at him. Then Taff arrived, shaking drops of rain from his wig. He was greeted with shouts of ribald joy. 'What do you want for your wig, Taff?' asked someone.

'All of twenty-five pounds,' he said.

'Put me down for a couple.'

'You cannot get them now, look you,' said Hughes. 'They are not making them any more.'

'It's insured, of course,' said Lachlan with a ghastly nonchalance.

'No, it's not that.' Then someone asked him about his Judy, to which he replied. 'She was a good girl, whatever,' and with this sounding oddly in my ears, I fell asleep.

Taff became more and more communicative each day. We soon heard the full story of the wig, of his miserable childhood, spent mostly retreating from the thoughtless laughter that everywhere met him until someone taught him not to hide his baldness but insist on it, brazen it out, disarm the mockers. The story of his first timid essay into the streets of Cardiff after dark was a triumph. You could just see his tentative advance, the coy uncovering in the corner lamplight, and the drab, sidling out of the darkness to peer at him, at first suspicious, then intrigued enough to go off with him.

'Bloody skite of a thieving Welshman,' said Lachlan savagely, with reference I suppose to the old rhyme, 'Taffy was a Welshman, Taffy was a thief,' though in this case he had no evidence whatever. But I thought Taff was superb.

The story provoked a round of amorous reminiscences. They were rough accounts of appetites casually appeased, no more valuable to them, I noted, than any other appetite. ('I didn't know whether to go to the flicks or pick up a Judy.') Then Hughes started in again. I knew what he could do, but I was not prepared for him to evoke a whole gallery of women. He talked quietly, with no marked inflections but the Welsh cadence, yet there they were; this girl with her pride and self-pity; this other with her flaunting assurance, and that one there who was saving to go for a trip to Penzance: it was masterly. By this time Lachlan could hardly keep still. There was a crude honesty about the other stories, the callow glee of the child who scrawls in public places, and this made them easy to laugh off. But when Hughes was talking, there was something so direct and intimate about them that some sort of action was necessary. Why didn't Lachlan go, the silly tit? Why did he have to sit there, with his eyes fixed on Taff, and his chin so tight there was a twitch below his lip? He leapt up suddenly, dived into his locker, and returned with a book which he threw down open on the table and with a tigerish concentration began to read. I saw what it was, and my bowels seemed to wither. It was the New Testament which the Chaplain had given him a few days before. Hughes stopped. There was a hush as they all saw it, and then came a burst of obscenity so spirited and intense that it seemed to strike Lachlan and engulf him. He began to read aloud and his voice grew higher and had the shrillness of a priest chanting an exorcism. I was wondering just where it would all end, when he snapped the book shut and rushed out with his head down.

The next day he asked to be transferred to another mess, but was refused. I reminded him that he had only ten days to go.

A few nights later I was writing a letter when I saw Taff emerging through the hatch. He was being paid out gently like a sack from the top of the ladder, and when I went to secure him at the bottom, I found to my surprise that my opposite number was Lachlan. Hughes was stupid with drink. His eyes were dull and opaque and his face like a clot of yellow putty. I noticed then that he didn't have his wig, and made some remark about it, but he didn't seem to hear or understand, and rolled into his hammock as he was, hat and all. We took off his hat and boots and let him be.

It appeared that he had baulked at the gangplank and then worked back to the dockyard gates in search of help. There Lachlan had found him, wigless, and magnificently at peace, crooning a soft Welsh song.

Next morning, we were awakened not by the bugle, but by a roar from Hughes.

'It's gone!' he shouted. We shot out of sleep, the light snapped on, and Hughes was on the mess table, shaking us, stamping and shouting, pushing a distraught, grimacing mask inside the hammocks. 'Where is it? Where is it? Which of you bastards has robbed me? Get out, you rotten lot, and I'll fight you! Get out, get out, get out!' And seizing the ropes of a hammock, he emptied its occupant on to the table, and began on the next one. It was Lachlan's. Hughes had barely touched the ropes, when Lachlan sprang out on to the mess table.

'Now then, Hughes, what's the trouble here? Why can't you let a man sleep?' And the old authority rang in his voice. Hughes, checked, faltered.

'It's gone,' he said stupidly.

'What's gone? Explain yourself, man.'

Hughes pointed to his glossy skull. 'It's gone,' he said again.

'So that's it!' Lachlan said. 'So that's what all the fuss is about, is it? Well, we'll soon have that jacked up. Come on, men,' he said in the old masterful voice, 'everybody out. Hughes has lost his wig, and there'll be no peace till he finds it. We can't have that here, you know. Come on now, out you get.'

I marvelled. This was the old, the authentic Lachlan, miraculously reborn. Once again we were in the grip of those brisk imperatives. We rolled out. Turned out our lockers. Emptied our kits. No wig. Then someone remarked that he had gone out with it on, and I remembered that he had been without it when he returned. We would have thought of this sooner had it not been quite so bloody early.

When the full import of this news reached him, Hughes sat down and rocked with misery.

'What have I done? What have I done? I that was the shining light, look you, what am I now? A cut tomcat, no less, a gelding, slinking about ashamed of the light of day,' he moaned in Welsh on a long note that was like a keen.

The boys sniggered openly. He looked so squat and wretched, sitting there, rubbing his fingers over his head as another would through thick hair. We asked him where he'd been, and it appeared that he'd spent the whole evening at a house in the Gorbals, and we suggested he go there and make a search. But he shrank in a panic from going back, like an oyster without its shell. For some reason he asked me to go for him, and Lachlan who was standing by me, asked to come too.

I had the pleasant feeling, as we watched Glasgow from the top of a bus, of indulging in something rather daring with neither obligations nor consequences. The house was dirty, and the door was opened after we had knocked for some time, by a tired looking dark girl, who looked at us resentfully.

'What's that you're saying? Mister Hughes and his wig? How should I know? No, he didn't leave it here, put it on him myself.' She spoke in the harsh Glasgow accent; somehow I had expected them all to talk in Cockney and call you dearie. I saw Lachlan peering at her with a fascinated, tense look. She felt his stare, and dropping suddenly into an arch coyness, asked him if he was a friend of Mr Hughes, because any friend of his was O.K. by her too. Lachlan at once assumed the look of a small boy who has just soiled his clean rompers. He told her we were going on draft the next day.

'Pity,' she said, and closed the door slowly.

'Fancy women living like that,' he said on the bus back. 'You wonder they could sink so low.'

When we told Hughes of the failure of our mission, an enormous gloom seemed to settle on him. We assured him that he would find another sometime, but it did not comfort him. He seemed overwhelmed, not by the loss itself, but by the duplicity of a fate which had arbitrarily snatched from him his only protection against a mocking, hostile world, and any shelter from rebuff he once had dropped away from him, leaving him vulnerable and alone.

He sat there, in deep dejection, while we packed our kits for draft that night. Lachlan was in splendid fettle, supervising everything, radiating big-brotherly goodwill. Once or twice I saw his gaze fall compassionately on Taff's dispirited figure, and finally, obeying an impulse which one could watch from the moment of its conception, he went and sat beside him.

'You know,' he said, 'a man doesn't want to let himself get too down-hearted.' I winched, as Lachlan's thick hand fell heavily on Hughes' shoulder. 'You want to keep your grip. This won't do, you know. Now, do you know what I would do in your place?' Hughes shook his head mournfully. 'Go ashore tonight and just tell the world you don't care. Get it? You don't care! You don't care!' Hughes clasped his hands behind his ears, threw back his head, and howled. 'Emotional crowd, the Welsh,' said Lachlan to me later.

Hughes didn't look up as we left, not even as Lachlan sprinted past him with his: 'Cheerio, men!' Half an hour later we were bound for Portsmouth, and I never saw Hughes again.

Lachlan and I parted soon after this: his first appointment was to a minesweeper and mine to coastal forces. I did not see him again for over two years when we had both returned home and found ourselves one night on the same tram. We greeted each other coolly, appraisingly; the casualness proper to two men forced by circumstances to know each other very well, yet not friends nor ever likely to be. But he surprised me as I was leaving him by asking if I would care to come round one evening. 'I'd like you to meet the wife,' he added with some diffidence.

The wife! My memories of Lachlan became suddenly vivid and I was faintly shocked. But I was curious too, and I said I would.

It was an awful evening. Esmé Fyffe was small and fair and had known Lachlan since he was so high. She had a grim, steadfast gaiety that after half an hour made me want to slap her. She had the further misfortune to be 'interested in things'. Any remark, however casual or oblique, seemed to release some ratchet in her brain, and with a whirr she was off. For hours this went on. God, it was exhausting. But Lachlan didn't seem to mind.

When Esmé went to prepare supper it was Lachlan's turn. I had news of some of the boys I had known, how the rehearsals for *Elijah* were going, and what was wrong with the Junior Chamber of Commerce. There really was nothing to choose between them, I thought. Lachlan married was Lachlan single twice. How much longer?

There was a low rumble at the door and Esmé appeared wheeling a rickety tea-wagon. It stumbled over the carpet jiggling a heap of cakes, and drops of milk spat out of the small silver jug.

'I think we'll let it draw a moment,' she said, and covered the pot with a large yellow cosy. Something about its quality caught my eye. I looked again. Was it possible? I walked over to the wagon. There could be no doubt about it. This was Hughes' wig, somewhat disguised with a wide, loosely knitted border, but quite unmistakable.

'This is rather remarkable,' I said at length, looking at Lachlan.

He met my eyes composedly. I wondered if he was seeing little Taff Hughes, as I was, sitting wretchedly, rocking his head in his hands.

A tremor crossed his face.

'It was for his own good,' he said.

## JOHN REECE COLE                  **It Was So Late**

The moment he was left to himself he moved over to the long window overlooking the grounds, still thinking, Why had it to be here, in this house, of all places? Outside there was no wind and the sun slanting against the motionless branches made shadow patterns on the lawns. The native shrubbery stood out darkly against the burnt copper of the oaks. He remembered how the coming evenings would be soft and still, with mist slowly gathering around the trunks. Later there would be rain and the black water of the creek would swell and sweep away spinning clusters of leaves and dead twigs. And after the rain reflectionless pools would lie under the trees and in the hollows of rotting logs.

A man wearing a shapeless hat and carrying a gardening fork stepped out of the trees and walked across the bottom lawn. Jennings! he thought excitedly, almost upsetting the forgotten cup and saucer in his hand. Then he remembered, Jennings had been an old man. He must have died years ago.

A quiet voice interrupted his thoughts, 'Autumn, everything is dying . . . the season of decay.' It was the young man with scanty blonde hair, wearing a clerical collar, whom he had noticed earlier sitting in a corner alone. They stood for a moment without speaking, looking out into the greying light. 'It's always rather sad, don't you think?' the curate continued.

Behind them a faded voice had risen uncertainly above the flickering conversations, ' . . . greatest pleasure to welcome these brave boys back into our midst.'

They turned and sat down respectfully. It must be the mayor, he thought, noticing the winged collar and the dark, carefully pressed suit. The voice wavered, then with a confident spurt became louder, '. . . if I may so express myself, these gallant knights of the air, who by their fine record of service with the Royal Air Force, have added lustre to the name of New Zealand. These men to whom we. . . .'

He glanced around at the other uniformed figures. Alan was slumped in his chair, his brow puckered, staring hard at the end of his cigarette. Michael, his face studiedly expressionless, was fiddling with the strap of his wrist watch. Rex had been trying to attract his attention. He was leaning forward so that he was partly screened from the rest of the room by a high-backed mahogany chair. He was making deprecating gestures and grinning desperately.

Reluctantly, inevitably, his gaze shifted to Mrs Chatterton, the hostess. She was sitting with her head inclined towards the speaker. Her hair that he remembered having glimmers of grey was now white, and harsher lines marked her strong immobile features. Thinking of the first time he had seen that cold implacable face, he felt again the shock and sharp thrust of rising emotion.

He was holding his mother's gloved hand as they walked up a tree-lined drive towards a big house, when they came upon a tall lady walking in the garden.

'Good afternoon,' his mother said.

'Well?' the lady demanded.

'I. . . I answered the advertisement. . . for a maid,' his mother faltered.

'Oh, indeed.' The inescapable eyes held them for several moments. 'Well, if there is anything you wish to know ask Mrs Johnston, the housekeeper.'

'Why so serious?' Mrs Wells said, lowering her wide hips into the chair at his side. He continued to stare at the bone-white knuckles of his still tightly clenched hands. Groping for a reply, he began, 'I was—'

Mrs Wells interrupted, 'I was only saying to Mrs Chatterton—Oh, here she is! So nice of her to have the "welcome home" here when there wasn't a hall available. Hello, my dear! I was just saying to Flight Lieutenant—'

Mrs Chatterton swept past and stood for a moment by the window. Then she turned to Mrs Wells. 'That girl, wherever can she be? Her car isn't in the garage yet!'

'Well, she's young,' Mrs Wells said feelingly. 'When I was her age—'

'I don't know what she does with all her time,' Mrs Chatterton complained.

'Well, she has her Red Cross work, my dear,' Mrs Wells defended.

'You should be thankful, Mrs Chatterton,' Mrs Keeble interposed in a thin, high voice, 'that there are no longer any of these soup kitchens and charity bazaars, or she might spend all her time there, like my Grace and Jeannie did before they were married.

Mrs Keeble was the wife of Old John Keeble, headmaster of Woodbury. Mrs Chatterton glanced absently at her nervous features, then, dismissing her, continued, 'I do wish Margot would hurry. She might consider me sometimes.'

Margot, he thought, feeling his way back through dim years. Then everything sharpened, came into focus. He saw again a green trellis gate open and a little girl wearing a blue embroidered dress come through. She walked over to where he was sitting at the bottom of the kitchen steps. She was dragging behind her a large wax sleeping doll, and each time its head bumped on the gravel its closed eyes flickered open.

'What is your name?' she demanded.

'Ronny,' he replied. 'What's yours?'

'My name is Margot Chatterton.'

Then she said suddenly, 'See that car. It belongs to my father. Father says next year we will have two. . . .Have you got a car?'

'No.'

'Why doesn't your father buy you one? Where is your father?'

There were rapid footsteps on the drive and a voice called sharply, 'Margot, come here at once!' It was Mrs Chatterton. 'Haven't I told you to keep away from there?'

In the afternoons after school he would sit by the window of the small back room that he shared with his mother, waiting till she could find a moment to slip in and get him something to eat. Sometimes, when there had been visitors, she would smuggle him in something special, such as a cream cake or a chocolate biscuit, which she would take out of a pocket in her black dress under her white apron.

Often he would feel very lonely, waiting, feeling the faint pangs of hunger, listening to the subdued, conflicting noises of the big house. Jennings, the gardener, would stop and talk to him when he was working nearby. Once he had brought him an old cap-gun that he had dug up down by the creek. Sometimes he would see Margot playing on the far lawn. He began to look forward to hearing her bright chatter when she bombarded the gardeners with excited questions, or to watching her movements as she played with her toys. So that later there was always an emptiness when she was not there.

One day she noticed him and ran over to the window. When she smiled he could see how the freckles crinkled round her eyes. 'What school do you go to?' she asked. 'I'm going to school soon. To St. Catherine's. Is that were you go?'

'No, I go to Marsh Street.'

'Oh.'

For a moment she seriously traced with the toe of her shoe in the loose soil of the border garden. When she looked up she asked, 'Where is your mother?'

'She's busy.'

'I know something.'

'What?'

'I won't tell, see!'

'What is it, then?'

'The gardener told me.'

'Who, Jennings?'

'Yes.'

A chair grated on the verandah and Mrs Chatterton called, 'Margot.'

Margot turned and ran to where her mother was sitting, shaded from the sun by a rattan blind. 'If I have to tell you again—'

'Mother, mother, I know why the little boy hasn't got a father. It's 'cause he was killed at the war.'

'Margot, go inside at once.'

Mrs Chatterton stamped her foot, her voice broke shrilly. 'Margot! Do as I say, at once! And don't have so much to say for yourself!'

Then it was Saturday, Margot's birthday. Watching Jennings set up the tables for the party, by the fountain in the sunken garden, he remembered how the previous day Jennings had leaned his brown hairy arms over his shovel and said to his mother: 'It's a new country, gal. You don't have to depend upon anyone here, not like at home. You've been out here long enough to know that—plenty of opportunity! I'm old . . . doesn't matter now.'

Mrs Johnston arranged the spread. Watching, he forgot about Jennings; he ceased to wonder why he often told his mother she shouldn't work there any longer. He couldn't look away from the tables. There were plates of feathery cakes bursting with cream, frail white and pink meringues, chocolate cake, a variety of biscuits, some covered in coloured tinsel paper, and finally the birthday cake, encrusted with icing, with five candles on top. Mrs Chatterton came out when the games were finished and watched Mrs Johnston arrange the guests around the tables. The boys wore dark jackets and starched white collars; the girls, white silk dresses, and most had bows in their hair.

He leaned against the window sill, listening to Margot's voice, brighter and quicker, rising above the others. Then he saw that something was wrong. Margot had got down from her place at the top of the table and was shouting, 'I won't. I won't!'

Mrs Chatterton moved towards her, but she turned and ran, stopping with her back to the pond. Her cheeks were flaming as she cried, 'I don't want to sit next to Grace and Maurice! I want Ronny to be here. Ronny. . . .' Mrs Chatterton tried to grasp her daughter's arm but she jumped, evading the outstretched hand, and stumbled against the low stone rim of the pond. For an instant she struggled to hold her balance, then all the children shrieked as she flopped backwards into the water.

When he could bring himself to look again, Jennings had got Margot out of the pond, and Mrs Johnston was trying to get the tittering children back to the tables. Mrs Chatterton half led, half dragged her soaked choking daughter over to the house. As they approached, he moved back from the window into the shadows. His heart was racing and he felt sick, and somehow guilty.

'Well, how does it feel to be back?' asked Old John Keeble, peering shrewdly down his long nose.

'It's rather early to say.'

'I suppose the old country has, well, as they seem to say nowadays, taken a pounding?' Then, scarcely allowing him to reply, Old John went on, 'I must say everyone over there stood up to it wonderfully. Plenty of spirit, eh, Flight Lieutenant? I'd like to go home again some day, just to have a look around. It's surprising how one becomes attached to this little country. I came out here thirty five years ago, straight from Oxford. Never thought I would stay; there was so much I missed, the finer things. One settles in, though, takes root. . . It's comfortable here, that's it. . . .'

He was aware of the keen gaze again. 'Now, let me see. . . . What year would you have been in?'

'I beg your—Oh, I see. I. . .I didn't go to college.'

'Oh.'

'Lieutenant, you haven't had a thing to eat!' Mrs Wells interrupted. 'Can I get you anything? Another cup of tea, then?'

'No thank you.'

Outside there was the sound of a car being braked sharply, and then the distant boom of a heavy door closing. Mrs Wells was speaking to him, but he could hear only the rhythm of her voice. Out of the corner of his eye he saw Mrs Chatterton leave the room. 'Yes,' he said, 'yes,' struggling to regain the drift of the conversation. Then he heard Mrs Wells say, 'Oh, here's Margot. Now isn't she beautiful? Just like her mother used to be!'

Mrs Chatterton was crossing the room, accompanied by a tall young woman.

'Isn't she beautiful?' Mrs Wells persisted.

'Yes . . . Yes, she is,' he said, feeling weak.

Then Mrs Chatterton was standing before him. 'Now, what is your name again?' He felt the blood rising in his face, and he couldn't find words. Mrs Wells came to his rescue. 'Brent,' Mrs Chatterton repeated. 'Of course. I simply cannot remember introductions now. Flight Lieutenant Brent.'

He was looking into a pair of clear light eyes and he felt his lips moving and heard a voice unlike his own acknowledging the introduction. The eyes smiled automatically, then flicked down to the decorations beneath his wings. 'Quite a collection!' Margot said, arching her eyebrows.

'Oh, those,' he said awkwardly. Then in a floundering attempt at humour, 'They gave them away. Must have had too many left over.'

'Will you have a cup of tea, dear?' Mrs Wells asked.

Margot shook her head—'Thank you.'

'What have you been doing, dear?' Mrs Wells inquired.

'Nothing very interesting, I'm afraid,' Margot smiled sociably.

When Mrs Wells was out of hearing, she turned back to him, saying, 'A cup of tea! Hell, a gin would be more like it. God, what a life. You can't even get anything decent to drink!'

'That's the hell of it,' he said. But she missed the irony of his tone. She was gazing around the room at each of the uniformed figures in turn. Finally she said, 'I suppose you're glad to be back.' Then unexpectedly, 'The roads are just dreadful nowadays. We went for a run out to Newhaven this afternoon and had to crawl all the way. Soon as the needle moved over fifty we got shaken to pieces. It was simply brutal!'

'I see,' he said.

'There was nothing to do when we got there. Sybil wanted to go in for a swim, but it was simply freezing. There's nothing to do anywhere these days, for that matter.'

'How about your Red Cross work?'

'Oh, that. It's only a few hours a week, and it's just about finished now, anyway. Mother wouldn't let me go into a hospital full time.

Once I tried to get overseas. I was keen then. You know, Florence Nightingale, and all that. But I never got an answer to my application. I think mother must have had something to do with that, too.'

'Margot,' Mrs Chatterton called.

'Margot.' An echo awoke in the past.

There was a thud, thud of small feet in the passage, changing to a quick slap, slap on the boards, where the rugs ceased in the servants' quarters. Then small fists were beating against the door. His mother put down her darning and opened the door. Margot stood in the passage in her nightgown. Her hair was damp and had just been combed, leaving the ends straight and spiked.

'I want to see Ronny,' she said.

'You'd better go back, Margot. Your mother will be angry,' his mother told her.

'Ronny,' Margot called. There were little points of light dancing in her eyes. When he moved up beside his mother, Margot bent down and grasped the hem of her nightgown and pulled it up to her chin. 'See,' she squealed, 'I've just had a bath!' She stood with her feet planted apart and her toes turned in, revealing her body, still flushed from a brisk towelling. The points of light in her eyes were racing. Then she was stamping back along the passage, her excited laughter rising above the sound of her mother's voice.

'Margot,' Mrs Chatterton insisted.

'Yes mother.'

'I want you to meet Flying Officer Grayson. He was at Woodbury with your cousin Roger.'

'A cigarette?' The curate held out a silver case.

'Thanks.'

'I was rather sore at missing out on the show,' the curate said. 'Actually I was in camp for three months, but they turned me out. Apparently the old heart is not what it might be.'

He tried to think of a reply, but his attention kept wandering. 'I don't think you missed much, really,' he said. He could hear Michael Grayson's lisping, 'Ve'y nice . . . Ve'y fine indeed.' Good old Michael. One of the best, he thought. Margot was answering, her head tipped slightly to one side, a fixed social smile on her lips. Dressed in white, she appeared almost illuminated in the darkening room. His eyes lingered on her costume, shaped by her hips and the full thrust of her breasts. An image from the past returned, and thinking of how Margot had obviously forgotten it all, he smiled. Then he was shaking, struggling against a mounting desire to laugh.

He held himself tight, aware that the curate was speaking again.

'It's possible you did more real good being out of it all,' he replied, noticing that Margot had left Michael and was now standing with her mother. Her lips were moving and he tried to separate her voice from the surrounding conversations.

'What I say is, where is all the money coming from?'

'So we had to stooge around until the pathfinders dropped their flares.'

'. . . time they lifted petrol restrictions altogether.'

'Ve'y nice.'

'. . . almost impossible to get servants. And you daren't say a word to them.'

But Margot was talking in a low tone which did not reach him. Her head was slightly bowed, she suddenly seemed to him dispirited, subdued. Still talking, she turned absently in his direction and with a gathering shock he became aware of the change she had undergone. Her face, for the moment unprotected by its cultivated responses, was empty. Her eyes were old and vacant. Their dancing animation that had been so much part of her memory was gone.

The curate's voice brightened. 'You really think so—' He stopped, seeing the officer's changed expression.

He was still looking at the delicate lifeless face, pain and anger mounting in him, spreading, choking. He gazed round the room, his anger giving way to dull wonder. 'I didn't realize . . . I wouldn't have thought that even all this could have . . .' His voice tailed off.

'I beg your pardon?' The curate was looking at him anxiously.

'I didn't—' He made an effort to dismiss his thoughts. 'I didn't realize that it was so late.'

Mrs Wells turned to Mrs Keeble. 'What a pity the Flight Lieutenant has to leave so soon he's awfully nice. . . . What dear? Yes, that's him shaking hands with the Mayor.'

He paused at the door and glanced back into the room. Rex was speaking to an attentive group, illustrating his remarks with sweeping movements of his hands. Margot was walking with a studied flowing movement to where Alan was sitting alone. Her face was calm, imperious, bored. Mrs Chatterton was resting her head against the back of her chair, her cheek bones prominent in the sunken flesh. As he watched, the white lids dropped for an instant over her eyes, like the blinking of an old harsh-voiced bird. The curate stood by the window, thoughtfully peering out into the thickening light, which was slowly blacking out the dying trees, the rotting leaves, the silent decay.

He turned and stepped quickly out of the room. Mrs Wells' wide, moist eyes stared after him; but she could see only the light slipping backwards and forwards on the swinging glass of the doors. 'War is dreadful,' she said. But Mrs Keeble had moved away, so she continued, speaking her thoughts aloud. 'He's been through so much. You can see it all in his face.'

ANTON VOGT                     # The Accident

When Johnnie's sharp bushman's axe sank into his foot two toes were completely severed. They lay there on the ground like caterpillars that had forgotten how to crawl. But his immediate concern was with the rest of his foot. The blow had fallen sharp and swift, leaving no time for pain. There was only a numbness and the warm feel of blood bathing his foot stickily. Now a hammer was beginning to beat in his brain, and nausea gripped his bowels deep down asking him to be sick. But he had been hurt before. As he worked he was conscious of hands damaged, the sawn-off stump of the index finger on the right hand; the left hand with the little finger neatly lopped off by the doctor. The hand had been crushed that time, but had miraculously recovered. The bush brooded and when the time was right struck back. The tall trees stood where the seed fell before man came. But when the axe struck, like Samson they drew down their destroyers. Johnnie, binding his foot firmly with the kerchief he wore round his neck, said to himself: 'The cows'll never get wise to this lot. . . .'

*          *          *

It wasn't until he had made a good job of the bandage that he began to hobble out. He had been ringing trees, working without a mate. He knew that Ben and Sailor were felling; they'd be thinking of morning tea. Well, he'd get them the morning off, and nothing lost. He used the axe as a stick, hopping on the sound leg. The foot was starting to throb now and he could feel the strain in his head, a dull hurt, a wound that was not merely physical, himself dying. Panic struck him, all the old fears, blood-poisoning, tetanus, the uncertainty of life and death. The trees loomed up, hating him. From the ground their roots struck upwards, eager to trip or to wound. The damp earth, soggy with long rains, the leaves, rank and half rotten, smelled of death. Involuntarily he shuddered. 'I've had enough,' he said. 'By Christ, I've had enough. After this lot they can keep their bleeding bush.' He stumbled painfully, catching the bad foot on a stump. Cursing, he saw the blood splotched with mud, the soggy lump of bandage oozing freely. Well, he had good blood. 'Plenty of red corpuscles,' the doctor had said: 'You'll never die of anaemia anyway.' No, by Christ, the bush gave you no chance for that, nor old age either. It got you somehow, some of you or all of you. The bush or the mill: the axe or the saw. Some blokes thought they were smart, but it got them in the end. Or else rheumatism from being wet, with the rain always falling and the sweat, and the wait around for the engine and the cold ride home. 'You get a big screw in the bush,' they had told him. 'A quid a day without overtime. . . .' Yeh; and you went screwy yourself if you hung around long enough. The hammer in his brain beat more loudly; it beat like the rain on the roof of his shack, insistently, trying to remind him of something he had forgotten, buried deep down somewhere where it was no use looking. As he moved forward he disturbed a branch, weighed down with water. The heavy shower caught him, but he was already wet. Under the hill where the mill houses were it rained every night. The low cloud hung over the bush so that everything was permeated by water, trees and earth and men turned to a wet slime. It made trees grow, Sailor said. But then Sailor was used to water. He wouldn't mind water that way, in oceans; on a windjammer maybe, with the sails spread and the wind whistling and the spray coming salt on the smooth hard deck. In the bush the hollows between roots bogged, furrows were creeks, depressions great pools full of water-newts and crawlies. Even when it wasn't raining you got wet through ten minutes after starting, and you stayed that way all day, winter and summer, sweating and freezing. And all the time working heavily, using your hands and arms, straining your back and your guts. . . . Well, he'd had his share and he was getting out light.

Coming out on an open patch where the beech had been cleared and the bracken grew tall and thick, he startled a deer. They stood there looking at each other: the man, crippled and without a gun, the deer, a half-grown stag, frightened but proud. Then the deer broke and ran. Johnnie cursed his luck. You chased them all day with a gun, and when you went out without one they came walking. Well, one bleeding cow at a time was plenty. Skins were worth two quid a pop, but your own was worth a darn sight more. You got something even for bits of it. He remembered the story about the bushman who had lost his thumb; according to his cobber he had cooked it. Said he wanted to see what it was like. . . . They'd argued the toss, whether it made him a cannibal or what. Well, he wasn't trying anything as fancy as that. 'Compo' was enough; enough to take him out of the bush and keep him out. Till next time. . . . He hobbled on, more cheerful remembering the man with the thumb. As he made his way towards Ben and Sailor he crossed patches of bush already cut. The remains of the old line were still visible; the sleepers grown soft and almost rotted away, the bits of iron that remained porous with rust. Bracken and blackberry grew heavily, hiding the low ramp. Between the trees the sky was overcast, but to the south it was clear. They were in for a change. In the distance he heard an axe bite into wood, and then the answering call from another axe; and now the tattoo sang in his head like the rhythm of his pulse, Sailor and Ben keeping time with the loss of his blood, swinging and flinging, easy and sure, but never too sure, with the tall trees waiting to catch them . . . And then Ben saw him coming and ran forward to meet him.

*         *         *

All day long they worked in the bush, always together. It became second nature with them to know what the other was doing. Ben and Sailor, the people would say at the mill; never just Ben or Sailor. Like David and Jonathan. It was safer that way too. It was surprising how often accidents happened through poor combination. People worked in different rhythms, the ebb and flow varied. Put a slow man with a quick man and they'd kill each other. It wasn't that you worked slow or worked fast. It was like two clocks: they'd both do the same speed finally, they'd keep the same time. But the pendulums varied; they varied in length and weight, they had different rhythms. They ticked differently. In the bush you had to synchronize, or else the trees fell on you, or the axe went into you, or else you got knocked up in some other way. If you didn't get knocked up you got on each other's nerves, and once you got rattled the bush did the rest. There were too many funerals in the little mill settlements; too many for the population. The bush was always ready to strike back. It wasn't a matter of brains either. There's more than one way of having brains. A man might have it with figures or with language, and still be a dumb cluck with tools, or handling a horse or an engine. Or keeping alive in the bush with the trees after him, waiting for him to make a mistake, waiting for his cobber to make a mistake, waiting for them to get out of step. . . . And ready to hop in and beat them up with a few thousand feet of timber, with ten tons of wood, with all the malice of centuries. . . .

Ben worked with Sailor and Sailor talked; not always, but always slowly, spacing the flow with grunts as the axe struck. Ben went to work each day like the rest of the men, with his crib and oil-skin, riding out on the engine. The women at the mill could hear the whistle and they'd look out and watch the engine go out, the smoke merging with the low clouds. And then they'd be swallowed up by the bush. Ben's wife hated the mill. She hated the tall trees and the brooding hills and the rain that never stopped falling. But Ben loved the feel of the axe and the smell of the leaves. He loved to startle the red deer. He listened to the birds and knew their song. He loved the feel of the soft grey fur of the opossumes he caught each night in the traps he set where they worked. He would watch the bases of the trees for tracks, and when he saw fresh marks he set traps. Because he knew the ways of the bush he always got something, although sometimes it would be only a big bush rat. But best of all he loved to listen to Sailor. Sailor was Ben's adventure. Ben's wife didn't know Sailor; to her he was just a drunken ne'er-do-well. Ben learnt to keep quiet about Sailor. But every day he heard some new story about China or Brazil or Madagascar or Ceylon or Siberia, or some other place where Sailor had lived crudely but well, drinking, fighting, making love; using his senses and his imagination as Ben did in the bush, glorying in himself. And Ben was a fair mate, giving as well as taking. He knew every tree in the bush, every shrub, every bird and insect; every living thing. And like Sailor he gloried in it, gloried in his mastery. In neither was there any conceit. Their pride was the natural pride of craftsmanship. From the first night they had met, leaning over the pub bar, they had clicked. They recognized themselves in each other. They were curiously similar for all that they had scarcely a feature in common. They were similar in action, in humour rather than in looks. They loved hunting and eating and drinking and yarning—and laughing with the women when Ben's wife wasn't looking. What was more strange they liked working, especially working together. They loved the smooth swinging rhythm of the axe, the synchronous movement of bodies, the skilled judgment of weight and balance, the nicety of timing that gave them mastery over the great dumb trees. Ben and Sailor, working today wholly absorbed, didn't see Johnnie until he was almost on them. Ben stayed his axe, wiping the sweat off his face. Sailor did likewise, the stroke falling rhythmic and neat, the pause coming cleanly. Then he saw Ben run forward.

Johnnie saw Ben coming and stopped. He grinned seeing the other man run. 'One day they'll both run under a train together', he said to himself, 'And whose fault will that be?' Ben caught his arm and he sat down and Ben called out something to Sailor, and then he couldn't remember anything except that it was raining and he was out walking and he only had one boot on; and the other boot was hidden somewhere, and there were leaves everywhere, and it was no use looking because there was only one boot and all the time it was raining, and it wasn't any use looking. . . .And the trees stood there like sentinels saying, 'You can't get away. We'll get you. It's no use trying to get away. We'll get you, we'll get you. . . .' And then the showers came drowning their voices, and the boot went sailing away on a river of blood. . .

\*     \*     \*

The mill houses clustered under the hills. The road from the station passed through three miles of bush, mostly second growth. The road followed the old line, and remains of the old mill made an untidy splodge of rotting timbers. Over the stumps of the cut trees bracken and blackberry grew fiercely. Parasitic plants flourished. Mosses covered the eroded roots of the living and the dead. Sinewy creeper strangled the gnarled trunks, reaching far into the arms of giant trees still standing. Survivors of the first and second cuttings, they stood proudly among the rubble. They were like old men. Around each hung a spirit, an emanation, a will to be and to survive. Even the stumps seemed to say, 'We hang on, and we are renewed. You lop us off, but we sprout. Our death is a new birth; in decay we give life.'

The road came to an end at the mill. On the wall facing the road a humorist had carved the inscription 'World's End'. On either side, close together, there were five small houses. Behind the mill there were two shacks. Against two of the houses there were garages, one a big sprawling barn for the lorry, the other for the owner's car. Through the open door it stood lop-sided, jacked up on an empty kerosene case: the track was hard on axles. All the houses had wood-sheds. Ben's had a fowlhouse and run, and most of them had small strips of garden. But where the gardens finished the bush began. In winter the tall trees shaded the sun; but then the sun didn't shine much in winter anyway. The low cloud hung over the hills. The ground went soggy. Up at the mill they threw great logs into the bog to get the truck clear. Further down it was easier: the subsoil was shallow and the road tolerable. If you had speed up you could make it. If you didn't you got to work with scrub to give the chains a grip. The houses were small wooden boxes with tin roofs. They had squares cut out of them for windows and slits for doors. They were bleached by the weather to a dull grey and the grey roofing rusted to a dirty brown. A mill only lasts so long, and it wasn't much use throwing paint around if the timber gave out. The smoke came from the chimneys all day. There was no wood shortage. Inside the women put up curtains, and used embroidered cloths when they invited each other to afternoon tea. At night the men came in full of mud and slush. They bathed, carrying kerosene tins of hot water from the copper in the wash-house. After tea they sank into time-payment chesterfields, listened to time-payment radios run on batteries; they looked through the sporting results in the weekly, and usually fell asleep before supper from sheer exhaustion. But some of the men went down to the station with the last lorry and stayed down there. If they couldn't get the driver to stay they walked back drunk or fell asleep on the way. Sailor knew every puddle and stone on the road from the pub. 'Like Mark Twain on the Mississippi,' he'd say, 'I know every shoal blindfold. Whoah there! Three points to starboard or you'll be up to your bloody neck,' he'd yell. And by God you would be. The liquor oiled Sailor's tongue, and somehow made him grow. Ben liked getting drunk with Sailor, but Ben's wife didn't like him splashing the money. 'You've got to get out of here,' she'd say. 'This is no place to bring up kids. We've got to save and move out, into town maybe.'

Today she hung over the tub washing his sweaty shirt and singlet and socks. The copper was well stoked up. There was no shortage of water either. All through the winter the tanks overflowed, corrugating the gardens and paths and carrying the soil into the creek. But in spite of the wet the slabs smouldered night and day on the tip at the side of the mill. She could see the smoke now as she leant out of the window shooing the neighbour's cat from the fowlrun. Outer shavings, no good for timber, they were good fire-wood in any language but not worth the transportation. The cabbages sprouting in the small dark plot grew on wood ash and humus. So did the nasturtium in the bed under the wash-house window, that startled her with its fierce growth, smothering the wall and producing leaves like saucers. It was a world of growth and decay. But chained to the tubs and the range, and insulated from a childhood home and friends in town by miles of mud and slush, Ben's wife brooded like the bush, only more fiercely, hating the small box-like house and the sooty smell of kerosene lamps, and the torn clothes and dirty feet of her children smearing the grime of the yard on the one good carpet, the two good chairs; resenting the coarse thick socks, the greasy singlets; hating the low cloud that cut off the horizon, levelling even the hills. Today she hung over the tub, knowing the scene too well, reliving the day that was today, yesterday and forever unless something happened; unless. . . .

With a start she saw the procession coming from the mill: men moving slowly, men carrying something. . . .Men walking slowly, carrying someone. . . .Suddenly she ran, her heart beating wildly, clasping her hand to her side in an agony of fear. 'Ben, Ben, Ben!' she cried. A wild hysteria shook her so that she did not see; so that she was unaware of other women running. . . . Until at last she was there, and Ben was holding her hand and saying, 'All right, old dear. It's only Johnnie, and it's nothing serious.'

*          *          *

Johnnie lived by himself in one of the shacks at the back of the mill. He had his meals with Sailor's wife, who ran the boarding house. It wasn't a boarding house really. She had her own kids to look after and the house was full as far as beds went; but all the men who weren't married had their meals there. She got twenty-five bob a week from them, and the house rent free to run things that way. There wasn't much in it. Besides Sailor and herself and three kids she had six men to wash and cook and cut sandwiches for; and once every week she went down to the pub and got shikkered. She was up at 5 o'clock most mornings, and when she went down to the pub on a week-night she didn't go to bed at all, but just started in on the sandwiches: seven big lunches for the men, and three smaller ones for the kids who went in to school on the second lorry.

When she found it was Johnnie who was hurt she took over the way she always did. While they were waiting for the lorry to come back she took care of the foot. 'How did you do it, kid? Meat shortage isn't as bad as all that,' she said. She worked over him steadily and easily like she did over the sandwiches, and then she lit a cigarette and stuck it in his mouth. 'Feeling better?'

And Johnnie, who had come to hearing Ben's wife yell out, thought, 'Now everything is a big fuss, but it's nothing really. A man can live without toes.' And suddenly he realized that he had passed out and he coloured, wondering what they'd think. Well, Christ almighty, accidents were always happening and it was always the same, except that he had never passed out before.

*          *          *

Andy was a great fellow with the men. Andy was in the bush for the wood he could get out of it, but he was a fair boss. When there was anything on they were never stuck for the lorry. And when there was anyone hurt there wasn't a quicker man to get things moving. In his younger days Andy had been a crack bushman himself. He had come away from the chops with big money in his belt, but he had stuck to it. And when the chance came he went in for his own mill. No man ever made anything on wages, so Andy paid wages and collected on footage. The little mill was Andy's creation: with no Andy there would have been no houses. There would have been no street with five boxes with squares cut out of them for windows on either side, no cabbage or nasturtium in the cleared beds, no chickens behind the wires, no clothes props or tin chimneys with the smoke always coming, no slab heap smouldering against the rain, no mill stuck in the heart of the bush with the inscription carved, 'World's End'. Also there would have been no community of thirty souls poked away in the back of beyond, though God knows where they would have been had they not been there. Sailor on the high seas perhaps, and the others in nooks and crannies where the world's work is done. . . . For without the mill settlement there would have been so many feet of timber less, so many fewer cheese crates, so many less houses in the suburb . . . So when a man got hurt Andy saw to it that he went to hospital in his car or in the big truck that took the heart out of the bush and took the sweat out of the men and lined Andy's pockets and built a fine bank balance, though Christ knows he deserved it.

To Johnnie, sitting up gripping his leg to stop it from flopping when the bumps came, no three miles were ever longer. He could feel the blood drain from his face and the blue vein thump high up. He wanted to talk, but said nothing. Ralph, driving, leant forward and thought, Thank God I'm out of it. Shoving his foot down, feeling the power, he said: 'I got mine snigging.' He showed his elbow, the joint projecting, the flesh scarred deeply with the vicious marks of rough surgery still visible. Johnnie nodded. 'Everyone gets it sooner or later,' he said. The foot throbbed, and he could feel the soggy bandage spilling. They were passing the small school with its clean cream walls and the pointed roof like a church. Through the pines planted evenly along the south of the cleared patch that made a playground he could see the children out for lunch. Some of them came running to the gate, hearing the lorry. They waved and he waved back. Suddenly his mind was at peace. Twenty miles to go, but a good road from here on. In an hour the doctor would be cleaning up the mess. As the school disappeared behind the trees

Johnnie caught sight of a slim blonde girl standing in the doorway. He could feel the blood come to his face, a hot wave running up to his ears, making them scarlet. He looked around, but Ralph was busy negotiating the railway crossing where one train passed each night and morning but where the signpost told you to Stop, Look and Listen.

\*  \*  \*

Young Johnnie sat on a stone under a tree and ate his lunch made of white bread sandwiches with mince and blackberry jam, smeared on thick so that the purple came through like dye. He had been kept in for putting gum in Pat's hair. Now as he ate his lunch he watched the other children playing rounders. The girls and boys played together, the big ones with the little ones, and when the ball went over the fence into the scrub they all went over to look for it. Young Johnnie liked playing rounders and he liked coming down to the cream school with the red roof and hoisting the flag for Miss Thomas even though he couldn't sing the King in tune. Miss Thomas was a blonde and very beautiful, especially when someone was naughty and she flared up and her blue eyes were like ice with a flame in the middle of them cutting into you. It wasn't only with children that she went like that. He had seen her once with big Johnnie, tearing into him so that he, little Johnnie, had got frightened. Mister, she called him; no-one ever called anyone Mister in the mill settlement unless they didn't belong. But then Miss Thomas lived at the farm near the school, and anyway she had come from town. Looking through the school porch, Johnnie could see her at her table with her head down and he suddenly wondered what she was thinking about. And then he heard the lorry coming and crammed the last mouthful down and crumpled the paper and ran to the gate, and Miss Thomas came out to look too. The lorry didn't stop but went right on, and big Johnnie was sitting very white and he waved at them; but then they noticed that the lorry was empty and they knew that something was wrong. Little Johnnie saw Miss Thomas come out and heard her ask in a funny kind of voice who was in the lorry, and saying, 'Johnnie? Why, Johnnie's in the bush. . . .'

They stood and watched the lorry cross the line and veer past the station on the way to town, and then they went on with their rounders.

Ralph came back about sundown and said everything was O.K. Johnnie would be right in no time, and no complications. Young Johnnie and the other children had a great time running wild around the school playing cowboys and Indians while waiting for the lorry; but now they were getting peevish. While they were having tea Johnnie heard his father and mother talk about accidents, and when he went to bed he could still hear them talking and his Dad saying, 'Anyhow, he'll get compo.' Then he heard his Dad go out, and he lay there in the dark thinking about Johnnie who was hurt until he felt quite bad about it.

\*         \*         \*

That night Andy drove down to the pub himself to ring up the hospital. Ben and Sailor and Sailor's wife and Dave, the sawyer, went down too. While the ring was going through they went into the pub parlour. There was a good fire getting under way. There were no customers in the pub except after hours. The law said you could only drink until 6 o'clock; but the men from the mill, or from the few outlying farms, or the small dredge working up Mura Creek had a fat chance of getting in before that. So since there was nothing else to do they broke the law. The pub stood open for all the world to see, with a light in front and a good fire in the parlour. It was good to get in out of the rain and stand drying yourself in front of the fire, and warming your inside too, even if the stuff was getting so weak that you needed a stiffener to get a kick out of it. It was civilized drinking, with women present and no rush, sitting down to it when you got dry; with the radio throwing out a good tune that made you forget the green bush and the tough going and the small boxlike houses. Tunes from the bright lights and the big streets, London and New York, and all the other places you wouldn't see, unless you were like Sailor but it was too late for that now. For good measure they had dragged in an old piano from the disused parlour at the back, and the sawyer Dave played: catchy tunes that had them singing and sometimes swinging it. Then the dingy parlour with its splotchy walls and cheap-jack couch and old red chairs became alive. Dave would thump, keeping time with his body till the hair got in his eyes and he had to throw his head back to keep it out. There was big drinking done, with everyone in. You put down ten bob and there wasn't much change, but you wouldn't put down any more for a long time or maybe at all, unless you were one of the cows who never went home. Sailor could take more than any of them, and when old Martin the publican got too shikkered to deal anything out Sailor used to take over. There was one thing about Sailor; he could take any amount himself, but when he was behind the counter he would never give it out to anyone who couldn't take it. Instead he'd fix up a bed with his coat out in the passage and tuck you up there, and every so often he would go out and see if you were O.K. At about 1 o'clock most Sunday mornings old Mrs Martin would turn on a bit of supper, good hunks of bread and cheese and a cup of tea. If you were hungry she would sometimes let you get to work over the open fire with bacon and eggs, but if you wanted that you had to pay for it.

Well, when Andy got through the nurse said, Yes, Johnnie was O.K., nothing to worry about. And Andy thought anyway he's insured; thank God for that. He went back into the parlour where the men were drinking with two men from the dredge. They were drinking beer straight but Sailor's wife was mopping up gin and looking a bit glazed already, although it meant nothing except that she was getting away from the cooking and the sandwiches and the house under the hill with the bush leaning on it. She always got that glazed look but she was good for a few hours yet. They were telling yarns, and Ben was just going to tell the one about the maid with housemaid's knee when Charlie from Mura Creek came in with his wife, and two kids so he told them them the one about the Irishman and the Maori instead. It looked like being quite a social evening and no-one worried much about Johnnie now that he was going to be O.K. They started pouring the stuff down steadily, feeling the warm glow rising inside, and not taking any notice of the rain when they went outside.

\*     \*     \*

But up at the mill little Johnnie heard his Dad come in late and knew by the way he laughed when he tripped over his boots on the back porch that he was drunk and would have something for him, but when he came in he asked, 'How's Johnnie, Pop?' And his Dad sat back on the bed and laughed. Johnnie's all right, young feller; he's in the money.' And he explained to young Johnnie with a lot of flourishes the current meat prices, so much for one finger, so much for two fingers, so much for a hand or an arm; so much for a toe, and so on until he had young Johnnie laughing. And then suddenly he got up and went outside again and was sick on Mum's flash nasturtium.

\*     \*     \*

Big Johnnie lying in hospital felt the leg ease. The sheets were starched cool and smooth, and there was no sag in the bed like the one in his shack. The walls were white, and he realized suddenly that the walls of his shack were dirty and the air was never sweet, but always foul from old clothes and tobacco and spilt beer. Christ, there were worlds within worlds and all of them different, but linked somehow. You opened or shut doors. Chance did it mostly, a job took you there. And so you went down a mine or on a dredge or into the bush, and after a few days you had been doing it all your life and you let it happen to you. . . . Until one day the weight came down too hard and you fought back or cracked up. Everyone cracked up sometime, some on booze or women, some on horses or against the law. You couldn't go on day after day, with the wet and the weight of the trees bearing down on you. Now he was out of it, and he wasn't sorry. Through the ward window before the blinds were drawn he could see trees. Trees separately were good things. He could see them standing detached, poplars and pinus insignis, planted trees with spaced lawns between them. Further back, even here, the hills were thick with native bush; but it was beaten back with axe and saw and fire, the stumps standing black, the cattle grazing in the rubble. When the nurse came in with a cup of tea he smiled, and she noticed that even one of his teeth was missing.

*    *    *

Next morning was Saturday so young Johnnie went out with his Dad and Sailor. He had his crib with him for morning tea and rode out on the engine. When the whistle blew he turned and waved to his mother until the houses and the clothes lines were swallowed up by the trees, and you couldn't tell what was smoke or mist or steam rising as the sun tried to break through. Young Johnnie liked riding on the engine and no one had to tell him to look out. After an accident everyone was careful. When Ben and Sailor got to work he hung around for a while. But at morning tea he asked where big Johnnie was hurt, and later when they went to work again he went over that way. He was thinking about big Johnnie and what they had said, and suddenly he realized that all night he had been wanting to look. He had a funny kind of feeling inside him, a sort of knot that made him breathe queerly. He ran forward, noting the ringed trees, big Johnnie's work. And then he came to the place. In an open patch before a native birch he saw the thing that had made Johnnie faint. Not the toes, lying like dead caterpillars, for the rats would leave nothing so choice lying about for a whole day and night. What young Johnnie saw was what big Johnnie had forgotten and then suddenly remembered. What young Johnnie saw was that no one should have seen, and ten to one no one would ever have seen among all that slush and rubble and the creeper fighting for life among the tall trees, if big Johnnie hadn't been little Johnnie's hero and if little Johnnie hadn't been lying awake half the night wanting to look. He saw a big red boot standing there obscenely with half an inch of water in it and the instep gnawed by a bush rat, but no mark on the smooth round toe. With a little cry Johnnie ran forward and picked it up. With a queer twisted look on his face he threw it far, far into the scrub. Then he walked back to where Sailor and Ben were working.

DENNIS McELDOWNEY    **By the Lake**

The fact that ash from her cigarette dropped occasionally into the dough she was mixing didn't worry Michael's mother over much; sometimes she took it between her floury thumb and forefinger and wiped it on her apron, but mostly she just stirred it in until it was enveloped in dough and could no longer be seen.

But Mr Payne, sitting on the sofa in the kitchen window reading a book and whistling idly through his teeth, did annoy her, not because he was reading or whistling through his teeth, though he seemed to do these things not as other men but in a manner solely designed to irritate, but because she didn't like Mr Payne. She didn't reason her dislike and she would have freely admitted that he had many admirable qualities, but he was small, and she regarded small men as she regarded weeds that got in the way underfoot and spoilt the view.

Michael, who danced round her to look in the bowl from one side and then from the other, and then scrambled behind the table to get a still better view, and wanting to make men from dough with currants for eyes and waistcoat buttons to be baked in the oven only for him even when she told him that he would have to wait for tomorrow morning when the dough was risen—Michael was also a nuisance. So she said pleasantly.

'Wouldn't you like to take Mr Payne for a walk round the lake?'

'No,' Michael said.

'But I'm sure Mr Payne would like to go.'

Mr Payne sighed and put down his book. Though small he was tactful.

'Oh, all right,' Michael said.

They went along the passage and from the front door into the first paddock, well covered with bones, some bones bleached white, one or two where the dogs had just eaten with the newly torn flesh still clinging at the joints: clambered through the wire fence and walked down the clearing where the grass was sharp and scanty on the unfertilized high country soil.

'Didn't the Maoris come this way going over to the Coast for greenstone?' Mr Payne said.

'I think they went round the lake and up to the pass the way they take the sheep after shearing,' Michael said.

They came to the end of the flat ledged between hill and the valley where the homestead stood and looked at the lake glowing blue in the sun. From here the ground sloped quickly to a stream grown with willows, and flattened to where the lake rose and fell on the shingle.

'I can show you something about that too,' Michael said. 'Ted showed it to me.'

'Who's Ted?' Mr Payne said.

'He was our shepherd. He was here last year when we came, but he's dead now. Dad says he was drunk. They never found him. They only found his boots by the lake.'

The hill rose on the left, dark with trees below, but burnt brown on the barren top. Near the water there were clumps of flax and raupo. Michael ran down the slope with Mr Payne following behind, and pulled aside some flax growing by a bare face on the hillside.

'There's just room to get through,' Michael said, and he crawled through the hole in the rock near the ground.

'Come on,' he said, 'there's plenty of room inside.'

There was a tall cave inside, sand floored and still and dimly lit, apparently from a hole further up, the wall deepening to shadows on the far side.

'Does your father know about this?' Mr Payne said.

'He hasn't found it yet. Ted said the old Maoris said something would happen if you told about it.'

'Why?'

Michael pointed to a ledge of rock where, half-hidden from the filtered light, were a row of human skulls, yellow with age, looking impassively into space.

'Good God!' Mr Payne said.

'There are fourteen of them,' Michael said calmly.

Mr Payne's eye went curiously down the row. 'Fifteen to be exact,' he said.

'I thought there were fourteen when Ted brought me here. It's funny to think they used to be alive isn't it? I wonder what's in that dark part over there.'

Mr Payne thought, his father ought to know about this. They might be valuable. The museum people would be interested anyway. There might be axes and things. He kicked a hole in the sand with his heel.

'There's another hole here Mr Payne,' Michael called.

'Don't go too far,' Mr Payne said. All for greenstone, he thought, walking over these hills and along by the lakes and over the rivers and mountain ridges and through the pass into the bush on the other side. Probably bare-footed and not much clothing and most likely there was snow to go through. I suppose these poor beggars died on the way. Now I wonder where that boy is.

'Michael!' he called.

There was no answer, not even an echo.

'Michael!' he called louder. This time there was a faint echo that called again, 'Michael,' and Mr Payne found himself looking again at the row of yellow skulls.

There were sixteen of them now.

As he pushed his way through it the air in the cave was heavy on his shoulders and tried to hold him back, and the walls of the entrance hole threatened to close in and crush him. Clouds were coming over the lake as he emerged and the surrounding hills were sharply reflected in the greying water; but Mr Payne did not stop to look. He ran heavily along the shore, stumbling over stones as he went, and up the ridge towards the house. Near the top, he heard Michael's mother calling, 'Michael!'

Pulling hard at his legs he slowed down as he reached the top and saw Michael's mother along the clearing, leaning on the fence by the paddock with the green grass and the bones.

'It's you Mr Payne is it?' she said, politeness and contempt for small men struggling in her voice. 'You look puffed. Where's Michael?'

'When I left him . . .' Mr Payne began, and then he stopped.

'Would you mind asking him to collect the eggs before tea?'

'Not at all,' Mr Payne said, and he turned, and walked again towards the lake.

DAVID BALLANTYNE        **And The Glory**

1

The hell with it, Larry thought, seeing the customer out of the corner of his eye. He went on stowing cigarettes on the shelf. It was twenty-eight minutes past five, he had to hurry and fill the shelf before half past so's he could meet the boys on time.

'Two packets of Golden Virginia, please.' The voice was hesitant, the sort you could pretend not to hear.

Larry picked up another carton of cigarettes. Quickly he ripped off the top, grabbed several packets, inserted them between others on the shelf.

The customer coughed.

Larry concentrated on the cigarettes, amused at the thought of the bird kicking his heels. The bastard should pull his finger out and buy his fags earlier in the day.

'I say, how about some service?' The voice was firm this time.

Hell, thought Larry. He turned to attend to the dope.

But Myers, the floorwalker, was already behind the counter handing over two packets of Golden Virginia.

'Thanks a lot, Mr Myers,' Larry said, turning back to the shelf.

'Just a moment, son. This is not my job. You're here to attend to the customers. There's two more waiting.' Myers spoke in a sharp whisper.

Annoyed at the way Myers spoke, especially at being called son, Larry attended to the customers.

When the narks had gone Myers, who had remained back of the counter watching, moved close. 'I saw you, Scott,' he said. 'You deliberately ignored that person. What's going on? This the way you always attend to your job?'

'I was hurrying to get the shelf filled, Mr Myers. I looked around when I heard him talk.'

'You heard him when he first came in. I was watching you, Scott.'

'I'm sorry, Mr Myers.'

'Watch it in future. You're here to give service.'

Myers walked away.

Greasy bastard, Larry thought, angrily jamming packets of cigarettes on the shelf.

## 2

Larry grabbed the beer, gulped half of it down straight off. He sighed and looked at the other three standing with him in a corner of the private bar. 'I needed that,' he said.

'Where's the fire?' asked Tom Duggan, another counter assistant.

'That damned Myers is on my tail again,' Larry frowned. 'Reckoned I wasn't looking after the customers. You got to give service, he says.'

'Well, were you?' Duggan asked.

'I was trying to get those cartons of fags on the shelves before half past,' Larry said. 'It was pretty late. I reckon no joker can expect service that late.'

'Customers come first, you know,' said Allen, who worked in the hardware department.

'Look, Myers is always getting onto me,' Larry said. 'I can't do anything, can't keep anybody waiting a second and he's behind the counter bawling me out. Hasn't he got anything else to do? What a soft bloody job some jokers have!'

'Forget your miseries,' Duggan said. 'Have another beer.'

Larry sulked. These jokers didn't understand the snitch Myers had on you, seemed to think it was right that Myers should always be tormenting you.

Waiting till Duggan had taken the glasses to the bar to be filled, he said: 'You think they'd encourage a man to stay with them. The way things are these days it's easy to get another job. Wonder what they'd say if I gave my notice, got another job?'

'Forget it, Larry,' Allen said. 'Say, there was a sheila down my section today; boy, I bet a joker could make her on a cup of coffee.'

Offended at Allen's casual disregard of a serious matter, Larry frowned moodily into his beer, sipping it slowly so's he didn't finish ahead of the others and have to pay for the next round.

He glanced at Ryan, the tall well-dressed clerk from the upstairs office. Ryan was a keen type, eager to get ahead, willing to talk of his own ambitions, not so willing to offer sympathy to others.

Larry waited till the others had discussed the girl, then he interrupted: 'Had your promotion yet, Tom?'

'Got a ten bob rise last week,' Duggan said.

'Funny that, you know,' Larry said. 'I been there about the same time as you, Tom, and I haven't had a rise yet. Wonder if Myers put my pot on.'

'It might come through this week,' Ryan said. 'Used to get sick of waiting myself. But it came through.'

'No, I bet Myers has been up to his dirty work,' Larry said. 'Don't like that sort of thing.'

'Well, I've found Myers a pretty good bloke myself,' Allen said.

'Doesn't trouble me,' Duggan said.

'Hey, Tom, coming to the races on Saturday?' Allen said. 'Taking the old man's car, and there'll be some grog.'

'Sure enough,' Duggan said. 'That include Kay?'

'That's what I mean. You and Kay and myself and Doris.'

'Do *you* good, Larry, to get out somewhere on a Saturday,' Duggan said.

'The mother-in-law's coming down on Saturday,' Larry said. 'Anyway, I have to take the kid for a walk. Pam reckons she has enough of him in the week, it's my turn on Saturdays.'

'Married life!' Duggan said.

'Won't see me getting hitched for a few years,' Allen said. 'Takes me all my time to keep myself on my pay.'

'Trouble with you, you got married too young, Larry,' said Duggan. 'Think of the fun you could be having.'

'I'm not complaining,' Larry said, watching Allen dig for the money for the next round.

'Just old Happy-go-lucky!' Duggan laughed.

Larry was sore. What business was it of theirs if he was married? No outsiders could make you feel any different about your marriage than you already felt. And, when all the worries of married life were considered, didn't that still leave something to be said for it? It was hard to believe this when you were down in the dumps and Pam was in one of her fretful moods and the kid was squawking, but it was not so hard other times when you got home and tea was ready and Pam was there to listen to you and sympathize.

He looked anxiously at the clock. It was five minutes to six. He hoped they took their beer easily so's he could get out of paying for his round.

### 3

Hands in pockets, shoulders hunched, he strode bitterly up the street from the pub. He'd wipe them, have nothing to do with the morons. They knew he was scratching along on a few miserable quid a week, had a wife and child to support, and it wouldn't have harmed them to wait till tomorrow night for his shout. They couldn't have enjoyed gulping down a beer right on the tick of six. He thought how each anxious moment nearer six o'clock had been a minute nearer his saving his last half-crown. Then, he might have known it,

Duggan must look at the clock, sink his beer and demand that you shout.

He'd knock off going to the pub. Obviously he could not afford it; but, after standing behind a counter all day, it was good to relax a while before going home. There were not many other pleasures and, besides, he figured what he spent on beer week-nights would total no more than what most jokers spent on their Saturday bashes, and seeing he never drank on Saturdays it worked out even.

No, he would not knock off drinking; a man had to have some pleasure in life. But he'd knock off drinking with the fellows from the store. He had enjoyed their company in the past, but he'd noticed an unsympathetic attitude about them recently. He'd find another pub and drink alone, and to hell with them.

He fingered the two pennies that remained from the half-crown and his anger increased; he knew nothing would make him change toward those jokers, they had shown they were not real friends. They were almost scornful when he attempted to explain how Myers had humiliated him, had not offered suggestions as he hoped they would. Bloody morons. Why bother with them? But for them he could have trammed all the way home; as it was he'd have to walk to the end of the first section, catch the tram there.

He walked close to the shop window, the stealthy walk that accompanied dusk and humiliation. Keep the head down, the shoulders hunched; ignore the passing people, the cars, the trams.

No tram was in sight when he got to the end of the section, so he walked on. Anyway, he thought, he couldn't stand the shoving, the smell, the jolting, of a tram. He wanted to think of himself, consider the problems that were growing every day. At least, in times and moods like this the problems were greater; some days it was as though he had every right to be satisfied with life—a comfortable job, a wife, a child, the prospect of a State house, good health . . . what more did anybody want? What more had he ever wanted?

He felt through his pockets for a cigarette, found a butt and lit it. Why moan? .

He walked on home.

4

Pam was waiting for him at the bottom of the stairs. She was crying. And, upstairs, the kid was bawling its lungs out.

'What you standing down here for? Can't you hear Dickie bawling?'

'Where have *you* been? Why didn't you come home?'

He ran up the stairs. She followed.

'This damned crying,' he called back at her.

He opened the door to the apartment, the sound of the child shrilling in his ears. The place was in darkness.

He cursed, flicked down the light switch. Nothing happened.

'What's up with the lights?' he asked.

'That's what's wrong,' she said. 'They came and cut them off.' She wiped the sleeve of her smock over her face.

'What the hell they do that for?' he said.

'They said the bill wasn't paid,' she said. 'Larry, didn't you pay the bill? I told you this'd happen.'

'I went in this morning and paid it,' he said.

She moved across the room to the sofa. In the bedroom the kid was choking up long sobs.

He looked down at his wife. Her helplessness irritated him. He wanted to say something to her that would make her sit up and look as though she had some life in her, but suddenly the anger he felt toward the power board was more important than any irritation.

'God, I'll fix this,' he said. He stamped from the room. 'I'll show them!'

He rushed up the second flight of stairs to the meter. He was examining it when the landlady came from her room with two candles.

'Oh, Mr Scott, the power board men told me they were cutting off your power and I wondered if you'd like these candles.'

'They told *you* they were cutting it off, did they?'

'They said the bill hadn't been paid.'

'Fine thing! Telling other people *my* business! Matter of fact the bill was paid this morning. You know how much? The huge sum of seven shillings and sixpence!'

'It's awful,' the landlady said. 'Well, I'll give the candles to your wife.'

He called Thanks as he hurried downstairs.

He ran along the street to the corner dairy. 'Can I use the 'phone, Mrs Mills?' he asked, his hand already around the receiver. 'The power board cut off our power. The bill was paid but they went right ahead.'

'It's terrible what they do,' said Mrs Mills.

'For the huge sum of seven and sixpence,' he said as he dialled the power board number.

'Inquiries? Look, my name's Scott. 36 Patterson Street. My power's been cut off. What's that? The bill hasn't been paid! Look, the bloody bill was paid at ten o'clock this morning. I made a special trip from work just to pay the magnificent sum of seven shillings and sixpence. Now, I want those lights put on again smartly . . . What's that?'

The voice mumbled that it was there to answer inquiries; connecting power was not in its scope. The matter would have to wait until the staff reported for work in the morning.

'Like bloody hell it will! What's the engineer's number? Those lights are going to be put on tonight.'

Fiercely he dialled the engineer's number. A woman answered. The engineer was out for the evening, she said.

'Listen to me,' he said. 'I'm a married man with a child. Name's Scott. I got home from work just now and what do I find? My lights cut off! My wife needs power to heat milk for the baby. And I want my tea. What? Hasn't the bill been paid! It was paid this morning. The magnificent sum of seven and sixpence. You tell him I got to have those lights on tonight.'

He let the woman say how sorry she was, then dialled the Mayor's number. The Mayor was out. He told the person who answered the 'phone what had happened, got the number of the power board chairman.

The power board chairman was home. 'Look, my power's been cut off. I want to know the reason why. Nothing to do with you! My God, this has got a lot to do with you. That power's going on tonight or you'll hear more about this. My bill was paid this morning and your fellows came up this afternoon and cut off the power. All for the sake of the huge sum of seven and sixpence. I *can't* wait till morning! I want that power on tonight!'

He listened to the chairman saying he'd get in touch with somebody, told him he certainly better get in touch with somebody or he'd tell his story to the Mayor tonight if it was the last thing he did. More would be heard of this, he told the chairman.

He stood back from the 'phone.

'Are they going to do something?' Mrs Mills asked.

'They better,' he said. 'I left enough noise. Something will happen all right.'

'What a terrible thing to do,' Mrs Mills said. 'You'd think they'd have some sense, wouldn't you?'

'All for seven and six,' he said. 'Be different if it was a tenner. Think I'll ring the engineer again.'

This time the engineer was home. 'You don't have to ring the chairman and the Mayor with your troubles,' he said.

'My oath I'll ring the Mayor,' Larry said. 'I'll ring the Prime Minister if those lights aren't put on tonight. I don't care how you get them on but they got to be on tonight. And I'm thinking of suing you anyway for spreading lies that I haven't paid the bill.'

He walked cockily from the dairy, sure the board would make

things jake. He thought with satisfaction how he'd told off the bureaucrats. Christ, the thing was ridiculous. Cutting off a family's power for the sake of seven and six! Well he'd put the servile little bureaucrats in their place.

He returned to the apartment to wait for the power board men.

## 5

Larry sat on the sofa, looking at the glow of the electric light bulb. Pam was frying bacon and eggs, Dickie was squatting in a tub of water on the floor.

'I asked those jokers how much it'd cost the board to send them here tonight and they said about a quid each for them and a quid for the joker that drives the truck. That's about three quid it'll cost them for the sake of seven and six.'

'Yes, Larry,' Pam said.

'I certainly got some action,' he said. 'Nobody's going to push us around, honey.'

'Watch Dickie, will you, Larry?'

He leaned over the child, tried to grab the soap from him. 'Give Daddy the soap, Dickie. That's the man.'

'No, no, no.'

'That's no way to thank your old man for the trouble he's gone to tonight,' Larry said, rubbing the soap in Dickie's hair. 'Hold your head back. That's the boy.'

Made a man feel good knowing he had guts. He wasn't going to be trampled on by anyone. Nobody was going to push Larry Scott around.

What insignificant things his worries of earlier in the evening now were! The Myers affair had been very trivial; probably Myers had a good deal of justice on his side, was only doing his job. And there was nothing wrong with being married, as the boys knew; they'd only been kidding you, you shouldn't take them seriously. They were good sticks.

He looked up from the tub with a smile. Boy, wait till he told this to the jokers tomorrow! He'd hang on till they were in the pub, then he'd give them the whole story. Concentrate on the amount of the bill, then how you rang the engineer, the chairman and the Mayor, threatened to ring the Prime Minister. Mention the idea of suing the board for spreading lies about you.

He wished it was tomorrow night so's he could be telling the story to the fellows in the pub.

'Better dry him now, Larry. He's been in there long enough.'

'Yes, love,' he said, lifting his son out of the water.

# The Blind

The house is old. Early colonial. Its wooden walls are faded; weathered a pale, green-tinged ochre. They soak up the rain and darken, like damp clay.

Above the broken-lipped chimneys rises a small octagonal-shaped turret room, a great suspended prism of windows where, at certain times, opalescent pools of colour melt, drift and glister over the glass. One frill of scallops runs round beneath the spouting while between this and the windows shines an insertion of blue and frosted panes. Like a bubble the little room upstairs lets through the outside light in contrast to the verandahs which have been half closed in at the corners with a geometry of red and purple glazing and gloomily dampened by a knitwork of shrubs. The great belly of bow windows is draped in velvet, the glass being patterned with lace roses and perpetually half-drawn bottle green blinds, blinds that curb the lace impatient to sneak outside with the wind.

Lillas Howell stood at one of the turret windows. She could have put out her hand and touched the winding wistaria heavy with flowers that curtained a downstairs verandah, but her big ringless hands, glazed, nobbled, faintly freckled from age, lay resting on a wet chamois leather and a piece of white jap silk, worn almost transparent. Her drawn-back hair was iron grey, fuzzy where it escaped from a tortoiseshell pin; her features were strong; the expression was dour, the short-sloped line between the brows deep, puzzled, frowning; and the reddish-purple frock, reaching high and tight around a prominent throat exactly matched the little cobweb of thickening veins on each cheek. And yet the face suddenly changed, the eyes brightened and the sparse sandy brows lifted eagerly as sheets in the yard beneath strained from their lines, cracking like whips.

'Mother,' Lillas shouted, 'it's a grand day for the washing.'

And the answer came, tremulous and irrelevant. 'As sure as my name is Ellen-Christine Howell that's an angel with long curls looking in my window.' The tone ranged from thin soprano to broken contralto. It was the voice of a very old woman. Lying deep in her bed, the soft, collapsed, simple looking face framed with a neat plait of white hair showed among the many frilled pillows.

'You're seeing things, mother. I've told you it's nothing but a nor'west cloud,' the daughter said, her smile going.

'Look at his beautiful eyes,' the old woman went on. 'I wonder what he thinks of this wicked world. And don't you go whispering about me to your sister. I want the binoculars. Do you hear me? Bring them at once.'

Lillas trod heavily down a creaking, carpetless stairway; very narrow; but by the time she came up again bringing the binoculars her mother was asleep. She returned to the kitchen where her sister was lifting shut the little iron door across a grating, in front of the stove, with a short, bow-shaped handle. The woman turned to Lillas.

'As mother used to say, this range just eats up the coal,' she said.

'But you've forgotten to turn down the damper. Can't you hear the flames gallivanting up the chimney, Nell? Before we know where we are we'll have all those clean night-gowns ruined with soot.'

Nell slipped the fresh ironing from a high drier and stood nursing it, folding the things into her apron with arthritic shaky hands while Lillas drew down the pulley cord, winding it round a hook on the wall. The mellowed lengths of bamboo swayed and creaked above their heads. A red and blue checked cloth for dusting the bars hung over one end. Nothing had been changed in fifty years. The golden hammer of an eight day glass-cased clock whirred and struck eleven.

'These stairs will be the death of me, Nelly. I'm weary to the bone, and I don't like the look of mother at all. She's cantankerous. She's getting quite queer. We shall have to move her down to the big bedroom.'

'And put up new curtains then, Lillas dear?'

'Indeed we won't. Where's the money for curtains? There's still some life left in mother's old red serge. If we hang lace ones underneath. And that'll cover up the borer and keep out the glare. Maybe they'll keep out some of mother's angels if there's less light.'

Nelly nodded.

The two women paused, burdened with memories, between them the kitchen table scrubbed into a grey map of smooth hollows and knife cracks.

Years ago the mother had slept in the turret room with the younger children. One of them had been born there, brought in a basket carried by an angel, so had believed the children. Divided from the plushy rooms and varnished dados downstairs the airy retreat for children had protected the late James Howell from their early crying. Later the room fell into disuse. From the northern windows there had been a fine view of their garden and orchard until, after the father's death, they had been forced to sell half the property. The boundary then ran through the rose garden. A new house sprang up and new children played over a tidy lawn where once the young Howells had filled their pinny pockets with apricots and pears. At first the mother lamented her loss day and night, but after a while she transferred her tin box of wills and insurances to the turret room for extra safety and so she was able to make this box an excuse for spending some of each day staring from the windows, noting every movement of her neighbours, as if by knowing how often they changed their sheets she was able to possess them in return for the loss of her land. When she became deaf and bedridden she forsook her domination of the house and returned to this room, where she had slept for the last three years, the tin box under her bed, its keys hanging round her neck in a black satin bag.

But she had been seeing things for weeks.

And so they carried her, wrapped in blankets, down into the core of the house, through the kitchen, along the hall, under the chandelier that had been her pride, past the picture she had painted on silk. Nelly turned a loose cream doorknob. It was cool and dim in the spring-cleaned bedroom but for a beam of dustmotes that sloped from the blind down to a foot-worn rose on the carpet. The old reddish furniture had been wonderfully polished, the white curtains starched and all the fussy gilt handles rubbed up. The cleanness was like a scent, Nelly thought, but the leaves were surely further than ever from the garden outside.

The mother seemed smaller now in the large double bed, in the larger darker room where the space was swallowed up by a massive mahogany wardrobe with crystal-handled tiny drawers running down each side of the full length mirror, the mirror alone giving back some sense of distance and of reflected though subdued light. Here, among yellowing faces staring from ornate gilded frames she lay quiet enough although once she cried out sharply that there was a man in her room, near the wardrobe, with waxed red whiskers. The sisters hastened to soothe her, to pass it off lightly, for hadn't she always been fanciful and superstitious they told each other; hadn't she always wept if she saw the new moon through glass. Hadn't she always suspected every man who knocked at the door, of evil intentions.

But they heard no more of the man in the mirror and she was easy until the day the young Presbyterian minister came to call on the Howells.

She asked him at once, wasn't the manse damp? 'It has been damp from the beginning. I think it's built over a stream,' she said. 'They must have been wicked elders to buy such land for a minister of

God.' And then she whispered to the young man, though loudly and hoarsely in her deafness, that he put her in mind of her own little Jamie who died. 'Wrap up warm, Parson,' she told him. The young Reverend Lawrence moved up closer to Ellen-Christine's bed. He chatted pleasantly shouting a word every here and there in the old woman's ear.

She kept nodding her head as if she were understanding, then her mouth fell open and she dozed while the sisters poured and handed tea, but she woke with a start crying 'Bless me', and tugging at the minister's sleeve she began to whisper that the *man* had come back. He was over there by the wardrobe making glad eyes at someone and, sure as eggs were eggs, it was Tom Mathias, her poor dear Nelly's rogue of a husband.

Lillas Howell went on talking, from long habit ignoring her mother's mumbo jumbo but the mother's cracked voice shrilled at them; her wrinkled arm rose up out of the pink knitted sleeve, pointing and quivering.

'Pity's the day you set eyes on my Nelly. Have a care, Tom Mathias. Maggie Moyle's leading you a pretty dance, the bissom, just like you led my poor Nelly. Nab him Parson. Spring off your tail Lillas. O my poor heart. He's slipped through your fingers. He's run off—in his father's gig—with my brandy. My head! Stop it, can't you stop the noise of the wheels.'

'Now mother,' Lillas said quietly. 'Don't fret yourself and drink a little tea.'

'He's stolen his father's gig, has he! That'll hurt the old man. But who'll pay the piper, you girls——' she moaned now lying still, her nose and her eyes outlined with blue and the face like wax. '—his little bairn, Nelly's new born bairn sleeping in its crib—but don't think father and I are made of money—don't tell the parson I'm dotty——'

For the young parson it was just another old woman with a wandering mind. He'd seen such things before. The sun made his face hot, burning in under the half-drawn blind. Next door the neighbour trundled his child on a barrow of leaves down the path, past a hedge. The young laurel leaves at the top were gleaming. In the wardrobe mirror the reflections were tinged with a disconcerting yellowish hue. 'Our Father——' the parson began to pray.

Nelly Mathias was shaking. That dead and dreadful past that she had tried to outlive through Oliver her son. She rose up and carried away the tea cups. Hurt? She had nothing in common with the young parson but her nerves were not what they used to be, and for the life of her she could not speak for herself. I've been happy, mother, she longed to answer, but she knew that nothing she could ever say would impress her family, or the town for that matter, like the stale tale of her husband Tom going off in his father's gig with the fast handsome widow Magdalen Moyle. Humbly she washed the thin china cups, carried them to the dresser. It dismayed her to hear her feet shuffling across the worn linoleum, to see that her slippers were familiarly shaped with the same bulges and worn down heels she had watched coming in her mother's shoes. She emptied the tea-pot, rinsed it, and left it upside down to dry; she carried the blue-rimmed strainer to the back door and threw away the tea leaves on to a mound under some geraniums. She unpegged tea towels and put away the peg basket on a shelf beneath the mangle, taking care to drape the mangle with its turkey red cover. The family habits were now fitting her like her own gloves. How often she had told Oliver stories of her life in this house, and yet now that she had come home she felt as if the very hooks and shelves were intent to destroy the last of her youth, as if the damp drab walls were compelling her to accept old age. And what an effort, a burden, had become this struggle with the dust that would keep rising up between the widening cracks in the floor boards. Even though it had all been done in the morning she could see even now the tiny heaps of yellow dusty powder near the legs of the umbrella stand, and in the slanting afternoon sunlight the dumpy turned legs showed up their lacework of borer holes.

Nelly Mathias came slowly into the front of the house to find Lillas.

Lillas was speaking with a school girl. The girl's hair, tied by a ribbon, hung down her back in a heavy tail, coarse shining kinky hair, and she was fiddling with a long end of braid knotted about her tunic.

'This is Mary,' Lillas said. 'You remember Mary's mother, Kathy Essler, Nelly?'

Essler, Nelly thought. Kathy Essler, the young Irish servant blushing to the roots of her black hair. And now, so soon, Kathy's likeness, Mary.

'I remember your mother as if it were yesterday, Mary,' Nelly said.

But Mary had to go. She would tell her mother how bad poor Mrs Howell had been taken. Her mother would be sorry. The sisters watched Kathy's daughter flying down the hill beyond their garden, steering her bicycle with one hand, the other pressed on the crown of her white hat. The brim blew back from her rosy face and at the end of the brick wall she waved. Then the bicycle raced out of sight.

'She's a headwind every stone of five miles,' Lillas sighed.

'Don't fash yourself, Lillas dear, the girl's young,' Nelly whispered. Tears came into her eyes. But Lillas thought her sister wept for their mother.

'Shut the door,' she said briskly. 'We'll be having dust all through the house.'

It seemed that the Reverend Lawrence thought the mirror in the wardrobe was giving Mrs Howell her fancies; but even if something, something sudden, should be done about it, first they must send for their brother Will who had always, Nelly remembered, when all was said and done, been able to twist their mother round his little finger.

Will Howell, the lawyer, was shocked to see the change a few months had brought, to see his mother so much at all their mercy —no more ruling the roost, no more keeping up of appearances. The tight plaited wreath of hair above her soft shrunken face reminded him that at last old age had placed her beyond vanity, not that he would remember her like this, but rather how she had with long strokes brushed her hair down from the wide pink parting into a snowy flying cape and then, separating it into three strands had fluffed it up, rolling it over her two fingers, and finally stabbed it with pins into the shape the world knew her by—not this tidy wreath that other hands had woven.

At first he made a pretence of conversing with her, sitting close, shouting simple questions, but he could no longer reach the mind he had known, so he held her brittle fingers and listened to her memories. She was wandering through the eighty odd years of her life, living in whatever time she chose. Although he knew emphatically that his mother's mind had gone to pieces it still left him feeling an outcast, when he saw that the child she doted on was neither himself nor any of his living sisters but Jamie, a boy who had died before his parents emigrated. Will Howell had always banked on his mother's affection. Now it seemed the Prodigal son had come home, a figure in a glass; a delusion. That his mother's mind was failing was one thing, but to see her wanly smiling and crooning to the empty mirror left him with a feeling that was close to shame. For Lillas this mirror-gazing was just another daily worry. What, indeed what would be left for Lillas when she need no longer answer mother's life-time of habits? For poor old Nelly a word in passing was enough to send her hysterical with a theatrical kind of sympathy; it made his blood boil to hear her speak of little Jamie in the present tense: 'Little Jamie's lost in the heather with his grandpa Baillie Howell, and they've nothing but a communion cloth to keep out the cold, Will'—it was as if she really believed the twaddle his poor mother told them. And worse than this were the long solemn lustful faces of neighbours who gathered round the door in the evenings to be astonished, lugubriously beguiled, by stories of Ellen-Christine's latest fancies.

To end it all he came to a quick decision. They must remove the wardrobe. No, not that, for she had never cared for changes. They must cover up the glass, tell her they were sparing her eyes from the light.

Lillas took a long length of lilac print and hung it over the mirror, leaving the little drawers showing, and seeing the stuff again the mother was pleased, for she remembered that from lilac print she had made the children's sunbonnets and she thought for a long time about how well it had worn and she was calm again. For days she was calm.

But one morning, all at once her sickroom bell, crazily tinkling, brought them all running. She was moaning, her head turning slowly towards them. 'Are you stone deaf?' she whimpered. 'Listen, Lillas. O Nelly there's a little child lost in our roof, up under the rafters. Mammy, mammy mammy. It's lost. It's under the rafters, crying, Nelly; mammy, mammy mammy. It's lost. Go and look.' The last flicker of vivacity, of suspicion, had died down in the once large eyes which were filmy now and small under the drapery of the lids, and the cheeks were never without tears lying passively in the first met wrinkle. There was no rest for Lillas and Nelly for morning noon and night, no matter how hard they worked to keep the sickroom fresh, except when she slept they must answer her bell until each one was dropping with tiredness, they must pretend to be searching, high and low, for the lost child calling, for the silent sobbing that only the deaf could hear.

Mammy mammy—Nelly would hear it in her sleep. It was a wee bit of a cry a long way off but in the dream she would hurry between narrow walls, just as a long time ago, after Tom had left her, she had hurried to her own child, to the white cot in the room at the end of the back hall.

Since she had come home Nelly had been given a spare room. She lay there now trying to sleep. There was little in this room but its bed and table; a photograph of herself as a girl, with a cloud of long waving hair tied on top; but the features were fogged and the large placid eyes seemed to know nothing of life. Once she had seen her mother kneeling on this very same yellow hearth rug, going through the servant girl's trunk, feeling right down to the bottom. Triumphantly her mother had held up a slipper and shaken out from the toe two little silver earrings, two crosses. The girl had been packed off with tight-lipped advice and the crosses returned to a green leather jewel box. To the vault of the family's past.

Shall I not be stifled——? yes, mother had often thrilled them to the marrow with her dramatics, and she'd learned all her lines from the theatre itself, not from books. Mother had always been a simple soul, ruling the roost, but simple tastes. I met a little cottage girl. She liked putting out the crumb tray to the birds. Where had all the birds gone when the orchard was cut down?

Into the Mathias pine trees across the gully? Mathias—her name and Oliver's all these years. An old man—old Donald Mathias, going like the Lord of Creation, in his knickerbockers, down the main street, on a daily tour of inspection; down the winding track his father's bullocks had travelled, carrying wool; the name of a Scottish village painted on his five-barred gate in the tussocks; hard as nails; mean as dirt.

An old man. Near with his money. But an old man. No little Oliver had ridden on his knees. She had taken all she could from old man Mathias and his childless daughters. She had disowned him just as his son had disowned her. Hadn't it been enough to endure his screaming and cursing and keening over his stolen gig and grey? She had looked but once, before she left her home town, into his sagging face, and had passed him without recognition. Hard as stones, little Nelly Howell, the youngest of five, father's pet. She had left him, jogging in his pony cart up the long hill to his sonless house, his knees covered with a fur rug, his hand blue and slack on the rein. That town house was still there, a stone's throw away, and for all she knew there might be Mathias kith and kin sleeping under the sodden greening slates, watching small new busy houses springing up on the land where their stables and pigeon house had once lured romantic boys and girls. But she—she had had to watch the Mathias full slack lips and handsome disguising moustache re-shaping on her son's face.

*          *          *

When Nelly Mathias woke she felt stifled. Her throat was dry. Her heart was going at top. She had had a dream and in the dream she had seen little Jamie leading Tom across a street. Tom was walking with timid shuffling steps, and together he and the child went up to the door of a public house. There Tom had stood underneath a splintered glass verandah roof while the rain poured down on him, and he was playing on a toy concertina as if his life depended on it. His face, blank and leering, looked kind of daft until suddenly he began to bawl like the raving loony old drunks who had scared her stiff as a child; but when he turned round to go inside the pub she read Come into the garden, Maud, hanging in a golden text across his shoulders. Then Jamie had danced up to her shaking a sailor cap and whispering, A penny for the Guy, sister dear. But just as she put out her hand to touch Jamie's curls the tenderness that had welled up in her was bitterly quenched by the sight of her Celtic grandfather, Baillie Howell, standing high up above her in a pulpit, thumping and haranguing with his clenched fist, and his long white Scottish beard was burning round the edges. She was choked by the dust that rose up and clouded out of the pulpit cushion, while Baillie Howell shouted Adultery and Charity until she saw dimly, through the dust, that the pulpit was really a small white box, narrow, with six silver handles.

The relief that the dream was over. But she left her bed. Who were they, who were Lillas, Will, and herself to take away sight from the dying? She must go and take down that old bit of lilac from mother's wardrobe mirror. She must go now.

NOW.

She slipped into the windowless hall where it was still dark and began to grope her way along, feeling the bubbled up patches on the wall paper, patting at doors, running her hand along the umbrella stand, the way she had trodden that very hall as a child, but then much faster, in a frenzy to be past the hump-backed shadow thrown by her father's black coats. If only she were not so stupid and weak, blind as a bat in the darkness, toddling past the skirting boards like a done old man tapping gutters with his white stick. And she must have taken a step too few before turning, for her face met thick musty-smelling cloth, the velour of winter coats, the coats of the dead or departed that had been saved for a rainy day, and she knew that the tiny knocking sound was the rim of a bowler hat rocking on its hook. Cold rushed through her, the old guilty fear at disturbing taboo possessions; daring to open mother's best umbrella in the hall and bring bad luck on the house; mother; mother going with a thin ebony brush all over father's hard hat, her ring clicking on its brim. It used to hang on Sundays at the back of the church in the cloakroom where the elders left their hats and umbrellas. It was all muffled in there with solemn whispering under the low ceiling and the heads were bald and the beards were white. And then she had followed father's slow tread; his coal black boots. She had always been in time under father's wing.

She pushed at the wall to free herself but her loose hair had wound round one of the coat buttons and, fumbling for it with chilly fingers she thought, it used to be mother's hair, the silvery rolls enclosed in the white net, that had snagged on father's waistcoat button when he kissed her. She started to weep and giggle.

'Lillas,' she called softly, 'Lillas.'

At once, almost at once her sister came towards her and untangled her hair, and Nelly, following Lillas, walked slowly back to the spare room. In the doorway she saw that it was morning; the light was coming, showing up little wreaths of silver on the wallpaper. A gust of wind whirled out the curtain, fanning on her face.

'Feel the nor-wester blowing up, Lillas,' she said. But Lillas Howell elbowed away the meshes of curtain and clasped the blind, pressing around its frail papery edges with her big vein-rippled hands. Then she began to draw it down letting it slide over the window at a snail pace that hushed the click of the roller, and dark slipped over the walls and took away the colour from the wreaths, the gleam from the glass.

'Mother's gone, Nell,' the elder sister said and drew the blind down beneath the sill holding it there for a moment before letting go, for the spring had a habit of jerking back with a snap.

'You didn't call me,' Nelly whispered, going cold.

'Dinna say that. Dinna. She went in her sleep,' Lillas answered without turning round.

But Nelly Mathias knew she had been called, only she had gone too late to give back the mirror, and so nothing could be altered. Ever. She pressed her hands to her ears. Now she would hear the poor bairn crying in the rafters until Kingdom Come.

A little gust blew out the blind, tapping the slat and cord bobble gently against the wall. Lillas Howell slipped her hand in behind it and closed the window.

The house is old. Early colonial. Its wooden walls are faded; weathered a pale, green-tinged ochre. They soak up the rain and darken, like damp clay.

O. E. MIDDLETON      # Coopers' Christmas

As I get off the bus this morning and sniff the first cloying smells from the meat works I don't mind. The gang of chamberhands who usually dawdle along behind me are already crossing the loci tracks up in front. They look almost eager.

When I turn the corner into the timber yard Des and Lofty are standing by the stacks ready for work although it is only five to six. I climb into boots and overalls and we start loading seasoned timber into one of the skips. I can see Lofty's eyes are bleared from one of these late two-up sessions he's always talking about but he doesn't give us his usual commentary. Just keeps bullocking like the rest of us. Three, four, five skips we push into the cooperage and put through the planer, and old Gerty grunts and grinds away and spits out faced boards for the tailer-out to stack by the goose saw. Sid is on the saw again and that monotonous chopping whine goes on without a break as he cuts stave-lengths four at a time. Sid is really working today.

We are all ready for smoko when the hooter goes at 7.45, but when it is time to start work again we rush the last hand of draw and show and hurry back to our jobs.

Tony, the leading hand, tells us that we still need forty casks to complete the order that came in the day before yesterday. As soon as the last of these is made and loaded on to the railway truck we can knock off, he says. But the foreman wants no drinking before we finish work. He say machinery and beer don't mix.

And so the morning goes on with Des and Lofty and I pulling down seasoned timber from the racks in the yard and feeding them through the planer; old Bongo shaping and jointing the staves, and the five coopers raising-up casks, steaming and winching them and trundling them, still hot from the drying fires, to stacks near the loading door.

In the yard it is hot and dusty. Some of the four-by-ones we are handling are very long. They ripple and bend in our hands like fishing rods as we break them out of the stacks and balance them across the go-carts. The sawdust showers from them and sticks to our sweat. Every so often Des and Lofty wipe their mouths and look down the road to see if the beer truck is coming. Lofty says if the weather stays like this for Boxing Day he'll take the boat out and try for some snapper. Des tells us that with the family he's got he'll have to do a month's overtime to pay for all the presents he's had to buy. He says he's told his kids he's going to nail boards across the chimney next year.

At morning tea time Tony starts throwing off at Little Spike again for the way he acted last Christmas. Little Spike is six foot two and has a reputation for being a hard case when he is steamed-up. The old hands say that he once chased a cat round the rafters of the cooperage in his stockinged feet because she tipped over his beer. From the things Tony and the others have said since I came on the job I gather that the cooperage is a pretty wet place over Christmas and New Year. It seems that some of these boys can really drink. I begin to think that the months of tough yakker I've spent in the timber yard are at last going to be rewarded.

Des and Lofty and I are all walking a little awkwardly now. The sawdust and sweat are chafing us under our overalls, but we keep pushing timber into the factory.

Every few minutes or so one of the coopers comes to the door and holds up his fingers to let us know how many casks are needed to complete the tally.

The beer truck comes round to the lunch room at 11 o'clock.

The hoops are on the last cask by 11.45, and the trump calls out all hands to load the railway wagon. We all work like mad and the wagon is loaded and sheeted by lunch-time.

As I take off my gloves and walk back into the factory all the machinery is still. In the washroom everyone is splashing water and making wisecracks.

I decide that nothing less than a hot shower will shift the dirt that has caked on my skin in the past six hours, so I get quite a shock by the time I go into the lunch room. At first I think I must have come into the wrong place. The men who sit at the tables with their lunches and bottles of beer don't look like my workmates. Their faces are washed, their hair is combed and the clothes they wear are not the ones they usually come to work in. But the poker game is in full swing.

Sid deals me in and Des raises my bet. I go up again and he does the same. When I finally see him he lays down a pair of bullets to my three ladies. I feel a bit of a heel because he is usually much more cautious and there is only one empty beside him.

It isn't long before everyone is doing a lot of talking. Lofty starts a sing-song in the corner and the trump comes in and calls us gentle-men and wishes us the very best.

I keep winning steadily and soon there is quite a pile of silver beside my tea mug. Nobody is really playing seriously. They're all talking about what's going to win on Boxing Day.

By two o'clock there is a regular procession going to and from the urinal. When my turn comes to deal I can't get sense out of anyone. I know that there were only five dozen bottles among the twelve of us so all this tipsiness is a little out of place. I drained my fifth warm bottle-full ages ago and have been on the scrounge ever since.

Well I keep the game going and every so often somebody fills my mug. All the time I'm expecting Tony to say there is more beer on the way, but with two of his bottles still untouched he's well on the way himself and seems to have forgotten that terrific thirst he talked about all morning.

By four o'clock several of the boys are quite hopeless and when I see Sid filling the cat's saucer with beer I figure it's time to pull out.

On my way out through the cooperage I notice Little Spike's legs sticking out from an empty tallow cask where he is having a snore-off. Over by the timber the trump is trying to put out his smouldering cigar butt with a stirrup pump.

On my way home in the bus I count my poker winnings and find that there are nearly four pounds in my pocket. You can buy an awful lot of Dally plonk for four pounds. It's not the way I planned it, but perhaps I'll have myself a real slap-up Christmas after all.

PHILLIP WILSON      # The Wedding

A week before the day, Betty bought a new hat.

'Do I look nice in it?' she asked in the morning when she tried it on, taking it from the box filled richly with tissue paper. 'Does it suit my blue dress?'

'I don't like the idea of this wedding much,' he replied.

'But Alan, you don't like any social function.'

'Not where those relatives of mine are likely to be present,' he said, thinking how each one expected to be remembered when they all looked about the same to him, the old aunts with their grey hair and glasses, and the uncles, retired but still dangerous they hoped, ogling each unfamiliar fresh young face. ' "How are you?" they will say,' he cried, mimicking the old feminine falsetto. ' "So glad you were able to come. When are you coming down to see us again?" '

'Alan, you make me laugh,' she said, 'but I'm being serious.'

And what other strange fauna would emerge from their retreats for the occasion, he wondered. Cousins who had married badly and who chose this opportunity to bring their offspring to be admired? Or embarrassed relatives of the bridegroom whom no one knew anyway, and whom he himself he expected, would greet in uncomprehending sympathy as long-lost friends while the others, the authentic relatives he had somehow omitted to see in his short-sightedness, scowled murderously in the background? It was a grim prospect, but he supposed he had to go. A fortnight earlier he might have made an excuse, have absented himself from town for the day on some office pretext, if only he had thought of it in time. But now there was no chance of escape. She had bought a new hat, and no matter what argument he produced he would have to go.

He fidgeted about the house that morning, cut himself when he was shaving, dug ineffectually for a while in the garden, and retired to the back of the woodshed for a smoke. But there was nothing he could do to delay it any more. At ten she called through the kitchen window, 'Come and get changed, dear. We don't want to be late.' And he had to get into his best suit, change his socks, brush his hair, knot his grey tie and polish his shoes, until finally the door banged behind them as they set off for the bus.

What injustice, he thought as they bumped over the tram rails by Parliament Buildings, that he should be subjected to this ritual humiliation, led like a lamb to the sacrificial. And as they approached the church door (he couldn't remember whether or not they would have to kneel) he felt his blood rush from his heart. He was relieved when they saw Andrew, Aggie's brother. They stopped talking to him as long as possible, standing with their backs to the entrance, waiting until he thought everyone else was seated. Then they strode in to the nearest pew and sat looking at their prayer books. The organ began to play, and under its murmur Betty glanced around. Immediately she began to whisper.

'Isn't that Aunt Mary over there? And beside her in the green coat, isn't that Aunt Jeannie all the way up from Roxburgh?'

'Oh, yeah. They'll all be here.'

She giggled. 'Uncle Albert's got fat in the last few years.'

He recognized his bald head, shining in the shadow of a pillar like a dim bulb, and he resented them all, the tie of blood. 'The winners must have been kind to him,' he replied.

But after a while he became reconciled to meeting them again, so that by the time the organ roared out its triumphant march and Aggie walked in on his Uncle Garland's arm he was almost in a fit state to enjoy the ceremony. He was not yet completely happy, but he knew the first barriers were down, and with the cocktails at the reception afterwards he hoped his manner would at least approach that of the normal social creature he had on these occasions to try to be. There was only one bridesmaid, and Betty couldn't resist speaking out loud in her excitement. 'Oh, organdie!' she said. 'How beautifully Fay is dressed.'

'Fay?' Alan said.

Something came into his mind and he looked at her again. Yes, he thought, an American soldier had been her lover during the war. He felt himself slipping into the old family pattern, and the memory of her came back like the scent of faded flowers. The sight of those angular Scottish aunts brought it back to him, because they had been so narrow, so provincial in their small islanded taboos and loyalties, because they had said, when it all began, 'How sad her falling for a chap like that. Why, for all she knows he might be a released convict, they say there are some in the American army.' They had been so suspicious, those southern aunts, their privacies untouched by war's invasions. 'Of course, we know nothing whatever about the man's family background. And why should she want to marry'—he remembered how they had hesitated at the word—'a foreigner?' It was something they hadn't liked because they didn't understand it, he reflected. Like sullen sea birds they had rejected him, because he was an American, not British, because he was of mixed blood. Negro, Italian, Jew—it was all mixed up in him, they had imagined. It stood out, he remembered Aunt Jeannie had said, in his finger nails (what a canard) and in his too wavy hair and his brown eyes. American. They couldn't tolerate such a thing in the family. And they had never learnt either, he thought, what war does to us, breaking down those tottering fences, making strange links—as wonderful, in some ways, as the excitement of actual gunfire in what it did to a man.

So that was Fay. He leaned over to speak to Betty about her, but the sacred moment of union had arrived, and her attention was as rapt as if a birth was taking place—or a death. He continued to brood, and he recollected, while the responses were spoken and the group moved out to the registry, that even her father had tried his hardest to prevent their engagement. Gorbal, they called him, after the Glasgow slums where he had made his name in the trade unions before coming out to New Zealand to satisfy his wife. He had given way in the end only on her mother's insistence. But what had happened afterwards? With the turmoil of his own part in the war coming between in his memory he couldn't for the life of him recall. She couldn't have married the fellow anyway, since there she was—unless rumour was right and she had left him, a ne'er-do-well scraping out a miserble existence in the cotton fields of Georgia. Perhaps, he smiled at the fantasy he was building up, she had come back from the States especially for the wedding.

'I wish you would sing, dear.'

'Hmm?'

He discovered they all had their hymn books open and that the organ was blaring again. But he found he couldn't sing, when he looked down at the page over Betty's shoulder. The words were familiar, but the tune was different from what he remembered having carolled as a boy. He opened and shut his mouth in time with the rhythm, hoping Betty wouldn't notice he was thinking of something else, as his thoughts drifted off once more. What had happened to her? He fingered the grey patch at his temple. But he couldn't at that moment remember.

While the voices murmured in the little room at the back, and a sudden burst of laughter floated out, Betty kept up a running fire of questions and instructions.

'Who is that sitting over there?'

'I don't know.'

'Try and remember then. It's your family.'

'I'm trying.'

'At least it can't be a relation of yours. He hasn't got that dreadful nose.' Was a nose that distinctive? he thought. It was the twist in it of course, supposed to be the Cameron blood. 'I hope you know what you're going to talk about at the reception.'

'Oh, they do it for you. All the family gossip. That's really what they come for.'

'Alan!' she said with a little laugh that was largely apprehension at the way he might behave. 'Don't be so bitter.'

'Huh,' he replied. 'As if you care.'

But he tried to brighten himself up as they looked at the wedding presents. 'A hundred quid's worth,' he heard someone remark behind them, and it wasn't so bad after all. Eventually he managed two sherries before Aunt Jeannie came bouncing up to them, a cup of coffee in her hand. He had been wondering when she would come, and now all he could think was that she looked ridiculously young, and seemed to be enjoying herself immensely.

'Which side of seventy?' he said to Betty.

'I'm so glad you were able to come, Alan,' she cried, adjusting the hearing aid in her left ear. 'I was hoping I'd meet you. Do you like your new job?'

'Oh,' he said in embarrassment, 'it's not bad.' He blushed. 'I quite enjoy it really. It's quite interesting.'

'I'm glad. Some of the boys have found it so hard to settle down after the war. I suppose you'll be getting a car soon. You should be able to afford it, with no kiddies.'

'Car?' He tittered at her in his nervousness. 'I hadn't thought of it.'

'But surely. Everyone has a car.'

'We public servants are so underpaid, auntie.'

'Well, you didn't have to join the government.'

He realized she still considered him a failure. And besides, his politics would always rankle her. Her dead husband's money was like a shroud over her old ideas. Things like improving the lot of the southern Maoris, which she had written to him about when he was still a student, no longer aroused her interest. It had changed her whole outlook on life.

'And your Mum and Dad? How are they keeping?' Her eyes were like little steel balls, he thought. She was inexorable.

'Not bad,' he said again. 'They said they were all right, last time they wrote. I'm sure they would have liked to be here, but it's so far for them to come. His spectacles clouded suddenly. Gas had got his father in 1917, while she was probably bouncing on plush by a hot fire.

'Well, I'm glad to hear they are well.'

He struggled for the right social words. 'When are you going back?'

'What?' She jiggled her hearing aid.

'When you going home?' he shouted.

'Tonight.' She sparkled gaily at him. 'I don't want to be away too long this weather.'

'But it's warmer up here.'

'Oh dear no. Give me good old Otago any time for a warm winter. You can never get warm in these hotels.'

'Jeannie!' A spinster with a beaked nose came up and they went away without another word. He sighed.

'I know that one,' Betty said. 'She's after her money. I could tell by the look in her eye.'

'Do you think so?'

But it was probably true anyway. They were all after her money, even himself he supposed, except that he was too proud to admit it. The whole family was waiting for her to die, so they could share the spoils and achieve their belated revenge on the one who had married a fat bank account.

'She's the widow of Uncle George, the one who fell off a haystack.'

The afternoon went on. The crowd circulated gaily—like a kaleidoscope, he thought, coloured broken fragments that clotted into curious patterns as the speeches were made, the toasts drunk, and the self-conscious couple feted. Then 'For They Are Jolly Good Fellows' was sung, while a solemn youth played boogie in a corner.

He saw Betty get a word at last with his cousin, flushed beside the wedding cake. 'Congrats Aggie,' she said. 'You don't know how lucky you are, marrying a schoolteacher.'

'Why, thanks, Betty.'

'Mrs Harris now, isn't it?' Alan said as he came up.

'Yes.' She literally beamed at them, while two infants bellowed behind her. She was absolutely on top of the world and would have said so, he felt sure, if she'd had the words. But all she came out with was, 'Fancy you getting along.'

'Oh, I'm not such a recluse.'

He smiled as somebody else, Uncle Albert he saw, claimed her attention. And as she poured out her triumph and innocent graciousness into the room with all her star-shining eyes, warm cheeks and lips, and teeth like bright pearls in the electric light, his heart glowed for a moment at her happiness before his gloom returned. He wondered how soon it would be before disillusionment came, and lit a cigarette thinking of hours on a clock, days on a calendar, and years of love-making and then disappointment.

Betty kept near to him all the time, thrilled with everything in her quiet way, her sharp eyes seeing and remembering every incident that could brighten future hours of letter-writing.

And he, with no one to talk to, he knew so few of them, yet trying to keep his poise within the family circle, said to her in a conversational way, 'What happened to Fay?' He hadn't spoken to the girl, hadn't seen her even since the ceremony. For all he knew she might have gone away, and he wanted to speak to her.

'Don't you remember?' she said. 'I—oh, tell you later. I've just remembered something I wanted to say to Aggie.'

At about two o'clock, as he was searching among the litter of plates and glasses for another asparagus roll, he saw Fay push past the door with tears in her eyes. Sadness tugged like a thread between them, and he wanted to go to her. He was stretched on a burning rack of sympathy as the details of her story came back to him at last.

He remembered the young soldier, the American, completely in love with her as she had knelt beside him at the fireside in those winter evenings, her head against his knee. He remembered the afternoon jaunts they had made to the museum and art gallery, to the Katherine Mansfield memorial and Massey's tomb. He remembered the nights at the pictures and cabarets, the week-ends at Otaki and Palmerston. It had been the big romance of the year for everyone, even the southern aunts in their purity having become reconciled to it by that time. And then his Division had gone off to the Pacific and he had been killed at Iwo Jima on the first day of battle, in the last weeks of the war. But what could he do about it, he thought as the door closed behind her. What could a man do to salve wounds that time would not heal?

'Alan.' Betty was beside him. 'Are you all right? You look pale. Is your leg hurting?'

He took off his spectacles and wiped them. 'Did you see that?'

'See what? You don't seem——' She sniffed. 'Have you had too many cocktails again?'

Her obtuseness struck him like a blow. It was a thing about her he still hadn't got used to. 'No,' he said, feeling his old fatigue and the afternoon collapsing on to his shoulders like a crumbling bank of clay. 'You know I don't like these weddings, dear. Why don't we go home now that all the important people have gone?'

'But I don't see——'

'Come on.' His leg had been hurting all the time, and now it throbbed into his consciousness. 'I'm sure everyone's noticed your new hat by this time.'

'Why, it was a glorious wedding,' she said as they walked down into the city. 'Didn't you enjoy yourself once you got there?'

It was strange, he thought, how sometimes she could see right through him, and at others it was as if his feelings were hidden from her by a brick wall. Because although he wouldn't admit it to her, he did feel elated now that it was over. He supposed it was partly the relaxation of nervous tension. He had screwed himself up to a great effort, and had come through with reasonable success. But it didn't mean anything.

'I wonder if Fay will marry someone else now Aggie's done it,' Betty said, and he realized with a shock that she was bound to have remembered the whole story.

'Why not?' he heard himself say. 'Those young girls soon get over things. They're too full of life to feel sorry for themselves for long.'

'I declare, Alan, you've never said a thing like that before.'

But he wondered if it was true. There was a point of defeat beyond

which once the human spirit had gone it could never recover itself.
How many disappointed girls spent their lives lamenting a lost lover,
enduring the years only as hollow urns containing the ashes of a
dead past? If the will to live was weak, or the thrust of circumstance
too strong to resist, life could be a retreat into the cavern of memory,
and the young lovers become aging grey spinsters, embittered relics
of a time that everyone else had forgotten, virgins weeping before
the image of irrecoverable happiness. Would that be Fay's fate, to
become a living sacrifice upon the altar of family solidarity? He
wondered if she would ever escape her future, any more than he had
been able today to escape from his past. For a moment people like
Fay and himself felt within their grasp the tiny private visions they
had built up in their minds: hers of freedom through a great love, his
of a heroic idealistic protest against Uncle Albert, Aunt Jeannie, and
their code of wealth, property, and the family sticking together, the
barren preservation of the species. Yet how often did the individual
succeed in achieving his desires? To him the family was a symbol of
the society which had got him into the war, the real source of the
wound that had given him a stiff leg and turned his hair grey. How
could anything worthwhile be accomplished against such intoler-
ance and narrowness? One man's resistance was not enough against
life measured out in coffee spoons, the ever-increasing confinement
of behaviour, these rules he had to obey which were other people's
rules, the pressures which fitted everyone, despite their most furious
struggles, into the appropriate mould so that they soon ceased to be
individuals at all, but became merely colourless, recognizable types
which could be classified and slotted correctly into the social pattern
around them. He felt that once he might have become a hero to his
conscience, but now there was some psychological block, his war
neurosis he called it, that held him back. The shattering exploding
violence of that holocaust had engulfed him and burst the tender
membranes and very pulsing arteries of his heart's amplitude. In
that incredibly sickening shock of furious conflict the silver bubble
of his desire had cracked and he had fallen stone-like to the bottom
of the well of humanity, doomed to exist for the rest of his life a
hungering schizophrene. Yet it still flamed and flickered there, the
vitality and desire, and deep within him he had that other secret, the
hope that one day some outrageous event would force him into a
corner where he would have no option but to become a renegade if
he was to preserve what was left of his personal integrity. The day
had not yet arrived, perhaps never would arrive, but Gauguin-like,
he thought, he waited.

'Did you notice how cleverly I got you out of that?' Betty said
making a generous movement towards him as they stood waiting at

the bus stop. 'We didn't have to say goodbye to any of them. A clean get-away.'

'I suppose it was because I was thinking about Fay and everything, but I didn't notice it at all.'

He felt a brutal anger rise in him against the community whose blunders had brought about these present defections, which had destroyed Fay's happiness just as surely as it was slowly bringing him to heel after weakening in bloody battles his ambition to live according to his own ideals.

'You funny man.'

'Funny? Did you think it was funny?' He saw the frown start between her eyes. 'You mean Fay?'

'Everything,' he said. 'You know as well as I do what an ordeal this wedding must have been to her.'

'But Alan, Fay was just unlucky.'

'Sure. Even if the family had let her marry him, it still wouldn't have stopped the Japs from killing him when they did. But she would at least have had a younker to remember him by. That's what I mean. They ruin her life with their cold Puritanical narrowness, and then years afterwards they pretend to make up for things by giving Aggie a flash send-off. It's crazy.'

'They try to do their best. Don't you think they have their compassion too? Perhaps they have realized their mistake.'

'But who in God's name decided that Fay should be bridesmaid? They can never see beyond their little old wives' conventions until it's too late. I tell you I hate it. The whole damned set-up's as sterile and destructive of happiness as any other code of behaviour which stops reasonable people from doing what they want to.'

'You're exaggeratng.'

'I tell you I saw her,' he said, 'and she was weeping. It was a terrible affair. The whole thing simply broke her heart.'

As they waited for their bus the wind which had been silent all day suddenly began to blow at last. Without any warning it swept around the corner with an incredible fury, so that he grabbed at a verandah post for support. Betty lost her balance and stumbled a few steps under the inexorable force of its attack as it began to carry her away. He reached out and seized her, and she thumped up against him, soft and warm. 'Darling,' she said. Her eyes sparkled with glee as his hat was lifted high into the air, whirled along the tram lines among galloping sheets of newspaper, bits of straw, a cloud of dust, all in flight towards the other end of the street. He rushed after it, seized it and jammed it on his head. The wind blew his coat out, phantom-like behind him as he beat back against it towards the footpath.

And then with surprise he saw her: Fay standing beside Betty on the corner, radiant as her hair blew about her face and colour whipped into her pale cheeks, Fay laughing at him, laughing into the wind, laughing hysterically at life's little ironies. He felt he made a ridiculous figure as the wind battered against him. What a fool I am, he thought. She had already forgotten. He had been right the first time. Another man, somewhere battling against the wind, standing ready behind the next corner to raise his hat politely and say, 'Good afternoon,' was waiting for her. The wedding was over. The family was dissolving away, the aunts and uncles returning to the craggy Waitaki wilderness from which they had come, to brood once more over their Calvinist consciences. And already, with the risen wind, he too felt free. The icy bonds of death had released him from their sad clutch. What did it matter how they thought or acted, when he could still escape them? He sprang into the air and landed with a jolt on the pavement beside her.

'Hullo there, Fay,' he said.

'Isn't this terrible?' she shouted. With one hand she was holding onto her hat, and with the other pressing her skirts down over her knees. He thought she looked beautiful. She had made a remarkable recovery.

'Why don't you come out?' he said, as the bus rolled into sight down the road.

'Yes,' Betty said. 'Come home and have another drink. We may as well continue the celebration.'

'I'd love to,' she replied, 'but I have made other arrangements.'

'Oh?' Betty said. 'Other arrangements?'

'Yes.' The bus stopped and they got on. The wind continued to blow, making a high whistle as it rushed around the corner of the shops behind them.

'I'm sorry,' she said, laughing up through the window.

'Well, any time,' Betty said. 'Come out soon.'

'I'd love to,' she repeated.

The bus started to move. Betty waved and Fay lifted her gloved hand to wave back. 'Good-byee!' The wind caught her dress and lifted it up above her thighs. She beat it down and walked out into the street. Alan watched her cross to the other side, high-stepping, serene. Then he relaxed back into his seat.

'I told you. It's like I remarked a few minutes ago. You always exaggerate things,' Betty said.